RAISING KANE

Elisha Kent Kane and the Culture
of Fame in Antebellum America

RAISING KANE

Elisha Kent Kane and the Culture of Fame in Antebellum America

Mark Metzler Sawin, PhD

AMERICAN PHILOSOPHICAL SOCIETY

Philadelphia • 2008

Transactions of the
American Philosophical Society
Held at Philadelphia
for Promoting Useful Knowledge
Volume 98, Part 3

ISBN-13: 978-1-60618-983-2
US ISSN: 0065-9746

Library of Congress Cataloging-in-Publication Data

Sawin, Mark Metzler.
    Raising Kane : Elisha Kent Kane and the culture of fame in antebellum
    America / Mark Metzler Sawin.
        p. cm.—(Transactions of the American Philosophical Society held
    at Philadelphia for promoting useful knowledge, ISSN 0065-9746 ; v. 98,
    pt. 3)
    Includes bibliographical references and index.
    ISBN 978-1-60618-983-2
       1. Kane, Elisha Kent, 1820-1857. 2. Fox, Margaret, 1833-1893. 3.
    Popular culture—United States—History—19th century. 4. United
    States—Intellectual life—19th century. 5. Explorers—United
    States—Biography. 6. Spiritualists—United States—Biography. I. Title.

G635.K2S39 2008
910.92--dc22
[B]
                                                          2008052864

CONTENTS

Alas! in vain poor I together scraped
All that man's science till this day hath shown;
And all that his imagined shaped,
I in ambition's dreams have made my own.
A weary task it was—a sullen strife,
And now I sit me down, helpless, alone,
No new power comes—no strength—no spring of life.
Not by a hair's breadth higher is my height,
Far—far as ever from the Infinite.

—Goethe, Faust (1808)

I cannot rest from travel: I will drink
Life to the lees: All times I have enjoy'd
Greatly, have suffer'd greatly, both with those
That loved me, and alone; on shore, and when
Thro' scudding drifts the rainy Hyades
Vext the dim sea: I am become a name;
For always roaming with a hungry heart
Much have I seen and known; cities of men
And manners, climates, councils, governments,
Myself not least, but honour'd of them all…

Tho' much is taken, much abides; and tho'
We are not now that strength which in old days
Moved earth and heaven, that which we are, we are;
One equal temper of heroic hearts,
Made weak by time and fate, but strong in will
To strive, to seek, to find, and not to yield.

—Alfred Lord Tennyson, "Ulysses" (1842)

We countenance each other in this life of show, puffing, advertisement and manufacture of public opinion; and excellence is lost sight of in the hunger for sudden performance and praise....

Self-trust is the first secret of success, the belief that if you are here the authorities of the universe put you here, and for cause, or with some task strictly appointed you in your constitution, and so long as you work at that you are well and successful. It by no means consists in rushing prematurely to a showy feat that shall catch the eye and satisfy spectators. It is enough if you work in the right direction.

       —Ralph Waldo Emerson, "Success" (1870)

ACKNOWLEDGMENTS

While writing this book I was helped by many people in many ways and I gratefully take this opportunity to offer them my thanks. First and foremost, I thank William H. Goetzmann who introduced me to Elisha Kent Kane and directed my doctoral research in the American Studies program at the University of Texas at Austin; this book would not exist without him. I also thank Howard Miller, Michael Winship, and Janet Davis for their guidance and encouragement during my years of graduate study. The administrative and research librarians of the American Philosophical Society—Martin Levitt, Robert Cox, and Roy Goodman—provided exemplary assistance and insight in my efforts to "Raise Kane," and their colleague, Mary McDonald, skillfully guided this manuscript to press. Aaron Richman and his staff at A Good Thing Inc. patiently crafted my text into a book, and Martin Jones lent his prodigious skills to indexing and editing the final draft—this book's polish is due to them; any errors are mine. Eliza and Timothy Cope Harrison, and Robert and Elizabeth Reid provided me with encouragement, hospitality, and a better understanding of the Kane family. Russell Potter, Charles Cowing, and Matthew Grow each helped guide me to valuable resources. I also graciously acknowledge the American Philosophical Society's Grundy Fellowship, the University of Texas's University Fellowship, and Eastern Mennonite University for their generous financial contributions to this project.

The odd and lonely process of writing a book necessitated a great deal of support. Tom and Ruby Sawin were always there when I needed them. Shawn Brumbaugh and Jennifer Richardson provided essential camaraderie during my years at the University of Texas. So too did many fellow students: Ben Chappell, Paul Erickson, Eric Eliason, Bill Fagelson, John Haddad, Matt Hedstrom, Laura Hernandez-Ehrisman, Marike Janzen, Sarah Mullen, Danielle Brune Sigler, Joel Silverman, Lee Smithey and Cathy Turner. The supportive community in and around Eastern Mennonite University is too vast to list, but I owe special debts of gratitude to Mary Sprunger, for her encouragement and guidance; Peter Dula, for his many hours of thoughtful and provocative conversation; and Shawn and Susannah Gerber Lepley, for their life-balancing friendship. I must also thank my companions in the Mid-Atlantic American Studies Association—Simon Bronner, John Haddad, and Charlie Kupfer—for their passionate convictions and good-humored sanity within the larger world of academia.

Finally, I thank my family. My wife, Erika Metzler Sawin, has accompanied me throughout this entire journey. Over the past fifteen years we have launched two academic careers while also creating and maintaining a circle of friends and family that are off-kilter and wonderfully quirky enough to make our existences meaningful and our house a home. For this and many other reasons she has my constant love and gratitude. And our children, Cora and Isaac, have spent the first years of their lives teaching me what is most important. I hope I can return this lesson some day.

Introduction

⚜

I remember as a young man taking an evening walk northward along one of the many dirt roads that grid the wheat-covered expanses of Kansas. When I reached a crossroad I stopped on its slightly elevated crown and looked back over the undulating fields toward the silo and barn that marked the beginning of my evening walk. Although the farm was still clearly visible, it was reduced in stature. The red of the barn and white of the house, the concrete gray of the silo, and the glint of tin from the machine-shed roof were still vivid, but less obvious. What had loomed largely about me before was now only a sliver of color on a stretching horizon. This reduction hid details from view, and I found that without the obvious reminders afforded by immediate proximity, my straining eyes and struggling memory could no longer recreate the scene I had so recently left behind. I could no longer confidently state the color of the flowers by the front porch, the number of steps to the backdoor, or the height of the corn growing in the garden. As I stood there gazing over that short space that separated me from where I had been, I suddenly had the strange sense that I was not looking back over distance, but time. As I began my walk back, I wondered that upon my return I would be able to learn again the color of the flowers, the number of steps, and the height of the corn, but though this would gain me precise, quantifiable facts about my immediate past, no amount of effort would ever allow me to recall other details. The moment of my departure was forever gone. The gust of breeze that crossed my face, the swallow that flitted overhead in the evening sky, the curve of the cat's tail as it rubbed past my leg when I stepped down from the porch to begin my walk; all of these were blurred by time, and what memory did not preserve, imagination could only recreate using the clumsy facts I could still retain and gather. This is the challenge and the curse of the historian.

For the past decade I have been trying to peer back across a century and a half at a young man named Elisha Kent Kane. I have returned to the narrow streets and stately buildings of Philadelphia that were home to his youth. I have read and reread the hundreds of letters that were written by his hand and read by his eyes. I have studied the precisely cut engravings and dark, scratched daguerreotypes that record his image, and I have tracked down the grandnieces and nephews that still tell stories of their long-dead ancestor. I know Elisha Kent Kane well, and yet I do not know him at all. The following is my story of this man's life. It is not a biography in the strict sense of the term because I have decided to tell my version of Kane's life not as the story of a man, but as the story of a time. Elisha Kent Kane, or "Dr. Kane" as he was known and celebrated during the 1850s, grew up in, and became the hero of, an era filled with hope and fear. Though no one person can be a perfect archetype for an entire nation or era, Kane's life in many ways reflected the life of antebellum America because both he and his country struggled to make a name for themselves on the world stage during the 1850s, only to have their plans tragically come to an end—divisivness and internal strain ended Kane's life and tore apart the unity of the United States.

The pages that follow introduce an anxious, driven, sickly, brilliant, adventurous, and insecure young man who turned himself into a national icon. As I have noted, looking back over time is not a precise science, and as such the following story gives an impression—a "glimpse" as antebellum authors were fond of entitling there memoirs—of what life was like in the years leading up to the U.S. Civil War. Though forgotten today, Dr. Kane was one of the most celebrated heroes of this tumultuous era. During his thirty-seven years of life, this physician from an aristocratic Philadelphia family accomplished an amazing amount. He traveled through China, East Asia, North and South America, India, Europe, Africa and the Arctic. He also fought in the Mexican-American War, made two highly celebrated journeys to the far north in search of Sir John Franklin and the fabled Open Polar Sea, had a turbulent and troubled love affair with spirit-rapper Margaret Fox, and wrote one of the most successful books of the period. When he suddenly and unexpectedly died in 1857, he was such a celebrated figure that the nation mourned his death for nearly a month as his casket wound from Havana to Philadelphia via steamboat and rail in a funeral procession that, to date, is still matched only by Abraham Lincoln's. As one of his many effusive obituaries noted, "Dr. Kane was a man of whom the country became more proud with every new revelation of his character.... Gallant, brave, heroic, smitten equally with a love of science and a passion for adventure, he possessed the mental force to convert the dreams of imagination into reality."[1]

These "dreams of imagination" were those of both Elisha and the nation, and an examination of these dreams provides insights into both the man and the country. Elisha's youthful quest to become a "man of importance" reveals much about masculinity during his era, and his relationship with spiritualist Margaret Fox exposes aspects of antebellum religion, gender, and class relations. Kane's explorations exemplify the romantic spirit that inspired the young nation, and his efforts to write and market books about these adventures show much about authorship and book production during the time of the American Literary Renaissance. On a larger level, and most significantly, Elisha's life-long drive for fame paralleled America's efforts during the same decades to become a major player on the world stage.[2] Elisha Kent Kane achieved the fame he sought, but he was then transformed by his popularity because, even as the nation's regional differences threatened to unravel the union, each region embraced and transformed him into their own version of the larger-than-life "Dr. Kane," an Odysseus-like hero who guided his men through the horrific perils of the harsh arctic world and, by analogy, was capable of guiding his nation through the ominous storms on its horizon. This was the Faustian price of Kane's fame—the nation came to expect a level of perfection and heroism far greater than he or any human was capable of providing. In life, Kane could not sustain the perfection that the nation expected of Dr. Kane, but his sudden death in 1857 allowed the public image of Dr. Kane to become larger than life. Unimpeded by the foibles and faults of Elisha Kent Kane the man, Dr. Kane could become all things to all people. Men, women, and children; scientific, religious, and popular societies; military, literary, and political groups in the North, South, and West all turned Dr. Kane into their own idealized hero. As governments, institutions, churches, and learned and civic societies fell over themselves to commemorate Dr. Kane, many people came to believe that his heroic example of overcoming great odds could even restore order to the chaotic nation teetering on the brink of a civil war, however, this "dream of imagination" was not to be. Just as Kane's dream for a stable life of fame and fortune shattered just as it was fulfilled, so too did the nation's first optimistic era and identity come to a crashing close as mortars began raining down on Fort Sumter in April 1861. Dr. Kane's heroic stature was one of the many casualties of the Civil War, for, as soldiers noted a few bloody years later, Dr. Kane was the hero of a bygone age. He was "the last hero of the United States of America." The union failed, and the new nation that was forged from its pieces brought with it a new set of heroes.[3]

These pages tell the story of Elisha Kent Kane and the era that made Dr. Kane its hero. My goal for this work has been to "raise Kane" from the past and to use him to explain the culture and country in which he lived. This, of course, is an imperfect science, because even though Kane was emblematic of his age, he was, after all, just one man among millions. His thoughts and actions were ultimately and uniquely his own, not those of the nation. To follow my opening analogy, I have gone back and counted the steps and recorded the color of the flowers, I have even attempted to recover and reveal the flight of the swallow in the sky. But as I realized on that evening years ago under a vast Kansas sky, much of what lay behind us is truly gone. What I offer here, then, is a careful and sympathetic but necessarily incomplete glimpse of one man and the era in which he lived.

1 New York *Times* (February 18, 1857), 5.

2 Several books on Kane have influenced my manuscript. George Corner's *Dr. Kane of the Arctic Seas* (Philadelphia: Temple University Press, 1972) is an excellent biography of Kane and provides a starting point for all subsequent Kane scholarship. William H. Goetzmann's *New Lands, New Men* (New York: Viking Penguin Inc., 1986) contains a brief but solid examination of Kane in the context of the "second great age of discovery," and David Chapin's *Exploring Other Worlds: Margaret Fox, Elisha Kane, and the Antebellum Culture of Curiosity* (Amherst: University of Massachusetts Press, 2004) uses the lives of Kane and Margaret Fox to demonstrate how high-, middle-, and low-brow culture embraced "curiosities" in a variety of manners and for different purposes. Two dissertations have examined Kane as well. Barry Allen Joyce's "As the Wolf from the Dog"; American Overseas Exploration & the Compartmentalization of Humankind: 1838-1859," (Ph.D. diss., University of California, Riverside, 1995); and Matthew J. Grow's "'Liberty to the Downtrodden': Thomas L. Kane, Romantic Reformer" (PhD diss., University of Notre Dame, 2006). Grow's excellent study of Thomas Kane and the Kane family will be published under the same title by Yale University Press in 2009.

3 Thomas Leiper Kane to Robert Patterson Kane (May 17, 1862), APS Robert Patterson Kane papers.

CHAPTER

1

Heroic Desire:
Elisha Kent Kane, the Man

❧

In the early part of the nineteenth century Philadelphia was an energetic city of opportunity. Though its rival New York would pass it in size and commerce by the 1820s, the "City of Brotherly Love" remained a vibrant and active place. Its wharves bustled with trade as five hundred ships from foreign ports arrived each year, providing a constant supply of both news and goods from across the globe. Philadelphia served as a hub of trade and culture as a major port and the nation's first industrial center, bringing together the new country's disparate regions. Many Southern families established business offices and residences in Philadelphia and spent their summers in its cooler climate. In Philadelphia they met and formed partnerships (both business and marital) with their Northern countrymen, many of whom journeyed south to Philadelphia because of its strong banking system and commercial opportunities. This regional diversity created a lively civic and political culture. Philadelphia's partisan newspapers and institutions raged against each other over the issues of the day, and early labor unions and social reform agencies emerged in the shadow of Independence Hall, to challenge the nation's emerging cultural systems. More refined pursuits also flourished in the midst of this commercial and political fervor, making Philadelphia the "Athens of America." Before the Smithsonian was formed in the 1840s, Philadelphia's American Philosophical Society, which also housed the remains of Charles Wilson Peale's eclectic museum of national and natural history, served as the repository for the nation's treasures. Music and the theatrical arts abounded thanks to the Musical Fund Society that formed in 1820 and established Musical Fund Hall by the middle of that decade. Overall, thanks to much farsighted civic planning (most notably by the city's most famous adopted son, Benjamin Franklin), Philadelphia had a feeling of cleanliness and order compared with the chaos that plagued the nation's other urban centers. But perhaps most importantly of all, Philadelphia during the antebellum period still exuded the powerful sense that any American could come to its streets and, just as Benjamin Franklin had done the century before, rise from obscurity to fame and fortune. All it took was hard work, ingenuity, gumption, and, as Franklin himself noted, the ability to portray yourself correctly in the public eye—to "not only be in *reality* industrious and frugal, but to avoid all *appearances* of the contrary."[1]

Like many other families, the Kane family came to Philadelphia during the early nineteenth century, hoping that the city's bustling business and culture would improve their fortunes. As a young man, Elisha Kane (Elisha Kent Kane's grandfather and namesake) came back to the United States after his own father had fled the country as a Tory during the Revolutionary War. He and his brothers established Kane & Brothers, a trading company that moved goods between the hinterlands and New York City, and then on to Europe. Elisha had a pioneering spirit and established and operated the company's far-flung trading posts, most notably one among the Oneidas close to Cooperstown in upstate New York. He was a shrewd and successful businessman, and some in the community viewed him with suspicion. In 1792, Cooperstown native Moss Kent, who was a cousin to the Kane family, thought about marrying Elisha's sister, Sally. He saw this as advantageous because the Kanes were wealthy merchants and he expected the union would "add to my Happiness & advance my Prosperity to many *Thousand*." Ultimately , he decided against the union, however, because his brother warned that he had "little respect for most of her connections."[2] The inland trade Elisha oversaw helped Kane & Brothers expand, but he eventually grew weary of living in the hinterlands of the new nation. In 1793, he thus sought a more "civilized" society in which to plant his growing family, and so settled in Albany to run the company's primary storehouse. In Albany his young wife, Alida Van Rensselaer, a member of a prominent Dutch family, bore him two sons and a daughter before passing away. In 1801 Elisha moved his family to Philadelphia and soon established himself as a businessman of some prominence. He was elected a charter director of the newly formed Philadelphia Bank in 1803, and he remained influential in city commerce until his death in 1834.[3]

As a member of this wealthy but socially unestablished Philadelphia family, Elisha Kane's eldest son, John Kintzing Kane, ambitiously sought to enter the higher social spheres of the city. Philadelphia was established and largely controlled by several prominent Quaker families, and thus money and commercial success alone were not enough to gain high social standing. As British traveler

Alexander Mackay observed in the early nineteenth century, compared with other U.S. cities Philadelphia's class lines were the most "distinctive" and "difficult to transcend."[4] After graduating from Yale in 1814 and being admitted to the Philadelphia Bar in 1817, John gained a foothold into Philadelphia's upper society when he married Jane Duval Leiper, a celebrated beauty from a prominent Philadelphia family.[5] Jane's father, Thomas Leiper, was a Revolutionary War hero, a close friend of Thomas Jefferson, and a successful businessman and real estate speculator who constructed the nation's first horse-drawn railroad in 1809. He was also involved in local and national financial institutions, serving as a director of the Bank of Pennsylvania and the First Bank of the United States. Jane's mother, Elizabeth Gray, was also from a well-respected Philadelphia family, her father having served as speaker of the house in the Pennsylvania State Legislature.[6]

By the 1820s, John Kane had established himself as an able lawyer with a substantial and influential clientele. Like other ambitious young Philadelphians, he sought to increase his fortunes through the traditional channels of career, marriage, and investment, but what made him unique and ultimately successful was his ability to understand and use a powerful new force in America—the popular press. John's big break came in 1828 when he wrote a pamphlet entitled "A Candid View

Portraits of John K. Kane (1836) and Jane Duval Leiper Kane (1824). Reproduced from original paintings by Thomas Sully. Reprinted in *Century Magazine* (Aug. 1898).

FROM PHOTOGRAPH OF PORTRAIT BY THOMAS SULLY.

FROM PHOTOGRAPH OF PORTRAIT BY THOMAS SULLY.

THE HON. JOHN K. KANE, FATHER OF DR. KANE.   JANE DUVAL LEIPER KANE, MOTHER OF DR. KANE.

of the Presidential Question." Signing himself "A Pennsylvanian... pledged to the dogmas of no partisan leader," and with "nothing to hope from either candidate," he offered his "dispassionately formed" opinion of Andrew Jackson and his presidential opponent, John Quincy Adams. His pamphlet portrayed Jackson as a self-made man with heroic attributes—a man "quick to resent an injury, and as quick to forgive one." It then condemned Adams as an elitist who was raised in the lap of luxury and, like the "head of the house of Stuart... has never forgotten an enemy, or remembered a friend."[7] This pamphlet was popular and effective because it targeted the new, greatly expanded voting public. By 1828, most white men, regardless of wealth or property, could vote. These men were the political powerbase of the country, and Jackson and his supporters in the newly formed Democratic Party knew that they had to appeal to their sympathies to win elections. Kane, like several of Jackson's other key supporters, had an excellent feel for public sentiment and used this knowledge to construct a type of campaign literature that stressed the hard-work, innate morality, frontier toughness, and common-man attributes of their candidate, a strategy that produced the slogan, "Adams can Write, Jackson can Fight!" This tactic was very successful in America's new political climate, and Jackson easily won the 1828 election.[8]

After his victory, Jackson, like all politicians of the time, rewarded his supporters by appointing them to influential offices. Although John Kane didn't immediately win a position himself, he did gain many powerful friends because of his allegiance to Jackson. Then in 1832, while supporting Jackson for his re-election bid, John was granted his first official federal job when Jackson called him to Washington and made him one of three commissioners to work on spoliation claims in which France agreed to pay the United States 25 million francs in restitution for attacks made on neutral American ships during the Napoleonic wars. This job kept John in Washington for the better part of four years and provided him with frequent social and official visits to the White House.[9] During this time it was widely rumored that his skillful pen was frequently brought into service for Jackson, especially during the hotly contested Bank War, when the Whig party forced a conflict between Jackson and Nicholas Biddle, head of the Philadelphia-based Second Bank of the United States. Jackson won the Bank War by illegally removing federal funds from the National Bank and preventing its charter from being renewed. This caused the National Bank to collapse in 1836 and, a year later, the nation's economy followed suit as a massive economic depression hit only months after Jackson left office, plaguing the political career of Jackson's hand-picked successor, Martin Van Buren (or "Van Ruin" as the public soon dubbed him). Aiding Jackson in the Bank War hurt John Kane's reputation in the eyes of many of Philadelphia's elite (the fall of the Second National Bank greatly hurt Philadelphia's economic stature as national banking shifted to New York City), but it gained him national political power in the young Democratic Party. In 1838 he led the Democrats in the "Buckshot War," a Pennsylvania election dispute that grew so heated that the militia was called in to protect the legislators from the mobs that swarmed the state capital in Harrisburg. A few years later, during the Presidential election of 1844, Kane campaigned tirelessly to pull Pennsylvania, a critical swing-state, into the Democratic camp. In May 1844 he wrote to his son of his efforts, "I took charge of the *Pennsylvanian*, and in a few leading editorials brought out the democrats of the Legislature and of all the counties on the same side. Meetings were called: I presided. The Whigs were confounded."[10] A month later he was still hard at work. Kane wrote political biographies of the Democratic presidential and vice-presidential candidates, James K. Polk and George M. Dallas, and published them in newspapers and as pamphlets. He also wrote a widely circulated pamphlet that explained the party's pro-annexation of Texas position. Most importantly, Kane also published what became known as the "Kane letter," which showed Polk, who had historically supported free-trade, as willing to back protective tariffs, thus calming the fears of the many pro-tariff voters of Pennsylvania. This document had a huge political impact as many voters saw it as a masterly compromise between the protectionists and free-traders, and, as Polk's only public statement on the tariff issue, it made him look solid in his beliefs as opposed to his opponent, Henry Clay, who had made dozens of statements on the issue during his long political career, many of them contradictory. Clay's campaign portrayed Polk as a political nobody (Clay's reported response to Polk's nomination was, "Who's James Polk?"), but John Kane and Polk's other supporters embraced this critique, painting their candidate as a political outsider and man of the people.[11] In the months before the election, Kane wrote home saying, "We shall elect our candidates, I think; and if we do, I shall have friends at court in Polk, [and] Dallas."[12] The "Kane letter" largely contributed to Polk winning Pennsylvania and thus the election, and, as John had predicted, his efforts did not go unrewarded. Though his hopes for a cabinet position were not realized, he was appointed attorney general of Pennsylvania in 1845, and Polk made him U.S. District Court Judge of Eastern Pennsylvania the next year, a position Kane held for the rest of his life.[13] John Kane was now a powerful man, and he used his political savvy and understanding of the popular press to promote his pet projects, such as the completion of the Chesapeake and Delaware Canal and the founding of Philadelphia's Girard College, Second Presbyterian Church, Academy of Fine Arts, and Musical Fund Society. In the years that followed his judgeship, he became a prominent Mason and a longtime officer and eventual president of the American Philosophical Society. By the time of his death in 1858 he was one of the most powerful Democrats in the nation.[14] As a biographical sketch noted, "Judge Kane did not aspire to be conspicuous as a politician," but instead viewed himself primarily as "a writer of other men's speeches—a prompter of the stock performers on the stage, who could find his sufficient reward and enjoyment in seeing the drama enacted of which he might have claimed to be the author."[15] This ability to quietly pull the strings of public opinion through the shrewd use of the popular press—to be, as he wrote in his autobiography, one of the "men behind the curtain, that taught the wires how to move"—was a hugely powerful skill and one that Judge Kane passed on to his sons.[16]

As a U.S. judge, John Kane could not easily be removed from power, thus enabling him to hand down decisions from his courtroom on the second floor of Independence Hall with little fear of personal economic impact. But there were other costs. While his judgeship made him politically unassailable, it did not shield him from public scorn in the tumultuous years leading up to and following the hugely controversial Fugitive Slave Act of 1850. Although his political opponents insisted that he used his court as a bully pulpit for the benefit of the largely pro-slavery Democratic party, Kane's legal decisions show a much more complicated story. He was a powerful political operative for the Democrats, but he also took his duty to administer the law fairly and without bias seriously. In the years following the Fugitive Slave Act, Judge Kane ruled both for and against slave owners trying to reclaim escaped slaves, and he made these ruling with little regard for the public outcry that accompanied each decision. As a staunch Democrat concerned about keeping the South solidly behind the Democratic Party while also maintaining enough Northern support to swing elections in their favor, Kane was keenly aware of the political ramifications of his decisions. Judge Kane also felt the tension of this issue within his own family because his second son, Thomas (Tom), who served as his judicial clerk and court commissioner, was a staunch abolitionist who, with great fanfare, resigned as court commissioner when the Fugitive Slave Act required that he help capture and extradite fugitive slaves. Tom's vocal resignation caused such a public fury that Judge Kane threatened to jail his son for contempt of court, which only increased the furor. A year later Tom, still serving as his father's court clerk, sent Thanksgiving food to the abolitionist "traitors" and fugitive slaves his father was holding in prison during the *Christiana* case, an act that was widely praised by abolitionist papers and condemned throughout the South. Family tension only increased when Tom's younger brother, Robert Patterson (Pat), became part of the black prisoners' legal defense team.[17] Throughout all of this, however, the Kane family remained dedicated to each other, and each was willing to promote the welfare and ambitions of the others.

On February 3, 1820, Elisha Kent Kane was born the first child of John Kane, then a young lawyer, and his wife, Jane Duval Leiper Kane. During Elisha's early years, the family lived in the heart of Philadelphia, on Walnut Street between Seventh and Eighth, and then at 100 South Fourth, each location also housing John Kane's law office.[18] During these years Elisha's constant companion was his brother Tom, who was just two years his junior. Elisha and Tom were bright, energetic boys full of adventurous spirit. Elisha's childhood drawings depicted exciting scenes of battle and heroism—soldiers fighting with drawn swords and exotic turban-clad warriors galloping on horseback.[19] Despite his exceptionally slight stature (thirty-four pounds at age eight) Elisha was drawn more to outdoor adventure than books. According to family legend he devised and executed an elaborate plan to scale their three-story house when he was just a young boy. Judging from this and other accounts, he was anything but a disciplined student in his younger years.[20] William Elder, a close friend of the Kane family, noted that, "Elisha earned the character of bad boy, while he was in fact exercising and cultivating the spriit of a brave one. Goody-good people, very naturally, did not understand him then."[21] By the time he was a young teen, however, Elisha began applying himself to his studies. While away with his mother and siblings for the summer, he responded to his father's pointed queries by assuring him that he "would rather be a smart boy and clumsy play fellow" than the other way around.[22]

By the age of seventeen, Elisha was a gifted scientific observer, and he hoped to pursue a career as an engineer or natural philosopher. His father pushed him to attend his alma mater—Yale—but Elisha was denied admittance, primarily for his lack of classical languages. He opted instead for the University of Virginia, where he was not required to meet Greek and Latin requirements and could concentrate on his primary interest—science. Robert Patterson, Elisha's cousin, had entered the University of Virginia the year before and this was another major draw because Robert provided Elisha with a ready roommate and friend. Kane matriculated in 1838 and quickly proved himself to be an excellent scholar. He studied primarily with William Barton Rogers, who taught physics, geology, mineralogy, and civil engineering. At that time, Rogers (who later became the Massachusetts Institute of Technology's first president) was in the midst of mapping the geological formations of the Blue Ridge Mountains, and he invited Elisha to join him in this endeavor. Elisha enjoyed these rugged outings and hoped to pursue a career in geology or engineering, but these hopes ended when he suffered a severe attack of rheumatic fever in the fall of 1838.[23] Elisha returned to Virginia after a time of recovery at home, thanks to the university's granting him special permission to live in a vacant room in the library that afforded him a less stressful and better-heated environment than the dormitory. He again excelled in his work, and by June 1839 Patterson reported that Elisha stood "among the best in all his classes" and was "with Mr. Rogers in his laboratory every evening."[24] But within a few months, Elisha suffered another major rheumatic attack, again forcing him home to recover. At this time, his physician warned him that he should not pursue any active occupation because, given the damage that had been done to his heart, such strain could cause him to die "as suddenly as from a musket shot."[25] Shaken and depressed by the idea of a life of inactivity, Elisha languished in bed, apprehensive about what future awaited a sickly young man.

In his study of American manhood, E. Anthony Rotundo noted that "each culture constructs its own version of what men and women are—and ought to be," and that American definitions of manhood were changing during the antebellum period.[26] A strict separation of men and women's spheres emerged with the rise of industrialism and a market economy. Women were in charge of the home and were expected to preserve the "civilized" attributes of self-sacrifice, compassion, and religious morality. Men occupied the "worldly" sphere, the brutal environment of the new industrial nation, where fortitude, strength, endurance, and cunning were necessary for survival. These spheres changed the relationship between men and women as women were increasingly confined to the home and seen more and more as consumers, not producers, of goods. Women lost their status as help-mates (partners in the economic support of the family), especially in more affluent families, and came to be seen as childlike dependents. They were "kept," largely helpless people who preserved the morality of the family by maintaining a sheltered home away from the harsh realities of the world. Men, on the other hand, were expected to meet the harsh world head on. Through perseverance, hard work, and fortitude they were expected to "rise," mastering skills and increasing in wealth and prestige. Success in this male sphere at times necessitated brutal actions. Men were to be "honorable," but first and foremost they were to ensure the survival and protection of the family, even if that meant going to morally questionable extremes.[27]

As the nineteenth century progressed, characteristics of the ideal American man shifted. During the colonial and early national period, a man was defined by the roles and services he provided his community, the "goodness" he could do; but by the early nineteenth century, manliness became increasingly defined by the ability to make money and get ahead. As this shift occurred, ministers, local magistrates, and philanthropic gentlemen lost prestige whereas shrewd and aggressive businessmen, speculators, politicians, and adventurers rose in the eyes of the community. Because of this, by the 1830s a "manly man" was a mixture of the older model of manhood, that valued civic responsibility and selfless service, and the newer kind of man, that exhibited qualities of stoic and daring bravery, flamboyant mastery of skills, and a general aggressiveness. These lessons began even in boyhood as "traits such as size, strength, speed, and endurance" were valued in most games boys played, whereas weakness, emotional tenderness, and passive characteristics were often mocked and scorned as they made a boy "vulnerable to predatory rivals."[28] According to Rotundo's analysis, the shifting meaning of manliness meant that by the late-1800s, "the bad boy was now the hero" and "the good boy had become a sort of wan villain, a dull, weak, submissive husk of a child. The bad boy was manly, the good boy was effeminate, and virtue simply did not matter."[29] Though this is overstated (i.e., virtue did still matter and the constitutions of both heroes and villains ran a wide gamut from hulking to puny throughout the century), it is true that the ideals of manliness shifted during this era, moving the attributes of aggression and passion from vices to virtues.

This shift in what it meant to be a man impacted men coming of age during the antebellum era, and Elisha was no exception. He was small, just over five feet tall and never more than 125 pounds. As a child, he made up for his diminutive stature via robust and aggressive actions. But at the age of fourteen he suffered several attacks of rheumatic fever, which sapped him of his energy, and by the age of eighteen, it was apparent that he had suffered serious heart damage. How was he to make it in the world as a small, sickly man? This question plagued both Elisha and his father. John Kane was a robust and energetic man. In his younger years he displayed intellectual prowess as a politically savvy lawyer, but also physical power as one of the bravest (and most reckless) members of the Philadelphia Hose Company. Late in life he wrote with much bravado and undoubtedly a good deal of exaggeration that his fire-fighting career ended only after he had a bad fall from the steeple of the flaming State House.[30] An ambitious and assertive father, he encouraged his sons to adopt similar characteristics of daring and fortitude. When Elisha was fourteen and struggling with illness and schoolwork, his father wrote, "Stick to it, my son, the reward will come.... It would be a miserable world, if we had no difficulties to encounter: one of the best enjoyments we can have is that of reflecting on a duty, well performed by overcoming many obstacles."[31] He took an active role in Elisha's education, telling his wife Jane to stop spending so much time instructing his sons in music and drawing (subjects Elisha enjoyed greatly) and to instead focus on mathematics and writing, which he felt were "more important branches" of learning for young men.[32] Because he made his reputation by his own pen, John often advised Elisha on the finer points of writing, and his advice shows that he viewed writing as a manly and influential pursuit: He noted, "Don't strike out a bold thought or a strong word hastily: tameness is the more natural fault of a young writer."[33] In a letter of encouragement to Elisha, he praised his intellect, noting that he had "talents as good as Heaven is in the habit of giving," but chastised him for not working harder to develop them. He noted that skills "are acquired by practice, by self denial, by effort, by perseverance" and that Elisha was currently lacking these characteristics. He closed with the charge, "I hope, I expect, I am sure of much from you. Get well quick, & see that you do not disappoint."[34] When illness forced Elisha home from college, his father was both concerned and dismayed to watch him languish in bed. After a few weeks he was

no longer able to bear this and ordered Elisha to get up and get back to work saying, "If you must die—die in the harness."[35]

This stern command invigorated Elisha. Certain that his physical condition
would not allow him to pursue his hoped-for career as an engineer and naturalist,
he adopted a different plan of study. In the fall of 1839 he apprenticed himself to
Dr. William Harris of Philadelphia and began studying medicine at the University
of Pennsylvania, a choice that his family heartily supported. Elisha was a diligent
student, a hard-working resident at Blockley (now Philadelphia General) Hospital, and an impressive researcher. During his three years of medical training he
gained considerable hospital experience, established himself as a skilled doctor,
and published an article in the *American Journal of the Medical Sciences* on kiesteine,
a substance found in urine that can be an indicator of pregnancy.[36] His family
and peers were impressed by his efforts. His brother Tom wrote their father, "Is it
not delightful to see how the Doctor is coming on? He has that in him which can
make a great ornament & honour to his parents, nor does it seem slow at develop-
ing itself."[37]

Though medical school afforded Elisha many successes and the potential for
a lucrative and prestigious career, it was a difficult time for him. He was often
sick and continually agonized over his own worth: What good was a sickly doctor?
A sickly man? At times these thoughts depressed Elisha almost to the point of despair. Dr. William Marcellus McPheeters, the senior resident physician and Elisha's
immediate superior at Blockley, recalled an occasion when he and Elisha were
treating a "miserable, squalid, diminutive, and deformed pauper." Noting that this
man had a very attractive wife, McPheeters jokingly wondered what she must think
of her husband. He reported that Elisha replied, "It is to save some lady just such
reflections as these that I have made up my mind never to marry."[38] A few months
later, Elisha tried to explain to his parents the pain and frustration his continual
illness caused him, but he found them unsympathetic: "No one who has not experienced the suffocating state of low spirits induced by heart disease would do
other than you would do and have done—laugh at my explanation."[39] At other
times , however, his illness drove him to succeed. Reflecting on Elisha's demeanor
during his time at Blockley, Dr. McPheeters noted that Elisha was always aware of
"the gravity of his disease" but that it did not "affect the buoyancy of his spirits,
or to abate the ardour with which he pursued the objects of his ambition."
McPheeters even suggested that "the uncertain state of his health had a good deal
to do with his subsequent course of life, and the almost reckless exposure of himself to danger."[40]

To the surprise of his family, upon graduation from medical school in March
1842, Elisha did not try to establish himself as a physician in Philadelphia, but instead continued to do scientific research. Throughout his medical training, Elisha

conducted experiments both in medicine, and in the larger field of natural science. When his brother Tom traveled to Europe, Elisha continually pestered him for various specimens of plants, animals, and minerals; he also kept Tom busy hunting down the latest and best equipment for various laboratory projects.[41] In the month after Elisha's graduation, his father was bemused to note that Elisha had captured some "dear little rats" for his experiments, but that they had promptly escaped, forcing him to commandeer his kid-brother's guinea pigs "to comfort him in his study."[42]

Full of ambition but trapped in a sickly body, by the spring of 1842 Elisha came to the conclusion that he had two options in life: to quietly live a restrained, docile existence for fear of overstressing his weak body; or to throw caution to the wind and vigorously pursue his dreams of greatness and adventure, knowing that such activities could kill him. In May 1842, seemingly without any discussion with his family, he made up his mind. He abruptly left his family's house and moved into Lapedia, his uncle George Gray Leiper's country estate outside of Philadelphia, where he began a daily routine of exercise and strenuous activity. In explanation of his actions, he wrote his parents that he left the confines of their house because, while there, he felt "as if death had his grip upon my larynx." William Harris, his supervising physician during medical school, endorsed this decision. Elisha told his parents, "Should Harris be correct, [this treatment] would cure me, if wrong it would kill. The first was my hope and the latter my anticipation and thus I left you." He concluded:

> I hope to come back to you a new man—hope of life is for the first time urging me on and the very hope is worth a host. For the first time I begin to see that a life of usefulness may be before me, and for the next six months I intend to devote soul and body to this one great possibility. Eating, drinking, sleeping, riding, sweating and better than all forgetting—Living the life of the body that I may hereafter live that of the mind.... I will seek to expel Rheumatism, exercise to gain strength... and anticipate a time when I may settle down as a practicing physician.[43]

During this active summer in the company of his attractive and attentive cousin Mary Leiper, Elisha's health greatly improved. This convinced him that an active life was essential to his health and he thus began to entertain the idea of becoming a navy surgeon. His father had suggested this career during Elisha's final months of school, but Elisha shunned it because he then felt it would be both overtaxing and overbearing. He hated the thought of being under military command, having thoughtlessly to obey orders from others; however, by June 1842, with his health steadily improving, this option began to look more appealing. He wrote a letter to the Navy Board of Examiners requesting a position, and this letter is telling of Elisha's temperament at that time. After giving a standard account of his qualifications, he inserted a paragraph of personal testimony that was almost confessional in nature. He began, "I have been a somewhat desultory student, guided too often by the inclination of the moment in the selection of my topics. I have of course lost much time and have learnt few things as accurately as I could wish. I have, however, incidentally gained acquaintance with enough of French to read it with pleasure. I am a tolerable draftsman, and have practiced the delineations of morbid anatomy, not without satisfaction." He then admitted that his primary research and study had been in obstetrics (hardly a useful skill for a navy doctor), but explained that "since the change of purpose" that brought him before the Board, he had began new, more pertinent studies. He concluded, "I come, therefore, to be examined, with a consciousness of the absence of special preparation."[44] Though his application was favorably reviewed and accepted by the Navy Board of Examiners, no positions were then available. Elisha thus spent the winter of 1842-1843 attending lectures at Jefferson Medical College in Philadelphia, trying to improve his medical skills.[45] In January 1843, tired of waiting for a commission and feeling his health again failing from lack of activity, Elisha wrote to Navy Secretary Abel Upshur, inquiring about the possibility of shipping out on a merchant vessel in an effort to improve his health through more strenuous activity.[46]

This request shows Elisha firmly immersed in the popular ideas and culture of his age. In 1840, Richard Henry Dana's memoir, *Two Years Before the Mast*, became hugely popular. As a young man, Dana had been a promising scholar at Harvard until an acute attack of measles forced him to drop out. Fearing that he was losing his sight, and having found no cure in the common medical treatments of the day, Dana signed on for a two-year voyage as a common sailor, hoping that "by an entire change of life, and by a long absence from books and study" he would regain his health and manly energy. His book outlined his two-year cruise aboard a merchant vessel and vividly showed how it turned him from a sickly man into a powerful "jack tar" capable of hoisting the mainstay and negotiating exotic lands, as well as writing a popular book.[47]

This book said exactly what Elisha wanted to hear. He *could* beat his disease; he *could* live a life of adventure and greatness. All he needed was to go to sea—to travel the world and examine it with pen and magnifying glass in hand. The navy seemed the obvious option, but after his initial rush of enthusiasm about its prospects, he began to grow lukewarm. He wanted to travel and explore the world as a free-thinking man of science, not as a duty-bound, subservient naval officer. As an independent, strong-willed young man, the idea of military discipline horrified him. He knew what he did and did not want to do and could not tolerate the idea of "the routine life of a subordinate" that naval rank would impose on

Portrait of Elisha Kent Kane from May 1843. Reprinted in *Century Magazine* (Aug. 1898).

him.[48] This explains why he jumped when a far more appealing opportunity presented itself.

Following the Opium War of 1837-1842 between China and England, China was forced to surrender Hong Kong and open several "treaty ports" to British commerce. Not wanting to miss out on this new trade opportunity, the United States quickly organized a diplomatic mission to China, hoping to negotiate commercial treaties and potentially to gain a hold in China's forbidden capital, Peking (Beijing). Daniel Webster was initially chosen to head this sensitive diplomatic mission, but when he resigned his cabinet post early in 1843, Massachusetts statesman Caleb Cushing was appointed head of the delegation. Upon hearing of this mission, Elisha's father used his political connections to get Elisha a position on this mission, a popular idea apparently as Webster also insured that his son Fletcher would be on board. To ensure himself a place, Elisha wrote directly to Cushing and volunteered to serve as an "honorary" member of the delegation; this meant that he would not be paid for his service and would have no official navy rank. This freed Elisha from the naval regulations he so despised and gave him the option of leaving the expedition and traveling on his own.[49]

In the early months of 1843, while awaiting the expedition's departure, Elisha put together an elaborate scheme. He planned to travel with the delegation to China, but to then leave it and travel to the Philippines. Once there, he would set up a medical practice in Manila that would serve the many foreign vessels passing through its active port. In preparation for this endeavor, he secured letters of introduction from Philadelphia residents who had connections in the Philippines. He and his father were both certain that he could make a hefty income in such a position while also expanding his reputation by writing medical and popular articles about his adventures as a foreign doctor.[50]

On May 24, 1843, with Elisha happily aboard, the *Brandywine* left Norfolk and crossed the Atlantic to the African island port of Madeira, only to cross back to Rio de Janeiro, Brazil, before crossing once more to India; this circuitous route was typical as it allowed sailing vessels to take advantage of prevailing winds and currents. During this trip, Kane discovered another reason to avoid a career with the navy, sea sickness, a condition that plagued him the rest of his seafaring life. One thing that helped him keep his mind off his discomfort was a young boy named William Henry Weaver. Orphaned at a young age, Weaver was placed in the care of William Robinson, who arranged for him to ship aboard Cushing's expedition as a midshipman. Kane took Weaver under his wing, serving as both an instructor and mentor. He had Weaver keep an unofficial logbook of the journey and instructed him in basic medical skills. This instruction and companionship delighted Kane and turned into a life-long friendship with Weaver.[51]

While in Rio, Kane observed the celebration of Emperor Dom Pedro II's marriage to Princess Theresa Christina of Bourbon and attended the massive reception that followed. He also spent a few days climbing in the Organ Mountains that surround Rio. From Rio the *Brandywine* sailed for Bombay (Mumbai) by way of the Cape of Good Hope, arriving on October 25. Cushing had not accompanied the mission to this point, choosing instead to meet up with it in Bombay. He was delayed, however, and this gave Kane a month in India with little to do but study and explore. He poured over books on mathematics, navigation, and European languages when confined to the ship, but spent most of his time roaming the area, visiting the sculpted caves at Elephanta and Karli and crossing to Ceylon (Sri Lanka) with several British officers to join in an elephant hunt near Kandy.[52]

Elisha kept a detailed journal of his experiences and medical observations during this time so he could send them home for publication. His family took these efforts very seriously; in the fall of 1843 his father took a class at Thomas Jefferson medical school so he would "be learned in physiology by the time I receive your first [manuscript] for revision." He encouraged Elisha, "Don't fail, as circumstances permit, to make yourself remembered here anew by writings on any subject whatever, medical, scientific, or narrative. I can use everything you send me."[53] A few months later he wrote back, assuring Elisha that he had put his journal to good use, passing along the official reports and editing the rest to "publish to the rest of the world in the newspaper."[54]

Cushing's ship finally met up with the *Brandywine* in late November, and, with the delegation complete, they set sail for the Bay of Canton on December 9, arriving on February 27, 1844. During this long trip, Kane became fast friends with Daniel Webster's son Fletcher, who served as secretary to the legation. Webster was both amused and impressed with Elisha's manic quest for knowledge and experience. He noted that even though Elisha was already an accomplished physician, "he seemed to think very lightly of his acquirements" and was "continually looking forward to something beyond... evidently annoyed when not engaged in something, and always restless unless busy,—for hours in the stateroom buried in mathematics, and then next seen at the masthead or over the ship's side."[55] Upon arrival in Canton (Guangdong), it was quickly apparent that the negotiations would take a very long time as the Chinese made every effort to delay the Americans; they did not even let the delegates set foot on Chinese soil, so all negotiations were held at a temple in the Portuguese trade-city of Macao. Peter Parker, a doctor and missionary who had worked in that region for years, served as the delegation's primary interpreter. Because Parker was an experienced physician, Elisha, as assistant surgeon to the expedition, was not needed. This allowed him to leave the delegation in March 1844 and travel with the *Brandywine* to the Philippine Islands, where it was to inspect supplies left in Manila by the U.S. East India Squadron.[56] This was exactly what Elisha had hoped for when he joined the delegation. In the Philippines he would have no official duties and could thus explore the islands, especially the main island of Luzon, where he could begin laying the groundwork for a medical practice in Manila. But before he left Macao, his plans were shattered. He discovered that to practice medicine in Spanish-held Manila he would need permission directly from Spain, which he did not have. He also learned that his idea was not as unique as he had thought; there were already several European doctors with well-established practices in Manila. He wrote his family of this disappointment and they feared he would be "full of disappointment" and "gloomy," and undoubtedly he was for a time.[57] Once in Luzon, however, it was not long before Elisha's adventurous spirit propelled him to a new and more exciting plan of action.

In the 1840s the line between scientist and adventurer was blurred. In fact, the term *scientist* was not yet in common usage or readily defined. According to the *Oxford English Dictionary*, in 1834 the British Association for the Advancement of Science actively debated what to call their members, feeling that the commonly used term *philosopher* was "too wide and too lofty." The word scientist—derived in comparison to those who do art being called artists—was debated but ultimately dismissed because they felt the term "was not generally palatable."[58] This lexicographical confusion was telling of the profession as a whole. Science was not yet a professional discipline; it was an activity done by skilled amateurs and generally trained "natural philosophers." There were certainly professionals who were doing science, most notably renowned German scholar Alexander von Humboldt, who was then compiling vast amounts of meticulously collected data into a massive, universe-explaining series of books he humbly entitled, *Cosmos*; but even such professionals acknowledged and happily used data collected by well-educated laymen who traveled the globe recording what they saw. This is what Elisha wanted to be— a "man of science." From the time of his data-collecting trek across the Blue Ridge Mountains with William Barton Rogers during his days at the University of Virginia, Elisha had remained an avid student of nature. In 1843, at the age of twenty-three, he was in an exotic land filled with questions and curiosities that he longed to examine, and it was to this pursuit that he readily applied himself.

Within weeks after his arrival in the Philippines, Elisha set off for Taal Lake, a location famous for its active volcano that rises 1,000 feet out of its waters. Accompanied by Baron Diedrick von Loë, a young Prussian baron he met in Manila, and led by native guides provided by a local clergyman, Elisha hoped to inspect the volcano. Upon arrival, Elisha recorded that the volcano's mouth was two miles in circumference and dropped more than one hundred feet to a beach of volcanic ash surrounding a steaming lake that bubbled around several sulfur-covered cones protruding from its surface. Loë was surprised, and their guides horrified, when Elisha decided to descend into the crater, cross the beach, and collect a specimen of the bubbling liquid to see if it was sulfuric acid. Loë consented to assist in this daring feat only after Elisha hastily penciled a note that absolved him of any blame in what Loë felt was likely to be Elisha's demise.[59] With the help of their reluctant guides they fashioned a rope out of bamboo and dug eight holes for the guides to brace themselves in as they lowered Elisha to the beach below. Loë was to follow him down, but their makeshift rope would not hold his heavy frame. At this point, the native guides began to abandon their stations, leaving Elisha stranded. Quickly grabbing Elisha's pistol (which didn't actually work), Loë waved it in their faces, and as Elisha wrote in his journal, "after an interesting jumble of Tagolog & Spanish [Loë] succeeded in conveying the conviction that any man who spoke, or laughed, or changed his betel nut, or quit his hole, was to be instantly shot through the head."[60] Loë forced one of the guides, Isidro, to follow Elisha down the rope. This act saved Elisha's life because by the time Isidro made it down the rope, Elisha had passed out from the fumes. Isidro tied Elisha's limp body to the rope so Loë and the others could pull him out of the crater. After Elisha revived, the group began their trek back to Manila, but before long the guides abandoned Elisha and Loë and joined local natives in aggressively protesting Elisha's profanation of their sacred volcano. The two explorers sought shelter in a thicket and fired their pistols until local friars came to their rescue.[61] When he was safely back in Manila, Elisha recorded this story in prose full of romantic and youthful flare. It is impossible to know whether the discrepancies in his story (e.g. first his pistol does not work, then he is firing it to scare off natives) are the errors of hasty writing or the result of artistic embellishment for heightened effect, but either way the deed and its vivid telling demonstrate Kane's ability to construct and record a thrilling adventure justified by scientific inquiry. His journal from this time includes this and several other exciting tales, each clearly written with publication in mind.[62]

Shortly after this adventure, Elisha received a large package of letters from home, responding to the letters he had sent them from India and Canton. His father wrote him a joyous letter, holding him up as "the flag bearer" for the family and praising his "unchanged purpose of mind and heart" despite hardships. A life of seafaring and adventure were clearly gaining Elisha the manly virtues his father and the larger culture so respected. His father exclaimed that, "It was delightful to find your affections growing warmer and... your manly determination gathering energy from thoughts of home. You are moving onward gallantly, my son,—and however fortunes may seem to vary for the time, I feel that you must and will succeed.

From William Godfrey's *Godfrey's Narrative of the Last Grinnell Arctic Exploring Expedition, in Search of Sir John Franklin, 1853-4-5* (Philadelphia, J.T. Lloyd & Co., 1857).

DR. KANE DESCENDS INTO THE CRATER OF A VOLCANO.

Indeed, I am proud at heart of you."[63] But this parental praise had its limits. Within a few months, the family letters changed in tone as they learned of Elisha's desire to leave the delegation permanently and to keep exploring the world on his own. In a letter back to his son, Judge Kane again praised his spirit and assured him that funds were available for his full support during Cushing's mission (up to $1,000), but then demanded that once the delegation ended, he was to "come home." He stressed, "No outer Island, no South American project, but home, home to us, and to such welcome as no man has a right to think coldly of."[64]

These family letters show the multidimensional expectations of manhood in the 1840s. Elisha was praised for his fortitude, his daring, and his ability to push forward despite adversity and disappointment. These traits exemplify the powerful independence that was of "ultimate value" in antebellum male culture; however, even though independence was praised, the traits that defined manhood in the decades before—especially, loyalty and duty—were also still expected of a young man.[65] As his father pointed out, Elisha's "manly determination" was growing because of his adventurous spirit as well as because of his growing affection and "thoughts of home" that his prolonged absence inspired within him. In early 1844, the Kane family was on the cusp of becoming a "big family" in Philadelphia. Tom was studying in Paris and planning to become a lawyer. The Kane's next eldest son, Robert Patterson (Pat), was also thinking of law. Thanks to his political activities and the spoils of party politics, John Kane was on the verge of great things; he would be Pennsylvania attorney general within a year and a U.S. judge within two. Elisha was expected to come home and contribute to the family, too. This conflict between independence and duty illustrates the changing currents of manhood—the shift between the eighteenth-century ideal of service and duty, and the post-industrial, later-nineteenth-century ideal of rugged and aggressive independence. For his sons, John Kane did not see independence and manly determination as ends in and of themselves, rather, they were the means to achieving the more important role of manhood, providing for your family and community. To him, a man rising in the world simply for the sake of personal gain was verging on improper, even sinful. He wrote Elisha, "You have seen the world, and have learnt valuable lessons that books can never teach: you have gained a name and position among men, and honourable ones both: and you have tried our affections and your own, and have strengthened them by the trial.... Now there is no reason in the world for your continuation away from us."[66]

Elisha and his brothers Tom and Patterson respected, even revered, their father, but they also chafed against his authoritarian nature. Like Elisha, Tom also suffered from a frail, sickly body and had sought to cure himself via a trip to Paris for a year of study and recovery. He was heartened by Elisha's increased vigor and wrote his parents that he was tired of being sickly, exclaiming, "I will try and feel like our brave Elish', and believe that at all events it is better to 'die fighting.'" After learning of Elisha's travel escapades from their parents, he praised Elisha's efforts and his driven, independent nature. He explained, "You are pleased with his deeds and jests so far—eh?—but wait till you see what is to come, if his life stands up to back him staunchly. I know him... even unto the most interior nakedness of his heart's core. All of his written words, only tell me truistically that as Elisha Kent Kane was, so he is and ever will be world without end. Amen."[67] When Tom returned home in the spring of 1844, he was convinced that Elisha's adventures could be made into a great adventure book, and that such an effort would help the family's cumulative reputation in the world. Not wanting Elisha to pass up any opportunities for adventure, and dismayed by Elisha's latest letter that recounted how he passed up an excursion because it was too costly, he scolded Elisha for not being more daring and extravagant. He exclaimed, "Damn your 'resisting temptation'— damn and double damn your having lived so cheaply, says T.L.K."[68]

Whether Elisha took Tom's advice or had overstated his frugality and restraint in the first place, it is certain that he did not live a monastic life in Manila. A letter from Baron Loë to Elisha alluded to them "drinking gin and water from morning till evening and smoking again from twilight till dawning. Loë also bemoaned the fact that a recent escapade without Elisha—one that involved a fine "collection of Tuchan and Mestizo women"—was not "equal to what we have seen on our trips."[69] Though Kane was a skilled and disciplined doctor and student of science, he was also a young and exuberant twenty-four year-old free for the first time from the confines of a very proper home. Independence more than duty was on his mind.

In May 1844, Elisha returned to Macao and took up his station with the American legation. He enjoyed the pomp and ceremony of the negotiations and described the elegant events fully to his family. He was especially impressed with the drinking game, "Chin-chin," that had the Americans and their Chinese hosts gulping larger and larger quantities of wine-flavored rice liquor. He noted that the dinner ended when they finally, "toasted the Emperor of China, hip-hipped him, hurrahed him, hiccupped him, and withdrew." In the same letter, however, despite (or perhaps because of) his father's wishes, he announced that he had decided not to return home with the delegation. He enthusiastically reported that he had resigned his post, participated in one final official dinner, and then two hours later "was in a chartered boat, armed to the teeth, and threading the ladrone dangers of the Canton River. I was a freed man."[70]

Elisha declaring himself a "freed man" was a declaration of double meanings. He was happy to be free of the delegation and again able to explore on his own, and this was certainly the meaning he meant for his parents to understand, but more importantly, by refusing to return home, he was directly defying the wishes of his domineering father, a rebellion also worth celebrating. Elisha's impetuous decision came as no surprise to his friends aboard the *Brandywine*; they knew him as a young man who thrived on risk and adventure. Fletcher Webster noted that in

Macao, Kane often set off alone on "excursions always attended with a good deal of personal danger," and that he had "explored the whole town itself before we, of slower motions, had commenced." The ship's chaplain, Rev. George Jones, further noted that Elisha had "a great enthusiasm in manner.... He seemed to be all hope, all ardor, and his eye appeared already to take in the whole world as his own."[71]

When Kane left the delegation, he traveled down the Canton River to the busy harbor of Whampoa (present day Huangpu), and set up a temporary medical practice to gain funds for further travel. He teamed up with young English Surgeon Michael O'Sullivan, and the two of them managed a hospital boat that serviced foreign ships coming into port. He also engaged in some exciting and experimental medical practices; at one point he helped medical missionary Peter Parker in an amazing surgery in which they removed a basketball-sized tumor from a man's head. Elisha worked for about six months in Whampoa and earned nearly $3,000.[72] This success inspired him to pursue again a practice in Manila. He wrote to Washington Irving, then U.S. minister to Spain, and asked him to secure permission for the endeavor.[73]

Kane gained a new sense of independence and power while working in Whampoa, earning his own keep for the first time in his life. He began to see himself not as the son of John Kane of Philadelphia (though his father still loomed large in his thoughts), but as an independent man. He was an explorer, determined to understand new lands and new peoples and to turn these discoveries into significant contributions to the scientific community. When his family got news of Elisha's adventure, their reactions were mixed. Their letters from this time show that Elisha, Tom and their parents were all struggling with what role sons should take in the family. Tom returned from Paris in the spring of 1844, and was initially excited about Elisha's adventures and their potential for adding to the family's prestige, but after several months in the confines of his parents' house, his feelings about Elisha's absence began to change. As the eldest son at home, he was expected to guide his four younger siblings' entrances into proper society, and this was no small task. This responsibility began making him jealous and bitter about Elisha's freedom. Tom tried to lure Elisha back home, noting that many older physicians were about to retire, thus opening great opportunities for young physicians. He also noted that the social scene was ripe with opportunity as well; of a ball he attended he said: "The gentlemen were shocking creatures indeed.... Bad dressers and bad talkers: they are totally ignorant of what a 'woman' means and to crown all, are generally very awkward and very ugly. I am pleased to see them so vulgar & provincial—on my own account—and yours—if you shall soon be with us."[74] But by the end of the year, when Elisha refused to return and proposed staying abroad for another ten years, Tom grew bitter and blunt. He wrote to Elisha, "You must not and by Christ's life you shall not stay to practice at Whampoa."[75]

Tom's resentment was twofold. He more than Elisha subscribed to the older ideal of masculinity and thus felt duty bound to his family and community. Unlike his elder brother, he would be a community and social activist his entire life and invest huge amounts of time, energy, and money into maintaining "the family." Despite this, however, Tom also wanted to be independent and not restrained by family control. The same pen that begged Elisha to come home to his duty also recorded Tom's longing for Elisha's independence. In September 1844 he wrote: "I appreciate... the blessedness of independence, because of my experience of the antagonist state. At this moment, kind as I must say the progenitor dual are, I would—not have your heroism in practicing physic in a Chinese... swamp—but do almost anything else!"[76] A few months later, in a letter he kept from his parents' eyes, he proposed a "brotherhood" between himself and Elisha. Together they would make their own way in the world. Frustrated with their family he exclaimed:

> If you were here, what in the devil do you suppose I would care for them? Why we'd make light of them all, and rub through the world, right finely till both were able to make the Declaration of Independence. If you want my place, as lighting rod to carry off the electric shocks of the progenitors, formerly yours, then I'll put into execution my idea of going to practice at New Orleans, leaving you the onus—the duty, which alone keeps me here, of taking care that Bess & Pat & John get in good society—of which without something done there is at present no chance.[77]

Continuing with this idea a few days later, Tom wrote, "I can see damned plain now that you have been freed from our cramping [and] are rebelling for two of us." He felt that Elisha's actions had forced their parents to accept them both as independent young men, and he was right to some degree. In a letter from this time their father wrote, "Indeed, dear Elisha, as to yourself we have mingled feelings always, and all of us. Our hearts would call you home at any price, and it is only our reliance on your judgment and affection that makes us tolerate your absence."[78] Their mother expressed similar feelings. She resigned herself to his independence, and though she still grieved his absence, she consoled herself by comparing him with several of his "lounging companions." Noting several young men of Philadelphia society she exclaimed, "I cannot understand how these aforesaid young men can calmly occupy the paternal home, be fed and clothed by the overtasked strength of a Father no longer young, and refuse every offer that might contribute to their own support, absolutely preferring a life of utter idleness & worthlessness."[79] The Kanes wanted to keep their sons close and involved in family activities, but they also understood and even admired the spirit that carried them away.

Craving independence but wanting to maintain family reputation, Tom began laying out plans for Elisha and his future—plans that would establish them in

Portrait of Elisha, Tom, and John K. Kane from May 1843. Courtesy of Special Collections, University of Virginia Library. This image captures much of the tension that lay beneath the surface of the Kane family. Sitting beneath the proud but critical gaze of their father, Elisha and Tom both appear young and determined, but focused in different directions.

proper society and free them from the more odious pressures of familial obligation. Having worked out a careful budget, Tom concluded that all that stood between them and a life of independent success was $1500. This amount would allow them to rent offices and living space just off Washington Square (a fashionable business district) and to cover their daily expenses for more than a year, giving them time to establish their law and medical practices. Given their exceptional abilities—"Are we not able to push our way better than the dull driver cattle of the common herd?"—Tom was sure that within four years they would each be leaders in their professions and "at the head of society."[80]

The correspondence between Tom and Elisha at this time shows a deep and intimate relationship, one that would continue for years to come. The affection and loyalty they expressed, and the joint plans they made with each other, sound to the modern reader more akin to the bonds of marriage than of fraternity. Such a relationship was not uncommon in the antebellum period. Young men often developed deep, almost marriage-like relationships with a close friend or brother. Because the general assumption for middle- and upper-class men was that marriage came only after the establishment of a career, young men often left their childhood homes for some kind of partnership with another young man. This relationship could take the form of a formal joint business venture, but more often it was an informal relationship of mutual support. Sharing a dwelling and resources was common, and this bond often remained intact up until the courtship and marriage of one or both of the men.[81]

Unbeknownst to Tom, as he was planning their Philadelphia-based future, thousands of miles away in Whampoa, Elisha was also reconsidering his life plans. Just as rheumatic fever had ended his career goals eight years earlier, in December 1844 illness—this time "rice fever" (probably cholera)—again confounded his plans and forced him to rethink his future. Discouraged with his life and disgusted with his frail constitution, he decided to sail for home. A surviving journal written the day before his departure shows the anger he felt as his pride of manly self-sufficiency was replaced by feelings of sickly inadequacy.

> China had been my first field of action and responsibility. It was here that casting off the dependence of a child I assumed the self-sustaining duties of a man.... I felt myself improving in my profession and advancing in experience. My present success redeemed all my previous failures—it exceeded all my expectations. My debts had been paid, my position established and, in a little heaven of self-satisfaction, I was looking forward with almost childlike delight to what? To day dreams....
>
> This then was China.... I at last felt that I could gladden those I loved by an account of my success, and a hurried letter gave vent to my hopes. Three days after its completion and one before its departure, I was delirious—for three weeks my life was despaired of, and when at last I awoke from the stupefaction of a frightful fever it was to feel, not that disease had crushed my energies, nor sickness broken down the pride of manhood, but that both were useless—Nature's frail instrument the carcass had broken down.[82]

On January 25, 1845, after selling his portion of the Whampoa medical practice and abandoning his plans for further travel, Elisha shipped out from Macao, discouraged and heading for home; however, his fortunes again changed. After a few days at sea, Elisha's health improved and his spirit of adventure returned. What was to be a quick trip home extended into a six-month journey that spanned much of Asia, Africa, and Europe.[83] The few surviving letters from this time show Elisha in good spirits and back to his intrepid self. In March 1845, his seven-year-old brother, Willie, wrote that he had "laughed very much" at Elisha's previous letters, but was now refusing to write "quite so much as I have done till you write to me how you escaped from the indians and the shark."[84]

Elisha sailed from Macao to Singapore and then on to Borneo and Sumatra, stopping briefly at both islands before he headed for Galle, Ceylon, which he reached on February 19. He crossed over to India soon thereafter and explored its eastern coast, perhaps as far north as Calcutta. While in India, Elisha met the wealthy nobleman, Dwarkanath Tagore (grandfather of poet Rabindranath Tagore), who was planning a trip to England to visit Queen Victoria's court; he invited Kane to travel with him. The only record of this part of Elisha's journey comes from William Elder, a friend of the Kane family, who wrote a biography of Elisha in 1857, that was constructed from family letters and remembrances. Elder claimed that before Elisha left with Tagore, he spent "some months... in a tour of exploration through the interior of India, including the ascent of the Himalaya Mountains." Elder's facts are then contradictory: He said Kane traveled with Tagore by sea to Suez, which would have meant a sailing route through the Red Sea, but also claims that he visited Persia and Syria, which suggests that Elisha sailed up the Persian Gulf and traveled overland to Suez. Whichever route he took, it is clear that some of Elder's story is exaggerated because Kane arrived in Suez by April 3, giving him only a month and a half to have made it there from Ceylon, leaving little time for exploration or overland travel.[85]

By mid-April, Kane was in Cairo and, thanks to a letter of introduction from Tagore, he obtained safe conduct for travel in Egypt and membership in the prestigious Egyptian Society of Cairo.[86] On April 15 he hired a boat and pilot and headed up the Nile, bound for the pyramids. In Dendera, disaster struck. Kane wanted to inspect the site's famous ruins and went ashore for the night. When he returned the next morning, his boat, along with all the trunks containing his collections and papers, was gone. He discovered the boat downstream, lodged on a sandbar and emptied of its contents. He had fortunately taken his money with him and was thus able to continue his travels. A few days later he recovered his pocket watch, which he saw in the possession of his interpreter, who escaped during the ensuing scuffle.[87]

Though sick over the loss of his artifacts and journals from the past two years, Kane continued his trek, making it to Thebes sometime before May. Awed by the monuments there, he wrote home, "there is something so vast in the dimensions of these colossal ruins that I cannot embrace details; and, indeed, I almost fear that

I shall leave Thebes without a definite impression of anything but magnitude." He spent hours exploring these monuments and enthusiastically adopted the local lifestyle, wearing "native dress, with a beard so long that I have to tuck it in."[88]

While in Thebes, Kane learned that the German Egyptologist, Richard Lepsius, was just across the river, working at the great temple in Karnak. Lepsius had recently become a foreign member of the American Philosophical Society, an honor he had learned of via a letter from the society's secretary, John K. Kane. Elisha's name alone thus gained him welcome with Lepsius. They spent several days together, Kane enthralled with Lepsius's work and Lepsius glad to have a learned companion. Over the next weeks, traveling by camel, boat, and on foot, Kane visited the ruins at Luxor, Karnak, Abydos, Saqquara, Serapeum, and Masara, as well as the Valley of the Kings and the two statues of Amenophis III.[89] The Colossi of Memnon (two massive statues of Amenhotep III) was the stage for another of Elisha's fantastic tales of exploration and daring. According to his account, he believed that Egyptian hieroglyphics were "nothing more nor less than a great library of monumental history, where all that is wanted is the patient labor of a reader." Thus, when he reached this monument, he immediately set off to read the tablet perched on the pharaoh's knees, not the top side of it, which was easily read by climbing to the statue's head via an easy route up the back, but the underside of it, which he was certain was also engraved with small hieroglyphs. As Elisha told his family, this presented a challenge because the ten-inch thick tablet was thirty-five feet above the ground and the only way to inspect it was to climb the statue's massive legs and suspend yourself beneath it. Elisha reported that he stripped down to his pantaloons and began the difficult task, though his guides warned against it. Within minutes he was stranded, unable to move either up or down. Fortunately, his boatman found a guide who climbed out onto the tablet and pulled Kane up to safety with his sash.[90]

This story casts light (and a degree of doubt) onto all of Elisha's former and later accounts of his adventures. He passed this story onto his family, and they put it to good use, publishing it in newspaper accounts and, eventually, recounting it to his biographer.[91] In his and their telling, this escapade is self-deprecating, because it shows a young man determined to risk life and limb for the attainment of knowledge, but doing so with more bravado than wisdom. The account never notes whether there were any hieroglyphs on the underside of the tablet, only that Elisha got himself stuck and had to be saved by his guide, a story thematically similar to his account of his descent into the Taal volcano. Elisha and his family publicized these stories later in his life, when he was about to set off on what many viewed as a foolhardy mission to the arctic, and in this context, these early tales were clearly designed to show that he had always been a daring and courageous man of science, willing to face danger for the sake of knowledge, but also that he had matured—his earlier recklessness had been tempered into well-experienced wisdom. These stories were thus key to helping establish Elisha's public persona, but, at least in the case of the Colossi of Memnon, they were also hugely exaggerated or simply untrue. The Colossi are massive statues, but their tablets are only twenty feet off the ground and are easily and completely visible from beneath. There would have never been any reason for Elisha to need to climb to inspect them, and if he had, it would not have been a difficult climb.

In May 1845 Elisha parted with Lepsius, and soon thereafter received an injury to his leg. Whether it was inflicted by "thieving Bedouins" as he later suggested, or by some less dramatic means, he returned to Cairo and then pressed on to Alexandria to seek medical attention. While there he developed a high fever that incapacitated him for several weeks. When he was traveling among the monuments he had sent several boats to Alexandria full of artifacts he planned to ship home. The anguish of his illness was thus heightened when he learned that none of these boats made it to Alexandria with their cargoes still intact.[92] Still ill but wanting to press on with his travels, he left Alexandria and arrived in Athens on June 10. He spent the next few weeks visiting the ancient cities of the area, including Thebes, Livadia, Mount Helicon, and the Pythos oracle at Castri. He then traveled up the Adriatic and through northern Italy and Switzerland to Paris, which he reached by July 13.[93] This comfortable trip through the lands of European antiquity revived Elisha's spirits and he no longer relished the idea of returning home. He contemplated putting his plan of a Manila based medical practice back into action and audaciously wrote his father, asking him to use his influence in this effort.[94] He also bluntly confessed his "Anti-Home resolve" to Tom and sharply stated, "For God sake don't urge me homeward." He felt he was doing exactly what he should be doing—gaining experience and influence—and asked Tom whose fault it would be if he returned home prematurely.[95]

Tom's reply was sharp and direct. Addressing Elisha's question he flatly stated, "I do not mind answering you that it would be mine.... You may think it better to stay away just as sincerely as I, that you should return. We have seen the world... with fundamental ideas of very different colour and relative dimension." With a sarcastic bite he then continued, "I am not in possession of all the facts belonging to the case. I do not know [what] breezes, paseos and muchachas there may be... to console for deprivation of Philadelphia redbrick & green window shutters, Quaker formalities, half cut provincialisms and Puritan forced virtues, and above all its hard labour at solitary confinement." Pressing further he noted, "I do not know even, what kind of a fellow you are and whether, after living as you have lived, you can be content to drive the one horse gig,... or apply the energies which have moved Pashas and Prince Tagores... to conciliating aristocratic Messieurs,... humbugging Hospital Managers and Guardians of the Poor."[96] Tom's tone then shifted, however. "You talk much about your changes. I also have changed and if I have changed in any one thing—it is that I have learned the value of ambition—the true value." Tom told Elisha that he too had had "grand dreams." Inspired no doubt by the possitivist philosophy of Augusta Comté, which he greatly admired, Tom confessed that he had dreamed of nothing less than beginning his own religion. "By Jove it was a grand scheme!" he exclaimed. "A religion suited to the 19th century—a religion containing all things and influencing all conduct of life of man, nation, & government—emancipating women, slaves, industrial classes—a religion containing [in] itself the principle of its own change and amelioration... a religion of movement." Tom had spent much of the early 1840s in Paris, trying to regain his health, but also mixing with many of the era's most progressive thinkers. Even though he would become an ardent reformer and activist in later years, in the summer of 1845, the struggle to establish himself as a lawyer in Philadelphia, his poor health, and the inane, grinding demands of society life had crushed his spirit. As he explained to Elisha: "I lost my noble aspirations for the good of my species;... I, the Moses grew faint hearted. There was no one to say 'It is I, be of good cheer, be not afraid.'"[97] Tom thus pronounced himself a realist who had given up on changing the world and achieving worldly renown. "I value fame for what it will bring in the Market. *Nota Bene*—Price payable in Annuity insured for Life and Life only." He urged Elisha to accept this as well and to stop pursuing fame for its own sake. In a sly analogy appropriate for a nineteenth-century man of science, he noted, "If I have again any longings for immortality of remembrance—and all that sort of humbug—I will waste fifty dollars at my death to procure the deposition of my bones in an asphalt envelope (like that of amber round bugs)... which will make a fine fossil of me for the investigation of the race which is to succeed man."[98]

Tom then again requested that Elisha return home and assured him that if he did so, his travels of the past years would gain him an ample amount of fame and financial gain. "You have already earned enough reputation to be of profit to you as a Philadelphian. Write a really good book of travels—tell some really marvelous stories of Medical Experience, and you can easily be puffed enough to prepare you for being a busy practitioner and a gift of the gab Lecturer. Succeed in achieving this... and no one can gainsay that you will be first Ceasar of the Village." Tom confessed that he was tempted to leave Philadelphia for New Orleans where he could establish a lucrative law practice and get away from Philadelphia society, but he assured Elisha that he would prefer to stay and work together to preserve and enhance the family's fortune and place in society—"This is a chief reason why I have urged your coming to stand at my side." Writing again in a tone of brotherly affection and jest he concluded, "With your person, prestige and moustache (don't cut it off till after you show it at home) we can make some capital—

Map of Elisha Kent Kane's Travels, 1843-45

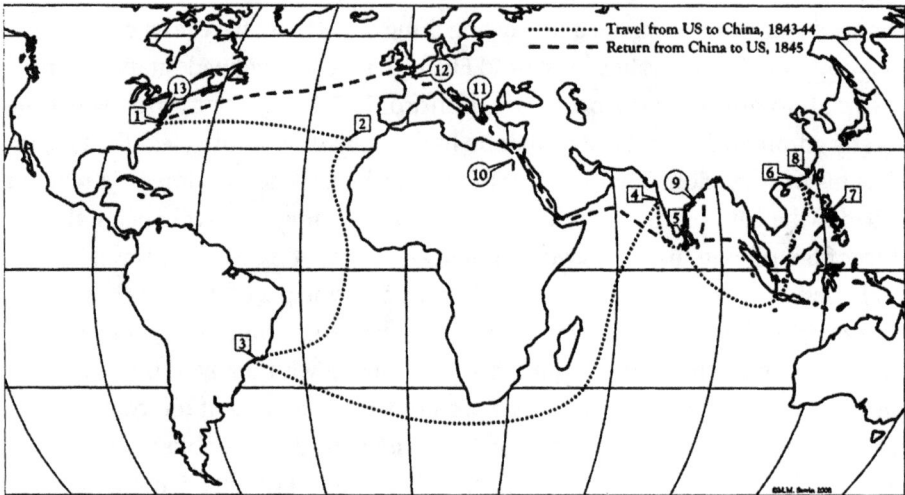

Map by Author, 2008.
1.   May 24, 1843, left Norfolk with the Cushing Delegation aboard the *Brandywine*.
2.   Following the common trade route, the expedition crossed to Madeira.
3.   The expedition then crossed back to Rio, taking advantage of prevailing winds. Kane explored Rio and the Organ Mountains in September 1843.
4.   Arrived in Bombay (Mumbai) India on October 25. Spent November exploring the area and the sculpted caves of Elephanta and Karli.
5.   Sailed to Ceylon (Sri Lanka) and joined a British regiment in an Elephant hunt near Kandy. The entire delegation left from Colombo on December 9, 1843.
6.   February 27, 1844, arrived at the Portuguese trade port of Macao in Canton Bay. Negotiations began, lasting until August when the treaty was signed.
7.   March 1844, Kane left the delegation to explore the Philippine Islands and Taal Volcano.
8.   In late May Kane rejoined the delegation. He resigned his post on June 25, leaving for Whampoa (Huangpu) to set up a medical practice. He became ill and left for Singapore on January 25, 1845.
9.   February 19 arrived in Ceylon (Sri Lanka) with renewed health. Perhaps traveled as far north as Calcutta, but there is no documentation of this portion of his trip.
10. April 13 arrived in Suez. Proceeded to Cairo and then south up the Nile to Luxor, Karnak, and the Valley of the Kings. Robbed, injured, and ill, Kane went to Alexandria in late May.
11. By June 10, Kane was in Athens. He toured several ancient Greek sites before taking a steamer to Trieste and then crossing northern Italy and Switzerland into France.
12. During the summer of 1845 he toured Paris and considered another stint as a foreign doctor, but under pressure from his family, he went to England to catch a ship back to Philadelphia.
13. August 6, 1845, returned to Philadelphia as one of the best-traveled men of his era.

even if you don't want to get married.... If you will come home to stay, I will have myself admitted to the bar by Winter and we will put into operation our plan of the joint offices."[99] This letter worked. Though still somewhat hesitant about his decision, Elisha returned to Philadelphia in the late summer of 1845.

Conservatively estimated, Elisha traveled nearly forty thousand miles during his two-and-a-half year trip. He crossed the Atlantic four times; cruised the waters of the Indian and Pacific Oceans as well as the Mediterranean, Red and Adriatic Seas; and visited five continents. This extensive journey made him one of the best-traveled Americans of his day, and Tom was accurate in thinking that the story of these travels could be turned into a successful book. The U.S. reading public was then clamoring for travel narratives from exotic lands. It was at this same time that Herman Melville, another young man who took to the sea in the early 1840s, turned his seafaring adventures into a series of popular books, beginning with *Typee* in 1846 and including *Moby-Dick* in 1851. Elisha had the skills for such a project; his letters home show a lively, energetic writing style, and his surviving sketches show that he was capable of drafting rich illustrations to accompany his text. Piecing together his surviving notes and journals, Elisha began this project upon his return home, writing up a narrative of his time in the Philippines.[100]

During the three years Elisha was away on his worldwide wanderings, his family had been busy at home. His brother Patterson had grown from an energetic sixteen-year-old to a dedicated nineteen-year-old law student, and Tom was prepared to pass the bar and begin his own law practice. The most important change, however, came thanks to the political spoils of the 1844 election that gained John Kane the post of attorney general of Pennsylvania.[101] The Kane family Elisha returned to was one of far greater political power and social position than the one he had left.

Given the Kane family's new prominence, after Elisha's return neither he nor his parents wanted him to remain in the Navy. Elisha had been perpetually seasick during rough weather and his aversion to military discipline had only grown stronger during his time with the delegation. Though proud of his accomplishments while abroad, his family was now anxious for Elisha to settle in Philadelphia permanently; they wanted him to establish a medical practice, not to continue wandering the globe as a naval surgeon. Withdrawal from the navy was not a problem because it had never called him into service. This left Elisha free to return to civilian life and set up a medical practice in Philadelphia. Although he still longed for further travel and adventure, Elisha acquiesced to his family's wishes and settled in Philadelphia to set up a practice, earn some money, and publish a narrative of his adventures. Following Tom's plan, they rented an office on Walnut Street and Elisha began establishing himself within the medical community by keeping a "full round of engagements."[102] He worked on his book and also began to translate French medical works for publication. He wrote to Henry Selden, a friend returning from Paris, and asked him to bring with him, "any medical work suitable for a translation—short and marketable, [that] meets your eye."[103]

During this time, Elisha also rekindled old romantic relationships and began some new ones as well. He maintained a close relationship with his cousin Mary Leiper and also began seeing another cousin, Helen Patterson, the sister of his University of Virginia roommate, Robert Patterson (marriage between cousins was quite common at this time).[104] How intimate these relationships became is impossible to tell, but Elisha was certainly sexually active at this time. In addition to medical texts, he also asked his friend Seldon to send back prophylactics: "Do not forget my gossamer envelopes for the pistolet d'amour—for already I need their protecting influence."[105] It is unlikely that his relationship with his cousins ever became physical; the object of Kane's carnal affections was another young lady, Julia Reed. This relationship soon haunted Elisha when Julia became pregnant.

Elisha's behavior at this time, even though outwardly condemned by proper society, was common. Middle-class moral guides and "purity preachers" strictly forbid all sexual acts before marriage; they railed against even the thought of such acts, noting that lust and masturbation led to loss of vigor, insanity, premature death, and hell.[106] The enforcement of such purity was pushed to extremes—one doctor created a device that, when worn by a young man, would ring a bell if his penis became erect—but this strict morality of sexual abstinence was far more successful in theory than in practice.[107] In fact, according to one scholar's study based on American marriage and birth records, between 1800 and 1840, one fourth of brides walked down the aisle pregnant. This number was actually down from earlier times; one third of brides were pregnant between 1761 and 1800.[108] More important than the fact that young people were having premarital sex in the mid-1800s, however, are the unspoken rules that largely governed their sexual behavior. Middle and upper class men of the era adhered to two contrasting sexual ethics. One was the strict moral code just noted, in which sexual self-restraint was of the utmost importance. The other was a more "natural" morality, one that assumed that as innately aggressive beings, it was necessary for young men to have a release for their sexual energy. This idea was not printed in any tract or preached from any pulpit, but evidence from birth records and hundreds of personal accounts show its pervasiveness.[109] This meant that there was a double standard when it came to sexual expression. Toward women of their own class who were potential wives, men tended to follow the strict morality of proper society, but toward women of a lesser social standing, the latter ethic applied. Elisha's different actions toward his cousins and toward Julia Reed illustrate this double standard.

It is difficult to piece together Elisha's relationship with Reed—he never publicly mentioned her and little correspondence survives—but evidence shows that they must have begun seeing each other in the fall of 1845, soon after his return to Philadelphia. The first record of their relationship is a letter from John Taylor, Jr., dated January 4, 1846, and written in reply to a letter Elisha must have sent in late December. Taylor was Elisha's cousin by marriage, who lived in Hazlewood, Virginia. Elisha asked him for help in finding a place to hide Reed during her pregnancy. Taylor's lighthearted response clearly illustrates the double-ethic of antebellum male sexuality.

> My Dear Doctor, <u>Private</u>
>
> I think there can be no doubt that our young Lady may find a pleasant place of temporary abode in Harrisonburg, Port Royal, or in the country, a point intermediate between these two.... How awful 'tis that these women will now & then get themselves with child. Would it not be a good plan for the Lady to pass herself off as the widow of some one who has died by train, small pox, or salt water, on his way to the south where her husband had relations?—Her situation would render such a tale plausible & proper to stop for a while in Hburg....
>
> Woman are the bane of men—I got along morally enough in Richmond for the first ten days, when I stumbled upon the smartest piece of youthful flesh, young 18. I soon got word that she was the paramour of a member of the Legislature, & staid with him every night—I passed the day of Sunday with her & my God! added to her beauty she is intellectual, a shade under the nubian size, with coal black hair, & the sweetest & whitest bosom in the world. Ye Gods! what a form. She has written to me to come again to see her, & I will....
>
> What an ardent lover must you be Elisha. I have heard you generally leave a mark on anything which you touch. I am more fortunate....
>
> Sincerely yours, J.T.J.[110]

An indiscretion such as Elisha's was clearly far from exceptional for men of his social class, but such affairs were still an embarrassment if detected, so Elisha needed a way to hide Julia Reed, at least until she gave birth. He did not follow Taylor's suggestion; instead he kept her in Philadelphia under the care of fellow physician C.C. VanWyck. Elisha devised an elaborate plan to keep himself distanced from Reed: He never went to VanWyck's office but instead had his brother Patterson deliver all his messages, signing himself under the false name of "P. T. Hunsenker, Esq." Elisha felt it was "a thing desirable for all parties" to keep the whole situation as quiet as possible, so he designed the arrangements to prevent Patterson from ever meeting Julia. He agreed to pay all her expenses, but, in a letter to VanWyck, instructed him to make her think that the money was "uncertain in its continuance and dependent <u>absolutely</u> upon her caution with regard to my name." He added ominously, "Make her feel this."[111]

Kane hoped that Julia would be willing to give up the baby once it was born, but she refused. He asked VanWyck to keep pushing her on this point, and just to be sure he was covered, he wrote several notes, which VanWyck was to deliver to her depending on her ultimate decision.[112] VanWyck found this plan acceptable and wrote Elisha a reassuring note saying, "Do not annoy or distress yourself about final results. You have done as much as & more than could be asked of any individual in a like fix—you rest therefore under no moral or other obligation towards this girl... in my opinion you ought to rest quietly by night in view of what you have agreed to perform."[113]

Among Kane's papers is a contract for indenture, stating that Margaret Jones Smith is giving her six-week-old girl, Eleanora, to John Smith Jones. The contract is in ink but the names (obviously pseudonyms) are filled in with pencil, and even though it is officially stamped, it does not appear to have ever been enacted.[114] It is thus unlikely that Julia gave up her child. One of the last records of this affair comes in a coded but sharply written letter from Patterson to Elisha. Along with a bill for $76.29 for medical expenses and prolonged care, he told Elisha "that poor Paul Hensenken... became a Papa." He explained that things got complicated and that he had "been obliged to lend him some of your money" because Hensenken's "fair one" suffered greatly during labor. "Her physician told me that owing to injuries she had received at a former period in her life, her delivery gave rise to severe ulcerations of one of her legs."[115] Elisha paid these final bills and never looked back; there is no evidence that he was ever in contact with Julia again.[116]

This affair with Julia Reed explains why Elisha shipped out again just nine months after returning home. The early months of 1846 found him scrambling both to hide his sexual indiscretion, that was growing more and more obvious with each passing day, and to gain a military position that would get him out of town. Elisha was successful in both efforts. Julia remained hidden (it appears that other than Pat, none of the family ever knew of the pregnancy), and the impending war with Mexico gave him a legitimate excuse to drop his medical practice and again seek military service; this time he gained a position as assistant surgeon in the U.S. Navy. Indeed, both Kane's contemporary and modern biographers concluded that Elisha's sudden career change in 1846 was the result of the "exciting new chance of adventure" offered by the impending war.[117] Although it is certainly true that Kane did aggressively pursue the chance to participate in this war, his sudden decision to abandon his new medical practice and rejoin the navy was driven as much by the desire to avoid scandal as to gain adventure. This is apparent in a cryptic letter he wrote his beloved cousin, Helen Patterson, just a few weeks later. Now in Boston waiting to set sail on his new commission, he wrote pleadingly, "Dearest Helen,... My affection can do you no harm, it interferes not with your prospects nor your pleasure, it resigns all obligation, demands nothing, and thinks not of itself. —Love me then, dear darling Nell, for you have seen your last of poor Elish.... I cannot revisit Philadelphia." He then referred to "Julia the pure and Julia the impure" and shamefully admitted that she had written him, regretting that he had not said farewell, and then "in humility—only blessed me." He closed, grieving that he was "absent and alone, on the eve of a perilous voyage, and perhaps never to see you again," and asked her to "remember me kindly, as one who has once been your lover but is now your friend."[118]

Though sad and forlorn, Elisha must have been a bit comforted that the impending war was the perfect justification for his sudden departure. Diplomatic relations between Mexico and the United States had been strained since Texas declared its independence in 1836, and war was imminent by December 1845. John Kane, who was intimately connected with the Polk administration, had the most recent intelligence from the disputed territory. It is thus not surprising that in March, two months before Congress declared war, John was already writing to Secretary of the Navy, George Bancroft, trying to get Elisha a promotion and thus an advantageous position in the navy.[119] The navy did not grant Elisha's promotion, but it did commission him aboard the frigate *United States*, the flagship of a squadron sailing not for Mexico, but for Africa, to patrol the slave trade off the West African coast. Though this assignment made Elisha "bitterly bitter," he accepted it. He reported for duty in Charlestown, Massachusetts, on May 5 and shipped out at the end of the month.[120]

While Elisha was in Charlestown waiting to sail, the Kane family was kept busy by Tom's new obsession—the Mormons' evacuation of Nauvoo, Illinois, and their trek to the west. When Tom realized that Elisha was reneging on their joint office plan, he too tried to get a position in the military, but the army turned him down because of his frail health. His parents wanted him to go on a trip through upper New York to visit family members and recover his health, but on May 13, 1846 (the same day Congress declared War on Mexico), Tom discovered another option. He attended a rally held by Jesse Little, an Elder of the Mormon Church, and there learned of their forced exodus from Nauvoo, Illinois, to the trans Rocky Mountain West. As both a philanthropist involved in social reform and a young man looking for adventure, this was a hugely tempting cause for Tom. Within a few days he accompanied Little to Washington to help him gain governmental support. Though Polk and his cabinet were not supportive of Brigham Young and his followers, they recognized that the Mormons could fill a much-needed gap in the United States' war with Mexico. California was sure to be a key battle site of the war and Polk needed to find a way to get troops there quickly. The Mormons were already more than halfway there—Tom estimated that fifteen thousand were then camped along the Missouri River near present day Omaha, Nebraska. If a battalion of men could be pulled from their numbers, this force could march to California quickly and inexpensively. Although this plan proposed (and indeed eventually necessitated) the longest military march in U.S. history, Little saw it as a wonderful opportunity; the military salaries of the five hundred Mormon troops could finance the group's migration across the West. The Mormon battalion also sounded wonderful to Tom because it would provide him with a chance for adventure and prestige. He would travel with Little to Fort Leavenworth and deliver the order to organize the Mormon battalion. He would then go on to the Mormon camps to help organize and train the five hundred "volunteers" for military service. Tom's optimism even prompted him to speculate that he could serve as the battalion's commander and, after leading them in victorious battle against the Mexican troops in California, his family's political connection would make him a good candidate for the first governor of the newly formed California Territory.[121]

This opportunity invigorated Tom. He was finally following in Elisha's footsteps. He had always been the timid, "good" brother. He had gone on an excursion through the Southeast as an eighteen year old, and, while in Mobile, Alabama, had written his mother, telling her of his companions' wild ways and confessing, "For my part I don't know that ever I had an appetite for excitement... but rather long too much for the quiet joys of home."[122] It was Tom who always felt dutybound to stay at home while Elisha roamed across the globe. With a cautious spirit and a body built more for bed-rest than boisterous adventures, Tom felt pale in comparison to Elisha, who had overcome his illness and reveled in daring exploits. But now was his chance to be the adventurer. It must have been with some satisfaction that Tom learned that his father so disapproved of his actions, seeing them as too risky. As the newly appointed attorney general of Pennsylvania, he wanted Tom to stay in Philadelphia and work with him in legal matters. He called Tom's plan "the variest hallucination that ever afflicted an educated mind," and wrote Elisha asking, "Was there ever such blindness of judgment?"[123] Patterson asked Elisha to negotiate the tension between Tom and their father, and Elisha wrote Tom from Boston, recommending that he should avoid rushing into anything, but also admitting that he could "feel the tingle of healthy excitement which would urge you... to select these wild fanatics, and that western world as the scene of your exploration."[124] This qualified encouragement was enough family endorsement for Tom. He would go west with Elder Little and the Mormons.

Tom and Elisha wrote letter after letter during the month of May, discussing their upcoming adventures and the best ways to turn them into successful books. Though the tales of his earlier adventures were still incomplete, Elisha was consoled by the fact that his routine commission to Africa would provide him with time to complete the project and the opportunity to gather more exotic tales. He was also sure he could write medical articles of a caliber far beyond those being published in the United States at that time. Tom agreed and strongly encouraged him: "Write your book materials and your medical case notes, and if I live, you shall only fall behind [Washington] Irving & [Robert Lewis] Stephens in reputation. You shall certainly be the lead writer of your profession and, ere two years after your return, shall be one of its head lecturers."[125]

Although he supported Elisha's writing, Tom also had literary ambitions of his own. He was sure he could produce a popular account of his trip; his book would describe new Western lands as well as an inside account of the Mormon migration and the "queer life, yankee and fanatic" of Brigham Young and his Saints.[126] Before he left, Tom contacted Philadelphia publisher Carey & Hart. They were interested in his project and promised "famous success" for the book, but refused to give him the cash advance he wanted to help subsidize his trip.[127] Though this discouraged him, he was convinced that, given the current conflict with Mexico, it was best for him and Elisha to delay their publishing projects anyway. On the last day of May he wrote Elisha that a "publishing bookseller told me... that since our foreign difficulties 'the trade' was at a stand still and that if you had contrived to edit your book before your departure he would have advised its being held back for a time at least. So you see you have not lost much time after all."[128]

After nearly a month of waiting, the *United States* finally sailed for its first African port, Praia, Cape Verde Islands. During the nine months Elisha spent on the *United States* it made two cruises from Praia to Principle Island in the Gulf of Guinea, calling at the major ports of Sierra Leone, Liberia, and Ghana along the way. These trips were largely uneventful, leaving Elisha time to write long descriptions of all that he saw. In a letter to his mother he dedicated seven pages to verbally painting a picture of Praia, noting that "every ripple of its dark bay becomes a crescent spangle and its shoreline is haloed with the white glories of the surf."[129] But such florid descriptions could only entertain an adventurous young man for so long. As the ship's medical officer he had some interesting cases, but this did not break the monotony. He wrote fellow Philadelphia physician, Robley Dunglison, "Of all the miserable blanks in one's existence the most miserable is an African cruise."[130]

Things were better when the ship was docked. While in Brazil with the Cushing legation three years earlier, Kane had met Francisco Felix de Sousa, a famous Brazilian slave trader associated with the powerful West African slave-trading kingdom of Dahomey. When the *United States* docked at the Dahomey-controlled town of Ouidah in southern Benin, Kane spent two days with de Sousa's sons, who gave him a tour of their slave factory. Careful not to offend his hosts with any judgmental questions, Kane gained their confidence and learned all about their methods to elude British and American naval vessels (such as the *United States* itself) stationed along their coast to prevent the exportation of slaves. Elisha was even allowed to join the de Sousa sons on a caravan to meet "King Gezo," a Dahomey leader who supplied many slaves for trade. Kane was amazed by Gezo, who wielded absolute power over his subjects. He executed men for sport and kept dozens of women as his wives. Like several other Western travelers to this region, Kane wrote of the King's exploits with a sense of horror and awe, recording all the gory and salacious details.[131] Even though Kane was appalled by the slave traders' cruel treatment of their human chattel, after meeting Gezo, he wondered whether slavery was not the better of two terrible fates.[132] An intriguing side note to Kane's visit to King Gezo is that he seems to have helped the king with a rather intimate problem. Tom Dillard, the fleet surgeon aboard Kane's mission, wrote Kane some months later: "Your friend... inquired after you, and wishes you to send him some <u>drops,</u> more powerfully <u>restorative</u> and <u>invigorating</u>, than those you administered to him! His numerous wives, they say, complain that you did not benefit and <u>strengthen</u> their liege Lord and sovereign as much as they desired and expected."[133]

As the *United States'* mission dragged on, boredom caused tensions to rise aboard the ship, especially between Kane and line officer Lieutenant George A. Prentiss. The two quarreled often and twice their spats resulted in Kane challenging Prentiss to a duel. Prentiss wrote back a firm refusal each time, pointing out what Kane already knew, that "while our official relations remain as they are [Kane outranked Prentiss]... the consequences would be disastrous to <u>me</u> whatever the event, while <u>you</u> would go unscathed."[134] These dueling challenges are telling of Elisha's feelings at this time. The practice of dueling came to America during the Revolution when class lines were fluid. Challenging someone to a duel became a method of establishing your social standing as a gentleman—it meant that your honor was so important that you were willing to kill or be killed to preserve it. The practice was first outlawed in the United States in 1801, and was largely ended in the North by 1804 thanks to the establishment of liable and slander laws that gave gentlemen legal recourse to settle slights against their name, and because of the infamous duel when then Vice President Aaron Burr killed Alexander Hamilton on the "field of honor." The practice remained alive in the South until the Civil War, however, due largely to the South's heightened social code that stressed personal honor above all else.[135] That Elisha continually challenged a lesser officer to duel suggests that he felt insecure in his standing. As a young officer with little sea experience, Elisha was threatened by the superior knowledge of George Prentiss, a well-seasoned sailor (Prentiss would go on to become a well-decorated Union commander). This meant that any time Prentiss contradicted his opinion, Elisha felt insulted and feared that his reputation among the other crewmembers was diminished. Elisha never meant for these challenges to result in actual combat; rather, they were theatrical gestures meant to delineate social status and built on the unspoken assumption that resolution would come via apology or some other face-saving gesture, and not through violence.

As Elisha was aboard the *United States*, his family was again going through major changes. A little more than a year after becoming attorney general of Pennsylvania, John Kane resigned to accept a new position—judge of the U.S. District Court for Eastern Pennsylvania. Judge Kane loved his new position because it provided life tenure in a job with great potential for public exposure, a hefty salary, and the power to appoint a clerk with a $1,500 per year salary, a position he gave to his son Tom. In a letter to Elisha, John happily announced that he was "on the whole so placed that I would not change for any office in the nation."[136]

Tom's life had also changed in the fall of 1846. His Western trip had been a great success. He traveled extensively through what is now Kansas, Nebraska, and Iowa, and recorded all he saw in meticulously kept journals and sketchbooks. He met up with Brigham Young and his followers along the Platte River near present-day Omaha, Nebraska, and from among their numbers he helped to organize the five hundred-man "Mormon Battalion." Once mustered, this battalion began an arduous march across the Great Plains to southern California, but Tom was not with them. Soon after arriving at the Mormon's "Winter-Quarters" in Nebraska, he became gravely ill. Tom, who was initially skeptical about Young and his "Saints," was soon humbled by their kindness, because despite their desperate conditions and meager resources, they extended him every hospitality as they nursed him back to health over the course of several weeks. By the time he returned to Philadelphia in October 1846, he was a firm supporter (though not a member) of the Church of Jesus Christ of Latter-day Saints, and he committed himself to helping them in their continuing evacuation of thousands of their members from Illinois to the Great Salt Lake basin. Mormon Elder Orson Spencer joined Tom in Philadelphia and was amazed at his energy for their cause. He reported to Young, "Col. Kane... is nothing daunted, but thinks the best method of operating upon [Polk's] Cabinet is through the press and the conversion of public opinion."[137] During November and December, Tom flooded Eastern newspapers with heart-wrenching accounts of the travesties committed against Mormons and the dire nature of their situation, having to face a harsh winter on the high plains. He published these articles anonymously and followed them with editorials, praising his articles and calling for further support of the Mormons. He wrote Brigham Young in early December, saying, "it was found next to impossible to do much for you before public opinion was corrected... [and so] it became incumbent on me to manufacture public opinion as soon as possible." Tom happily reported that his efforts "had been successful beyond my hopes" and explained that "my first feeler, of the bold kind, was put forth in the *Pennsylvanian* and its reception proved that I had fully prepared the public to receive the truth. This week I have begun the hard knocks.... Tomorrow morning myself and scribe start for New York, and if I can have there, any portion of the same success which I have had in my own city, I will consider the brunt of the battle over if indeed victory be not at hand."[138]

In November 1846, in the midst of his efforts for the Mormons, Tom accepted the position as his father's clerk. Though he was anxious to get on with his life, he did not want to make any plans without first consulting Elisha. From the many letters he wrote to his older brother in the fall of 1846, it is clear that Tom (and to a lesser degree, Elisha) saw their lives as necessarily intertwined. In a high-spirited letter, Tom demanded that Elisha come home, get married, restart his medical practice, and settle down so the two of them could begin their plans for financial and social success. He generously offered Elisha $1,000 per year from his $1,700 salary, explaining, "you can have a first rate office for $100. $200 will pay the livery of a horse and vehicle. $300 will give you a good wardrobe, and your pocket money certainly cannot stand you in $100 more. Your total expenses of living will then be $700 the year."[139] He noted that this money would free Elisha from having to worry about whether his medical practice would make a profit during its first years.

After explaining the financial portion of his plan, Tom moved on to its social elements: "You must marry.—Take any of the girls in town (which Judge Kane's son can) but marry you must." He explained that this was a necessary part of proper society and that it was high time for Elisha "to begin the domestic duties, set on your own eggs and leave off promiscuous cock pigeoning." He warned Elisha to do this soon, before too many years of sea-life made his face "look like unhealthy jerked beef." With his language turning to lighthearted slang, Tom exclaimed, "Now the damnition brides is waiting for you in their nuptshil chambers. I see three of em.... They was a piece put in the mornin' papers of one of them there chamin' creatures which, mentionin' all the facts desired relatin' to altars and baby clothes and such like, bust into the frantic ejackylation—Where be my Lijah?" He further noted that if Elisha would agree to come back it would also help their younger brother Patterson because he was currently cultivating "the acquaintance of three sweet damsels who will be glad to furnish forth the staff of life as well as its old hat, but he cannot in our well-regulated political family take quince & peach both, and fears through distraction to go without either.... He invites you to his aide to divide, and conquer."[140]

The same package that brought Tom's letter to Elisha also carried one from his father. Judge Kane praised his adventurous son, but suggested that it was time for him to come home and take up the responsibilities of a settled, adult life. "All I have to say pointedly and finally is this: Judge for yourself what is honourable, politic, best." If Elisha did this, Judge Kane promised that he and the whole family would do "all we can do to further your purposes to the utmost, means, action, influence, —all we have is yours."[141] These letters arrived at a time when Elisha was feeling alone and depressed. In a confessional letter to Tom he discussed all that had been troubling him for the past several months. He alluded to his affair with Julia Reed and the circumstances of his rapid departure from Philadelphia. "When I left you it was in such a state that I would have run to hell to escape a Paradise." He apologized that his departure came at a time when Tom was ill and their father's affairs were "nearly at a crises,"[142] and confessed that his selfishness had been so great as to be sinful, writing, "while I may be a very tolerable Elisha Kane the assistant Surgeon, I am a very poor Ilish Kane brother and son." He then made an honest assessment of his life:

> I am now 26 years old. In two years I will be twenty eight. Am I to be in the Navy as a career or am I to make it subservient to a more solid [life] at home?... But at the same time even in spite of home longings, excited (oh how much) by the dreary social waste around me—I am bound dispassionately to say that should domestic affairs remain unaltered I would much hesitate about resigning. It is difficult to give up a fine & increasing income—difficult to change a certainty to an uncertainty.... It is hard to commence a race in which I should have had already a long start of some years.... All these things have weighed upon me.[143]

After this internal debate, Elisha proclaimed, "I have at last stopped oscillating & made up my mind. I am going to try my tug at home—if possible to retain the Navy as a potential reserve in case of failure, but if I cannot do this... I am prepared to burn my bridge and resign." He compared his love and devotion for Tom to that of King David and Jonathan of the Bible, and then proclaimed, "Father and Mother need me, need us. Not me as I was nor you as you were, but both of us as we might be.... We will put each other right and... travel together! Together!!" Having come to this resolution, he concluded, "I cannot be wrong Tom in all this Joy... it would be a Holy Ghost Sin to resist this influence."[144]

At this same time Tom was also torn about his future. He had grand plans about settling down with Elisha and establishing themselves among Philadelphia's elite society, but his trip west among the Mormons had also whetted his spirit for adventure and rekindled his passion for social reform. These desires were made all the more profound by the general American sentiment of 1846, when Mexican-American War hysteria was at its height and tens of thousands of young American men were flooding army recruitment stations, anxious for adventure. The question across the nation was not who would have to go to war, but who would have to stay. In Tennessee, for example, thirty thousand men volunteered for three thousand positions, thus gaining it the nickname, the "Volunteer State." The war was a chance for young men to win glory in an exciting and exotic land, and to live out the fantasies of chivalry and daring that they had read about in the novels of Sir Walter Scott that were then in vogue.[145]

Despite his plans for an established life in Philadelphia with Elisha, his firmly held moral stance against violence and the expansion of slavery, and the promise of a lucrative job as his father's clerk, Tom could not resist the fervor of the time. He again pushed for a position in the army. Both amused and dismayed by Tom's actions, Judge Kane wrote Elisha, "Could you ever believe it! Your philanthropish-philosopher, anti-war, anti-capital punishment brother... is rabid for a chance of shooting Mexicans, and would march, if I did not forbid it, as third lieut. of a company of rowdy volunteers."[146] He was convinced that military service would "kill

[Tom] with ennué and camp duty," and so, respecting his son's wishes, used his political pull to have Tom considered for pay master or some other higher-ranking, noncombatant position in the army. Tom himself went to the White House to press his case in person, but despite these efforts, no position came available and he had to resign himself to staying at home.

On Christmas day, 1846, Tom wrote to Elisha. He explained his disappointment regarding a military position, but he also celebrated his forced alternative. He would be his father's court clerk, and with the money and time this would allow him, he would be able to assemble Elisha's adventures into a narrative that was sure to be a popular success. During the next several months he advised Elisha on what to write, how to write it, and what to do with it once it was written. He sent Elisha several clippings of articles recently written on Africa and insisted, "You must make the most of your time irremediably spent abroad, collecting materials; so as to be the Writing Doctor of Philadelphia." He instructed him to assemble any statistics he could on gold dust or the slave trade for a mercantile article; to put together a narrative article about some interesting incident for the *Democratic Review*; and to write an essay on some strange pathology for a medical journal. He confidently noted that, "This done,... you would stand the superior of the M.D.s every one—indeed for the matter of that; I do not know the man of them who has risen to the heights of a readable magazine contribution." He then closed by stressing the importance of writing an entertaining narrative because it would establish his reputation most broadly. He suggested a story "of slave ships, combats, cocoa nuts, Quashees, Mud Huts, Boarding parties, Fevers, Ivory, Palm Oil, Nigger Kings, &c. &c. cemented together by proper quantities of Blue Sea, Fire, Blood, and Tropical Sunshine" and suggested that he follow the style of James Gordon Bennett, the flamboyant editor of the *New York Herald*, who was famous for his sensational articles.[147]

Elisha took Tom's suggestions and sent several essays back to him. Tom critiqued these with great care; his biggest fear was that Elisha's narrative was too labored and ornate. "Remember, that your aim must be to prepare simple solid food as you have always a profusion of confectionery on hand." He felt that Elisha was at his best when he provided "a mixture of the touching and humorous," a style that came forth most readily in Elisha's "unguarded moments" of writing.[148] He suggested that Elisha write almost spontaneously: "Don't slant your paper. Fill notebooks of every kind with thoughts, hints, impressions, notes, facts, suppositions, whatever has at any time been in your brain."[149] Aside from these few criticisms, Tom was convinced that Elisha truly had a gift for writing and that his essays could easily be formed into a popular travel narrative. He calculated eighty to one hundred pages on India; fifty each on China, Ceylon, Africa, and Europe; and another hundred on the Philippines, bringing the total to three to four hundred pages. Tom believed this was the most marketable length for a book. He also instructed Elisha to "make a few more water colours if possible" as well as "small portraits of objects for wood cuts"; he was certain that a well-illustrated volume would sell best, especially if it included a few color prints. Tom closed his letter encouragingly: "know your time is not thrown away so long as you can write. Your style is improving rapidly—and I can see that you want nothing but practice. You have more imagination & fancy than any of the family and have only to break your faculties into harness."[150]

Elisha did not receive these comments until several months later because, in the first weeks of 1847, he became violently ill. By February fleet-surgeon Tom Dillard, fearing for Elisha's life, deemed him unfit for duty and sent him home via a passing merchant ship, and by early March, Elisha was back in Philadelphia and resting at home. After a few weeks of recovery, he began his writing again and started to take steps to reestablish himself in Philadelphia. He once again opened an office and began seeking patients; he even applied for a faculty position at the newly opening Girard College. But this did not last for long—wanderlust still pulled hard at his feet.[151] In April, and again in October, against his doctor's recommendation and his family's wishes, Elisha went to Washington to plead with President Polk for some opportunity to serve in the final days of the war with Mexico.[152] Unlike Tom, Elisha was successful in this effort. General Winfield Scott captured Mexico City on September 13, and although happy for the victory, President Polk justifiably feared that Scott and Nicholas V. Trist of the State Department (both of whom had become his political opponents) were negotiating with Mexico on their own terms and disregarding his wishes. He urgently needed to send a message to Mexico City and Elisha showed up at the right time. Elisha received special orders from H. L. Heiskill, acting surgeon-general, to gather statistics about U.S. field hospitals in Mexico; this served as cover for his real assignment, to hand deliver a dispatch to Mexico City ordering Trist home and Scott to forward duplicates of all his dispatches back to Washington.[153] Thus, on November 6, 1847, Elisha was off on another adventure, this time to Mexico.

The news of Elisha's sudden departure, and of his success in gaining a military position, angered Tom. He wrote Elisha, "I am trying very hard to realize [this] is true." It had been four years since Tom first laid out a life plan for their success in Philadelphia, and now, just as it finally seemed to be coming together for the second time, Elisha left—again. Despite Tom's disappointment, however, he continued to support his brother's adventurous ambitions, promising to "keep the office in trim until the orders to close it may come from you; so, you shall come home if you like to just what you started away from, with a little more love of quiet maybe; and a little more renown."[154] A daguerreotype of Elisha from this time shows him to be strong and determined, dressed in military garb and clutching a sword—truly a man of adventure. After he set off for Mexico, he wrote a letter back to his father justifying his sudden departure. Knowing that his family felt he was full of "fickleness and instability," he explained that "in sober truth" his actions were "urged by more direct and impulsive instigations of propriety." Although he was sure that his father would not see this as a sufficient explanation, Elisha reminded him, "Be all this as it may, now that the deed is done we must make the best of it." He then suggested that his service in the war could be good for the family's image and wondered if his father could make his service conducive "to the Kane family advancement." It is clear that this "family advancement"—or more accurately stated, Elisha's personal advancement—was the driving factor in Elisha's decision to go to Mexico. He was obliged to send regular dispatches back to Polk's administration, but he decided to send them via his family so they could edit them to suit his and their purposes best. He wrote, "Whatever reaches you, purify it by the family filter and send it in its clear state to its instructed destination." He explained, "The arrangements which I have made with the Bureau allow me to keep back any or all of my communications—publishing them, after my own revision under the auspices of the Department." Elisha asked his father and Tom to "make

From a daguerreotype of Elisha
taken in November 1847.
Reprinted in *Century Magazine*
(Aug. 1898).

extracts from my letters, work them up,... and then jouralise;—in a word puff me when you can."[155]

In this letter of explanation, Elisha included a second private letter for his father in which he spoke frankly about his relationship with Tom. He admitted that his actions and requests were "very selfish" because they promoted his own success at a time when Tom was feeling betrayed and struggling with his health and future. He also recognized the sacrifices Tom made for him, but felt they were often unnecessary and based more on self-pitying martyrdom than any practical purpose. "Tom has made great sacrifices for me but where has been their result? They have been sacrifices for they have wrought their full share of pain with him— poor fellow!—but what the devil else have they done[?]" Elisha insisted that his father force Tom to relax, look after his health, and advance his own career. If Tom did this, Elisha was very willing to come back home and work with him. "Tell Tom that this is my dream, that it all depends upon him." If Tom did not do this, Elisha simply felt he could not work with his brother. He closed, "Who, dear Father, would advise me to give up a competency in order to follow to the grave the only human being who could chose the dull path of an everyday working time awaiting profession[?]" He closed, "Tell this to Tom, but do not show him my remarks. They would give him pain."[156]

Tom and Elisha had an intense, loving, but often strained relationship. Elisha was a doer. His impulse was to leap at every opportunity for adventure, whether an expedition to China, an affair with a young woman, or an evening at a less-than-respectable club. Tom was a thinker. He was concerned about the moral, political, and social ramifications of his actions. He was deeply involved with issues of religious freedom, free-soil and free-labor concerns, and abolition efforts. He also fretted over the family's social and financial well being, even fearing that their association with his mother's family, the Leipers, would hurt their reputation—he compared their social influence to a degenerative disease that he cleverly termed "Leiprasy."[157] Though he often talked of and occasionally engaged in great adventures, he did so cautiously, even hesitantly.[158] Like his father, Tom was more comfortable at home, working quietly behind the scenes to influence others through politics and the press. Tom was a strong, dynamic person, but he relied on Elisha for much of his own identity. Judge Kane recognized this and told Elisha, "Indeed, Tom has no exclusive identity when you are in the case, and I believe at this moment he is content with his approaching lot, principally because it will connect him with you still more closely."[159] These different characteristics made Elisha and Tom a good team, but they also ensured that they would often disagree about which course of action was most appropriate. Although they remained close throughout their lives, Elisha's departure for the Mexican-American War marked a turning point in their relationship and clearly demarcated their fun-

damental differences. Like Elisha, Tom was a small, sickly man who often struggled with issues of his own power and worth. He twice traveled to Paris to recover
his health, and though these trips resulted in little physical improvement, they did
heavily impact his thinking. When he returned home from his second Parisian trip
in the summer of 1844 he was skeptical of organized religion, a firm supporter of
his father's Democratic party, and extremely devoted to reform causes. These first
two characteristics put him in a different camp than most other reformers of the
age, who tended to be religious evangelicals and staunchly anti-Democrat, but the
trajectory of Tom's life from 1844 on clearly illustrates his deep dedication to reform. He was often naïve, self-righteous, and even self-serving about his efforts,
but his desire to create a better world was sincere and drove his adult decisions.
This stands in fundamental contrast to Elisha, whose actions were consistently driven not by altruism, nor by a desire for scientific discovery and exploration
(though this is what he always claimed), but by an insatiable desire for fame. Tom
and Elisha both wanted to be well-known, successful, powerful men, but this was
a secondary desire for Tom; for Elisha it was primary.[160]

Following Elisha's departure for Mexico, Tom began to emerge as his own person. He wrote, "I find that I am learning to look forward with pleasure instead of
the contrary, to my moments of holiday inaction; and so become every day more
and more disposed to make them for myself."[161] He began to cultivate his love of
music again, visiting Drigo's, Elisha's favorite New York concert hall, as well as
many performances offered by Philadelphia's Musical Fund Society. He even began
singing himself and was anxious for Elisha to come back so they could do duets:
"Just imagine two such hells of noises as we would make...!"[162]

While Tom steadily worked at recovering his health and spirits and creating
an identity of his own, Elisha was having a grand adventure. Though he was officially connected with the navy during his mission to Mexico, he had no superior
officer and was free to make his own decisions. He traveled to Pittsburgh via rail,
canal, and stage coach, and from there to New Orleans by way of the Ohio and
Mississippi Rivers. He added spice to this routine trip by riding on the cowcatcher
of the train. He wrote a friend, "Never had I such a twenty miles.... I tore the heel
from my boot, and smashed my thumb on the drag chain;—but I held on; and
after it was all over, sneaked on to the cars, much relieved—a wiser and a better
man."[163] Elisha reached New Orleans on November 21 and sailed for Veracruz two
days later aboard the U.S. steamer *Fashion*, which carried a full load of civilian and
military passengers, as well as a cargo of military supplies and a deckload of cav-
alry horses. Soon after departure, a severe storm blew the ship far off course,
choked her pumps, and forced all aboard to bail water to keep afloat. After more
than a month at sea, the *Fashion's* luck changed and she was blown between the

reefs that protect Veracruz harbor, landing safely in early January 1848, with no lives lost.[164]

After his arrival in Veracruz, Elisha traveled with a party of officers to Perote and there joined a group of contraguerillas—"all Mexican skinners, bandits, and traitors"—that was traveling to Puebla. This group was headed by Manuel Dominguez, a "celebrated captain of robbers," who the U.S. Army hired in June 1847 to patrol the road from Puebla to Veracruz. He and his men stopped all Mexican parties while allowing U.S. troops and supplies to pass, collecting only a small fee instead of robbing them as they had been doing.[165] On January 6, Dominguez and his group encountered a company of about fifty Mexican troops near Nopaluca. A brief but bloody battle ensued in which Elisha, Dominguez, and about 125 mounted lancers attacked the small Mexican company, killing four privates, wounding several officers, and taking the whole company captive, including Brigadier Generals Anastasio Torrejón and Antonio Gaona. What Elisha did during and after the battle would become the first publicized event in the larger-than-life adventures that marked his public image in the years to come. The following account appeared in the March 24, 1848 edition of *The Pennsylvanian*:

> It is not clear to us how the doctor ranked in the party... but it appears that it was at his instance, if not at his order, that they engaged the enemy.... At one period of the charge, when Dr. Kane was some distance ahead of the rest of his company, his fine horse carried him in between a spirited young major and his orderly, who fell upon him at the same moment. The lance of the latter failed at the thrust, except so far as to inflict a slight flesh-wound upon the doctor, who, being able to parry the major's sabre-cut, ran that officer through the bowels. The fight over, Dr. Kane was attending to his own hurts, when the poor wounded youth seized him by his arm, crying, "Father! my father! save my father!" The renegade Mexicans, having determined to slaughter their prisoners, had commenced operations by attacking their chief man [Gen. Gaona], an aged person, who had surrendered to Dr. Kane. He was at the moment defending himself, bare-headed and unarmed, against his assailants. Dr. Kane saved him and numerous others; but it appears that he did so with great efforts, and at considerable personal risk.... He parried four sabre cuts that were made at him, and did not succeed in enforcing obedience to his order until he had drawn his six shooter, (which all Mexicans hold in mortal dread,) and fired at Col. Dominguez, the commander of the squadron.... As soon as the old general was rescued, he sat down by the side of the major, his son, to comfort his last painful moments. When the doctor observed that that individual was bleeding to death from an artery in the groin, he made an effort in his behalf. With the bent prong of a table-fork he took up the artery and tied it with a ravel of packthread, and the crude surgical operation was perfectly successful.[166]

This story that was written by Elisha and his family became the first of what would be many tales of Elisha's larger-than-life persona, "Dr. Kane." Although it was exaggerated to some extent, their tale was true in its fundamental details; the facts were later confirmed by General and Major Gaona, who also wrote personal accounts of the battle. All hyperbole aside, sometime during the battle or in the skirmish that followed, Elisha received a lance wound in the lower abdomen and his horse was mortally wounded. After Elisha and Dominguez's squabble subsided, the company regained some semblance of order and began the twenty-five mile trip to Puebla with their Mexican captives. With his own mount killed, Elisha road a captured horse, but he collapsed after a few miles and so rode in a cart with the other injured men. Upon reaching Puebla, Dominguez took Elisha to the U.S. troop quarters, and then marched General Gaona and his son to the Governor's Palace that served as the U.S. headquarters for the area. The commanding officer, Colonel Tom Childs, ruled that the Gaonas had officially surrendered to Dominguez, not to Kane, a decision that infuriated both Elisha and General Gaona. Gaona declared to a U.S. officer, "I respect the Americans. They are a brave and magnanimous people, but I have been captured by that man, who is a thief and a robber. My honor is gone."[167] This blow was lessened when Colonel Childs allowed the Gaonas to return to their luxurious mansion in Puebla under a loose form of house arrest. Gaona accepted this arrangement but insisted on making a

From William Godfrey's *Godfrey's Narrative of the Last Grinnell Arctic Exploring Expedition, in Search of Sir John Franklin*, 1853-4-5 (Philadelphia, J.T. Lloyd & Co., 1857).

DR. KANE DEFENDING THE MEXICAN PRISONERS.

public declaration that he and his son owed their lives to Elisha. To express their gratitude, they offered him the pick of their stables to replace his fallen mount. The Gaona family also began to prepare a fiesta in his honor, but Elisha fell deathly ill of "congestive typhus fever" before it could be arranged. The Gaonas took him to their mansion, where the general's attractive daughters nursed him back to health over the next several weeks.[168]

It took more than a month for the news of this battle to get back to Philadelphia, but once it arrived, the Kane family wasted no time in publicizing it. Elisha's story appeared in several articles in *The Pennsylvanian* and the *Pennsylvania Inquirer* during February and March under such headlines as "Gallant Conduct of Dr. Elisha K. Kane of the U.S. Navy," and "Romantic Incident of the War." Philadelphia was soon buzzing with news of their hometown hero. This is hardly surprising. Elisha had performed a heroic deed, and, just as importantly, he had quickly reported it to his family with full romantic flair. While recovering at General Gaona's house, he sent a letter home telling his story in detail. He enumerated point by point the parts he wanted played up, what effect he wanted them to have, and where he wanted them published. For his section on Dominguez and his men he wrote, "Work up these facts and publish in the *N.Y. Herald*, the others in the *N[orth] American*. I want for readers, which the subjoined will explain, a sort of excitement got up concerning this disgraceful corps."[169]

Having received this letter, as well as an accompanying letter from Colonel Childs verifying Elisha's story, Tom and Judge Kane got to work. They placed an exciting article, anonymously written, in Philadelphia's Democratic paper, *The Pennsylvanian*, and then clipped it and sent it to many other papers up and down the eastern seaboard, assuming correctly that these text-starved papers would happily pick it up. This was the same method Tom had used to spread his pro-Mormon articles the year before. When the first news of Elisha's battle reached Philadelphia, Tom wrote up what he could for the press, and on receipt of Elisha's letter, he provided a greatly detailed account for the March 24, 1848, edition of the *Pennsylvanian* noted earlier. Another letter from Elisha arrived just a few days later, again pushing Tom to get his story into the papers. Annoyed, Tom wrote back, "It is right that I should say to you seriously that I do not consider your interests to have been neglected by me during your absence. I send you by this mail two newspapers issued before our receipt of your letters... which report progress, and show that there has not been an absolute inactivity on my part." He bitterly explained that while Elisha had "been all this time casting ornaments for your whole life like those of a monumental column," he had been busy with the mundane activities of normal life and simply did not have time to get all of Elisha's deeds promptly into the papers: "I know it must be hard for you to believe... [but this] is nevertheless the fact, and you must content yourself with it."[170]

Tom then brightened and asked Elisha to send more details about his exploits because the story was still sketchy and he was having difficulty pushing it further without more documentation. "It is now three weeks since our very first letter came giving authentic news of you, from Colonel Childs. It was the first thing capable of being made the basis of a newspaperism. We have had no official notice, no extract from one, no dispatch, no newspaper American or Spanish, nothing of the kind." He explained that he was willing to do anything to promote the story, but reminded Elisha that he was dealing with newspaper men who have "their regular business habits, and their regular habits of thought," and thus wanted more substantiation of the story; such evidence was essential because he couldn't simply "take their opinions by storm."[171] Within a week of this letter, however, Tom was again constructing "newspaperisms." Quoting from "the American Star, of Mexico" he placed a long story on the front page of Philadelphia's *North American & United States Gazette*, informing readers that the "romantic adventures of this distinguished officer" were of special interest to them because they regarded "the fortunes of our townsman, Doctor Kane."[172]

Because of his injury and illness, Elisha did not leave Puebla until February 18; therefore, by the time he finally arrived in Mexico City, another messenger had already delivered an order officially dismissing Scott from his command, which made his message moot. With Scott gone, Elisha wrote an official statement regarding the battle at Nopaluca and submitted it to the acting commander-in-chief, General William O. Butler. In this statement he demanded punishment for Dominguez and official recognition of General Gaona's kindness and aid.[173] Soon thereafter the army surgeons ruled that Elisha's wounds made him unfit for duty and so ordered him home. In early April he traveled to Veracruz in a four-horse ambulance cart escorted by a company of dragoons and sailed for home after a few weeks delay, arriving in New Orleans in late July and reaching home in early August 1848. Though pleased with his adventure, Elisha was dismayed by his broken health and again feared for his future. En route he wrote his family, "I again return, a broken-down man. My hair would be gray, but that I have no hair. My hopes would be particularly small, but that I have no hopes."[174]

As he had done five years earlier, Elisha spent much of the summer of 1848 at his uncle George G. Leiper's Chester County estate. During this time he recovered from his wounds and worked on several projects related to his experiences in Mexico. He again wrote an account of his adventures for publication and outlined a forty-chapter book that would be a general history of the war accompanied by additional cultural, scientific, and personal information.[175] He also agreed to illustrate a book for fellow physician Richard McSherry, who he met while in Mexico. This book, *El Puchero: A Mixed Dish from Mexico*, came out in 1850 and included several engravings of battles and Mexican scenery, most likely based on sketches by Elisha.[176]

Elisha sent multiple petitions to the government for remuneration for his horse that was killed by Dominguez and his men, and though it took many months, he was eventually compensated.[177] His most ambitious project of the summer, however, was to gain official recognition for his efforts in the war. After a bit of pushing by Elisha and his family, seventy citizens of Philadelphia formed a committee and purchased a gold-sheathed ceremonial sword to present to Elisha for his "courage, conduct, and humanity," during the battle of Nopaluca.[178]

As the fall approached, Elisha applied for a post as a naval surgeon for the Philadelphia Navy Yard, but was denied because he had only achieved the rank of assistant surgeon and a full surgeon was required. He then pushed for a place aboard an expedition to the California and Oregon coast, but this also fell through. Frustrated and disappointed at his lack of opportunities, he agreed to take a routine assignment aboard the store ship *Supply*.[179] He was called into duty in February, but the ship was delayed for a month. During this time he wrote to himself, "My lonelyness is so oppressive and my heart growing so void and selfish with the saddened recollection of other days—that I am actually scared when I feel how much I changed." He hoped that the short trip would allow him "to recover that manly state of mind so essential to my future success, and to rouse myself from the selfish reverie into which I have now six months been indulging."[180] The *Supply* finally left the Norfolk Naval Yard on March 5, 1849, and reached Gibraltar by April 3. It stopped at several Mediterranean ports and then sailed for Rio de Janeiro, arriving on July 1. As always, Elisha began the trip violently seasick. He felt so ill that he believed he had tetanus and so bled himself several times, making conditions worse. Otherwise, the trip was only notable for its violent discipline—during the seven-month cruise all eighteen of the ship's seamen and three of her six petty officers were punished with the cat o' nine tails. As surgeon, Elisha had to attend each of these beatings, which only increased his dislike of military discipline.[181]

The *Supply* arrived back in Norfolk in early September 1849, and almost immediately Elisha signed on to the *Walker* for a surveying expedition of the Gulf states. The *Walker* was not scheduled to leave for several weeks, but his commanding officers refused to allow Elisha a brief visit home. He told his parents: "My very blood boils at the brutality of the Old commodore fool commanding here.... We cannot possibly leave for a fortnight—and brother surgeons have volunteered to act until I return, yet 'no' is the only answer vouchsafed." His family wanted him to leave the navy, but he stoically refused. "As to my application for a detachment, as I am a gentleman, I shall never make nor allow it to be made. While the hard collar of Naval Serfdom hangs around my neck I must and will do the duty of a bondsman." But though he refused to leave, he also hated to stay; he closed his letter, "Damn such a life."[182]

While waiting at Norfolk, Kane finished up the illustrations for McSherry's book on the Mexican War and helped him find a publisher. He also worked at securing himself a servant for his next voyage.[183] Elisha almost always had a servant with him, be it an official assistant assigned to him as surgeon, or a personal servant under his own employ. William Weaver, the young boy Kane met on his trip to China, stayed with Kane for several years, serving him as a personal servant while Elisha trained him as a physician, a career he eventually achieved.[184] When he tried to secure a new servant, his mother helped him find one but chastised him saying, "you require more waiting on than any member of the family—a bad habit I have always thought taught by your profession."[185] Sometime in late 1849 Elisha hired William Morton, a young Irishman who would remain with him for the rest of his life, twice following him to the arctic and attending to his wishes even in Elisha's final days.

As Elisha waited for the *Walker* to leave port, he had mixed feelings about his future. After several days he wrote to his brothers Patterson and Tom, "I have gone through that wonderful operation called 'making up one's mind', and... since then I am quite contented." He would go back to Philadelphia, but the analogy he used to describe this decision illustrates that he saw it as a kind of defeated retreat. He wrote, "my abscess has come to a head and I am oozing on in a purulent state of comparative comfort waiting for time and sunshine to scab me over. Depend upon it, dear fellows, the process is going on grandly and I shall return to you in an admirable condition for the elderly ladies, and for family practice—a splendid scab."[186] Elisha took this plan seriously enough to have Patterson rent him an office and living quarters on the first floor of 21 Sansom Street in preparation for his return.[187] Tom was thrilled: "You want to know what Tom says, do you? Well, Tom says just what he said when you went away—nothing more nor less: Come home—stay at home, and be damned to Uncle Sam's scant pocket money.... Come home I say and be no man's man—until you get married and then you will be a woman's."[188]

Despite his decision, Elisha still felt restless; the boil of adventure would not scab over. Just before the *Walker* sailed, he sent a letter to Lieutenant William Francis Lynch who had just completed a discovery expedition to the Holy Lands and was rumored to be putting together a new expedition to the arctic to rescue the missing English explorer, Sir John Franklin. Lynch's reply was a painful reminder of how his health affected his career, because Lynch, who knew Elisha from his time aboard the *Supply*, said, "There is no one I would select sooner than yourself in all that pertains to high moral and intellectual qualifications." But he then added, "As to the physique, I confess that I have misgivings.... A second in command can supply the place of the leader, but there could be no substitute if the medical officer were to perish." Lynch was not willing to risk taking a sickly physician aboard an arduous exploring expedition.[189]

The *Walker* left port soon after Christmas and by mid-January it reached Charleston, South Carolina. While ashore for a few days, Kane undoubtedly read that on January 4, President Zachary Taylor had officially advocated an arctic expedition and passed his wishes along to Congress for debate. This news fueled Elisha's restlessness. He wrote home to his mother about his current, dull assignment:

> Never before have little things formed so equilibrium disturbing an aggregate, never have trifles so taxed a man used to the graver vicissitudes of life.
>
> Could the Charleston Hotel burst out into a comforting conflagration and I descend from the fifth story with sixteen small children bundled into an entry carpet, or could even the Cape Fear Steamboat boiler have burst opposite the lighthouse so as to have enabled me pleasantly to float ashore on a tea box—with fat Mrs. Colonel Huger tied to my neck cloth in a state of strangulation—there would have been something to relieve the littleness and undo the miserable tedium of small adventures under which most hopelessly and without comfort I do now groan.[190]

Elisha still thirsted for adventure. The thought of settling down as a Philadelphia physician and resigning himself to "the miserable tedium of small adventures" was agonizing. He wanted more, and an arctic expedition would provide just such an adventure. He thus struggled about what to do next. In mid-February he wrote Patterson that he saw his present trip as a type of atonement for his previous reckless life and suggested that he soon expected to make a change. "Every pendulum has its downward undulation & should I live to see the young summer I will begin to go up again." His last line used an entomological analogy to address this change, noting that he was moving from "worm" to "butterfly."[191] A letter from the fall of 1849 helps provide a physical illustration of Elisha's mind at this time. Apparently at Elisha's request, Tom wrote out a detailed account of the content of their study back in Philadelphia:

> [T]he study is the same as when you went away... an Indian moccasin,... Boxwood snuff Box, Escritoire, Chinese Lantern, Two skulls, Luzon birds, Cock Hornbill,... Tomahawk, Horsehair pendant, Dr. Dwight, Rotten snakes in bottle, Seven Conchs, Chinese Marionette, Compass, Teapot, Pewter Inkstand, Pistol burnt at Taunton, Powder holder from Kinsington fight ground, Alligator Bird Calumet, Knee britches of deceased doggy, drum, ink bottle, Iguana, Sand Toy, Cock Plume, Sack of arrow flints, Globe, Pamphlets, Alarm Clock, Writing Desk, Tagalar Books, Labôts Chourineur, old Bible, Marshal's bâton, Rosary, Sea Weed, Fossil Rocks, Birch canoe model, English Bow, Ceylonese Fan, Canteen, Moccasins, Coral, Fowling piece.[192]

Elisha's room, and by analogy his mind, was crammed full of objects of science and adventure. This was the clutter and accumulation of an explorer, not of a staid Philadelphia doctor in a proper, green-shuttered office. By the first months of 1850, Elisha finally and definitively decided that he was a man of science and exploration, not a physician. Toward the end of February, he learned that Lynch was not to command the arctic expedition; heartened by this he sent a letter to the secretary of the navy, volunteering to serve at furlough pay (one third his usual salary), and hoping that the new commander would overlook his frail constitution.

He did not immediately tell his family of his application, but he did hint to his mother about his change of heart by comparing his two career choices. "Ah, my dear Mother! It is hard to give up the ghost among foul sheets and dirty napkins—Better die in the bloody struggle... better be lance struck or fever smitten than expire in a white washed chamber whose four walls are spotted with the expectorated muculi of your departed predecessors."[193] Three weeks later he told Tom of his plans, beginning, "My dear Tom—Brother, You are the only person to whom I can entirely confide sure of appreciation, and, if need be, of cooperation." He knew his family would see his decision as foolhardy, but he assured Tom that it was not; it was a decision he had made only after "careful analysis." Elisha's tone throughout was firm but apologetic. He knew his leaving would cause Tom pain, but he also knew that his mind was made up. He closed his letter, "God bless again both of us, or give us stony wills wherewith in spite of weak carcasses we may bless ourselves."[194]

On May 12, 1850, Elisha received a telegram officially detaching him from his assignment aboard the *Walker* and ordering him to report immediately for duty aboard the U.S. Grinnell Expedition in Search of Sir John Franklin. He made the trip from Mobile Bay, Alabama, to New York in seven and a half days, an amazing feat for the time, involving stagecoach, train, and ferry.[195] His family was far from pleased about this news, but they had resolved to support Elisha's exploration efforts once again. Tom noted, "It seems dreadful about Elish', but I know it's right. If he lives through it, he will feel ennobled for life."[196] His father added, "I cannot rejoice that he is going on this expedition; his motive is most praiseworthy, but I think the project a wild one, and I fear inadequacy in outfit." Then addressing both the nation's and Elisha's ambition he exclaimed, "Oh! this Glory! when the cost is fairly counted up, it is no such great speculation after all." Ultimately, Elisha's mother best summed up the family's feelings when she simply noted: "I have been sadly troubled... but it is vain to grieve. Elisha cannot live without adventure."[197] After a very quick stop at home to gather his belongings and say his goodbyes, Elisha was gone. Forty hours after his arrival in Philadelphia, he was aboard the U.S. Grinnell Expedition and on his way to the arctic.

As his ship, the *Advance*, left its New York harbor, Elisha Kent Kane, the sickly Philadelphia physician, faded into the distance, and Dr. Kane, the arctic hero, slowly began to come into public view.

1. Russell F. Weigley ed., *Philadelphia: A 300-Year History* (New York: W.W. Norton & Co., 1982). Franklin's quote appears in *The Autobiography of Benjamin Franklin* (New Haven, CT: Yale University Press, 1964), 125.

2. Alan Taylor, *William Cooper's Town* (New York: Vintage Books, 1995), 306.

3. Early Kane family history is covered in: George Corner's *Dr. Kane of the Arctic Seas* (Philadelphia: Temple University Press, 1972), 6-17; John K. Kane, *Autobiography: Myself from 1795 to 1849*, ed. Sybil Kane, (Philadelphia: privately printed, 1949); and Elizabeth Dennistoun Kane, *Story of John Kane of Dutchess County, New York* (Philadelphia: J.B. Lippincott, 1921). John K. Kane's autobiography was written in 1848 and published with additional information and a family tree in 1949. Though informative, neither it nor Elizabeth Kane's book is entirely reliable as they are based largely on John Kane's recollections and family stories told many years after the events described.

4. John Kane did not have a middle name at birth, but as a young man he adopted his stepmother's maiden name, "Kintzing" as his middle name. Information on Philadelphia's class structure as well as Mackay's quote come from Elizabeth M. Geffen, "Industrial Development and Social Crisis 1841-1854," in *Philadelphia: A 300-Year History*, ed. Russell F. Weigley (New York: W.W. Norton & Co., 1982), 330.

5. Charles K. Shields, "The Arctic Monument named for Tennyson by Dr. Kane," *Century Magazine* 34 (Aug. 1898): 482-92. In 1824, Jane, then a 28 year-old mother of two boys, was selected by the city to join the Marquis de Lafayette in opening a costume ball in his honor. Thomas Sully, the leading portrait painter of the day, portrayed her in her costume as Mary, Queen of Scots.

6. Angela Hewett, "An Introduction to Thomas Leiper," *The Bulletin of the Delaware County Historical Society* 45 (Summer 1994): 1-8. Edgar Richardson, "The Athens of America," in *Philadelphia: A 300-Year History*, ed. Russell F. Weigley (New York: W.W. Norton & Co., 1982), 237-38; Corner, 6-17; Henry Simpson, ed. *The Lives of Eminent Philadelphians* (Philadelphia, 1859), 648-50; *Dictionary of American Biography*, s.v., "Thomas Leiper."

7. John K. Kane, and Pennsylvanian, *A Candid View of the Presidential Question* (Philadelphia: Printed by William Stavely, 1828).

8. The growing importance of campaign biographies and character sketches are discussed in Scott E. Casper, *Constructing American Lives* (Chapel Hill: University of North Carolina Press, 1999).

9. Matthew Grow "'Liberty to the Downtrodden': Thomas . Kane, Romantic Reformer" (PhD diss., University of Notre Dame, 2006), 24-25.

10. John K. Kane to Elisha Kent Kane (May 27, 1844), BYU Thomas Leiper Kane papers.

11. Paul H. Bergerson, *The Presidency of James K. Polk* (Lawrence: University Press of Kansas, 1987), 17-18; Charles A. McCoy, *Polk and the Presidency* (Austin: University of Texas Press, 1960), 9-48. Both sides greatly exaggerated Polk's obscurity—he had

served as Speaker of the House (1835-39) and Governor of Tennessee (1839-41) before becoming President.

12. John K. Kane to Elisha Kent Kane (June 14, 1844), BYU Thomas Leiper Kane papers.

13. Thomas Leiper Kane to Elisha Kent Kane (Feb. 26, 1845), BYU Thomas Leiper Kane papers; John Kane, *Autobiography*, 36-42. John Kane's main rival for Democratic power in Pennsylvania was James Buchanan who was able to curry greater favor with Polk and thus gain a political advantage over Kane—Polk made Buchanan Secretary of State.

14. John Kane, *Autobiography*; Corner, 9-11; and Simpson, 613-18.

15. Simpson, 615. This sketch was almost certainly written by Thomas Leiper Kane, who appears as a contributor to this work and who was himself a skilled manipulator of public opinion.

16. John Kane, *Autobiography*, 42.

17. See Grow, chapter 7 "Fugitive Slaves" for an excellent analysis of the Kane family's internal struggles over the slavery issue. See also the *Pennsylvania Freeman* (Dec. 4, 1851), 3; William Wood to Thomas Leiper Kane (Jan., 23, 1851), BYU Thomas Leiper Kane papers; Thomas Slaughter, *Bloody Dawn: The Christiana Riot and Racial Violence in the Antebellum North* (New York: Oxford University Press, 1991); W.U. Hensel, *The Christiana Riot and the Treason Trials of 1851* (Lancaster, PA: New Era Printing Co., 1911); and Randall Hudson & James Duram, "The *New York Daily Tribune* and Passmore Williamson's Case: A Study in the Use of Northern States' Rights," *Wichita State University Bulletin* (November, 1974). A good view of how Philadelphia's elite society viewed Judge Kane's ruling in fugitive slave cases is available in Sidney George Fisher, *The Diary of Sidney George Fisher, 1834-1871*, ed. N.B. Wainwright (Philadelphia: Historical Society of Pennsylvania, 1967), 249-51.

18. Corner, 11.

19. See folder, "Notebook (Childhood)," APS Elisha Kent Kane papers.

20. Elisha Kent Kane to John K. Kane (June 10, 1828), APS Elisha Kent Kane papers. For Elisha's roof-climbing story see William Elder, *Biography of Elisha Kent Kane* (Philadelphia: Childs & Peterson, 1857), 22-25.

21. Elder, 21.

22. Elisha Kent Kane to John K. Kane (Sept. 16, 1831), APS Elisha Kent Kane papers.

23. James Park McCallie, "Elisha Kent Kane," *Alumni Bulletin, University of Virginia* 6 (1889): 103-6; Corner, 22-24. It seems Kane may have began taking classes at UVA in 1837 though he did not matriculate until 1838.

24. Robert Patterson to Mrs. Patterson (June 6, 1839), Dow Papers, Stefansson Arctic Collection, Dartmouth College Library.

25. Elder, 37.

26. E. Anthony Rotundo, *American Manhood* (New York: Basic Books, 1993), 1.

27. Issues of masculinity in this time period are discussed in depth by Rotundo as well as in Ann Dougas, *The Feminization of American Culture* (New York: Alfred A. Knopf,

1977); and Mark C. Carnes & Clyde Griffen, eds, *Meanings for Manhood* (Chicago: University of Chicago, 1990).

28. Rotundo, 42-44 and passim.

29. Rotundo, 265.

30. Simpson, 614.

31. John K. Kane to Jane Duval Leiper Kane & Elisha Kent Kane (Nov. 7, 1834), BYU Thomas Leiper Kane papers.

32. John K. Kane to Jane Duval Leiper Kane (Feb. 9, 1835), BYU Thomas Leiper Kane papers.

33. John K. Kane to Elisha Kent Kane (Feb. 17, 1839), BYU Thomas Leiper Kane papers.

34. John K. Kane to Elisha Kent Kane (March 2, 1835), BYU Thomas Leiper Kane papers.

35. Elder, 37. This "die in the harness" mentality is echoed in a later letter from Tom; he noted that he planned to adopt Elisha's "die fighting" mentality in the face of illness. See Thomas Leiper Kane to John K. Kane (Dec. 29, 1843), BYU Thomas Leiper Kane papers.

36. Elisha Kent Kane to U.S. Naval Board of Examiners (June 2, 1842), APS Elisha Kent Kane papers. For Kane's experiments with Kiesteine see Elisha Kent Kane, "Experiments on Kiesteine with Remarks on its Application to Pregnancy," *American Journal of Medical Sciences* 4 (1842): 13-37.

37. Thomas Leiper Kane to John K. Kane (Dec. 11, 1840), BYU Thomas Leiper Kane papers.

38. Elder, 43.

39. Elisha Kent Kane to John K. Kane & Jane Duval Leiper Kane (May 23, [1842]), APS Elisha Kent Kane papers.

40. Elder, 41.

41. Thomas Leiper Kane to Elisha Kent Kane (June 10 & August 11, 1840), BYU Thomas Leiper Kane papers.

42. John K. Kane to Elizabeth Kane (April 1, 1842), Kane family papers, Clements Library, University of Michigan.

43. Elisha Kent Kane to John K. Kane & Jane Duval Leiper Kane (May 23, [1842]), APS Elisha Kent Kane papers.

44. Elisha Kent Kane to U.S. Naval Board of Examiners (June 2, 1842), APS Elisha Kent Kane papers.

45. Corner, 33; Mary Leiper to Elisha Kent Kane (May 23, 1843), APS Elisha Kent Kane papers.

46. Elisha Kent Kane to Abel Upshur (Jan. 30, 1843), Navy Records, U.S. National Archives as cited in Corner, 33.

47. Richard Henry Dana, *Two Years Before the Mast* (New York: MacMillan Co., 1909, 1840), 5 and passim. For the popularity of this book, see *Carl Bode, The Anatomy of American Popular Culture, 1840-1861* (Berkeley: University of California Press, 1960), 221.

48. Elder, 100.
49. Caleb Cushing to Elisha Kent Kane (May 20, 1843), Library of Congress, Manuscripts Division, Caleb Cushing papers. The Navy commissioned Elisha on May 30, 1843, six days after he shipped out with the Cushing delegation. In 1846 Elisha, through his father, requested full wages for his service. See John K. Kane to Elisha Kent Kane (May 31, 1843), and John K. Kane to Vice President George Dallas (April 30, 1846), BYU Thomas Leiper Kane papers.
50. John K. Kane to Elisha Kent Kane (Nov. 16, 1843) and (May 25, 1844), BYU Thomas Leiper Kane papers.
51. Weaver's logbook, housed in the APS Elisha Kent Kane papers, is now the only complete account of this part of the journey as this section of the ship's official log is missing. For Kane's work with Weaver see William Robinson to Elisha Kent Kane (Oct. 10, 1845), APS Elisha Kent Kane papers.
52. Corner, 35-36; Elder, 55-56. Kane's journals from this time were lost; this information comes from the remembrances of the Kane family as told to Elder in 1857. The events do match with the logbook of William Weaver noted above. Corner did an exceptional job of piecing together Kane's travels from 1843-44, meticulously verifying and correcting Elder's exaggerated account. My telling of this journey relies heavily on his book as well as his research notes now housed with Kane's papers at the American Philosophical Society in Philadelphia.
53. John K. Kane to Elisha Kent Kane (Nov. 16, 1843), BYU Thomas Leiper Kane papers. Unfortunately Elisha's journals from this time period do not survive.
54. John K. Kane to Elisha Kent Kane (Jan. 28, 1844), BYU Thomas Leiper Kane papers.
55. Elder, 75-76. When writing his biography of Kane, Elder wrote many of Kane's friends for their remembrances of him; this quote comes from Webster's response.
56. Corner, 36-37.
57. John K. Kane & Thomas Leiper Kane to Elisha Kent Kane (May 25, 1844), BYU Thomas Leiper Kane papers.
58. *Oxford English Dictionary*, electronic ed., s.v. "scientist."
59. This note still exists in the APS Elisha Kent Kane papers. Hastily written in pencil it reads, "Being about to descend into the Crater for the first time since its great alteration, I would exempt my friends from all participation in my attempt and I beg that this may be forwarded to my friends at home should I not return. E.K. Kane April 14th Manila Time, Crater of Taal Forward to J.K. Kane Esq. Philada."
60. Folder, "Travel Notes," APS Elisha Kent Kane papers.
61. This story appears in the folder, "Travel Notes," APS Elisha Kent Kane papers; and Elder, 59-65.
62. See folder, "Manila Rough Notes," APS Elisha Kent Kane papers. Marks in the journal show that they were edited for potential publication and letters between Elisha and Tom allude to these journals as the foundation of a book.

63. John K. Kane to Elisha Kent Kane (Jan. 24, 1843), BYU Thomas Leiper Kane papers.

64. John K. Kane & Thomas Leiper Kane to Elisha Kent Kane (undated, c. Spring, 1844), APS Elisha Kent Kane papers.

65. Rotundo, 46.

66. John K. Kane & Thomas Leiper Kane to Elisha Kent Kane (May 25, 1844), BYU Thomas Leiper Kane papers.

67. Thomas Leiper Kane to John K. Kane (March 7, 1844), BYU Thomas Leiper Kane papers.

68. John K. Kane & Thomas Leiper Kane to Elisha Kent Kane (May 1, 1844), BYU Thomas Leiper Kane papers.

69. Baron Loë to Elisha Kent Kane (May 23, 1844), APS Elisha Kent Kane papers.

70. Elder, 70-73.

71. Elder, 76-77.

72. Corner, 41-42. *The Friend of China and Hongkong Gazette*, an English-language newspaper published in Hong Kong, contained several ads placed by Kane and O'Sullivan, informing foreign captains of their services. A clipping can be found in the APS Elisha Kent Kane papers and is reprinted in Corner, 41.

73. Washington Irving to Elisha Kent Kane (Feb. 8. 1845), APS Elisha Kent Kane papers.

74. Thomas Leiper Kane to Elisha Kent Kane (May 22, 1844) & (Sept. 3, 1844), BYU Thomas Leiper Kane papers.

75. John K. Kane & Thomas Leiper Kane to Elisha Kent Kane (Dec. 9, 1844) APS Elisha Kent Kane papers.

76. Thomas Leiper Kane to Elisha Kent Kane (Sept. 3, 1844), BYU Thomas Leiper Kane papers.

77. Thomas Leiper Kane to Elisha Kent Kane (Dec. 6, 1844), APS Elisha Kent Kane papers.

78. John K. Kane to Elisha Kent Kane (Dec. 14, 1844), APS Elisha Kent Kane papers.

79. Jane Duval Leiper Kane to Elisha Kent Kane (Dec. 5, 1844), APS Elisha Kent Kane papers.

80. John K. Kane & Thomas Leiper Kane to Elisha Kent Kane (Dec. 9, 1844) APS Elisha Kent Kane papers.

81. For a discussion of this see Donald Yacovone, "Abolitionists and the Language of Fraternal Love," in Carnes & Griffen, eds, *Meanings for Manhood* (Chicago: University of Chicago, 1990); and Rotundo, chapter 4.

82. See folder, "Whampoa Medical Affairs," APS Elisha Kent Kane papers.

83. Judging from the letters he quotes, William Elder had many letters that have not survived to the present. However, Elder's biography was purposefully hagiographic (commissioned by Kane's publisher to promote further book sales) and thus exaggerated the scope of Kane's travels.

84. Willie Kane to Elisha Kent Kane (March 19, 1845), APS Elisha Kent Kane papers.

85. Elder, 80; Corner, 44, 281-82n20. Corner speculates on each of these possible routes

and shows that a sea route is much more likely.

86. Corner, 44. Kane also gained membership in the Egyptian Literary Association. See Henry Abbott to Elisha Kent Kane (Dec. 2, 1845), APS Elisha Kent Kane papers.

87. See folder, "Notebook #7," and Elisha Kent Kane to John K. Kane (Aug. 3, 1845), APS Elisha Kent Kane papers.

88. Elder, 81, 84. This comes from a long letter excerpted by Elder. The original is not present among Kane's surviving papers.

89. Elder, 81-90; Corner, 45.

90. Elder, 90-95.

91. Though no surviving letters or journals directly tell this tale, Elisha clearly reported it home as the family used it some years later to help drum up support for his first Arctic adventure, see *New York Tribune* (June 8, 1850), 7; *Spirit of the Times* (July 13, 1850), 245; and Elder, 90-95.

92. Corner, 45-46; folder, "Notebook #7," APS Elisha Kent Kane papers.

93. Elder, 96-97. Elder notes that Kane visited "the Delphic oracle at Castri" but the Delphic oracle is in Delphi, not Castri. When Elisha was in Delphos (then known as Castri) he probably visited the oracle of Pythos, dedicated to the god Apollo.

94. Elder, 97. Though this letter is no longer among Kane's papers, I do not doubt its authenticity because Elisha proposed a similar plan a few months earlier. See Washington Irving to Elisha Kent Kane (Feb. 8. 1845), APS Elisha Kent Kane papers.

95. Thomas Leiper Kane to Elisha Kent Kane (June 8, 1845), BYU Thomas Leiper Kane papers. Tom quotes Elisha's earlier letter in his reply.

96. Thomas Leiper Kane to Elisha Kent Kane (June 8, 1845), BYU Thomas Leiper Kane papers.

97. Thomas Leiper Kane to Elisha Kent Kane (June 8, 1845), BYU Thomas Leiper Kane papers. For an in-depth discussion of Tom's time in Paris and his early thoughts about reform see Grow, chapters 2 "Europe," and 3 "Beginnings of Reform," 45-132; for a general overview of the era's religious reformers see Robert H. Abzug, *Cosmos Crumbling* (New York: Oxford University Press, 1994).

98. Thomas Leiper Kane to Elisha Kent Kane (June 8, 1845), BYU Thomas Leiper Kane papers.

99. Thomas Leiper Kane to Elisha Kent Kane (June 8, 1845), BYU Thomas Leiper Kane papers.

100. Thomas Leiper Kane to Elisha Kent Kane (undated, c. May, 1846), APS Elisha Kent Kane papers. This letter discusses a chapter Elisha sent Tom for review.

101. John K. Kane to Elisha Kent Kane (Dec. 14, 1844), APS Elisha Kent Kane papers; Corner, 10.

102. Elder, 100.

103. Elisha Kent Kane to Henry Selden (Sept. 1, 1845), APS Elisha Kent Kane papers.

104. See folder, "Mary Leiper to Elisha Kent Kane," and Elisha Kent Kane to Helen

Patterson (May 7, 1845), APS Elisha Kent Kane papers.

105. Elisha Kent Kane to Henry Selden (Sept. 1, 1845), APS Elisha Kent Kane papers.

106. See Charles Rosenburg, "Sexuality, Class and Role in Nineteenth-Century America," *American Quarterly* 35, (May 1973): 131-153.

107. John S. Haller, Jr., & Robin M. Haller, *The Physician and Sexuality in Victorian America* (New York, 1974), 191-234.

108. Daniel Scott Smith, "The Dating of the American Sexual Revolution: Evidence and Interpretation," in *The American Family in Social-Historical Perspective*, ed. Michael Gordon, (New York, 1973), 323.

109. Rotundo, 122.

110. J[ohn] T[aylor] J[r.] to Elisha Kent Kane (Feb. 4, 1846), folder "Letters to Dr. Kane," APS Elisha Kent Kane papers.

111. See folder, "Miscellany #1," APS Elisha Kent Kane papers.

112. Folder, "Miscellany #1," APS Elisha Kent Kane papers.

113. C.C. VanWyck to Elisha Kent Kane (May 27, 1846), APS Elisha Kent Kane papers.

114. See folders, "Miscellany #1," and "Miscellany #5," APS Elisha Kent Kane papers.

115. Robert Patterson Kane to Elisha Kent Kane (Nov. 12, 1846), APS Elisha Kent Kane papers. Other surviving letters show that Patterson knew about this whole affair and used false names to protect Elisha. It is evident that "Hensenker" is a pseudonym because they alternate spelling it "Hensenker" and "Hensenken." See folder "Elisha Kent Kane," APS Robert Patterson Kane papers.

116. Neither census records nor the Philadelphia directories provide any evidence of a Julia Reed in the Philadelphia area during this time—not surprising given that women were rarely listed in these sources. It is possible that she is the Julia Reed (daughter of Patrick Reed and Mary Dunn) who married Morgan Carson of Toronto in McKean County, Pennsylvania, in 1846 or 1847. See *Clan Carson Website*, www.clancarson.com/Bulletin%20Board.html.

117. Corner, 49; Elder, 100-01.

118. Elisha Kent Kane to Helen Patterson (May 7, 1846), APS Elisha Kent Kane papers.

119. Corner, 50. That John Kane had prior knowledge of the events in Mexico is suggested in the journal of Philadelphia merchant Thomas Cope who, on Dec. 13, 1845, noted that he sought advice from John Kane on the situation and Kane had "affected ignorance on the subject." *Philadelphia Merchant: The Diary of Thomas P. Cope, 1800-1851* ed. Eliza Cope Harrison, (South Bend, IN: Gateway Editions, 1978).

120. Corner, 50; Elder, 101.

121. Thomas Leiper Kane to Elisha Kent Kane (May 17, 1846), APS Elisha Kent Kane papers. For a fuller discussion of Tom's efforts toward the Mormons in 1845-46 see Mark Metzler Sawin, "A Sentinel for the Saints: Tom Leiper Kane and the Mormon Migration," *Nauvoo Journal* 10 (Spring, 1998): 17-27; and Grow, chapter 4 "Meeting the Mormons," 133-190.

122. Thomas Leiper Kane to Jane Duval Leiper Kane (April 16, 1840), BYU Thomas Leiper

Kane papers.

123. John K. Kane to Elisha Kent Kane (May 16, 1846), APS Elisha Kent Kane papers.

124. Elisha Kent Kane to Thomas Leiper Kane (May 15, 1846), APS Elisha Kent Kane papers.

125. Thomas Leiper Kane to Elisha Kent Kane (May 27, 1846), APS Elisha Kent Kane papers.

126. Thomas Leiper Kane to Elisha Kent Kane (undated, c. May, 1846), APS Elisha Kent Kane papers.

127. Thomas Leiper Kane to Elisha Kent Kane (May 27, 1846), APS Elisha Kent Kane papers.

128. John K. Kane to Elisha Kent Kane (May 31, 1846), APS Elisha Kent Kane papers. Tom included a note on the back of this letter, referring to the bookseller as "Moore" who is almost certainly William H. Moore of the Cincinnati publishing house Moore, Anderson, Wilstach & Keys who specialized in travel literature and medical books. See John Tebbel, *A History of Book Publishing in the United States* vol. 1 (New York: R.R. Bowker, 1972), 483.

129. Corner, 52-53; Elisha Kent Kane to Jane Duval Leiper Kane (July 13, 1846), APS Elisha Kent Kane papers.

130. Letter cited in Corner, 53, 283n8.

131. Note for example Richard Francis Burton, *A Mission to Gelele, King of Dahome* (London: Tinsley Brothers, 1864).

132. Elder, 104.

133. T[homas] Dillard to Elisha Kent Kane (May 12, 1847), APS Elisha Kent Kane papers. Dillard addresses Kane's friend as "King Freeman" but this is almost certainly the same "king", as Westerners often referred to African rulers by a number of different names and this was the only leader Kane met while in Africa.

134. George A. Prentiss to Elisha Kent Kane (Jan. 5, 1847), APS Elisha Kent Kane papers. Bickering between the two began in the fall of 1846 and Kane complained about Prentiss several times to his commanding officer, J.R. Smoot. See folder, "Elisha Kent Kane to J.R. Smoot," APS Elisha Kent Kane papers. Prentiss went on to be a celebrated Union navy commander during the Civil War.

135. Robert Baldick, *The Duel: A History of Dueling* (New York: Clarkson N. Potter, 1965). For an informative and entertaining history of dueling in America see, *The Duel*, prod. Carl Byker, PBS Video, 2000.

136. John K. Kane to Elisha Kent Kane (Nov. 11, 1846), APS Elisha Kent Kane papers.

137. Orson Spencer to Brigham Young (Nov. 26, 1846), in Albert L. Zobell Jr., *Sentinel in the East* (Salt Lake City, UT: Nicholas G. Morgan, 1965), 28.

138. Thomas Leiper Kane to Brigham Young (Dec. 2, 1846), in Zobell, 29-30.

139. Thomas Leiper Kane to Elisha Kent Kane (Nov. 12, 1846), APS Elisha Kent Kane papers.

140. Thomas Leiper Kane to Elisha Kent Kane (Nov. 12, 1846), APS Elisha Kent Kane papers.

141. John K. Kane to Elisha Kent Kane (Nov. 11, 1846), APS Elisha Kent Kane papers.

142. It is difficult to ascertain just what this crisis was. It may have been monetary; several of the family letters of the time discuss finances. More likely, it refers to Judge Kane's work and political life—at this time he was serving as Attorney General for the State and was prosecuting many of the men arrested in the anti-Catholic riots of 1844, a process that put him in the middle of harsh political crossfire.

143. See folder, "E.K. Notebook-Egypt, etc.," APS Elisha Kent Kane papers. Cited here is the draft of a letter to his brother Tom that appears in this notebook marked "confidential" and dated Dec. 1, 1846. Given its confessional nature it is likely Elisha never sent it—no corresponding letter appears in Tom's surviving papers.

144. Folder, "E.K. Notebook-Egypt, etc.," APS Elisha Kent Kane papers.

145. This strong, war-driven desire for adventure is well documented in Robert Johannsen, *To the Halls of the Montezumas* (New York: Oxford University Press, 1985), 29.

146. John K. Kane to Elisha Kent Kane (Dec. 24, 1846), APS Elisha Kent Kane papers.

147. Thomas Leiper Kane to Elisha Kent Kane (Dec. 25, 1846), APS Elisha Kent Kane papers.

148. Thomas Leiper Kane to Elisha Kent Kane (Feb. 12, 1847), APS Elisha Kent Kane papers.

149. Thomas Leiper Kane to Elisha Kent Kane (Jan. 24, 1847), APS Elisha Kent Kane papers.

150. Thomas Leiper Kane to Elisha Kent Kane (Feb. 12, 1847), APS Elisha Kent Kane papers.

151. C.C. VanWyck to Elisha Kent Kane (Aug. 27, 1847), APS Elisha Kent Kane papers. Kane and VanWyck both applied for the position of medical professor; VanWyck felt certain Kane would get it if the board of trustees decided to appoint a non-Quaker.

152. Corner, 57. Kane also wrote President Polk, requesting a position. See Elisha Kent Kane to James Polk (June 19, 1847), APS Elisha Kent Kane papers.

153. H.L. Heiskill to Officers of the Medical Department serving in Mexico (Nov. 5, 1847), reprinted in Elder, 111. Kane was to verbally deliver the message and so a copy does not survive. The message is quite certain, however, because the date of Kane's assignment matches with an entry in Polk's diary noting the commissioning of a "special messenger" for this purpose. See Corner, 58.

154. Thomas Leiper Kane to Elisha Kent Kane (undated, c. Nov., 1847), APS Elisha Kent Kane papers.

155. Elisha Kent Kane to John K. Kane (Nov. 12, 1847), APS Elisha Kent Kane papers.

156. Elisha Kent Kane to John K. Kane (Nov. 12, 1847), APS Elisha Kent Kane papers.

157. Thomas Leiper Kane to Elisha Kent Kane (Dec. 6, 1844), APS Elisha Kent Kane papers.

158. Though he was more hesitant than his brother, Tom was adventurous. He went west

with the Mormons and in the years following Elisha's death he founded his own community, Kane, in rural western Pennsylvania. He also became a brigadier general during the Civil War and his men described him as "a little coal of hell-fire." See Robert D. Hoffsommer, "The Bucktails," *Civil War Times* 4 (1966): 16-21.

159. John K. Kane to Elisha Kent Kane (Feb. 3, 1847), APS Elisha Kent Kane papers.

160. For Tom's internal motivations I am relying heavily on Grow's superb analysis of Tom's inner life at this time.

161. Thomas Leiper Kane to Elisha Kent Kane (Nov. 19, 1847), APS Elisha Kent Kane papers.

162. Thomas Leiper Kane to Elisha Kent Kane (Feb. 20, 1848), APS Elisha Kent Kane papers.

163. Cited in Corner, 59. A copy of this letter is in the Dow papers, Stefansson Arctic Collection, Dartmouth College Library.

164. Corner, 59-60; Elder, 112-13.

165. Statement made by Dr. George E. Cooper of Philadelphia (Dec. 1, 1848), quoted in Elder, 113-14. See also, A. Brooke Caruso, *The Mexican Spy Company: United States Covert Operation in Mexico, 1845-48* (Jefferson, NC: McFarland Co. Inc., 1991), 152-55.

166. *The Pennsylvanian* (March 24, 1848), 2.

167. W.W.H. Davis, "Three Pennsylvanians, Biographical Sketches of General Robert Patterson, James Madison Porter, and Elisha Kent Kane." This work is an undated, incomplete manuscript housed in the Bucks County Historical Society, Doylestown, Pennsylvania. Davis was in Puebla at the time and visited both Kane and the Gaona family who told him the story of the battle and its aftermath.

168. W.W.H. Davis, "Three Pennsylvanians, Biographical Sketches of General Robert Patterson, James Madison Porter, and Elisha Kent Kane."; *The Pennsylvanian* (March 24, 1848), 2; Elisha Kent Kane to John K. Kane (Jan. 16, 1848), APS Elisha Kent Kane papers.

169. Elisha Kent Kane to John K. Kane (Jan. 16, 1848), APS Elisha Kent Kane papers.

170. Thomas Leiper Kane to Elisha Kent Kane (April 7, 1848), in folder, "E.K. Kane letters to Dr. Kane," APS Elisha Kent Kane papers. This unsigned letter is marked "post dated April 7, 1848" and was written by Thomas Leiper Kane.

171. Thomas Leiper Kane to Elisha Kent Kane (April 7, 1848), in folder, "E.K. Kane letters to Dr. Kane," APS Elisha Kent Kane papers.

172. *North American & United States Gazette*, Philadelphia (April 13, 1848), 1.

173. Elisha Kent Kane to William O. Butler, reprinted in Elder, 121-22.

174. *Niles' National Register* (July 26, 1848); Elisha Kent Kane to Kane family (undated), quoted in Elder, 137.

175. See folder, "re: Mexico," APS Elisha Kent Kane papers.

176. See folder, "R[ichard] McSherry to Elisha Kent Kane," APS Elisha Kent Kane papers;

and Richard McSherry, *El Puchero* (Philadelphia: Lippincott, Grambo & Co., 1850). The documentation suggests that these illustrations were done by Elisha, but his name appears nowhere in the volume. The engravings themselves are in different styles and signed by two different makers: "Gilbert & Gihon" and "Butler Sc." It is likely that those done by Gilbert & Gihon were done for the work because they match the text well. Those by Butler Sc appear to be recycled from another general work on Mexico. The book was copyrighted through "the Clerk's Office of the District Court for the Eastern District of Pennsylvania" which was then manned by Tom Kane.

177. Elder, 135. In his application for remuneration, Kane was required to outline what had happened to his horse, thus providing a written record of the events at Nopaluca.

178. Statement dated "Philadelphia, February 8, 1849," reprinted in Elder, 132-33. That Elisha lobbied for this award is evidenced in a letter in which Tom tells him how others have gone about getting such an award, a process that Tom felt would necessitate connection with a "Hose Company or other crony gang." See Thomas Leiper Kane to Elisha Kent Kane (April 7, 1848), folder, "letters to Dr. Kane," APS Elisha Kent Kane papers. This sword was at the Kane Manor Inn in Kane, Pennsylvania, until it was auctioned off to a private collector in Sept. of 2003. See http://www.bobconnelly.com/kaneswords.html

179. Corner, 66.

180. See folder, "Miscellany #2," APS Elisha Kent Kane papers. Undated, but almost certainly from February 1849.

181. Corner, 66-67.

182. Elisha Kent Kane to Jane Duval Leiper Kane (Sept. 6, 1849), APS Elisha Kent Kane papers.

183. See folder, "R[ichard] McSherry to Elisha Kent Kane," and Elisha Kent Kane to Mr. Bier (Oct. 15, 1849), APS Elisha Kent Kane papers.

184. See folder, "Elisha Kent Kane to William Weaver," APS Elisha Kent Kane papers.

185. Jane Duval Leiper Kane to Elisha Kent Kane (Jan. 28, 1849), APS Elisha Kent Kane papers.

186. Elisha Kent Kane to Robert Patterson Kane (Oct. 27, 1849), APS Elisha Kent Kane papers.

187. See folder, "Kane, R.P. agreement with Mrs. Mary Martin (Nov. 8, 1849)," APS Elisha Kent Kane papers.

188. Thomas Leiper Kane to Elisha Kent Kane (undated, c. Oct, 1849), ASP Elisha Kent Kane papers.

189. W[illiam] F[rancis] Lynch to Elisha Kent Kane (Dec. 6, 1849), APS Elisha Kent Kane papers. For Lynch's expedition to the Holy Lands see W.F. Lynch, *Narrative of the United States' Expedition to the River Jordan and the Dead Sea* (Philadelphia: Lea & Blanchard, 1849). This expedition sailed aboard the *USS Supply*, which Elisha served on upon their return.

190. Elisha Kent Kane to Jane Duval Leiper Kane (Jan. 16, 1850), APS Elisha Kent Kane papers.

191. Elisha Kent Kane to Robert Patterson Kane (Feb. 15, 1850), APS Elisha Kent Kane papers.

192. Thomas Leiper Kane to Elisha Kent Kane (undated, c. Oct, 1849), ASP Elisha Kent Kane papers.

193. Elisha Kent Kane to Jane Duval Leiper Kane (Feb. 22, 1850), APS Elisha Kent Kane papers.

194. Elisha Kent Kane to Thomas Leiper Kane (March 8, 1850), APS Elisha Kent Kane papers.

195. Corner, 70, 80-81.

196. Thomas Leiper Kane to Robert Patterson Kane (May 14, 1850), APS Robert Patterson Kane papers.

197. John K. Kane & Jane Duval Leiper Kane to Bessie Kane (May 14, 1850), APS Elisha Kent Kane papers.

2

The Creation of Dr. Kane

❧

Today it is somewhat difficult to understand why, in the mid-nineteenth century, nations were so obsessed with arctic exploration. It was a vastly dangerous enterprise that yielded almost nothing of practical gain, and by the 1820s it was amply clear that, even if the fabled "Northwest Passage" did exist, it would be impractical because of the dangers of arctic navigation. It was also clear that any arctic land that could be claimed would be largely useless; no settlers were going to homestead amidst polar bears and glaciers. The arctic was and remains remarkably desolate: Why bother to explore it? One way to understand the arctic mania of the 1840-1850s is to compare it to the "space race" of the 1950-1960s and the continuing role of space flight today.

According to Roger Launius, chair of the American Space History Program at the National Aeronautics and Space Administration (NASA), there were five reasons America began its manned space program: scientific discovery, economic possibilities, military security and applications, prestige, and survival of the species (the potential to inhabit other planets). Of these reasons, however, prestige was by far the greatest. The U.S. government created NASA in response to the Soviet Union's space program, which in 1957 rocketed to the forefront of the space race with the successful launching of the first satellite, *Sputnik*. Two years later they went farther, crash landing a payload on the moon. John F. Kennedy made space exploration a priority for his administration. In a 1961 speech he declared that the United States "should commit itself to achieving the goal... of landing a man on the moon and returning him safely to the earth," and the Apollo space missions began soon after. They were a direct challenge to the Soviet Union, a bold promotion of American prestige, and every bit as dangerous and superfluous as any arctic adventure of the antebellum period. Launius noted that America continues its space program to this day because "it raises our stature as a people, as a civilization, as a nation." That the U.S. space program is the best in the world is a sign of the nation's prestige: "That's why we started flying them in 1961, and that's why, all other things being countervailing... we will not stop flying them now." He went on to note that in the twenty-first century, "Nations that want to establish their credibility in the world, like China, are seeking to do this, in part, by flying astronauts."[1] Prestige drove and continues to drive the exploration of space. Prestige, and to a lesser degree all the other reasons Launius listed, also fueled the drive for arctic exploration in the antebellum period and caused the United States to launch its own arctic exploring expedition in 1850. A brief history of arctic exploration is necessary to explain how a series of quixotic quests for a lost explorer and a mythical sea could create a sensation great enough to make Dr. Kane one of the foremost celebrities of his age.

It is difficult to determine exactly when European exploration of the polar northwest began. Norse legend always included some notion of these lands, and archeological evidence shows that Scandinavian groups settled in Greenland and far-northern North America as early as the tenth century.[2] The first modern exploration of the American arctic was by English explorer John Cabot. He traveled to present-day Newfoundland in 1496 and 1497, just four years after Columbus sailed to the New World. Cabot's son, Sebastian, capitalized on his father's discoveries by starting the Muscovy Company in Bristol, and as early as 1502, Bristol natives sailed to this "new found land" to catch and dry fish for export back to Europe.[3] Martin Frobisher furthered arctic discovery by reaching Ellesmere Island and what is now called Frobisher Bay during a series of explorations in search of the Northwest Passage in 1576-1578. The British crown charged him to seek out gold and to his great joy he discovered and mined what seemed to be the legendary El Dorado: It was only upon his return to England that he learned that his tons of glistening cargo was fool's gold. In 1585 John Davis rediscovered Greenland (it had been abandoned and forgotten by the Scandanavians a few hundred years before), permanently placing it on European maps. Twenty-five years later, Henry Hudson discovered Hudson's Bay, and his first mate, Robert Bylot, led two other expeditions in search of the Northwest Passage in 1612 and 1615, determining that Hudson's Bay was not the route. Bylot's brilliant pilot, William Baffin, led another expedition in 1616 and discovered the vast bay that now bears his name, as well as the openings to Lancaster, Jones, and Smith Sounds. This greatly increased knowledge of the North American arctic region and again inspired hope of a Northwest Passage. In 1631, however, Luke Foxe again explored Hudson's Bay, and though he discovered two northern outlets—Foxe Channel and Roe's Welcome Sound—upon return to England he declared that the frozen climate would never allow easy access to the Orient, and that if a Northwest Passage did exist, it was not practical. His findings killed interest in arctic exploration for the next two centuries, and though fishing and whaling vessels continued to go to these regions annually, within a few decades, scholars began to doubt the discoveries of Frobisher and Baffin and so removed their findings from European maps.[4] The only North American arctic discoveries of the eighteenth century came from the overland expeditions of Samuel Hearne, who reached the Arctic Ocean via the Coppermine River in 1771, and Alexander Mackenzie, who traced the Mackenzie River to its arctic mouth in 1789.[5]

Systematic arctic exploration only began again in 1817, and for reasons that had little to do with commerce and everything to do with national prestige. In 1815 England finally defeated Napoleon and found itself suddenly at peace for the first time in decades. This created a problem. England had an enormous navy and nothing to do with it. By 1817, ninety percent of all naval officers were unemployed and barely surviving on their half-pay, off-duty wages. Furthermore, after the Napoleonic wars, England cut its navy from 140,000 to 19,000 seamen, but kept all its officers. This meant that there was an officer for every three men in the Royal Navy and none of them had anything to do that could gain them promotion.[6]

Into this era of inactivity stepped John Barrow, Jr. As second secretary to the Admiralty, Barrow was officially in no position to direct the future of the British Navy, but his personal tenacity and obsession with arctic discovery became the driving force of the Navy for the next thirty years.[7] Though Barrow had never traveled to the north nor seen an iceberg, he was captivated by the idea of an "Open Polar Sea"—a perfectly calm, temperate ocean lying at the top of the world, peacefully secluded by a barrier of frozen ice and tundra. The idea of an open sea at the north pole was not at all new. Early Greek maps included *Amphitrites*, an ocean that circled the globe north to south, crossing the equator at a right angle. In 1527, memory of this, as well as speculation based on Magellan's voyage, prompted Robert Thorne, an English merchant and cartographer living in Seville, to advocate the existence of a polar route to the Orient. Not wanting to be out traded by the Spanish and Portuguese, who already had established routes to the Far East, Thorne urged the English crown to search for a shorter northern route to the Orient. With great confidence and little knowledge he boldly asserted, "there is no land uninhabitable, nor Sea innavigable."[8] England, and later Holland, sought a Northeast Passage over the continent of Asia, but by 1597 they were convinced that this would never be a productive trade route. Despite this, explorers Henry Hudson and Willem Barentsz both remained convinced that a northern route existed because they had observed conditions that suggested a warmer climate and open water not far beyond the eightieth parallel. Dutch theologian and cartographer Petrus Plancius and Russian Mikhail Lomonosov both supported this belief, theorizing that the arctic sea remained open because of the continuous daylight of the summer months. A few efforts were made to reach it, but each was blocked by heavy ice and their theories fell into disrepute. Hope springs eternal, however, and hope for an idyllic ocean at the top of the world again emerged in the 1770s. French explorer Louis-Antoine de Bougainville took up Plancius and Lomonosov's theory in 1772, and Swiss geographer Samuel Engel supported the idea in his book published the same year. Inspired by this, Englishman Daines Barrington presented "proofs" of the sea's existence to the Royal Society, which prompted the expedition of Constantine Phipps. He sailed north of Spitzbergen in 1773 and hit solid pack ice at 80° 36' N. This did not deter England. Just three years later they instructed Captain James Cook to return home from the Pacific via the Northwest Passage, or as Cook put it, "make my passage home by the North Pole."[9] Though Cook failed in this regard, a few years later Russian explorers found several open water tracts leading north off the Siberian coast. These open waters (*polynyas* in Russian) again sparked belief in the Open Polar Sea.[10]

So it was that when in 1817 whaling captain William Scoresby reported to the British Admiralty that unusually open ice conditions existed along Greenland's coast, John Barrow jumped at the chance to gain England the threefold discovery of the Northwest Passage, the north pole, and the mysterious Open Polar Sea. That the Russians were making progress toward this discovery inspired Barrow further. He proclaimed that he was not about to let England suffer "another nation to accomplish almost the only interesting discovery that remains to be made in geography."[11] He organized two expeditions for 1818: the first, captained by David Buchan, was to push north from Spitzbergen; and the other, commanded by John Ross, was to seek an "American route" through the mysterious Baffin Bay (Barrow was not convinced of its existence).

These two expeditions were just the first of twelve that Barrow sent out over the next twenty years. Although they made many discoveries, these expeditions were constantly crippled by Barrow's obsession with "proper" military procedure that did not allow him to recognize the idiocy of some of the Royal Navy's practices. Barrow, the son of a poor farmer, was a social climber that looked down on "low" members of society. This prejudice kept him from ever allowing whaling captains—by far the most qualified sailors for arctic conditions—any place of importance on arctic expeditions. Instead, he favored appointing well-connected officers from the upper crust of English society, even if they had no practical experience with arctic travel.[12]

Barrow's bigger blunder, however, was one that stemmed from British views of order, civilization, and propriety. The constant use of big ships (usually sent in pairs), with large crews laden with cumbersome objects and clothed in "proper" but ill-suited uniforms, meant that expedition after expedition floundered. In his chapter, "The Arctic defeats the Royal Navy," arctic scholar Richard Vaughan sardonically compared Barrow's effort to "repeatedly firing off projectiles at an invisible target while blindfolded."[13] Given this refusal to adapt to different methods of exploration, a disaster was inevitable, and it finally struck in 1845 when the *Erebus* and *Terror*, commanded by Sir John Franklin and holding a combined crew of 129 men, passed through Melville Bay and disappeared somewhere beyond the northwestern horn of Greenland.

Franklin and his men set sail for the arctic in the spring of 1845, assigned to seek the Northwest Passage via Lancaster Sound and Barrow Strait. This mission was controversial because of its leader. Franklin was a truly personable man, well liked by everyone for his gracious manner and good humor; unfortunately, he was not much of a leader or navigator. In 1820-1821 and again in 1826 he led expeditions up the Coppermine and Mackenzie Rivers to explore the Canadian coastline of the Arctic Ocean. Both of these expeditions nearly ended in disaster as Franklin lacked the leadership and preparation skills needed for these journeys. George Simpson, a rugged trader and the eventual head of the Hudson's Bay Company, met Franklin before his first trip and commented that he "had not the physical powers required for the labor of moderate Voyaging in this country; he must have three meals p[er] diem, Tea is indispensable, and with the utmost exertion he cannot walk <u>Eight</u> miles in one day."[14]

From 1827 to 1834, Franklin served as commander of a ship stationed in the Mediterranean and then as governor of Tasmania. Upon return to England, Franklin wanted one final and glorious adventure. At the age of fifty-eight and as the senior officer with arctic experience (though this experience was all land-based), he claimed the mission aboard the *Erebus* and *Terror*. His friend, the experienced arctic explorer John Ross, urged him not to go, warning that he would wind up "the nucleus of an iceberg."[15] He appealed to Barrow to stop Franklin, but Barrow insisted that Franklin was the man. Franklin was so confident in his mission—he was commanding the biggest ships ever sent to the arctic—that he and his officers brought their own fine china and silverware as well as a library of twelve hundred books. Ross promised to go looking for him if he failed to return by February of 1847, but both Barrow and Franklin saw this as only the paranoid worrying of an old explorer. With great fanfare Franklin left London on May 19, 1845. He and his crew were last seen by an English whaler on July 22, 1845; the *Erebus* and *Terror* were moored to an iceberg in Baffin Bay, awaiting an opening in the ice floes.

Portraits of Sir John Franklin (in the center) and his officers. From
Gleason's Pictorial Drawing-Room Companion (October 18, 1851).

When Franklin failed to return in 1846 or 1847, Ross tried to persuade the Admiralty to send out a relief expedition, but they were confident in Franklin and so delayed another year. But when Franklin failed to return in the spring of 1848, they too became worried, as did Franklin's tenacious wife, Lady Jane Franklin. In the following years she worked tirelessly to launch expedition after expedition in search of her husband. Ultimately the desire to discover Franklin's fate sparked more than fifteen expeditions and become the holy grail of exploration for the next decade; the romance of exploration tied with the tragedy of a lost hero made this search popular on both sides of the Atlantic. England, France, Denmark, Russia and the United States each sent at least one expedition in search of Franklin.

It is important to note that national prestige, not Franklin's rescue, was the incentive that lay behind most of the expeditions sent to the arctic. Well aware of this, Lady Franklin exploited the United States' desire to prove its place among the "first nations" of the world when she wrote to President Zachary Taylor, asking for aid in the search for her husband. She urged the United States to participate in this "noble spectacle" because the United States was one of the three great nations (along with England and Russia) that were "possessed of the widest empires on the face of the globe."[16] National prestige was at stake and Lady Jane made it clear that if the United States wanted to compete, its manifest destiny needed to extend north as well as west.

For the United States, there was further incentive to send an expedition—science, or more accurately stated, the desire to show Europe that its men of science rivaled those of the Old World. Matthew Fontaine Maury, one of America's leading natural philosophers and the father of modern oceanography, had come to support the Open Polar Sea theory. He postulated that this open sea, together with the waters surrounding Antarctica, governed the circulation of the currents of the world's oceans. In the early 1840s he devised an ingenious charting system to compile data on ocean currents, wind direction, and other oceanic information. By carefully examining this information he found that warm currents flowed south from the north pole, suggesting a mild climate at the top of the world. This evidence was further supported by the fact that whales caught in the north Pacific sometimes had harpoons from Baffin Bay whaling companies stuck in their hides. Because it was then believed that these whales could not survive the warm waters around the equator, the only possible explanation was that they crossed from the Atlantic to the Pacific via an ice-free Northwest Passage.[17]

Finding the elusive Northwest Passage and proving that the Open Polar Sea existed was of utmost importance to Maury, then head of the U.S. Naval Observatory and Hydrographic Office. Though his hypothesis was not made public until the publication of his book, *The Physical Geography of the Sea* (1855), his theory was clearly set forth in the navy's instructions to the U.S. Grinnell Expedition in 1850. These instructions, written by Maury, directed Captain Edwin J. DeHaven to begin searching for Franklin in Baffin Bay but then to press on northward along the openings of Jones and Smith Sounds, not southward, the logical (and indeed actual) route of Franklin's escape.[18] This clearly shows that the expedition was more about exploration and discovery than the rescue of Franklin.[19] It is a coincidental but telling fact that the larger of the mission's ships was named *Advance*, the smaller *Rescue*.

On May 22, 1850, the U.S. Grinnell Expedition in Search of Sir John Franklin left New York and cruised up the Atlantic coast bound for the arctic. This expedition was quite different than those launched by the Royal Navy. It was made up of only two small ships: the *Advance*, a 144-ton hermaphrodite brig that was smaller than a present day harbor tugboat and designed for maneuverability and speed; and the *Rescue*, an even smaller brig of just ninety-one tons. Both ships were heavily reinforced; the *Advance* was covered with a five-inch layer of oak planking and sheet-iron strips, and the first seven feet of her hull was filled solidly with timber. Her decks were double-planked with a layer of tar and felt between them, and the whole interior of the ship was lined with cork for additional warmth. Thus equipped, these small but strong vessels were ideal for arctic navigation.[20] The expedition had these well-equipped vessels not because the U.S. Navy was more enlightened than the Royal Navy, but because of the generosity of Henry Grinnell, a wealthy whaling merchant who intimately understood the trials and necessities of arctic navigation.[21] Disgusted by Congress's lack of response to Lady Jane Franklin's pleas for a U.S. search expedition, Grinnell donated two of his own ships with the understanding that the government would provide a crew and provisions. The result was that the U.S. Grinnell Expedition was equipped with the best possible boats but very poor supplies; Congress delayed funding until the last possible minute, giving the navy little time to properly provision the ships.[22]

After leaving New York, the Grinnell Expedition followed the North American coast through Davis Strait into Baffin Bay, crossing north and east into Lancaster Sound. The *Advance* and *Rescue* were not alone in the arctic; ten other ships were searching for Sir John Franklin in the summer of 1850. The Royal Navy sent four vessels—the *Resolute, Assistance, Pioneer,* and *Intrepid*—and renamed and reassigned two whaling ships—the *Lady Franklin* and *Sophia*—to help in the search as well.

Engraving of Henry Grinnell from the frontispiece of Volume II of Kane's *Arctic Explorations* (Philadelphia: Childs & Peterson, 1856).

British explorer John Ross had two privately funded ships—the *Felix* and *Mary*—as well as a supply ship—the *North Star*—in the area. Lady Franklin's personally funded *Prince Albert* was also on hand. The *Advance* met up with the *Lady Franklin* and *Sophia*, under William Penny's command, on August 19, just as they were nearing the mouth of Lancaster Sound. They exchanged news with the crew and learned where several of the other British expeditions were searching. Two days later the *Advance* encountered the schooner *Felix*, commanded by the seventy-three-year-old arctic veteran, Sir John Ross.

On August 22, just a day after parting company with Ross's *Felix*, they were hailed by the *Prince Albert*, captained by Charles Forsyth. In the days before, the tiny *Prince Albert*—roughly the same size as the *Rescue*—had tried to penetrate Prince Regent Inlet, but met impenetrable ice. Despite several of his officers' objections, Forsyth decided to head back for England. He did, however, agree to first make a quick trip to the mouth of Wellington Channel to pick up any news from the other expeditions. On their way they met the *Advance* and followed her through Barrow Strait.[23] Forsyth and his surgeon, William Parker Snow, boarded the *Advance* and Snow spent the afternoon with the *Advance*'s surgeon, Elisha Kent Kane. They spent the better part of the day exchanging stories of travel and adventure. Snow was both amused and impressed with the energy and intelligence that seemed to almost burst out of Elisha's small frame. He recorded later, "Rich in anecdote and full of pleasing talk, time flew rapidly as I conversed with him."[24]

On August 25, when they reached the mouth of Wellington Channel, the crews from both ships spotted two cairns on the shore of Cape Riley. They went ashore and found a note left by the *Assistance* and *Intrepid*, commanded by Sir John Ommanney. These ships had been there two days before and had discovered evidence of a Royal Naval encampment, almost assuredly made by Sir John Franklin.[25] Further traces were also found ten miles further up Wellington Channel on Beechey Island (actually a peninsula).[26] The *Rescue*, which had sped ahead of the *Advance* and *Lady Franklin* while crossing Barrow Strait, soon rejoined them and reported that they had met up with Ommanney a few days earlier and had shared in the discovery of the encampment.[27] The *Prince Albert* immediately took sail for England, carrying with it news of this discovery as well as letters from the crews of the *Advance* and *Rescue*.[28]

While DeHaven and Kane were ashore examining the cairns, the *Advance* drifted onto the rocks. After a few hours, DeHaven got his ship free and continued on to Beechey Island to investigate the other encampment. There he found himself in the midst of an arctic traffic jam. Captains William Penny and John Ross had both tried to pass west through Barrow Strait, but ice forced them to seek shelter at Beechey Island. This meant that by August 27, six ships were within a quarter mile of each other. DeHaven and Kane went ashore, joining Penny's search

Like all of Kane's full-page illustrations in his first book, this picture of Franklin's men's graves was a drawing by James Hamilton made from a sketch by Kane and then engraved by John Sartain. From Kane's *U.S. Grinnell Expedition* (New York: Harper & Bros., 1854).

party in their examination of the encampment, and while they were there, one of Penny's men came running to report that he had discovered three graves. They all scrambled to the gravesites; the three wooden headboards definitively proved that Beechey Island had been Franklin's winter quarters in 1845-1846.[29]

Though the British and American crews got along well, the discoveries at Cape Riley and Beechey Island became a source of tension because both American and British crews were present at the discoveries, and each wanted to claim them for their own nations. It also struck the companies as strange that Franklin built cairns to mark his location, but did not leave a note explaining his next planned destination—the common practice of arctic explorers. This led many of the commanding officers to suspect that Captain Ommanney, who had first found the cairns, had removed the note so he alone could make the all-important discovery of Franklin's whereabouts. Convinced of Ommanney's deception, Penny swore "to shoot him," and DeHaven said he would "up helm and go home" if he found the British captain had put their lives in danger for the sake of his own glory.[30] The captains knew, however, that this controversy had to be resolved at a later date because there was still more time to make discoveries, and the remaining groups needed to cooperate. The captains conferred and agreed to pursue each of the plausible directions: Penny would head west to Cape Walker, Ross would go south toward Prince Regent Inlet, and DeHaven would push further north up Wellington Channel. This plan was perfect for the U.S. Expedition because north was exactly the direction they needed to go to search for Maury's Open Polar Sea.[31]

DeHaven headed toward Cornwallis Island and hoped to push north up the western side of Wellington Channel. His ships reached Cornwallis on September 5 and began heading north, but they were soon stopped by pack ice. On September 10 they were again joined by Austin's and Penny's vessels, which were forced to the same location because ice blocked their westward route through Barrow Strait. Two days later a terrific storm blew up, threatening to destroy all seven vessels. The *Rescue's* anchoring cable snapped in the gale and she was carried out to sea. Once the storm ended, DeHaven decided to abandon the mission because it was too dangerous to risk being forced to winter in that desolate area. After finding the *Rescue* on September 13, he ordered the two ships cabled together and set sail for home, but this plan was foiled two days later. Ice formed around the ships and locked them into an ice floe that pushed them north, past their original stopping point, and further up the western side of Wellington Channel. Trapped in the ice, they drifted helplessly north for several weeks, during which time they discovered and named the far northern portion of Devon Island, "Grinnell Land."[32]

On October 1, the crews resigned themselves to being stuck in the ice for the winter and began preparing for the total darkness that would soon be upon them; however, the floe suddenly broke apart, barely giving them time to scramble back aboard their ships. Their renewed hope of freedom was short lived, however, because they were soon again frozen into pack ice, this time moving south. During the long, dark winter, the crew suffered terribly from scurvy. Because DeHaven was desperately ill, Elisha took the health of the crew into his own hands. He ordered them to get out into the air for exercise (even in minus fifty degree weather) and increased their rations. The crew's morale increased a bit, probably not because of Elisha's efforts, but because the ice floe was pushing them further and further south, toward warmer, open water. Finally the pack broke apart on June 5, 1851, freeing the *Rescue* and, three days later, the *Advance*.

The ships headed south, making it to Greenland's Disco Island by June 17, where they stayed for several days to purchase much-needed provisions. Kane recorded that they "drank largely of the smallest of small beer, and danced with the natives, teaching them the polka."[33] He was fascinated by the rugged people of Greenland's shore, especially the women, but his finer senses, if not sensibilities, kept him at arm's length. He wrote, "What favorable impression that the mind gets through other channels can contend against the information of the nose! Organ of the aristocracy, critic... of all civilization, censor that heeds neither argument nor remonstrance... it bids me record, that to all their possible godliness cleanliness is not super-added."[34]

Women of Greenland from
Kane's *U.S. Grinnell Expedition*
(New York: Harper & Bros.,
1854).

The American expedition set off for the north again in late June, hoping to
cross Lancaster Sound for another season of exploration, but the *Advance* soon became entangled in another ice field. Fortunately they escaped this obstacle and,
after several days through rough seas, docked at Greenland's most northerly whaling port, Upernavik. There they found newspapers sent from home and greedily
consumed them. They soon again set sail and on July 9 met a whaler carrying mail
from the United States, including several letters for their crew. Elisha stayed up all
that sun-filled night to read his many letters from home. The next day they again
hit solid pack ice. Two days later they were surprised to be hailed by the *Prince Albert*, fresh from England, and this time under the command of William Kennedy.
The three ships stayed together for more than a month, battling to gain entrance
into Lancaster Sound. Kennedy gave up on August 13 and headed for home, and,
after another week of fruitless labor, DeHaven also turned south. The *Advance*
reached New York on September 30; the *Rescue* arrived a week later.[35]

It was aboard this arctic expedition that Elisha began his transformation from
Elisha Kent Kane to "Dr. Kane of the Arctic Seas." That the search for Sir John
Franklin made someone an international celebrity is hardly shocking; it was one of
the most publicized events of the era. But that this hero was to be Elisha—a sickly,
young surgeon aboard a largely unsuccessful expedition—is surprising. The story
of how Elisha became the celebrated hero of the arctic is an exceptional example of
nineteenth-century promotional effort as well as a tragic tale of the price of fame.

When Elisha volunteered for the Grinnell Expedition he asked his brother, Tom, to assure their family that "desire of change" and "craving after excitement" were not his incentives. He explained, "I am led by mixed motives; but upon their careful analysis as I am a man of honour, I believe the preponderating reasons to be creditable and worthy." He continued, however, "Of course I am aware of the process of self-deception where 'self' shakes the 'wavering balance' but I have tried my best to act according to a conscience." He noted that it was seldom in navy life that a mission of "self-sacrifice and privation connects itself with reward and self approval," but that "God knows both are involved in a volunteer expedition such as this."[36] In a similar vein, he wrote his brother, Patterson, to assure him that he would never thoughtlessly commit to such a dangerous expedition for mere fame: "Ambition is with me a very meagre abstraction." He did admit, however, that he was "not dead to the host of living influences connected with reputation.... I am not one of those who intend to let life drag idly, nor do I intend to cast to the winds the dearly earned experience of preceding years. The bullet and the lance, by some unknown Mercy, have spared me while friends were stricken by my side." That he had been "bowed down" by illness and injury but managed to survive gave him "the blessed boon of Hope" and led him to believe that it was his duty to volunteer for the dangerous arctic mission.[37]

Elisha felt he had to explain his actions to his family because they were not excited about his decision to go to the arctic. They wanted him to settle down to the life of a respectable physician, get married, and establish himself in Philadelphia society; but despite these wishes, once Elisha made his decision, his family supported him and did everything in their power to make the most of his actions. Elisha loved adventure; his family valued reputation and honor. Thus they yoked these ambitions to have them pull toward a common goal. If Elisha was going to be an explorer, then why not celebrate and "puff" his daring exploits to promote the family name? In the years that followed his return from the arctic, it is difficult to tell whether Elisha or his family most wanted him to become a celebrated hero. As seen in his earlier adventures, Elisha certainly encouraged his own promotion, but his family (and especially Tom) executed his wishes with an energy that shows they were fully supportive of this effort. When Elisha returned from the arctic he was pleased to find that the popular press was already singing his praises. This was exactly what he desired, but this publicity had little to do with his own actions and everything to do with his family's promotional efforts.

Just over a week after the Grinnell Expedition left port in 1850, the Kane family began promoting it. On June 1, a letter from a "gentleman of Philadelphia" appeared in Horace Greeley's New York *Daily Tribune*. This gentleman had "a friend" aboard the expedition and had learned from him of the great generosity of Henry

Grinnell and of the shoddy support of Congress. He suggested to Greeley that, "For the honor of New York you should find out and publish the amount of Mr. Grinnell's generous advances... [and] blow a trumpet for every cent he found himself out of pocket, and make Congress refund with interest."[38] Though it is impossible to know just who wrote this letter, evidence suggests that it came from the pen of Tom Kane. His father was a leading Democrat and the Kane family supported his party, but Tom's sympathies were more closely aligned with the political factions that would become the Republican Party. He was a devoted abolitionist and his support of free-labor and land reform, as well as his work with the Mormons, made him well respected among the social reformers of the Northeast. Greeley was interested in similar issues, and they had worked together on promotional efforts before—Greeley happily published Tom's pro-Mormon articles and Tom plugged Greeley's books in the Philadelphia press.[39] Tom was also a friend of Henry Grinnell and had worked with him to gather the materials Elisha needed for the expedition. This letter to the *Tribune* benefited all three of these men and framed the expedition in exactly the light the Kane family desired. Thanks to their efforts, the public was led to believe that the do-nothing Whig Congress and president paralyzed an honorable mission that was saved only by the efforts of noble citizens and sailors willing to risk their own lives and fortunes for the rescue of Sir John Franklin. That the Democrats in Congress delayed the mission in an effort to embarrass President Taylor was beside the point. Then, as now, political parties were more than willing to blame each other for their own misdeeds.[40]

The next week, an even more telling article appeared in the *Tribune* entitled, "Interesting Narrative. Surgeon of the Arctic Expedition." This article reminded people of the heroic expedition and called their attention specifically to Elisha: "We saw the announcement of his name among the officers with surprise. He has long been suffering from a combination of infirmities, the result of a series of adventures such as few men living have undergone, and such as even fewer would voluntarily embark in out of pure love of danger, and the spirit of seeing the wonders and the peculiarities of other parts of the globe." It recounted Elisha's adventures in South America, the Orient, India, the Nile Valley, the slave coast of Africa, and Mexico, noting with great detail his descent into the Taal Volcano, investigation of Vocal Memnon, and heroism in Mexico. It concluded:

> He had the rice fever in the Canton river, the plague in Egypt, the yellow fever at Rio, the congestive at Puebla, and the African fever on the coast. These, and wounds, and an organic disease of the heart, which he has had from boyhood, have been his preparations for the hazards he is encountering now.
>
> Altogether his history is eventful and thrilling for so young a man, and induces us cordially to hope that he may return from his last adventure with new honors and a restored constitution.[41]

Many newspapers reprinted this article and thus first introduced much of the nation to the heroic, young adventurer, "Dr. Kane." No articles about other crewmembers appeared in papers at that time—not even about its captain, Edwin J. DeHaven, who had led an equally exciting career, having traveled the globe aboard the Wilkes Expedition of 1838-1843.

A comparison of Kane and DeHaven reveals an important point. Being a hero takes more than heroic deeds. DeHaven had traveled more widely than Kane and was captain of the expedition as well as a skilled member of Maury's hydrographic team—far more impressive titles than Kane's position of assistant naval surgeon— and yet Kane, not DeHaven, became the celebrated member of the expedition. The reason for this is clear: Kane had the desire and the means to make his deeds known to the public; DeHaven did not. From the first days of the expedition, Kane was celebrated in the press and DeHaven went unmentioned. The result was that within a few years, Kane was a national celebrity (and this expedition commonly known as "Kane's First Arctic Expedition"), whereas DeHaven quietly disappeared. Both men performed heroic deeds. Both were heroic individuals. The only difference was the number of people who knew of their deeds. For DeHaven, it was his friends and family. For Kane, it was thousands thanks to his family's skillful use of the popular press.

Elisha's promotion had already begun long before he returned from the arctic. Throughout the trip he kept an extensive journal, complete with verbal sketches and scientific information, both written with an eye toward publication. DeHaven, who was no fan of pen and ink, observed this and readily made Kane the official historian of the expedition—exactly the job Elisha wanted. In addition to his journals, Elisha also wrote detailed letters to his family, hoping that opportunities would arise to send them back to Philadelphia well before the expedition returned. Such a chance presented itself first in upper Greenland when the *Advance* met the merchant ship *Emma Eugenia*. Elisha sent a detailed letter home, providing vivid accounts of their journey to date. He described his first sighting of an iceberg in a manner that readily conveyed the awe he felt. "In shape it was an oblong cube, about twice the size of Girard College—a great marble monolyth... a Parthenon floating on the ocean."[42] Just as Elisha wished, the Kane family did not keep this letter to themselves. Judge Kane read it before the American Philosophical Society and had it printed in its *Proceedings*.[43] The family (almost certainly Tom) also quickly got it into the popular press. The October 12, 1850, *Tribune* dedicated two columns to the long letter, proudly scooping their competitors with the first report from the American Expedition. Greeley headed the article: "Correspondence communicated for *The Tribune*."[44]

After Elisha's letter appeared in the *Tribune*, another account with sketchy details of the American Expedition appeared via information brought back in late-September aboard the *North Star*. This article of October 16 announced that John Ross had seen the U.S. Expedition and that it "had penetrated as far as any squadron, and at the departure of the last advices, the *Advance* had go[ne] aground, but no serious injury was apprehended."[45] Another article appeared two days later, this time with further news from the *Prince Albert*, which had reached England on October 1. This article cited William Parker Snow and told of the *Prince Albert's* last day of exploration, August 25, 1850, the day it and the *Advance* had arrived at Cape Riley and found the cairns and Franklin's camp. Though this letter mentioned that the *Rescue* was "beset with ice near Cape Bowen," it made no mention of the *Advance* or the fact that it was with the *Prince Albert* when they discovered the cairns.[46]

The next day another article appeared in the *Tribune*, this time credited to "private sources" (letters passed on from Henry Grinnell) and citing news from both Snow and "Dr. Kane, the head of the Scientific Department of the Expedition."[47] Kane's intelligence was dated "August 24, 5 P.M." and stated only that the crew was in good health and that the expedition was going well. Snow's report was a letter elaborating on the article of the day before, noting that he had met the *Advance* and found it "admirably adapted for the service," and her crew "all well" and a talented lot. He concluded by noting that off Cape Riley, the *Advance* "unfortunately drifted on shore, while her commander was examining the place," and that when the *Prince Albert* left, the crew of the *Advance* was "at work heaving her off, a job which was, no doubt, very soon accomplished."[48] This news alarmed many Americans, but another letter from Snow a few days later alleviated these fears. He reported, "I can confidently assert that there is no reason to doubt [the *Advance*] having been very speedily got off from her unpleasant position." He complimented the crew, saying, "Too much praise, I am sure, cannot be awarded to Lieut. DeHaven and his officers for their bold and seaman-like manner of handling their craft in the ice.... You have a fine set of officers, who will carry out the enterprise they are employed in and add to the glory of your national flag."[49]

These letters reveal subtle but significant issues of national pride in regard to exploration during this era. All of these articles were coming to the American reading public via letters by, or brought back by, members of English search expeditions. Though Snow complimented the U.S. Expedition and its crew, and continued to sing their praises in his book that came out the following year, his accounts were distinctly biased in England's favor. The events of August 25, 1850, at Cape Riley are important in understanding this. The *Prince Albert* and *Advance* were traveling together when they spotted the cairns left by Ommanney's *Assistance*, which had discovered Franklin's cairns. Members of both the *Advance* and *Prince Albert* went ashore and investigated Franklin's camp. After these events, Snow and the *Prince Albert* headed for home while the *Advance* sailed north, where, together with Penny, it discovered the three graves of Franklin's crew—an event unknown to Snow who had left two days before.

These events were the most important finds of the past three years. Both the United States and England were present when the discoveries were made and both wanted to claim them as their own, but Snow returned first and thus scooped the story. Though he later noted that DeHaven and his men were also at Cape Riley, his first report stated only that "Com. Forsyth of the *Prince Albert*... sent Mr. Snow to examine Cape Reilly [sic], where the remains of an encampment, consisting of five or six tents were found.... The *Assistance* had been there two days before and had left notice."[50] Snow did report the *Advance*'s presence at Cape Riley, but only by mentioning that she was grounded on the ice and trying to break free, not in the context of co-discovery.[51] Snow's coloring of these events were soon forgotten, however, because the *Tribune* found much better fare to print—several extraordinary letters from Elisha.

When the *Prince Albert* left Cape Riley in August 1850, Elisha used the opportunity to send letters home, including an important one for Tom. In this letter, dated August 23, 1850, Elisha instructed Tom to do exactly what Tom had already been doing, promoting "Dr. Kane." Elisha explained that within his packet of letters was one addressed to Horace Greeley, which stated that Tom would send him a full account of the expedition's travels "winnowed from the family Chaff-Bag." Elisha instructed Tom to edit his letters—"mend[ing] therein the inaccuracies of poor Elisha"—and to pass them along to Greeley as quickly as possible. He reminded him, "Time is, of course, everything to a journalist and I want you even before home deliver[y], to send him on a continuously concocted letter."[52]

Elisha also told Tom the specific events he wanted emphasized and how he wanted them to come across to the public. He wrote, "mention our unfortunate attempt to penetrate the 'middle ice' as far down as 73°50'. Do this regrettingly but without even the appearance of blame." He also instructed, "Say something too in enthusiastic eulogy of old Sir John Ross—this veteran, dear Tom, has left upon me sentiments of admiration tinged with sadness." Finally, he asked Tom to write "some Kane puffs" and to "send them with my respects" to Henry Grinnell.[53] This Tom did, and did well, writing Grinnell in Elisha's name saying, "the officers are in the daily enjoyment of the good things which your liberality has provided and all are ardently desirous to sustain the reputation of the Expedition which bears your name." Grinnell was so pleased with this flattering letter that he passed it along to Greeley, who printed it in the *Tribune*—exactly the effect Elisha and Tom desired.[54]

Despite this push for recognition, Elisha's letter to Tom ended contemplatively. He wrote this letter in the closing days of an arctic summer that would soon lead to a dismal and dangerous winter of perpetual darkness. Faced with this reality, Elisha became reflective and acknowledged that his quest for attention was questionable—"Alas my brother what humbugs we are"—but Elisha felt little regret for his actions because, for the first time in his life, he believed he was truly doing something that deserved such attention. "Out of the five expeditions which have wintered in this dreary sound and its appendages... Parry lost the *Fury*, Sir John Ross the *Victory* and wandered for four years in the ice, and Sir John Franklin has [been] missing five years. This is not very cheering, my brother Tom, but it will show you that at last I am in a situation of real and not mock heroics. I have a delightful sense of danger to keep me up, and you know that such stimulus is not uncongenial."[55]

Tom had followed Elisha's instructions to the letter, quickly presenting Greeley with a long article for the *Tribune*. After running DeHaven's official account of the expedition (taken from the report he sent back to the navy), Greeley printed Elisha's article, which provided far more detail.[56] For greater impact (and newspaper sales) he broke the article into two halves, running the first half under the bold heading "The American Arctic Expedition. Letter from E. K. Kane Communicated for *The Tribune*." This article covered the first months of the expedition and was accentuated by attention-getting subheads such as "A Storm Among the Bergs" and "Bears." The second half of the article ran the next week and discussed Inuit habits, the Crimson Cliffs, predictions of where and how the expedition would weather the winter, and concluded with a touching tribute to Sir John Ross.[57]

Elisha's prose was filled with well-constructed verbal pictures of the exotic arctic scenery, providing vivid images for American readers' imaginations:

This engraving is an example of the vivid arctic scenery described by Kane and was the frontispiece of his *U.S. Grinnell Expedition* (New York: Harper & Bros., 1854)

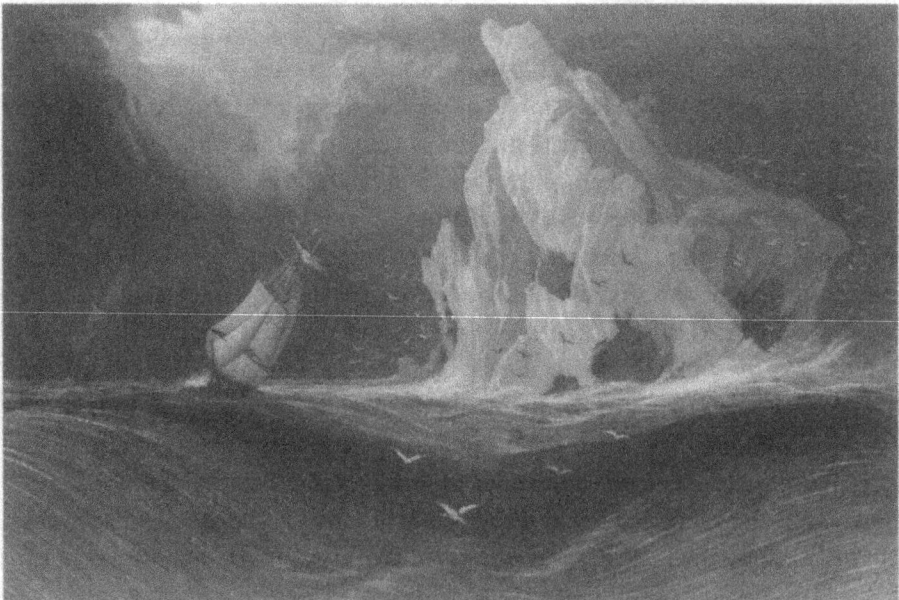

I have learned to believe in Turner, in my delight with the rich purple shadows of the slanting sun here; and the violet hues it gives to the reaches of white snow and the tranquil water leads that are like alcove looking glasses, unclouded by a breath of air....

> It is in these lingering hours that make the wedding of sunset to sunrise, the refractions are so regularly beautiful.... I have seen, in the course of a single night, regularly castellated feudal towers, glittering pinnacles with pennons streaming from them, mountains crimsoned with lava fires, oriental domes of golden tracery, and heaven knows what all of ideal architecture, mixed up with bizarre forms of hieroglyph and heraldry; things that have been and are, and things that imagination has never dreamt of; melting into each other like the phantasms of a dream.[58]

In this passage Elisha appeals to the antebellum public's knowledge of the popular paintings of the time done by the "romantic realists"—artists such as Thomas Cole and his fellow American painters of the "Hudson River School." Elisha explicitly noted British painter Joseph Turner when he addressed the deep hues of the arctic scenery, and his description of the changing images he saw reflected in the arctic twilight, moving from classical architectural forms to the destructive forces of nature, bear a remarkable similarity to Cole's popular five-part *Courses of Empire* series (1836) that depicted human civilization rising up out of nature, only to again be consumed by it.

Elisha's articles were a big success. For the first time, the American reading public was presented not only with the facts of arctic exploration, but with vivid and lively descriptions of what it was like to sail through an ice-strewn arctic sea. Through Elisha's pen, the arctic became a magical place full of the sublime danger and beauty that characterized the Romantic era's idea of nature as both a beautiful and terrifying force, a force that reflected nothing less than the mind of God. Judge Kane proudly wrote his son that his articles had "attracted much notice" and had "been reprinted everywhere, with infinite praise."[59] Tom added that his editing had done little; that the impact had come almost entirely from Elisha's prose. "[A]ll I did was to run your own pretty fancies... into an easier mould than I found them in, and modify somewhat the general form of the whole. Yet they took tremendously—were republished far and wide."[60]

The one thing these articles did not include was the plan already brewing in Elisha's head: He wanted to launch his own search for Sir John Franklin and the Open Polar Sea. Elisha, like many others, was sure the mythic open sea, or *Polynya*, lay beyond the ice pack around the eightieth parallel. While aboard the *Advance*, he came to believe that this hidden sea's mysterious waters also held the secret of the disappearance of Sir John Franklin. Writing home in August, Elisha obviously did not want this proposal put before the public because DeHaven's mission was

still actively seeking Franklin and it would have been presumptuous to discuss a
different search before the first returned; however, it was not too early to begin
putting the idea of such an expedition into the heads of potential supporters, just
in case Franklin's fate was not discovered. In the package of letters he sent home
with the *Prince Albert*, Elisha included a letter to Lady Jane Franklin, proposing that
her husband might be in the Open Polar Sea. Elisha's theory was that the summer of 1846 had been unusually warm, causing Wellington Channel to open. This
allowed Franklin to sail through it into the Open Polar Sea and then on to the
north pole itself. Though this channel gave Franklin's *Erebus* and *Terror* passage to
the Open Polar Sea, he was quite certain that it had probably frozen closed just a
few days later, trapping Franklin and his men in this beautiful but isolated ocean.
The likelihood that Wellington Channel would again open seemed slim, but a
more direct and likely route to the Open Polar Sea existed, Smith Sound, which
stretched north out of Baffin Bay. Elisha was confident that this unexplored sound
was the key that would unlock the mysteries of both Franklin's fate and the path
to the splashing, open shores of *Polynya*.[61]

Judge Kane passed Elisha's letter on to Lady Jane and then wrote his son, "I
have sent Lady Franklin your letters, & my abstract. I am sure it will give her pleasure to look over your argument: It has gone far to convince me, & I am not easy
of belief."[62] Judge Kane also presented Elisha's theory before the American Philosophical Society, where it received great praise. He wrote his son a few months
later, "The Philosophical Society has published in its bulletin your Upernavik calculations of the chances of finding Sir John, and Lady Jane Franklin has sent me
her thanks for it, and is now reprinting it in a pamphlet with other things."[63] The
American Philosophical Society was so pleased with Elisha's paper that five of its
members nominated him for membership into their prestigious organization of
science and learning; he was voted in on May 17, 1851, while still in the arctic.[64]

Though he was more than one thousand miles away and cut off from regular
communications, he was becoming a hero at home thanks to his family's efforts.
By January 1851, Tom and Judge Kane were already making plans for the book
Elisha would write about the expedition, certain that it would be a big success. Taking advantage of a whaling ship headed for arctic regions, they sent letters to Elisha explaining their ideas for the book. Tom wrote, "no matter what your
fortunes... your book is sure of being a success. The public mind is really in beautiful order for its reception,...you Franklins, have been steadily increasing in popularity, and will find every one of you are to come home heroes." He explained
that the book had the potential to "be the blasting bellows hell of a puff that will
send you through the world with a ten man power for ever after of doing the good
and great." He also said that, compared with other subjects (such as his own recently published account of his Mormon adventure), Elisha's arctic narrative would

be "greatly more popular" and would "make more sensation than any thing written by a Navy man in our day."[65]

Tom closed his letter with specific advice for the book. On writing style he stated, "you have no occasion for any reserves or breaks in your narrative—you can be perfectly unartificial, and write fresh from your notes of first impressions." Editing would take place at home, "you will have any amount of assistance from the big gun, our Father. He will bring up arrears, look to accuracy of statement and composition, and give the final polish which we could not hope to attain without immense labor." He then advised Elisha to make as many sketches of the arctic as possible, explaining that the book "must be an illustrated work—with vignettes and figured initials in artist style; and many of these,...this being the taste of the day." He concluded, "We have only two points to make; one is to make it the Official and Authorized Authentic Account of the Expedition; the other, to get it out in as short a time as possible after your arrival, so as to take the public interest before it flags and also to cut out the inferior authorship of your comrades."[66]

Aboard the *Advance*, Elisha had already become the official historian of the expedition and was planning the creation of his book, but neither he nor his family knew that his position as the narrator of the expedition was about to get a further boost from an unexpected source—William Parker Snow of the *Prince Albert*. When Snow arrived back in England in the fall of 1850, he immediately began writing up an account of his adventure. Although his book focused on the British discovery of the first signs of Franklin, it did mention the American expedition in a positive light, and especially its energetic surgeon, Dr. Kane. This portion of Snow's book was quickly reprinted by many American newspapers and magazines, thus propelling Dr. Kane into the limelight.[67]

The most impressive of these mentions was a ten-page article in *Harper's New Monthly Magazine*, complete with four large illustrations done by Harpers' engraver, Benson J. Lossing. This article dedicated nearly a full column to Snow's account of "Dr. Kane, the surgeon, naturalist, journalist, &c., of the expedition."

> Dr. Kane turned his attention to me, and a congeniality of sentiment and feeling soon brought us deep into pleasant conversation.... Our talk ran wild; and there, in that cold, inhospitable, dreary region of everlasting ice and snow, did we again, in fancy, gallop over miles and miles of lands far distant, and far more joyous. Ever-smiling Italy... sturdy Switzerland... France, Germany, and elsewhere were rapidly wandered over. India, Africa and Southern America were brought before us in swift succession. Then came Spain and Portugal... next appeared Egypt, Syria, and the Desert; with all of these was he personally familiar, in all had he been a traveler, and in all could I join him.... Rich in anecdote and full of pleasing talk, time flew rapidly as I conversed with him.[68]

The title illustration from
*Harper's New Monthly
Magazine* (April 1851) that
heavily "puffed" Kane and
began laying the groundwork
for the publication of Kane's
U.S. Grinnell Expedition.

This extensive coverage in one of the era's most popular monthly magazines gave Elisha national exposure. His family was ecstatic. A few weeks later another opportunity to send letters to the arctic arose and Tom and Judge Kane excitedly reported this news to Elisha. His father wrote, "Snow's book, plugging the *Advance* awfully, and yourself individually the most, has been in newspapers and reviews and magazines republished to the ends of the country." More than ever, "the publishers at New York expect a book from you," he reported, adding decidedly, "and a book they shall have."[69]

Tom reported that since Snow's mention, things had changed at the Kane household. "A flood of glory has rushed in at the doors and windows, that could not fail to carry everything before it.... You are expected home to be the biggest kind of Lion that has roared here since... the War of 1812." He then addressed "THE BOOK," saying, "This is the constant theme of my thoughts. It must be got out in all three months after your first settling down; yet it must trot the best foot foremost, yet it must be an omnibus of Science, Seacraft, Sentiment, and the Lord doesn't know what all, yet it must bind up the Record for all Posterity of our Family's Renown. Great Lord, what an anxiety it will be for a time!"[70]

Addressing the possibilities of publishers, Tom noted that he had recently been in New York and learned that "the best literary authorities," including a reader for Harper & Brothers Publishing, were excited about Elisha's writing. Of Harpers he said, "I regard it a capital thing that these gentlemen published Snow's Puff of Dr. Kane & colleagues, in their great magazine; not for the circulation of the same, but as a straw of showing... the probable demand for <u>the BOOK</u>. If you let them be your publishers, they must either get you out in handsome Immortality Style, or pay handsomely for Copy Right." He added excitedly, "The beauty of being put before the dear public in our Country is, that if it be in the right way, an official's fortune is made for life." He concluded, "God bless you, save you, keep you, sail you safe home—to spend what you have earned! For, for this once, you know I do believe you have earned your right to be honored and happy."[71]

The summer of 1851 progressed with no further word from any of the arctic expeditions, but as fall approached, whaling ships began returning from the far north with new information. As luck would have it, the first ship to bring news from any of the expeditions was the British vessel, *True Love*, which carried with it letters from the *Advance*. It was thus a letter from Elisha that provided the first news of the graves discovered the August before (they were discovered two days after the *Prince Albert* had sailed for home). British newspapers ran Kane's letter on September 13; ten days later the letter reached America and was reprinted widely—even in New York's newest paper, the week-old *New York Times*.[72] As with Snow the year before, in 1851 Kane was widely celebrated because his letter provided the newest news. Accounts from Captains Austin and Penny arrived just days later, confirming Kane's account, but the scoop belonged to Kane.[73] Because of this, Kane's name was already in the public's mind when, just a few days later, news reached New York that the Grinnell Expedition was only a few days journey from home. The *Advance* reached New York on September 30 and the slower *Rescue* a week later.[74]

The Kane family worked quickly. The day after the *Advance*'s arrival, Elisha's long and descriptive account of the expedition appeared in the *New York Times*. It is telling that this article, unlike his earlier letters, appeared in the *Times*, and not in the *Tribune* . As Tom had noted to Elisha in April, he felt that Harpers was their best bet for publishing a successful book and he was sure they were interested because their *Harper's New Monthly Magazine* had dedicated so much text to Snow's account of Dr. Kane. Harpers had launched this well-illustrated paper in June 1850, and, under the careful eye of their long-time reader and advisor, Henry J. Raymond, it quickly became one of the nation's most widely read periodicals, its circulation reaching 130,000 by 1853. Even before his editorship of *Harper's Monthly*, Raymond was already an experienced and busy editor. He had served as "first assistant" when Horace Greeley launched the *Tribune* in 1841, and later he helped to remake one of New York's other dailies, the *Courier and Enquirer*, all the while also serving as a reader and editor for Harper & Brothers. Unhappy with Greeley's tendency to crusade for every new "ism" that came along, and horrified by the sensationalism of James Gordon Bennett's *New York Herald*, in 1851 Raymond decided to begin his own paper to provide a balanced voice. With the financial backing of bankers George Jones and Edward Wesley, he vowed to give the public "All the news that's fit to print" and so launched the *New-York Daily Times* on September 18, 1851, thus firmly establishing himself as one of the most influential editors of the era.[75]

Given the flattering account of Elisha in *Harper's Monthly* and the knowledge that Harpers was the best publisher for Elisha's book, the Kane family felt it was advantageous to favor Raymond's *Times* with Elisha's exclusive story. Raymond gladly printed Kane's letter, noting proudly at the head of the article, "We are indebted to the kindness of Dr. Kane for an outline of the voyage, and for many incidents connected with it of great interest."[76] The Kanes' decision proved wise. Not long after they gave the story to the *Times*, Harpers agreed to publish Elisha's book—Raymond, no doubt, largely responsible for its acceptance. Ultimately, however, it was George W. Curtis, the well-known travel writer and "the editor" behind *Harper's Monthly*'s "Editor's Easy Chair" column, who negotiated the final contract between Elisha and Harpers.[77]

The *Times* did not rely solely on Elisha for its account of the expedition, however. The day after running his account of the journey it ran a long article about the "curiosities" the explorers brought home, saying, "we went on board the *Advance* yesterday, and through the courtesy of the officers, and Lieut. Lovell in particular, we are able to give a more minute account than has appeared." William I. Lovell was the second officer of the *Advance* and a "quietly companionable man."[78] He and Elisha became friends during the voyage and it does not seem Elisha perceived him as a threat to his position as spokesperson for the expedition. This perception proved correct for, by the next day, the papers again turned to Elisha for news of the expedition and Lovell faded from view.

On October 3, the *Times* dedicated almost a full page to three articles addressing the expedition. The first noted that the search for the Northwest Passage could no longer be justified on grounds of commerce, but speculated that it would continue to be "a motive to naval knight-errantry" because its existence had gained mythic importance: "The fleece of Colchis was never more eagerly sought—the location of El Dorado more profoundly speculated upon."[79] A second article noted further adventures of the *Advance*, and ended with an editorial calling for the government to honor Kane and his fellow officers: "Do not such men deserve from our Government some substantial as well as honorary notice?"[80] The final article addressed a meeting of the New York Yacht Club and noted a hearty toast to "Dr. Kane, of the Arctic Exploring Expedition." It reported that Elisha had responded to this toast "very modestly," and that though "the call upon him for a speech was very unexpected," he managed to offer a stirring toast to Grinnell and the other supporters of the expedition that was acknowledged with "hearty cheers."[81]

In the following weeks, both the *Times* and *Tribune* ran several other articles on the expedition. During this time, DeHaven, who was featured most prominently in the early articles, began to disappear, whereas "Dr. Kane" appeared with more and more frequency. Having no desire for the spotlight, DeHaven quietly turned in his official report and retired to his farm, ending his involvement with arctic exploration.[82] His exit from the scene left the stage wide open for Elisha, and he quickly stepped front and center. He energetically advocated his theory of Smith Sound as the key to finding both Franklin and the Open Polar Sea and began to push for a second American expedition to execute such a search. The success of his promotion of this idea is evidenced by the fact that, just eight days after his return from the arctic, the president of the Smithsonian Institute, Joseph Henry, sent a request asking him to deliver a series of lectures on his theory before both Congress and the public.[83] The navy, having received a lot of negative press for its lukewarm support of the expedition, sought to save face by granting Elisha a three-month paid leave from duty to lecture and write up his account.[84]

The day after the Smithsonian's request, the *Times* further publicized Elisha and his theory by reprinting his letter to Henry Grinnell that spelled out his beliefs about the Open Polar Sea, Franklin's whereabouts, and his suggestions for further exploration.[85] The Kanes were at work popularizing Elisha's theory as well. A day after the *Times* printed Elisha's letter, an article appeared in the *Daily Pennsylvanian* and noted that Captains DeHaven and Griffin of the *Advance* and *Rescue*, as well as "some of the officers of the British expedition" agreed with Elisha's hypothesis that Franklin was "hemmed in by the ice at a point to which these expeditions have not yet been able to penetrate."[86] Within another week Elisha was publicly associated with the Open Polar Sea to the extent that the son of eccentric scientist John Cleves Symmes—who in 1818 had proposed that the world was hollow and that there were "holes at the poles" that led to the concentric interior sphere of the world—wrote him, asking if he had further information to add to his father's theory.[87]

America had caught arctic fever. Papers across the country began running articles and poems about the tragic voyage of Sir John Franklin and the potential wonders of the Open Polar Sea. Boston's *Gleason's Pictorial*, a popular illustrated weekly paper, put portraits of Franklin and his crew on its cover in mid-October; *Harper's New Monthly Magazine* began laying the groundwork for its publication of Elisha's book by running a long, heavily illustrated article about his journey and theories about the Open Polar Sea; and New York's *International Magazine* ran "The Ballad of Sir John Franklin," by George H. Boker, a friend of Kane's.[88] This poem told of a whaler and a "little esquimaux" who warned Franklin of the dangers of the arctic at which "the stout Sir John" lightly laughed, saying that "Half England is wrong" if they were right. The poem then noted Franklin's hard trials and entrapment, and closed with Franklin saying, "Oh! whether we starve to death alone, / Or sail to our own country, / We have done what man has never done— / The open ocean danced in the sun— / We passed the Northern Sea!"[89] In this way, Boker's poem embodied both the heroism and tragedy that made up the romance of arctic exploration, while also expressing nationalist sentiment by subtly noting the ignorance and arrogance of the British Admiralty.

The amount of press dedicated to arctic exploration shows that it had captured the imagination of this era. Why it did so is more difficult to explain. Part of the explanation relates to the general spirit of that time—a feeling that scholars have rather loosely labeled "Romanticism."[90] The mid-1800s was an era when many Americans saw the world through the lens of sublime emotion and power. The Enlightenment thinkers of the generation before saw the world as an orderly and perfect place where everything fit neatly into the Great Chain of Being. This system of classification laid out all of creation along a well-defined continuum, beginning with rocks and earth, passing through progressive species of plants and animals, and ending with humans, angels, and God. Romantics also believed in this grand order and took great pains to carefully measure, test, classify and record nature in a precise manner; however, they also began to experience nature on an emotional level. Nature was orderly and precise, like the rings of a tree trunk or the spirals of a conch shell; but, it was also terrible and chaotic, like a thunderstorm crashing through the Rocky Mountains or a glacier crushing a rocky shore. Romantics' analogy for nature moved from the Enlightenment's coolly precise clock, wound and then ignored by a divine clockmaker, to a tumultuous and dynamic all-encompassing "whole"—something that necessitated both reason, as well as emotion, intuition, and feeling to understand. Alexander von Humboldt, the German explorer, philosopher, and scientist, was the quintessential Romantic man of science because he sought to see and understand all of nature and to capture it in its perfect completeness in his monumental, multivolume work, *Cosmos*. In these tomes, Humbolt showed how all of nature, including humankind, operated as a unified whole; they explained geological formations, the habits of hummingbirds, and even the nature of man, as Humboldt's section on history and scientific discovery showed the interrelationship of the sciences with the arts and humanities.[91]

It is evident in Ralph Waldo Emerson and his Transcendentalist movement that both the sciences and the humanities were coming to similar conclusions. Emerson, a "transcended" Unitarian minister, sought to understand the world through his philosophical wanderings. He ultimately arrived at the same conclusion that Humboldt formulated via his scientific explorations—that the universe, nature, humans and even God were all a part of the same unified whole. In the now famous passage from his 1836 essay, "Nature," Emerson contemplated his human existence within the context of the natural world and found that "all mean egotism vanishes. I become a transparent eye-ball; I am nothing; I see all; the currents of the Universal Being circulate through me; I am part or particle of God."[92] This essay became the foundational document of Transcendentalism, a movement that saw a direct correspondence or parallelism between spiritual truth and physical reality. As Emerson suggested in "Nature" and Henry David Thoreau (one of Emerson's protegés) tried to prove in his trip to Walden Pond, a person can come to understand the universe and even the mind of God (the "over soul" as Emerson put it) by studying the most everyday occurrences of nature: the sprouting of a bean plant, or the freezing and thawing of a pond. This philosophical movement, which included Emerson, Thoreau, Margaret Fuller, William Ellery Channing, Amos Bronson Alcott and many other thinkers and writers in the Boston area, had a profound impact on many of the writers of the American Literary Renaissance of the 1850s. Authors such as Walt Whitman, Emily Dickinson, and Nathaniel Hawthorne were all influenced by Transcendental thought, which had risen organically out of Romantic thought—the belief that nature yielded both scientific information and a window into the eternal. Skillful observation and a well-honed sense of the eternal were what was needed to understand nature, the universe, and God—to understand "the Whole."

To record and understand this "whole" was one of the major goals of this era of scientific examination; thus, the explorers of the Romantic age needed artistic talent as well as scientific precision to properly explain the new lands and new peoples they discovered. Their expeditions thus often included both scientists and artists to help document nature. The use of artists on exploring expeditions was not new to this era; it began in the 1760s with what William H. Goetzmann has called the "Second Great Age of Discovery"—the period when the primary goal of exploration shifted from conquest and colonization to scientific discovery and information.[93] The thing that did change with the Romantic explorers, however, was the way in which they expressed what they saw. Technical precision was the only goal of the artwork of earlier exploring expeditions; their art was designed to show exactly the order within nature. This was true even of Humboldt's works, which used stylized images to show the interrelationship of all of nature. The later Romantics also used stylized images to represent nature, but to a different end. They wanted to show the precision and interrelatedness of nature, but also its power and grandeur. Like the artwork of the earlier generation, their paintings were precise, representing each piece of flora and fauna exactly, but they were also emotionally dynamic, showing the blazing intensity of a sunset over the Amazon valley, or the cold, awesome power of an iceberg crushing a ship. A good illustration of this shift can be seen by comparing Alexander Humboldt's "Chimborazo" (1805) with Frederick Church's "Cotopaxi" (1862).[94] Whereas human figures did not often appear in the earlier era's images of nature, they did appear in Romantic era paintings, often as small, insignificant objects within a grand and towering scene. Humans were literally portrayed as "part or particle" of the whole—no more and no less. These dynamic representations of nature, painted by artists such as Thomas Cole, Frederick Church, Albert Bierstadt, and Thomas Moran, contributed largely to America's sense of Romanticism; as Goetzmann noted, their images of nature "became perhaps the primary influence of the formation of western civilization's Romantic yet scientific world view."[95]

This Romantic sensibility is also evident in the literary styles of exploration narratives. While the facts of earlier explorers' journeys—with the hardships, narrow escapes, and titillating discoveries—were exciting, their accounts of these events were often quite dull. These explorers were not writers and they made little effort to present their finding in a way that would appeal to the emotions, much less the public. Thus, their books (if a "popular" account appeared at all), were often little more than a slightly modified version of their official report. Although these were interesting, they were far from entertaining, and their appeal was limited to those who could get past the dull language of an official government document to see the exciting details contained within. An obvious example of this is the account of the U.S. Exploring Expedition (1838-1842). The expedition's leader, Charles Wilkes, who feared how his hostile crew would portray him, confiscated all diaries, logbooks, and journals from the expedition and insisted on writing the only account of the trip. He did so between 1843-1845, resulting in a tedious, five-volume account of the expedition. Upon reviewing it, Congress agreed to publish only one hundred copies of Wilkes' narrative, finding it too poorly written to justify a larger run. Although other publishers did reprint it in later years, it never sold well.[96] Later explorers, most obviously John C. Frémont, Henry Morton Stanley, and Elisha Kent Kane, broke from this mold by publishing reports of their expeditions written in a style that was both scientifically valuable and literarily thrilling.

Kane was very much a child of the Romantic era; the way he perceived and represented nature in his travel accounts tapped into its sentiment through scientific examination, literary grandeur, and powerful emotion. This is evident in Elisha's efforts to promote his second expedition to the arctic—an effort that began with his first Turner-inspired descriptions of the arctic and which continued throughout his lectures and speeches. In November 1851, at a dinner hosted by the British residents of New York in honor of the Grinnell Expedition, Elisha gave a speech that electrified the crowd and appeared in both the *Times* and *Tribune* the next day. He began by humbly admitting that the banquet was neither the time nor place to discuss the probability of Franklin's safety, but then apologetically launched into this discussion all the same, saying, "for the sake of the United States, for the sake of [Lady Jane Franklin],... for the sake of that humanity which makes us all kin, I

Engraving of Lady Jane Franklin
from [August Sonntag] *Professor
Sonntag's Thrilling Narrative of the
Grinnell Exploring Expedition to the
Arctic Ocean* (Philadelphia: James
T. Lloyd & Co., 1857).

LADY FRANKLIN.

trust that [the] search is not yet ended, and that the rescue of Sir John Franklin is yet reserved to his nation and the world."[97]

This speech, along with the announcement of his upcoming speaking engagement at the Smithsonian, attracted much attention on both sides of the Atlantic. Lady Jane Franklin was ecstatic about Elisha's promotion of her husband's rescue and recognized that his ability to capture the public's attention was invaluable. Elisha was pleased by her admiration and assured her that he would continue his efforts. He wrote to her, saying, "our press is favourable to continued search and it will not be difficult to keep the subject sufficiently prominent to sustain the emulative action of your own government." He also promised to pass up no opportunity "of bringing before the public my own convictions of the safety of the missing party as well as the incumbent duty which rests upon us to continue our efforts to relieve them."[98] Lady Jane gratefully responded, acknowledging the power of his public appeal and asking him to put his narrative into book form so his enthusiasm could be used to drum up support of further expeditions in England as well as America. "We are longing for the appearance of your book—it will I am sure be one of the most graphic, most touching and most eloquent of Arctic adventure if I may judge by the few specimens I have seen of your able pen."[99]

During this time the Kane family was busy with Elisha's upcoming appearance at the Smithsonian as well as with with the backlash that erupted after Judge Kane's ruling in the *Christiana* case (a murder/treason trial involving an escaped slave that provided one of the first direct challenges to the Fugitive Slave Act of 1850). Debates over Judge Kane's decision to try the accused for treason instead of murder raged in papers across the nation as well as within the Kane household. Tom and his father did not see eye to eye on the issue of slavery, and this caused Tom to resign his position as his father's clerk, but despite this rift, they were united behind Elisha.[100] Tom wrote to him praising his upcoming lecture and promising full family support. "All well, God bless you, and hurrah for our side."[101]

After celebrating Christmas with his family, Elisha left for Washington and there delivered a three-part lecture on the evenings of December 29 and 31, 1851, and January 3, 1852. Though the capital was in the midst of a crippling snowstorm, his lectures attracted capacity crowds. Because of the large audience and Kane's small stature, Smithsonian director Joseph Henry had the stage raised and asked Elisha to stand on an elevated podium.[102] On the first night, Elisha gave a general narrative of the Grinnell Expedition and concluded with his conviction that Franklin had pushed through Wellington Channel in the summer of 1846 and was trapped in the Open Polar Sea. His second lecture expanded on this theory and he illustrated it with several "well prepared diagrams" of the ice floes that had been reported by the expeditions of the previous years.[103] He also explained how Franklin's men could have survived in this area by noting that the "*Iglóo*, or snowhouse, of the Esquimaux is an excellent and wholesome shelter" and that the resources "for the support of human life are certainly surprisingly greater than the public are generally aware: Narwhal, white whales and seal—the latter in extreme abundance—crowd the waters."[104]

Before giving his final lecture, Elisha wrote to his brother, Patterson, to explain his future strategy. "My lecture was crowded and I think a <u>success</u>, but tonight I intend to do the thing much more <u>pretentiously</u>. I have prepared extemporaneous matter for demonstrative delivery." His goal was to push hard for the true object of his lectures, the promotion of a second expedition. He emphatically told Pat, "I'll succeed!"[105] Elisha knew that a second expedition hinged on the approval of Congress, so he began his final lecture by rhetorically asking all the questions he knew weighed most heavily on the congressmen's minds. "Why this search for an impracticable passage? Why all this risk of human life? And still more, perhaps, says some grave congressional debatory, why all this appropriation of National treasure, for an objectless, or, in the approved utilitarian phrase, 'a worthless chimera'!" Answering his own questions, Elisha explained that exploration often led to monumental events; exploration, he reminded them, "contributed to the geography of our globe the continent on which we live." He then cut to the real heart of the matter—money. Addressing those people "who look only to that more obvious utility, that is allied to some pecuniary scheme of individual or national profit," he noted that the explorations of Sir Humphrey Gilbert led to the discovery of the cod fisheries of Newfoundland, that Henry Hudson's led to the creation of the most lucrative fur trading company in history, and that Sir John Ross's had resulted in the establishment of Baffin Bay as one of the most profitable whaling grounds in the world.[106]

Though it did not cause Congress to begin organizing a second expedition immediately, Elisha's lectures did spark interest. Because of public interest, and a little prodding by Elisha, newspapers excerpted his speeches far and wide. Surviving notes show that Elisha wrote press releases of his own lectures for the newspapers, and that he clipped accounts from Washington papers and sent them on to New York's for republication.[107] This self-promotion worked and soon lecture requests flooded in from across the country and from many sectors of American society: the Mercantile Library Association of Montreal; the Philadelphia Methodist Musical Fund; the Amorers Literary Union of Springfield; the Providence Association of Mechanics & Manufacturers; the Camden Young Ladies' Institute; and the New London YMCA all wrote, pleading for an engagement.[108] The chair of the Cincinnati lecture board noted that his western city had "a very large literary taste, and fondness for attendance upon lectures of an educated and brilliant character," and offered Kane the enormous sum of $525 for a repetition of his Smithsonian lecture series.[109]

Elisha accepted many of these invitations and spent the next five months traveling from Maryland to Maine, delivering lectures that thrilled audiences with tales of arctic adventure, while pulling at their hearts and purse strings for the support he needed for a second expedition. He knew that Congress would never fully finance an expedition to Smith Sound, but he was confident that the money he raised via his lectures, along with the pressure of public opinion that they would generate, would be enough to force government sponsorship at some level. He worked diligently to keep his cause constantly in the public eye. The popularity of his lectures largely took care of this without his assistance, but when needed, he would run advertisements drumming up his cause. He wrote to one newspaper editor, saying, "Do me the kindness to insert the subjoined advertisement three times and forward to me your account. The object of my Lecture is to complete the scientific organization of our Expedition.... I know that such a motive will command the sympathies, as it has already, of that of the press... [and so] may I ask for my advertisement a conspicuous position."[110]

Though he was competing with big-name personalities on the lecture circuit that year (e.g. Ralph Waldo Emerson and Horace Mann), he did very well. He commanded large audiences and received universal praise. After a lecture in Baltimore, Elisha's uncle, George Leiper, wrote his daughter that Elisha had "made a decided hit here," and that his lectures attracted "a great variety of characters" from all sections of society. "There were those learned in the law and... skilled in physic...

and their deputies down to the shop boy who answered the prescriptions. Then there were the representatives of the church, from the high churchman to the retiring Quaker.... Then there were all denominations: the slouch hatted beau, the gay bonneted belle, the plain coat and the gay coat, the silk dress and the drab dress, the young, the middle aged, and those whose heads had been blossoming for many years and felt the frosts of many winters." He concluded enthusiastically, "You might ask who was *not* there."[111] F. M. Edselas was a child in 1851, but years later she remembered that Elisha's lectures at the Boston Lyceum were "the vital topic of the hour," discussed by men in "stores, offices and shops," and by women "at table and by the fireside, at the sewing cliques and quilting-bees." From her childhood perspective, Elisha's lecture was incredibly dynamic.

> It was to me no lecture, but a veritable reality, as I found myself in that land of the midnight sun, scurrying on snow-shoes, or in sledges drawn by the hardy Eskimo dogs, over trackless wastes, noting step by step the wonders found even there. Then as the brave explorer took us into winter quarters, where we were literally shut in by walls of ice, which perchance might become a living tomb, so real did it all seem, verily I felt my blood congeal with dread of the fate that appeared inevitable.[112]

Elisha's fame grew rapidly. William Wood (Tom's eventual father-in-law) noted that when he went to see Elisha speak in New York, the crowds largely ignored DeHaven and other members of the expedition present, but erupted into exclamations of "That's him!" when Elisha appeared.[113] Elisha was quite successful on capitalizing on this popularity and used it to help him gain funds for his proposed expedition. Though he complained that he made little money in Boston—he wrote his father, "These yankees have chizzled me"—he easily gained the support of Grinnell, who offered to back the expedition with both money and the use of the *Advance*.[114] His letters to Grinnell show that they both viewed the expedition as far more than just a voyage of discovery and rescue; it was a part of America's manifest destiny. America had expanded its borders from the Atlantic to the Pacific during the Mexican-American War of the mid-1840s, and during the early 1850s filibusters, most notably William Walker (notoriously known as "The Grey-Eyed Man of Destiny"), were trying to expand America's "destiny" into Mexico, Nicaragua, Cuba, and beyond. Elisha was certain that America's destiny lay north as well as south and west; he wrote Grinnell, "I think independent of any further search for Franklin, our Government should send an Expedition up in the northern regions—they will belong to us in less than 25 years, and we should know more about them."[115]

All these efforts had a profound impact on public sentiment, an impact that did not escape the notice of Lady Jane Franklin. Her niece and assistant, Julia

Cracroft, wrote Elisha, "[Lady Jane] is delighted to hear of the enthusiasm your lectures have everywhere created and... we must trust for the accomplishment of our hopes expecting the sending forth [of] another expedition from America."[116] They were distressed to hear, however, that his lectures were delaying the publication of his narrative, which they were anxious to market in England to promote further relief efforts. Elisha did intend to get his book out quickly, but his busy lecture schedule kept him from the project. In addition, Tom and Judge Kane—who planned to edit his rough journal into a polished narrative—were also busy with problems of their own. In July 1851, President Millard Fillmore had called on Tom for advice on making Brigham Young territorial governor of Utah, a position he did not want to grant Young if the rumors of Mormon polygamy were true. Although he knew Young well, Tom seems not to have known of the Mormon leader's multiple wives and thus swore to Fillmore that Young was not polygamous and advised him to make Young the governor because only he could successfully govern the almost entirely Mormon territory. In the summer of 1852, this act came back to haunt Tom when Orson Pratt, speaking for Young and the Mormons, publicly announced their practice of polygamy. Disgraced and comparing the betrayal he felt from Young to "the discovery of [your] wife's infidelity," Tom spent several months cloistered at home.[117]

At this same time the Kane family was also facing an emotional tragedy. Their youngest member, Willie, was dying. The fourteen year old contracted a fever in early summer that grew worse in the following months. Elisha, who was also fatigued and ill, withdrew from his lecturing engagements. He tried to cure himself, but when this failed, he checked himself into Dr. Robert Wesselhoeft's water cure clinic in Brattleboro, Vermont.[118] He returned home when Willie's illness grew worse, and made himself his brother's personal physician. He stayed by his bedside for weeks, but to no avail: Willie passed away on August 25, 1852. This event so profoundly affected the family that a few months later they moved away from Rennselaer—the mansion they had built on the outskirts of Philadelphia in 1848—and back into the city to escape the tragic memories that now infected the house.[119]

It was during this difficult summer that Elisha changed his focus, ending his lecture series and turning his attention to his book. Tom and Elisha agreed early on that the book would need to be profusely illustrated to sell well. Harpers had an excellent engraver, but Elisha felt his work would be better reproduced by an established London firm that was capable of producing the three- and four-color images he desired. His negotiations with these London firms fell through, however, because of cost.[120] By the summer of 1852, Elisha decided to produce his illustrations by hiring seascape artist James Hamilton to paint watercolors from his sketches and then to turn these paintings into mezzotints.[121] Hamilton had finished several of these paintings by mid-June, thanks to Kane's guidance and Grinnell's funding. Grinnell's son, Cornelius, who had become one of Elisha's closest friends, reported that Hamilton was doing excellent work and that his father was very pleased with the results; he had purchased several of the paintings and was proudly displaying them in a storefront on Broadway.[122]

Elisha was under pressure to finish his narrative because by June other members of the search expeditions of 1850-51 were beginning to publish their own accounts. The most serious threat came from Sherard Osborn, the British lieutenant who commanded the *Resolute*, one of the screw steamers in the flotilla commanded by Horatio Austin. Osborn's book, *Stray Leaves from an Arctic Journal, or, Eighteen Months in the Polar Regions*, was published in London in the spring of 1852 and reprinted in America a bit later. Lady Jane sent Elisha a copy in June 1852, hoping, no doubt, that it would inspire him to get his own account out as quickly as possible.[123] Osborn's book was especially threatening because he came to the same conclusion that Elisha was promoting, that there was an Open Polar Sea and that Franklin was in it.

Even closer to home, a member of the American expedition was also preparing to publish his account. Samuel P. Griffin, the commander of the *Rescue*, who had served as head of the expedition for several weeks when DeHaven was incapacitated by scurvy, was rumored to be negotiating with the *Literary Messenger* for the publication of several articles. Tom told Elisha of this, but reassured him that Griffin's writing was not a threat as it was "rather puerile." In fact, Tom felt Griffin's publication could work in Elisha's favor because it would "serve to keep up interest in the subject" until his book came out.[124] All the same, they needed to move quickly before more accounts appeared and satiated the public's interest.

Elisha made several efforts to get portions of his scientific findings published independently of the book. He sent descriptions of the polar bear and arctic fox to Victor Gifford Audubon, son of John James Audubon, who was then working on an illustrated work of quadrupeds to accompany his father's earlier ornithological works. Audubon thanked him for his submissions and noted that they would use his information on the arctic fox, but would have to place his new information on the polar bear in the appendix because they had already printed that entry.[125] Elisha also wrote up his findings on human exposure to extreme cold and submitted them to the Navy Bureau of Medicine for publication. Elisha was concerned that the navy would print this information before it was proved conclusively, but he stuck with the project because the navy deemed it "an important contribution to knowledge" and was thus willing to pay him while he wrote.[126] In the late summer, Elisha wrote an essay discussing the dispute with England over "Grinnell Land," the land mass the *Advance* discovered at the northern end of Wellington Channel. Though America claimed naming rights to this discovery, in late 1851 a British mapmaker, going off the reports of the Admiralty, labeled the spot "Albert Land." The mapmaker claimed (falsely) that Capt. Ommanney had discovered the area on August 26, 1850, thirty-four days before DeHaven claimed to have seen it.[127] This geographical discovery was the only one the Grinnell Expedition could claim and Elisha defended their naming rights adamantly. He discussed the issue with American historian and cartographer Peter Force, and with his help wrote up a long essay proving the discovery belonged to DeHaven.[128]

While Elisha was busy with these projects, Tom and his father were diligently reading through his journal and editing it into a coherent narrative for the book. This was not an easy task because Elisha's busy schedule kept him largely unavailable for comment and clarification. In March Tom complained of his "harum-scarum brother" to his soon-to-be father-in-law, William Wood, whom Elisha had stood up for a friendly meeting. In a letter of apology, Tom noted that "the nomadic relative, after leaving New York, ran through Philadelphia in the night, was next heard of in Richmond, Virginia; and... doing and leaving undone other things too numerous to mention, places me most particularly in the lurch."[129] It soon became easier to keep up with Elisha, however, because his health gave out. Tom wrote Wood in May that "The Book was advancing bravely" as it "was having the Soup sweated out of it, and flowing off, condensed, nutritious, and palatable." Adopting the terminology of the new steam-powered era in which they lived, Tom praised the family's rapid progress on the book, but noted that Elisha's "steam was too high. The 16 hours a day was too much for such battered machinery." He woke one night to a sharp cry and found Elisha with "blood running from both nostrils; nearly insensible, but bravely jagging his arm in the dark with a penknife, for purposes of venesection."[130] Too weak to even sit at a desk, Elisha again checked himself into Vermont's Brattleboro water cure clinic. While there, Tom kept him updated on the book. "[T]he introduction is in progress, and will not fail you. Perhaps we can do a good deal without you, for as I look into the volumes... I am surprised to see how little I would be content to change, and how large a portion can best keep the journal form. It is intensely interesting."[131] Their work went quickly, and by October they could see the end of the project. Tom wrote again, "We have read through half your book at least, and my mind is made up about it. The other half, if half as good, will make the whole a complete sell for the dear public." He then advised Elisha on the style of the remainder of the work. "Father is satisfied with me that it will be best very much cut down. You have picked many of the plums out of it for the rest of your cake, and the interest will be apt to pall after you have escaped the Pack and seem to be Homeward Bound. What do you say then to lightening ship by throwing overboard all that is not literally light reading?"[132] Judge Kane agreed and wrote, "Reading over the book carefully so far, I think it is 2/3 finished, & very good. The writing of the rest may occupy six busy weeks, counting in the revisal."[133]

While the Kanes were busy getting the text together, Cornelius Grinnell was handling all the publication negotiations with Harper Brothers. The big sticking point was the cost of illustrations. Both the Kanes and Grinnells wanted the work to be profusely illustrated, but the Harpers felt this would make the book "too costly, and put it beyond the reach of the masses." Elisha also wanted full control over the illustrations and to hire out much of the work, while the Harpers wanted to do all the work in-house. In August, Cornelius wrote Elisha, "I had an interview with the Harpers this morning with reference to the illustrations for your book.... The few specimens I have seen of the work of Harpers' Artist has not given me a very high idea of his abilities."[134]

Cornelius met with the Harpers again the next week and made arrangements with their engraver, Benson J. Lossing, to execute two engravings as specimens, which Elisha would have to pay for if he rejected them. Regarding the mezzotints, the only way Harpers was willing to include them was if Henry Grinnell was willing to bear their expense. Cornelius summed up his meetings with Harpers: "They are cold, calculating fellows, and I am always glad when I get out of their office. They pretended to admire your sketches very much, but they have no taste, or feeling for anything, except the accumulation of dollars."[135]

The dispute over the illustrations for the book went on well into the fall. It was finally agreed that Lossing would do all the small woodcuts, but not the larger images or mezzotints. Elisha was pleased with the paintings Hamilton made from his sketches and thus sought his advice on their printing. Hamilton contacted John Sartain, the Philadelphia engraver widely hailed as America's leading artist of that medium. Kane had already contracted Sartain to do a few small vignettes and Sartain agreed to expand this project to ten large images (eight by twelve inches) and ten smaller vignettes for the reduced rate of $1,300. He told Hamilton, "My charge ordinarily for a similar amount of labor would be nineteen hundred or two thousand dollars, it is therefore clear that the inducement is the opportunity it affords of producing a work that will repay in reputation, and in the pleasure derived from the style and character of the drawings." He warned, however, that he would not accept the project unless he could oversee the printing of the images. "If the plates are not very well printed the work will reflect no credit on any one, no matter how well engraved."[136] Hamilton passed this letter along to Elisha, along with a note saying that he and Sartain wanted "exclusive control over not only the printing but also over everything connected with the execution of the undertaking."[137] Elisha readily agreed. The amount of time, energy, and money Elisha put into the engravings show how important he felt they were to his narrative. They provided not only scientific precision via the detailed botanical and archeological sketches, but also Romantic emotion through the vivid and often ominous arctic scenes of gigantic icebergs that dwarfed the minuscule ships of the expedition.

By November 1852, though depressed by ill health and the loss of his brother, Elisha was well on his way to becoming a national celebrity. His lecture tour had been a grand success and his efforts to gain monetary support for a second expedition to the arctic were paying off—many were already calling for him to be the expedition's commander, a fact that he and Grinnell had decided upon but had not yet announced. His book, *The U.S. Grinnell Expedition in Search of Sir John Franklin*, was nearing completion, and thanks to the artistic skill of Hamilton and Sartain, the editing of his family, and the financial backing of Grinnell, it would be produced in stunning style. It would have an exciting narrative, hundreds of engravings, and ten dramatic two-color mezzotints—a certain success in this era of Romanticism.

So it was that in the fall of 1852 this young explorer, with his eyes fixed firmly on the arctic, suddenly found himself pulled into a much different adventure— one of the heart. One morning Elisha, like hundreds before him, decided to attend a showing of one of the curiosities of the time that had captured the attention of the public in a way that not even P. T. Barnum's Fiji Mermaid or Tom Thumb had been able to do. Walking the few blocks from his home at 36 Girard Street to Webb's Union Hotel on Arch Street, he climbed the stairs to the Bridal Suite and paid one dollar to witness the amazing "spirit-rappings" of the beautiful young spiritual medium, Margaret (Maggie) Fox.[138] Whether it was love at first sight, as Fox claimed in later years, is impossible to know. It is certain, however, that on that morning Elisha Kent Kane's life changed forever when he met the woman who was to become his lover, fiancé, and the one person so intertwined with his life that, upon his death, his family had to invest years of work and thousands of dollars to attempt to erase her from his public memory.

1. Roger Launius, interviewed by Liane Hansen, *Weekend Edition*, National Public Radio, (July 20, 2003).

2. There are several excellent histories of Arctic exploration; I have relied heavily on two. Pierre Berton, *The Arctic Grail: The Quest for the North West Passage and the North Pole, 1818-1909* (New York: Viking, 1988); and Richard Vaughan, *The Arctic: A History* (Dover, NH: Alan Sutton Publishing Ltd., 1994). All general information on Arctic exploration in this chapter comes from these two sources. The best source for maps of Arctic exploration is William H. Goetzmann & Glyndwr Williams, *The Atlas of North American Exploration* (New York: Prentice Hall General Reference, 1992), 38-31, 190-93, 198-201.

3. Vaughan, 55.

4. Vaughan, 74-76; Berton, 18.

5. Vaughan, 120-22.

6. Berton, 18-19.

7. Berton, 18-21. The Arctic was not Barrow's only obsession; he also strongly supported patrolling the China Sea for pirates and the West African coast for slave traders as well as the exploration of the Congo and Niger rivers. See Fergus Fleming, *Barrow's Boys* (London: Granta, 1998), 1-12.

8. Vaughan, 71.

9. Vaughan, 144.

10. John Kirtland Wright, "The Open Polar Sea," in *Human Nature in Geography: Fourteen Papers, 1925-1965* (Cambridge: Harvard University Press, 1966); Vaughan, 142-45.

11. John Barrow, *A Chronological History of Voyages into the Arctic Regions* (London: John Murray, 1818), 365.

12. Berton, 19-20.

13. Vaughn, 163.

14. Quoted in Berton, 67.

15. Quoted in Vaughan, 155.

16. Quoted in Nancy Fogelson, *Arctic Exploration & International Relations 1900-1932* (Fairbanks: University of Alaska Press, 1992), 11.

17. Matthew Fontaine Maury, "The Open Polar Sea," in *The Physical Geography of the Sea* (New York: Harper & Brothers, 1855). Most whales can survive the warm waters of the equator, but Maury was right in his observation—many whales do cross from the Atlantic to the Pacific via the Arctic Ocean, surfacing at holes that naturally occur in its icy surface.

18. George W. Corner, *Dr. Kane of the Arctic Seas* (Philadelphia: Temple University Press, 1972), 79-80.

19. This supports William H. Goetzmann's assertion that exploration in this "second great age of discovery," even when officially dedicated to a different purpose, was primarily concerned with scientific and geographic discovery. See Goetzmann, chapters 5 & 6 in *Exploration & Empire* (New York: W.W. Norton, 1966); and Goetzmann, "Introduction," in *New Lands, New Men* (New York: Viking Penguin Inc., 1986).

20. Corner, 83.

21. Unfortunately, no biography of Grinnell exists. The best source for information on his work with American Arctic exploration are Liz Cruwy's articles: "Henry Grinnell and the American Franklin Searches," *Polar Record* 26 (1990), 211-16; and "Profile: Henry Grinnell," *Polar Record* 27 (1991), 115-19.

22. Corner, 83-84.

23. Corner, 89-90; Berton, 178-79.

24. W. Parker Snow, *Voyage of the Prince Albert* (London: Longman, Brown, Green, & Longmans, 1851), 297.

25. Berton, 179.

26. Berton, 179; Corner, 90-92.

27. Corner, 92.

28. *New York Tribune* (Oct. 18, 1850), 8; and (Oct. 19, 1850), 5.

29. Berton, 180; Corner, 92; Vaughan, 156, 170.

30. *Searching for the Franklin Expedition: The Arctic Journal of Robert Randolph Carter*, ed. Harold B. Gill Jr., & Joanne Young (Annapolis, Maryland: Naval Institute Press, 1998), 60-62.

31. Corner, 92-93.

32. Information on the adventures of the Grinnell Expedition come from Elisha Kent Kane, *The U.S. Grinnell Expedition in Search of Sir John Franklin* (New York: Harper & Brothers, 1854).

33. Corner, 99-100.

34. Kane, *U.S. Grinnell Expedition*, 426.

35. Corner, 100-01.

36. Elisha Kent Kane to Thomas Leiper Kane (March 8, 1850), APS Elisha Kent Kane papers.

37. Elisha Kent Kane to Robert Patterson Kane (undated, c. March, 1850), APS Elisha Kent Kane papers. Elisha also assured his father that ambition and adventure were not his reasons for going to the Arctic. See Elisha Kent Kane to John K. Kane (May 18, 1850), APS Elisha Kent Kane papers.

38. *New York Tribune* (June 1, 1850), 4.

39. For the strong connection between Thomas and Greeley see Horace Greeley to Thomas Leiper Kane (June 19 & Aug. 7, 1849; June 30 & Dec. 1, 1850), BYU Thomas Leiper Kane papers. Also note Thomas Leiper Kane's pro-Mormon article and Greeley's supporting editorial in the *Tribune* (Oct. 16, 1846), 1-2.

40. For the political debate over the expedition see Corner, 76-78.

41. *New York Tribune* (June 8, 1850), 7; *Spirit of the Times* (July 13, 1850), 245. This issue of the *Tribune* also included its first long article about another young "explorer," spirit-rapper Margaret Fox, who would come to play an important role in Kane's life.

42. *New York Tribune* (Oct. 12, 1850), 3.

43. American Philosophical Society, *Proceedings* 5 (1848-55), 159-62.

44. *New York Tribune* (Oct. 12, 1850), 3.

45. *New York Tribune* (Oct. 16, 1850), 1.

46. *New York Tribune* (Oct. 18, 1850), 8.

47. *New York Tribune* (Oct. 19, 1850), 5. The article also misprints Kane's name as "R.P. Kane, M.D."—a telling sign that Greeley knew the Kane family through Tom, but not too well. Here he replaced Elisha's initials with those of his younger brother, Robert Patterson.

48. *New York Tribune* (Oct. 19, 1850), 5.

49. *New York Tribune* (Oct. 29, 1850), 5.

50. *New York Tribune* (Oct. 18, 1850), 5.

51. *New York Tribune* (Oct. 19, 1850), 5; and (Oct. 29, 1850), 5.

52. Elisha tried to send letters home earlier, once via Inuit on their way to a whaling port (these apparently miscarried), and again aboard the *North Star,* who refused to take them. See *New York Tribune* (Oct. 25, 1850), 2; and, Elisha Kent Kane to Thomas Leiper Kane (Aug. 23, 1850), in folder "Kane, EK to mother (Mrs. J.K. Kane)," APS Elisha Kent Kane papers.

53. Elisha Kent Kane to Thomas Leiper Kane (Aug. 23, 1850), in folder "Kane, EK to mother (Mrs. J.K. Kane)," APS Elisha Kent Kane papers.

54. *New York Tribune* (Oct. 19, 1850), 5.

55. Elisha Kent Kane to Thomas Leiper Kane (Aug. 23, 1850), in folder "Kane, EK to mother (Mrs. J.K. Kane)," APS Elisha Kent Kane papers.

56. *New York Tribune* (Oct. 23, 1850), 3.

57. *New York Tribune* (Oct. 25, 1850), 2; and, (Oct. 30, 1850), 2.

58. *New York Tribune* (Oct. 20, 1850), 2. Turner is English painter Joseph Turner who was famous for his Romantic landscapes.

59. John K. Kane to Elisha Kent Kane (Jan. 27, 1851) and (April 21, 1851), APS Elisha Kent Kane papers.

60. Thomas Leiper Kane to Elisha Kent Kane (Jan. 26, 1851), APS Elisha Kent Kane papers.

61. Though the letter from Elisha Kent Kane to his family outlining this plan is not among the family papers, its content can be inferred by his father's responding letters. See John K. Kane to Elisha Kent Kane (Jan. 26, 1851) and (April 21, 1851), APS Elisha Kent Kane papers.

62. John K. Kane to Elisha Kent Kane (Jan. 26, 1851), APS Elisha Kent Kane papers.

63. John K. Kane to Elisha Kent Kane (April 21, 1851), APS Elisha Kent Kane papers; American Philosophical Society, *Proceedings* 5 (1848-55), 159-62.

64. Corner, 104.

65. Thomas Leiper Kane to Elisha Kent Kane (Jan. 26, 1851), APS Elisha Kent Kane papers.

66. Thomas Leiper Kane to Elisha Kent Kane (Jan. 26, 1851), APS Elisha Kent Kane papers. Similar comments are also found in John K. Kane to Elisha Kent Kane (Jan. 26, 1851), APS Elisha Kent Kane papers.

67. See especially, *The Literary World* (March 15, 1851), 219, which appears to be the first American magazine article to mention Snow's book.

68. "Voyage in Search of Sir John Franklin," *Harper's New Monthly Magazine* 2 (April, 1851), 596-97. Snow was quite an adventurer himself. At an early age he went to Australia and engaged in mysterious (probably illegal) trade in the East Indies. He joined the English Navy and deserted, was arrested and punished, and then carried out his tour in West Africa. He worked as a newspaperman and unsuccessfully managed a hotel with his wife. He went to the Arctic in 1850 and later to Tierra del Fuego and Patagonia with the South American Missionary Society, which eventually fired him. He then moved to New York and met Charles Francis Hall, who was

working on another expedition to the Arctic. See Chauncey Loomis, *Weird and Tragic Shores* (New York: Alfred A. Knopf, 1971), 150-57.

69. John K. Kane to Elisha Kent Kane (April 21, 1851), APS Elisha Kent Kane papers.

70. Thomas Leiper Kane to Elisha Kent Kane (April 21, 1851), APS Elisha Kent Kane papers.

71. Thomas Leiper Kane to Elisha Kent Kane (April 21, 1851), APS Elisha Kent Kane papers.

72. See *New York Times* (Sept. 24, 1851), 1; as well as *The* (London) *Examiner* (Sept. 13, 1851), 583; *New York Tribune* (Sept. 24, 1851), 6; and *Daily Pennsylvanian* (Sept. 25, 1851), 1.

73. For the accounts of Austin and Penny see *New York Tribune* (Sept. 25, 1851), 6.

74. *New York Tribune* (Sept. 29, 1851) and (Sept. 30, 1851).

75. Raymond continued working for Harpers through 1856 before quitting to dedicate his time to the *Times* and his political career (he was elected lieutenant governor of New York in 1854 and became a major player in the birth of the Republican Party). For further information on Raymond see Eugene Exman *The Brothers Harper* (New York: Harper & Row, 1965); John Tebbel, *A History of Book Publishing in the United States* vol. 1 (New York: R.R. Bowker, 1972), 279-80; and, *Dictionary of American Biography* and *American National Biography s.v.* "Henry Jarvis Raymond."

76. *New York Times* (Oct. 1, 1851), 2.

77. It seems the Kanes sought to gain influence with Harpers through several channels. Tom talked with Rufus W. Griswold, a reader for Harpers and a powerful advocate for American authors and travel writers—Bayard Taylor was his protégé. See Thomas Leiper Kane to Elisha Kent Kane (April 21, 1851), APS Elisha Kent Kane papers; and *Dictionary of American Biography, s.v.* "Rufus Wilmont Griswold." For Curtis's negotiation, see Exman, *The Brothers Harper*, 359-60.

78. Corner, 85, 221-22. In 1854, Lovell would demonstrate his friendship to Elisha by serving as the acting master of the *Release*, one of the two ships sent to rescue Elisha from his second Arctic expedition.

79. "A Northwest Passage." *New York Times* (Oct. 3, 1851), 2.

80. "The Arctic Expedition. The Adventures of the Advance." *New York Times* (Oct. 3, 1851), 2.

81. "The New York Yacht Club." *New York Times* (Oct. 3, 1851), 2.

82. Corner, 102.

83. Joseph Henry to Elisha Kent Kane (Oct. 8, 1851), APS Elisha Kent Kane papers.

84. Navy Department to Elisha Kent Kane (Oct. 8, 1851), APS Elisha Kent Kane papers.

85. *New York Times* (Oct. 9, 1851), 3.

86. *Daily Pennsylvanian* (Oct. 10, 1851), 1. This story was printed anonymously; however, its content and prominent position on the front page of this Democratic paper strongly suggests Kane family influence.

87. John C. Symmes [Jr.] to Elisha Kent Kane (Oct. 20, 1851), APS Elisha Kent Kane

papers. For more on Symmes theory see Francis Spufford, *I May Be Some Time: Ice and the English Imagination* (New York: Picador, 1997), 64-78.

88. *Gleason's Pictorial Drawingroom Companion* 1 (Oct. 18, 1851), 1; *Harper's New Monthly Magazine* 4 (Dec. 1851), 11-22; and *International Magazine* 4 (Nov., 1851), 473.

89. Boker's poem first appeared in May of 1850, the month the Grinnell Expedition left. See *Sartain's Magazine* 6 (May, 1850), 323-34.

90. Like all broad terms, Romanticism is difficult to explain or define. My understanding, and the following explanation of Romanticism, come largely from the following sources: Goetzmann, *Exploration and Empire*, and *New Lands, New Men*; Russell Nye, *The Cultural Life of the New Nation, 1776-1830* (New York: Harper & Row, 1960); Lee Brown, *The Emerson Museum* (Cambridge: Harvard University Press, 1997); and Arthur Lovejoy, *The Great Chain of Being* (Cambridge: Harvard University Press, 1936).

91. See Douglas Botting, *Humboldt and the Cosmos* (New York: Harper and Row, 1973).

92. Ralph Waldo Emerson, "Nature" in *Ralph Waldo Emerson: Essays & Lectures* (New York: The Library of America, 1983), 10.

93. Goetzmann, "Introduction," in *New Lands, New Men*.

94. For a discussion of how painting styles shifted during this time period see Barbara Novak, *Nature and Culture* (New York: Oxford University Press, 1980), and *American Painting of the Nineteenth Century* (New York: Harper & Row, 1969); and James Flexner, *That Wilder Image* (Boston: Little Brown & Co., 1962).

95. Goetzmann, *New Lands New Men*, xiii.

96. See Herman Viola & Carolyn Margolis, eds. *Magnificent Voyagers* (Washington DC: Smithsonian Institution Press, 1985); and William Stanton, *The Great United States Exploring Expedition of 1838-1842* (Berkeley, CA: University of California Press, 1975) for a full account of the complex story of the publications that stemmed from this expedition—a process that took over thirty years.

97. *New York Tribune* (Nov. 5, 1851), 5; *New York Times* (Nov. 5, 1851), 1.

98. Elisha Kent Kane to Lady Jane Franklin (Nov. 15, 1851), APS Elisha Kent Kane papers.

99. Lady Jane Franklin to Elisha Kent Kane (Dec. 19, 1851), APS Elisha Kent Kane papers.

100. See articles in the *New York Times* and *Tribune* of Sept. 29, 30, and Oct. 1, 1851. For further information on the case see Matthew Grow "'Liberty to the Downtrodden': Thomas L. Kane, Romantic Reformer" (PhD diss., University of Notre Dame, 2006), 297-300; and Thomas Slaughter, *Bloody Dawn* (New York: Oxford University Press, 1991).

101. Thomas Leiper Kane to Elisha Kent Kane (undated, c. Dec., 1851), APS Elisha Kent Kane papers.

102. Corner, 102-03.

103. Descriptions of Kane's lectures at the Smithsonian appear in the *National Intelligencer* (Dec. 29, 31, & Jan. 3); and the *New York Times* (Jan. 10, 1852), 7.

104. *New York Times* (Jan. 10, 1851), 7.

105. Elisha Kent Kane to Robert Patterson Kane (undated, c. Jan. 1852), APS Elisha Kent

Kane papers.

106. Folder, "Lecture #1," APS Elisha Kent Kane papers.

107. The rough draft of one such news release appears on the back of a letter in the Kane family papers. See the backside of Elisha Kent Kane to J. P. Smith, APS Elisha Kent Kane papers. See Elisha Kent Kane to Robert Patterson Kane (undated, c. Jan. 1852), APS Elisha Kent Kane papers for evidence of his sending Washington newspaper articles on to New York papers.

108. All these requests, as well as many others, are housed in the APS Elisha Kent Kane papers.

109. D. Judkins to Elisha Kent Kane (Feb. 11, 1852), APS Elisha Kent Kane papers.

110. Undated copy of a letter in folder, "Kane, E.K. to ____, rough drafts and copies," APS Elisha Kent Kane papers.

111. George Gray Leiper to Martha Gray Leiper (Jan. 29, 1852), University of Virginia, Alderman Library, Acc. No. 5142-a. See also the Baltimore *Daily News* (Jan. 31, 1852), 1 for a similar account of the diversity of Kane's audience.

112. F. M. Edselas, "Boston Half a Century Ago," *The Catholic World* 62 (March, 1896), 733-746.

113. William Wood to Thomas Leiper Kane (Nov. 5, 1851), BYU Thomas Leiper Kane papers.

114. Elisha Kent Kane to John K. Kane (undated, c. Feb. 1852), APS Elisha Kent Kane papers.

115. Elisha Kent Kane to Henry Grinnell (Feb. 1, 1852), APS Elisha Kent Kane papers.

116. Julia Cracroft to Elisha Kent Kane (Feb. 20, 1852), APS Elisha Kent Kane papers.

117. Thomas Leiper Kane's date book (Dec. 28, 1851), BYU Thomas Leiper Kane papers. See also Grow, 228-38.

118. Thomas Leiper Kane to Elisha Kent Kane (two undated letters, c. July, 1852), APS Elisha Kent Kane papers.

119. Corner, 11. The family moved to 36 Girard St. A few years later, in 1855, they moved into "Fern Rock," a house they built on land adjacent to Rennselaer.

120. C. Hague to Elisha Kent Kane (Jan. 6, 1852), APS Elisha Kent Kane papers. The cost for three tint 11x15 images was 21 pounds 4 shilling for the first hundred copies and 4 pounds 4 shillings for each additional hundred copies.

121. For a brief but helpful work on James Hamilton's life and art, see Constance Martin, *James Hamilton: Arctic Watercolours* (Calgary, Canada: Glenbow Museum, 1983).

122. Cornelius Grinnell to Elisha Kent Kane (June 15, June 17, & Aug. 18, 1852), APS Elisha Kent Kane papers.

123. Lady Jane Franklin to Elisha Kent Kane (June 4, 1852), APS Elisha Kent Kane papers; Osborn's book was short, cheaply printed, and designed to be "a light, readable description of incidents... to interest the general reader and the community at large." See Sherard Osborn, "Preface," in *Stray Leaves from an Arctic Journal* (New York: G.P. Putnam, 1852). This book was part of "Putnam's Semi-Monthly Library."

124. Thomas Leiper Kane to Elisha Kent Kane (July 16, 1852), APS Elisha Kent Kane papers; Tom believed Griffin's letters would be in the "Literary Messenger," which seems to be a reference to the popular journal, the *Southern Literary Messenger* of Richmond, VA. If this is the case, then Griffin's letters were not printed, as they do not appear in this journal during 1852 or 1853. Literary Messenger may have also referred to one of many local papers by that name then existing in the United States. If Griffin's letters appeared in one of these, their impact would have been small because none of these papers had large circulations.

125. V.G. Audubon to Elisha Kent Kane (June 12, 1852), APS Elisha Kent Kane papers; John James Audubon, *The Quadrupeds of North America* (New York: V.G. Audubon, 1851-54), *s.v.* "Arctic Fox" & "Polar Bear." Though Kane was the one in contact with Audubon, he gave credit for the information on the Arctic Fox to the *Advance's* steward, William Morton, who also served as Kane's personal assistant and constant companion.

126. Tom Harris (chief of the Navy Bureau of Medicine) to W.A. Graham (Navy Department) (June 28, 1852); and, S.R. Addison (Navy Bureau of Medicine) to Elisha Kent Kane (July 17, 1852), APS Elisha Kent Kane papers.

127. Corner, 95.

128. Elisha Kent Kane to Peter Force (June 30, 1852); and folder, "Kane, E.K. Controversy on Grinnell Land," APS Elisha Kent Kane papers. This essay was reprinted in Kane, *U.S. Grinnell Expedition*, 200-09.

129. Thomas Leiper Kane to William Wood (March 8, 1852), BYU Thomas Leiper Kane papers.

130. Thomas Leiper Kane to William Wood (May 21, 1852), BYU Thomas Leiper Kane papers. Thanks to Matt Grow for bringing these letters to my attention.

131. Thomas Leiper Kane to Elisha Kent Kane (July 16, 1852), APS Elisha Kent Kane papers. Emphasis in original.

132. Thomas Leiper Kane to Elisha Kent Kane (Oct. 10, 1852), APS Elisha Kent Kane papers.

133. John K. Kane to Elisha Kent Kane (Oct. 13, 1852), APS Elisha Kent Kane papers.

134. Cornelius Grinnell to Elisha Kent Kane (Aug. 11, 1852), APS Elisha Kent Kane papers. Cornelius quotes the Harpers in his letter.

135. Cornelius Grinnell to Elisha Kent Kane (Aug. 18, 1852), APS Elisha Kent Kane papers.

136. John Sartain to James Hamilton (Oct. 9, 1852), APS Elisha Kent Kane papers.

137. James Hamilton to Elisha Kent Kane (Oct. 11, 1852), APS Elisha Kent Kane papers.

138. [Margaret Fox], *The Love-Life of Dr. Kane* (New York: Carleton Publisher, 1866), 21-23.

3

Rapping Spirits, Maggie Fox, and the Love Life of Elisha Kent Kane

W hen Elisha Kent Kane met Margaret Fox in 1852, he was a rising star. He was no longer just a well-traveled physician from Philadelphia, he was a hero on a mission. He had announced to the world that he was going to find and rescue Sir John Franklin from a location whose very existence was in question, a place that sparked heated debates and fired the imaginations of nineteenth-century Americans—the Open Polar Sea. This was quite a task for a young man, but because of his family's efforts and his skillful use of the popular media, thousands of Americans came to believe in his abilities. In this way, he and Maggie Fox were much alike. Like Elisha, Maggie was also a rising star. Though she was just a farm girl from rural New York, she had also dedicated herself to a seemingly impossible mission. She was trying to rescue humanity from the cold sting of death by venturing into the never seen but often dreamed of spirit world to bring back departed loved ones. To many this seemed a preposterous, even blasphemous, venture, but thanks to her family and supporters' clever use of the popular media, thousands of Americans rallied behind her. Unlike almost any other woman in America at that time, Maggie could understand Elisha at a fundamental level because she too led a life dedicated to adventure, exploration, and fame. They came from different social classes and operated within different fundamental belief structures (Elisha scientific; Maggie religious), but their goals were much the same. They both sought and achieved fame by getting the public to believe in a mysterious world that no one had ever seen and to support them in the exploration of this world. Even more importantly, having achieved fame, they both suffered from its dehumanizing influence. To seek to understand Elisha Kent Kane is to also seek to understand Margaret Fox because their lives were intertwined not only by romance, but by the realities of fame in nineteenth-century America.

On a cold winter evening in 1848, spirits of the dead descended on a small farm in Hydesville, New York, and began communicating via telegraphic "rappings" to two young girls, Maggie and Kate Fox, or so thousands (perhaps hundreds of thousands) of nineteenth-century Americans came to believe. Much like the "fanaticism" of Mormon leader Joseph Smith and his angel Moroni, or William Miller and his apocalyptic predictions that spawned the Adventist movement, many antebellum Americans saw the Fox sisters and their "spirit-rapping" as just another of the many outlandish new religious movements that sprang up during the fervent revivalism of their era. Critics dismissed the Fox sisters as nothing but two mischievous farm girls who had tricked their superstitious mother and neighbors into believing that the popping noises that sounded in their presence were messages from the spirit world. There was a problem, however. The people who went to see Maggie and Kate could not explain where the rapping noises came from, and even more troubling, the information the rappings spelled out was often eerily and inexplicably correct. The public's inability to prove or disprove the "spirit-rappings" resulted in a renewed and heightened interest in Spiritualism and propelled Maggie and Kate Fox to infamous stardom.[1]

Before the "Rochester Rappings" made their family infamous, the Fox family of Hydesville, New York, was much like many other rural families of the early 1800s.[2] In 1812, John Fox, the son of a blacksmith in Rockland County, New York, married a local girl, Margaret Smith, who came from an industrious family with ties on both sides of the U.S.-Canada border—as loyalists they had fled and prospered on the Canadian side of Lake Ontario during the American Revolution. As a young couple in a time of restless expansion, urbanization, and industrialization, John and Margaret sought a better life first in New York City and later in the far-western New York frontier. Between 1813 and 1820 they had four children—Ann Leah, Maria, Elizabeth, and David—before John, a severe alcoholic by the early 1820s, abandoned the family. For several years thereafter Margaret lived with her unmarried sister and raised her four children, most of whom left for work or marriage by 1830. Then, in the early 1830s, John returned as a reformed man; he was sober and a strict and observant Methodist. He and Margaret soon reconciled, and after moving across Lake Ontario to the tiny village of Consecon, Ontario, where John owned some land, they had two more children: Margaretta, who went by Maggie, was born in 1833; and Catherine, known as Kate, arrived four years later

A postcard of the Fox Cottage in Hydesville, New York, which was later
moved to Lily Dale, a spiritualist community in upstate New York.
Collection of Author.

in 1837.[3] During the decade after Kate's birth, the family moved frequently, bounc-
ing between farms in Ontario and rural New York, and a more urban existence in
the new Erie Canal boomtown of Rochester. Stability finally came in 1847 when
they moved to the little crossroads of Hydesville in Wayne County, New York,
thirty miles east of Rochester and within sight of their son David's farm. While
John built a house and struggled to find work as a blacksmith, they rented a small
cabin that many locals believed to be haunted.[4]

According to spiritualist believers, on New Year's Day 1848, John Fox woke
to the sound of quiet rapping noises sounding at various locations about the
house. As these noises continued over the next few weeks, he speculated that they
came from a nearby cobbler's hammering, dancing going on at their neighbor's
house, or rats. Mrs. Fox was unconvinced. She came from a family that believed
in supernatural forces and she began to fear that these noises came from otherworldly powers. As weeks passed and the noises persisted, Mrs. Fox became increasingly apprehensive. Finally, on March 31, 1848, the tension broke when Maggie
and Kate, then fourteen and eleven years old, began to play with the raps. They
told the raps to "do as I do" and then clapped four times, which the raps immediately repeated. Mrs. Fox, stunned by the response, began asking the raps yes-no
questions. Via this process she ascertained that the raps were coming from the
spirit of a man who had been murdered and buried in the cellar of their house.
Not sure what to do next, Mrs. Fox had her husband round up several neighbors
to witness the raps. News of the phenomenon spread quickly, and a crowd soon

gathered to listen to the raps of the spirit. It answered several of their questions and explained that in life it had been a thirty-one-year-old peddler who was robbed and killed with a butcher knife. This spiritual message was taken seriously enough that several people accused the former occupant of the cabin, John Bell, of murder. Bell quickly proclaimed his innocence and threatened litigation. This ended the accusations, but not the excitement surrounding the rapping spirit. By April 3 people from across the county flocked to the house and several men began to dig up the floor of the cellar. After going down three feet they hit water, and though they continued digging and bailing, the water eventually forced them to stop.[5] The Foxes left the cabin and moved in with their son David, but people kept coming to visit the now-famous haunted house. On April 12, the *Western Argus* of nearby Lyons, New York, reported, "The whole country is crazy with excitement and hundreds are flocking to the spot to hear the 'raps.'" Skeptical of the whole affair, it proposed a practical idea, "the establishment of a TAVERN in the neighborhood to accommodate those who make this a popular place of resort." It sarcastically noted, "Quite a 'living' business might be done."[6]

A local man, E. E. Lewis, collected statements from the Fox family and their neighbors and compiled them into a pamphlet that he quickly prepared for press. He also wrote a scathing editorial to his local newspaper, the *Newark Herald*, which had dismissed the whole thing as an April Fool's hoax. He noted that many "intelligent people" had visited the place and were unable to explain the phenomenon, but were brave enough not to simply dismiss it as humbug even though that left them "in the very UN-delectable state of doubt which arises from a fear of ridicule if one declares his true belief in such matters." He then challenged the *Herald* to "enlighten us in regard to the manner in which this 'hoax' is carried on." He concluded, be it "man, spirit, or devil—it is certainly one of the wonders of the age." In an article printed directly below Lewis's, the *Herald* ridiculed him. It noted that he was the author of the soon-to-be-released pamphlet on the Fox house and thus, "knowing that if the excitement should subside... it would materially injure the sale of his contemplated work, he has taken the above course, at the expense of veracity, to keep up an excitement in the public mind in hopes of realizing a nice speculation from the operation." It then pronounced him "either an ignorant fool, or a consummate knave" and accused him of helping to execute the whole thing.[7]

By mid-May, most of the local papers concluded that the raps were a hoax executed by Mr. Fox who, sitting on his wobbly bed, could produce the raps with just a slight movement. The *Western Argus* was sure this evidence would end the affair and reported that Mr. Fox, the "long-talked-of prince of humbugs... has at length 'given up the ghost'; and the duped 'spiritualists' who have flocked from all quarters to hear the 'Mysterious raps' and communicate with his ghostship, are essentially 'done for.'"[8]

This prediction could not have been more wrong. Western New York, known as the "burned-over district" because of the many religious revivals that roared through it in the first decades of the century, was filled with religious "seekers"— people who believed that God worked in powerful, mysterious, and magical ways. During the three preceding decades, these people had attended the heated revivals of Charles G. Finney, flocked to the prophet Joseph Smith and his Book of Mormon, embraced the teachings of Mother Ann Lee and her celibate Shakers, and joined John Humphry Noyes's sexually provocative "free love" community in Oneida.[9] In 1848, the "spirit-rappings" of the Fox family were a spark that could set the still smoldering burned-over district ablaze once again. All that was needed was a person to fan the flames by interpreting this strange phenomenon in terms that a religiously volatile public could embrace. This person was Maggie and Kate's eldest sister, Ann Leah Fox Fish.

Ann Leah (who went by Leah), was the Fox family's eldest child, more than twenty years older than Maggie and Kate. In 1827, at the age of fourteen, Leah married Bowman Fish and soon gave birth to their daughter, Elizabeth. A few years later Fish abandoned Leah, leaving her to struggle to support herself and her child by teaching piano lessons in Rochester. Leah had little contact with her family in Hydesville during these years and did not learn of the mysterious rappings until May 1848, when one of her piano students showed her the proof sheets of E. E. Lewis's pamphlet that their father, a printer, had brought home. Leah left for Hydesville that night and upon arrival found her family in a state of chaos. By this time people were beginning to suspect that Maggie and Kate were responsible for the rappings. Leah, who justifiably feared violence from the mobs that began to gather around the family demanding answers, left with Kate and instructed Mrs. Fox to follow by a different route with Maggie. They would rendezvous a few days later at Leah's house at 11 Mechanic's Square in Rochester.[10]

Once in Rochester, Leah, a shrewd thinker and a clever entrepreneur, quickly realized the potential of her younger sisters and slowly began to introduce them to the religiously radical families of Rochester. In her account of this time, Leah claimed she did this because the spirits, after terrorizing her household with poltergeist-like activities for several days, sent her a message via "God's Telegraph" that said: "You must proclaim these truths to the world. This is the dawning of a new era; and you must not try to conceal it any longer."[11] In later years, Maggie and Kate had a different version of this story. They claimed that Leah's promotional efforts were driven only by her desire for fame and fortune and that they, as young, innocent girls, were victims of her money-making trickery.[12] Whatever the motivation, the result was the same. Leah contacted Isaac and Amy Post and in them found strong supporters of her sisters' "spiritual gifts."

The Posts were well-known religious and political radicals. In 1827 they followed Elias Hicks (Amy's cousin) in a split from Quaker theology over their belief that a guiding inner-light, not the Bible, was the primary way God was revealed to true believers.[13] During the mid-1840s, the Posts enthusiastically embraced the two major radical reform efforts of the era: abolition of slavery and suffrage for women. Such notable reformers as Frederick Douglass, Elizabeth Cady Stanton, and Susan B. Anthony often visited their home, and the Posts energetically supported their reform efforts even though this made them controversial members of their community. By 1848, even the free-thinking Hicksites censured them for working too closely with non-Quakers in abolition and women's rights organizations.[14] The Posts thus began their own fellowship—the Congregational Friends of Waterloo—which had no hierarchical structure and placed all authority on each individual's relationship with God. The Fox sisters' spirit-rappings began just months after the formation of the Congregational Friends, and the Posts found in their raps an otherworldly confirmation of their theology—spirits were indeed speaking directly to humans. When the Posts visited Leah's house to commune with the spirits they found them manifested by familiar faces. A few years before they moved to Hydesville, the Fox family had rented rooms from the Posts and Amy and Isaac fondly remembered their vivacious young tenants.[15] This helped quiet any suspicion of chicanery the Posts may have felt. The spirits sprang to life around the young girls and the Posts were surprised and delighted to receive clear raps indicating "yes" or "no" to each of their questions. The structure of these early meetings between the Posts and the rapping spirits established an important part of early spiritualism because it dictated that the religious seeker set the agenda of the session. The spirits did not preach or instruct, they simply answered the questions they were asked, allowing the questioner to formulate their own interpretations and meanings.[16] It is not surprising, then, that the Posts found that the spirits supported their beliefs in abolition and women's rights, the latter being an issue very much on their minds. Amy Post and several other women who attended the Fox sisters' early meetings in Rochester were also helping Elizabeth Cady Stanton organize the Seneca Falls Convention, where she planned to present her "Declaration of Sentiments," a document that would become the cornerstone of the women's suffrage movement.[17]

Over the next few months, several Rochester citizens came to believe that the Fox sisters were able to communicate with spirits and began viewing them as the prophets of a new era of relations between the earthly and heavenly realms. Not everyone was so eager to believe, however, and Leah soon found herself evicted from her home because of neighbors' complaints about the rappings. At this time, Leah did not charge people to consult with the spirits. A committee, headed by Isaac Post, provided for the sisters' needs, so when Leah was evicted, they found her a "pleasant little cottage" on Troup Street where she could live in peace and continue supporting her young sisters and the spirits that followed them.[18]

During this time Maggie and Kate, each accompanied by an entourage of dedicated spiritualists, were often separated and taken to different communities to demonstrate the spirit raps. These events attracted little press attention because they were carefully regulated and consisted only of believers and their specially screened guests. This exclusivity led to a strong core of true believers who were willing to make great sacrifices for the new faith. Early believers included many respected community members, such as George Willets, a businessman and cousin of Isaac Post; John Kedzie, a jeweler; Reuben Jones, junior editor of the Rochester *American*; Edward Jones, a wool dealer; and ministers Asahel Jervis, Lemuel Clark, and Charles Hammond. These people came to the Fox sisters suspicious, but left convinced after hearing what they described as "communications... containing in themselves overwhelming testimony of spiritual power and foresight."[19]

Though shocking, the Fox sisters' "raps" were in fact congruous with a religious idea that had been gaining momentum among religious radicals for decades. Beginning in the 1740s, Swedish mystic Emanuel Swedenborg blended the ideas of several occult traditions with the burgeoning scientific and classification systems of the Enlightenment to form a new cosmology that asserted "correspondences" between the physical and spiritual world. His ideas heavily impacted many radical religious thinkers, ranging from Mother Ann Lee and her celibate Shaker communities to Ralph Waldo Emerson and his Transcendentalist break from Unitarianism. Most relevant to the Fox sisters, however, were the ideas of another New York resident, the "Poughkeepsie Seer" Andrew Jackson Davis. In 1844, at the age of eighteen, Davis was mesmerized during a public lecture, and in the following months he continued exploring the spiritual insights he experienced while entranced. With guidance from the spirit of Swedenborg and others, he soon developed a loosely defined system of "harmonialism" between the physical and spiritual worlds that rejected mainstream Christian theology and argued for a Harmonial Spiritualism that would lead to a "'Revelation' of the *Structures*, and *Laws*, and *orders*, and uses of the material and spiritual universe." Davis would dictate to a scribe while entranced (much as Joseph Smith had done with the Book of Mormon), and in this way he produced his first book, *The Principles of Nature, Her Divine Revelations, and a Voice to Mankind* (1847), which framed the way in which people understood the Fox sisters' raps the following year.[20]

In the fall of 1849, eighteen months after the raps first began, the Fox sisters enjoyed the loyal support of dozens of families. Séances continued on a regular basis—supporters took Kate to Auburn to meet fellow believers, while Maggie and Leah maintained a busy schedule in Rochester—but the influential men of the movement shunned public displays and aggressive proselytizing of the spirit manifestations. They were businessmen, church leaders, and respected members of their communities who feared that their spiritualist beliefs would bring public censure and ridicule.[21] This ensured that the movement would remain small—an insular sect—and not become a dynamic new religious movement like Joseph Smith's Mormonism or William Miller's Adventism, which both grew exponentially during the 1840s. In the fall of 1849, however, things changed. According to Eliab Capron, an early supporter of the Fox sisters, the spirits began demanding that their presence be made known to the world at large, but the Fox sisters' fear of notoriety caused them to "resist to the utmost all directions of that nature." This annoyed the spirits and consequently, during a séance run by Maggie and Leah, they curtly spelled out, "We will now bid you all farewell," and the raps went silent.[22] Days past and the raps did not return.

When the raps stopped and a quiet stillness fell over their household for the first time in months, the Fox sisters "declared that they were glad to be rid of [the spirits]" and "considered it a relief."[23] It was undoubtedly a welcomed respite for Maggie and Kate. The preceeding eighteen months had been exciting but bewildering. When the raps became public in the spring of 1848, Kate and Maggie's childhoods ended. The whirl of public attention transformed them from small-town farm girls into public figures embraced by some but scorned by many. Leaving their small cabin in the rural crossroads of Hydesville and becoming the center of attention among a group of affluent and worldly wise adults was certainly exciting. They traveled regularly, were well provided with clothes and other niceties, and enjoyed the company of energetic and articulate reformers who truly believed they could remake the world, whether through abolition, women's rights, or spirit manifestations. Though this was energizing, it was also exhausting. Kate and Maggie went from living amid a small, tight-knit family to being managed by aggressive adults who were more concerned about their own agendas than the girls' well being. They were valued not for themselves, but for what they could do. They were called "mediums" and this term is telling—they were to be passive object through which something else took place. No one wanted to know what they thought or felt; they were important only because the raps happened in their presence.

Kate was twelve in the fall of 1849, making it difficult to imagine that she had much say in the decisions that were made, whether by the spirits or other less ethereal beings. Maggie turned sixteen that October, an age when young women in a booming area of settlement and expansion were often regarded as adults—her mother was married at sixteen; Leah wed for the first time at fourteen. Maggie was certainly beholden to Leah, who had become her primary guardian, as well as to the many families who supported them because of the raps, but she was also old enough to have a mind of her own and to understand and question the decisions that were being made, even if she did not have the ability to influence those decisions directly. Leah's role is much clearer. By 1849 she had lived a difficult thirty-six years. Married at fourteen and abandoned with a child a few years later, she had struggled on her own for twenty years, supporting herself by teaching piano lessons to the children of Rochester's rising middle-class. The "Hydesville Raps" had changed everything, and for the first time she was living the American dream of upward mobility. Her parents moved from New York City to the far-western New York frontier, from Canada to the boomtown of Rochester in search of this dream, but it was never quite realized. The raps were Leah's opportunity for success and her sisters were the way to achieve it. It is difficult to believe, then, that she and the rapping spirits were not of the same mind about publicizing this new spiritual manifestation.

After twelve days of silence in the Fox house, Eliab Capron joined George Willets in calling on Leah and Maggie. Unlike Willets and the Posts, Capron was more aggressive in his desire to promote the spirits. It was he who took Kate to Auburn to gain converts and it was he who wrote one of the earliest books explaining and evangelizing the movement. It is not surprising, then, that when he entered the house the spirits broke their silence and he was "greeted with a perfect shower of raps." Using a tedious system of spelling out words via raps, the spirits again demanded to have their existence brought "prominently before the public" and Capron noted that they "proceeded to give their plan of the whole proceedings in minute detail."[24] The crux of their plan centered on the emphatic demand: "Hire Corinthian Hall," the newest and largest auditorium in Rochester.[25]

This time the group of Rochester supporters readily agreed, and to enhance the spirits' public premier, they ran a large advertisements in the Rochester *Daily Advertiser*, headed "Wonderful Phenomena at Corinthian Hall." This ad announced that, "The citizens of Rochester will have an opportunity of hearing a full explanation of the nature and history of the 'MYSTERIOUS NOISES' supposed to be supernatural, which have caused so much excitement in this city and other places for the last two years." The evening would consist of a lecture, followed by a demonstration of the raps, and end with the audience choosing a five-member committee. This group would meet the next day at a place of their choosing to investigate the raps in whatever way they thought fit. They would then "report at the next evening's lecture whether there is collusion or deception." Admission was twenty-five cents per person (fifty cents for a man accompanying two women) and the ad ended by proclaiming, "COME AND INVESTIGATE."[26]

This ad demonstrates one of the most important aspects of the spiritualist movement. Spiritualism can be seen as the logical outcome of the years of evangelical religious movements that preceded it. Beginning with George Whitefield and his dynamic, theatrical sermon style that stirred even religious skeptics like Benjamin Franklin, and continuing through the emotion-filled revivals of Charles Finney and other charismatic evangelists of the 1830s, many strains of American Protestantism had come to embrace the tactics of popular entertainment to draw

This ad from the Rochester *Daily Advertiser* (November 13, 1849) is similar to the ads for demonstrations of mesmerism, animal magnetism, clairvoyance, and phrenology that were popular in the antebellum era.

☞ PRICE REDUCED ☜

WONDERFUL PHENOMENA,

AT CORINTHIAN HALL,

On Saturday Evening, Nov. 17.

The citizens of Rochester will have an opportunity of hearing a full explanation of the nature and history of the "MYSTERIOUS NOISES," supposed to be *super natural*, which have caused so much excitement in this city and other places for the last two years. The whole directions in regard to bringing it before the public, have been given by these "mysterious agencies," and they have promised to give the public an actual demonstration of the sounds, so that they may know that they are neither made or controlled by human Beings. Let the citizens of Rochester embrace this opportunity of investigating the whole matter, and see if those engaged in laying it before the public are deceived, or are deceiving others, and if neither, account for these truly wonderful manifestations. After the lecture, a committee of *five persons* may be chosen by the audience to select any respectable and convenient room in the city, where the next day may be devoted to an examination of these manifestations, and report at the next evenings lecture whether there is collusion or deception. COME AND INVESTIGATE.

Doors open at 7 o'clock. Lecture to commence at 7 Admittance 12½ cents. Tickets obtained at the door.

nov13 dtf

a crowd. With no state-sanctioned church that the public had to attend or support, ministers joined entertainers in the hard task of filling seats to stay solvent—pews had to be full if offering plates were to be filled. Because of this, sermon styles moved from academic and foreboding to dynamic and exciting, hymns became moving and emotional, and even the professed message of God's will changed to be more loving and forgiving, and less judgmental and condemning. Religion, like almost all aspects of 1840s life, entered the new market economy.[27]

Spiritualism understood and embraced this trend. The spiritualists who rented Corinthian Hall believed they were bringing a wonderful new message from God to the world. They also knew that the way to spread this message was to make it exciting. It was no accident that their advertisement made the event sound more like an attraction at P. T. Barnum's popular American Museum than a religious revival. The first step in starting a movement is getting an audience, and this was exactly what the Corinthian Hall meetings did. On the first night, November 14, 1849, four hundred people showed up to listen to Capron's opening lecture, which made no assertion about what the raps were, but only what they were not—trickery. After his lecture, the audience was mystified as loud rappings thumped and bumped from many different places in the auditorium. The crowd was then asked to select a committee to investigate the mediums, Leah and Maggie, who were quietly sitting on the stage throughout the evening (Kate was out of town). This committee would report their findings the next evening—a brilliant strategy for assuring continued audiences and entrance fees.[28]

The committee met with Maggie and Leah the next day at the hall of the Sons of Temperance. After several hours of investigation they were unable to determine how the noises were made, which they reported the next evening. The audience was stunned and quickly appointed another committee, this time including Dr. H. H. Langworthy, the city's leading physician; Frederick Whittlesey, vice chancellor of the State of New York; and Judge A. P. Hascall, a former congressman. When this committee returned the next night and reported that they too were unable to detect any trickery, the audience was outraged. They appointed a third committee made up of vocal skeptics, including W. L. Burtis, who said he would give away his new beaver hat if he could not find the source of the raps, and Leonard Kenyon, who vowed to throw himself over the falls if he too was fooled. This group conducted their investigation in the offices of Dr. Justin Gates, who was also on the committee. They began by having three women disrobe Leah and Maggie, search their clothing, and then redress them in other clothes. By the sexual mores of the day, accepting such an investigation was scandalous, and though they complied, the ordeal was traumatizing—Amy Post ended this process when she heard Maggie and Leah's sobs, but the investigation continued. Next, sure that the trick was somehow done via that mysterious new force of the era, electricity, the committee asked the mediums to stand on feather pillows and glass plates to insulate them and thus foil any electrical gadgets that they may have been using. Leah and Maggie complied and the raps still sounded. They were then asked questions verbally, written on paper, and mentally. The raps answered each of them in a "generally correct" manner.[29]

Before that evening's meeting at Corinthian Hall, some members of the community learned that the third committee had also failed to find the source of the rapping and so prepared to disrupt the meeting and run the Foxes out of town; they were certainly either humbugs or witches, and either way they were undesirable. Josiah Bissel, a wealthy businessman and fervent supporter of such mainstream revivalists as Charles Finney, handed out fireworks to local rowdies who lit them in the auditorium, causing great chaos. Then, when the committee announced their findings, several men rushed the stage to grab Maggie and Leah.

Though these events terrified Maggie, this sort of violent reaction was exactly what Leah wanted. Maggie later testified that Leah had planned for this, knowing that "anything that might bear the semblance of religious persecution would promote her cause... by bringing to it both greater notoriety and widespread sympathy."[30] Such planning is evident in the events of the night. The moment the hall erupted, several men were at the ready and surrounded Maggie and Leah and escorted them home while the police were called in to put down the ensuing riot.[31]

In the months that followed, the Fox sisters stayed at the home of Deacon Alvah Strong in Rochester. There they were visited by hundreds of people who came to them out of curiosity or the desire to communicate with their departed friends and family members. Although many people left the sisters impressed if not converted by the rappings, others left sure of the girls' chicanery. One of Kate's former teachers, Mary B. Allen, bated her ex-pupil, saying, "I am interested in education, and I would like to know something about methods in the other world." She then asked how the spirit of her dead grandmother would spell the word "scissors." Using the common séance method of the time, a stick was dragged across a row of letters and the raps popped when the stick touched the desired letter. Under Kate's watchful eye the spirits spelled "sissers." "Oh," replied Allen, "that is just the way Katy Fox spelled 'scissors' when she was a scholar in my school."[32]

Such skeptical reports, however, did not keep people from flooding to the Fox sisters' séance table, bringing their money with them. It was at this time that Leah began suggesting a donation of a dollar per visitor.[33] It is not surprising that once money began to pour into the Fox household, a number of people in that booming, entrepreneurial area suddenly discovered that they too possessed the power to speak with the dead, and quickly began their own spiritual meetings. Some of these failed miserably and were run out of town, but others, such as Rachel Draper, did very well. Draper could "magnetize" herself and speak with the dead. In February 1850 she teamed up with the Fox sisters and together they channeled the spirit of Benjamin Franklin, who explained to a small audience how he used electricity and batteries to create a "spirit telegraph" that allowed him to communicate across the boundary of death. He ended by insisting that his audience write up what they had seen and get it into the papers. Albert Reynolds, Rochester's Postmaster and a leading businessman, did exactly that, and the story appeared in the February 26 edition of the appropriately titled *Daily Magnet*.[34]

In early March the *Rochester Daily American* directly addressed the phenomenon the Fox sisters had started, noting that "Mrs. Fish and her two sisters, the Misses Fox... have spent the winter in gratifying the taste and investigating spirit of all those inquirers who desire to search after 'things past finding out,' and with a devotion seldom witnessed, they have kept open house from morn till night, and often times from night till morn." Far from praising these efforts, however, the paper then noted that, even though "the manifestations were not for pay, a little box was kept for those who were kindly inclined," and as the young spiritual prophets began to see real-world profits roll in, Kate and Maggie developed "enough of the spirit of practical Christianity in them to believe the 'laborer worthy of his hire.'" Leah had been supplying her younger sisters with "what was necessary for personal adornment... including a few dollars for theatrical and other refined amusements," but was keeping all the rest of the money for herself. Maggie and Kate eventually demanded that Leah "fork over," and when she refused, they left her house, "and no sooner had they turned their backs... than the gentle rappings of the departed... hushed." With mocking tone, the article concluded, "Poor Mrs. F. had been tempted by mammon. She had fallen from her high estate, and admiring friends were seen like angels' visits, few and far between. But the hand of affliction came upon her—she relented—forked over—and the two kind sisters returned." The rappings and the crowds immediately returned as well, and were "admitted upon the same terms as formally."[35] This telling article shows that, despite their later claims to the contrary, even at a young age Maggie and Kate were keenly aware of their actions, and the financial gains they could achieve through their work as mediums.

With their relationship patched up, the Fox sisters took their séances on the road, traveling to Albany and Troy in April and May 1850. Unlike their earlier travels, these were promoted with extensive advertising and designed to attract large audiences, not just loyal believers. They made converts at each place, but they also ran into trouble. Clergymen in Albany sought their arrest for "blasphemy against the Holy Scriptures," and in Troy, a group of women publicly accused them of sexual improprieties—they were sure their husbands would not be nearly so interested in the spirits if the mediums were not attractive young women.[36] With spiritualism's entry into mainstream culture, the press had a field day, almost universally condemning the Fox sisters as humbugs, but disagreeing on just how the rappings were produced. A "Professor Loomis" declared that the raps were nothing more than a well-promoted explanation of the rapping noises that appeared all across the region, caused by the vibrations made from water rushing over its many dams.[37] Some papers were sure the raps were caused by a unique "electrical condition" in the mediums' bodies, and still others embraced the ideas raised by the Corinthian Hall committees—that the girls had lead balls in the edges of their skirts or were somehow popping their knees or toes.[38]

Horace Greeley, editor of the *New York Tribune*, was one of the few newspapermen in the country who took the raps seriously enough to actually investigate them. He sent a reporter to Rochester soon after the Corinthian Hall meetings, and although still skeptical, the *Tribune* reported that the raps could be "the precursors of more extraordinary developments," and suggested that "the judicious will look calmly and fairly as possible at all facts, and judge them by their own value."[39] Greeley continued to report on the Fox sisters in a balanced manner in the following months, neither supporting nor condemning them. Given this attitude, it is not surprising that when Leah decided it was time to take Maggie and Kate to New York City, and she gave Greeley advanced notice to ensure that he would be the first visitor to their séance rooms at Barnum's Hotel.[40] (It should be noted that neither Barnum's Hotel nor the Fox sisters were connected to P. T. Barnum and his famous museum of curiosities.) This trip to the big city was largely inspired by Eliab Capron, who in 1850 published *Singular Revelations*, a glowing account of the new movement. In a letter to Mrs. Fox he encouraged Leah to take Maggie and Kate to New York, noting that there they "might convince some of the best minds in the nation" of the power of the spirits. He worked to accomplish this by setting up a meeting with many eminent scholars, and though they offered to pay only expenses, he prodded Maggie and Kate, reminding them that many people liked to give presents to clever and charming girls.[41] Mrs. Fox initially disapproved of her youngest daughters essentially being exhibited in the nation's biggest city, but within a few months she relented.

The sisters arrived in Manhattan on June 3, 1850, and just as Leah had hoped, Greeley was one of their first visitors. He advised them about the promotion and execution of their sittings, suggesting to Leah that she raise the séance rate to five dollars per visitor "to keep the rabble away."[42] Leah ignored this advice and kept her rates at a dollar a head, but she did accept Greeley's offer to invite several of the city's most celebrated citizens to an introductory séance. Just three days after their arrival, many of the biggest names in American letters agreed to gather and investigate the mysterious "Rochester Rappings." Among those present were William Cullen Bryant, famed poet and editor of the *New York Evening Post*; John Bigelow, co-editor of the *Post*; Nathaniel P. Willis, popular poet, travel writer and editor of the *Home Journal*; George Ripley, literary critic for the *Tribune* and founder of the Fourierist utopian experiment at Brook Farm; George Bancroft, historian and former secretary of the navy; and James Fenimore Cooper, author of the Leatherstocking tales and America's best-known novelist. This distinguished group met at the house of writer, editor, and clergyman Rufus Griswold, and were soon joined by Leah, Maggie, Kate, and Mrs. Fox.[43]

Willis, famous for his insider accounts of the lives of the social elite, noted the appearance of the Fox family with his usual gossipy flair for detail. He described Mrs. Fox as "a stout lady, of the ordinary small-town type of maternity," and her daughters as "three young ladies considerably prettier than the average." He was a bit surprised that Leah was the spokesperson for the spirits and that "one of the virgins was not elected for that office." As the evening went on and the raps answered many seemingly unknowable questions, he and the rest of the group were quite impressed. Willis was especially struck by the sisters "combined good-humor and simplicity, and the ease and unpretendingness with which they let their visitors (from both worlds) have their own way." He noted that before the evening was over the sisters had "won the respect and liking of all present."[44]

These observations are telling of the gender rolls of the day, demonstrating rules of antebellum propriety that heavily influence the public's perception and reception of the Fox sisters. In antebellum America, men were expected to be moral, but their primary duty was to provide and support their families, which necessitated living and working within the hard and vicious world of industrial America, where moral traits such as compassion and forgiveness were seen as signs of weakness, not virtue. Operating in this worldly sphere forced them to do aggressive, even vicious things for the sake of survival. To counter this corrupting influence, women were expected to uphold the high moral standards that men were forced to compromise. Women, insulated in the domestic sphere of house and home, were to embody the highest aspects of Christian morality, especially traits such as compassion, passivity, and gentleness that were crushed in the public sphere. They were to be self-sacrificing, Christlike figures that inspired and protected their husbands and sons from the corrupting influences of the world.[45] This explains why Willis expected that the spirits would chose to speak through "one of the virgins" not the older, more worldly wise Leah—he and the rest of antebellum America saw young girls as the most pure, self-sacrificing, and passive members of society, and thus the obvious medium for spirits. It also explains why his confidence and positive feelings about the sisters were increased when he noted their "simplicity," "unpretendingness," and passive willingness to allow their visitors to "have their own way."

The evening was a huge success for the Fox family. Both Willis and Ripley wrote highly favorable articles about the evening, and these circulated nationwide, gaining the sisters much positive exposure.[46] This press attention resulted in one of those instances when history provides such perfect foreshadowing that it seems to have been written by an omniscient author. In the early summer of 1850, Elisha Kane asked his family to promote him while he was in the arctic, and they did this, sending an article to Greeley about his heroic pre-arctic endeavors. At this same time Leah was also courting Greeley for publicity, which resulted in the previously mentioned séance. Out of pure coincidence, Greeley chose to run both the Kanes' and the Foxes' promotional articles in the same issue of the *Tribune*, on the same page, side by side.[47] Thus, even though they were thousands of miles apart and had not yet met, Kane and Fox were already appearing together before the public eye.

With all this good press, it was not long before the Foxes' rooms at Barnum's Hotel were filled with visitors, including many of the city's most prominent residents. Maggie and Kate were the talk of the town—spirit jokes began circulating;

Lithograph of the Fox sisters by N. Currier of Currier & Ives fame
(New York: N. Currier, 1852). Collection of Author.

Mary Taylor, a Broadway soloist, popularized the song, "The Rochester Knockings
at Barnum's"; and N. Currier of Currier & Ives fame produced a lithograph of the
Fox sisters.[48] Leah set up a rigorous schedule of three, two-hour public sittings daily,
beginning at 10:00 A.M., noon, and 8:00 P.M. These were conducted in a large
room around "a long table with thirty seats," and then during the afternoon, the
sisters held private sittings for one or two people in small, intimate quarters.[49]

Although many people judged the Fox sisters as just another entertaining
sideshow attraction like those that P. T. Barnum brought to town, a significant
number of visitors were not willing to dismiss them as humbug. Because of this,

the Foxes always had two different audiences and thus offered two types of séances: the thirty-person group séance that emphasized the performance of dramatic spiritual phenomena, and the intimate one-on-one séance. These different séance structures had very different purposes. The large ("promiscuous," as Leah called them) séances were meant to dazzle, mystify, and entertain an audience. Tables would dance, heavy objects would levitate, and at times hazy figures would appear and deliver ghostly messages from such famous spirits as Benjamin Franklin and Thomas Paine. People attended these séances because they were great entertainment, an exciting alternative to plays, music, or panorama shows. Few of these people ever became believers in spiritualism just as few people who attend magic shows today leave believing in magic. These people went for entertainment and they were entertained—no more and no less.[50]

Such people accounted for most of the Fox sisters' audiences, but they were not the people who propelled them to fame and made them an important part of nineteenth-century culture. The Foxes' cultural power came from the individuals who attended the small, intimate séances and became firm supporters, or critics, of spiritualism. At these small séances people expected specific answers to their questions; so, unlike their large séances, the Fox sisters' goal at these gatherings was to explain and clarify, not to confuse and mystify. The people who attended these intimate gatherings generally fell into two categories: scientific or religious investigators, or people in search of spiritual or psychological comfort. It is difficult today to imagine that so many people were "taken in" by what seems such an obvious hoax. This was true at the time as well; most nineteenth-century Americans dismissed spiritualism as humbug and saw those who believed in it as slightly mad. The popular editorialist "Uncle Toby" noted whimsically, "When a man used to hear strange noises and see strange shapes, his experiences were termed hallucinations, and his 'red monkeys' and 'dancing devils,' were attributable to Holland gin; but now they are caused by Rochester spirits, Fox brand! The discovery fully accounts for the milk in a great many cocoanuts."[51] Even spiritualism's devoted followers shunned the most flamboyant mediums and balked at the outrageous claims they made.[52] Much of America was dubious if not completely condemning of spiritualism, but those who did come to believe did so for compelling reasons. A brief examination of a few believers demonstrates this and helps to explain how and why the Fox sisters' spirit rappings moved from an obscure oddity in rural New York to a surprisingly influential religious movement of the 1850s.

The people who generated the most press, wrote the most books, and caused the most publicity (negative and positive) for spiritualists were "spiritual investigators"—individuals who sought to explain spiritualism on scientific or religious grounds. Whether these investigators found spiritualism to be true and good or false and evil, they proclaimed their findings loudly and focused attention on the movement. One of the best examples of such an investigator is Robert Hare. Hare was a professor at the University of Pennsylvania (where he served as one of Kane's medical instructors from 1839-1842) and one of the most celebrated chemists of his era. He began to investigate spiritualism late in his life and, much to the surprise of his colleagues, became a convinced believer. He built such elaborate devices as the *Spiritoscope* to empirically measure, and thus scientifically prove, spiritual manifestations. With this evidence in hand, he published *Experimental Investigation of the Spirit Manifestations* in 1855. In this 460-page volume, Hare attacked the atheistic positivism of French mathematician and philosopher Auguste Comté, noting that under Comté's influence, "Religion and science [have]... been made to travel in opposite directions" thus destroying any hope for linking theology and science. Spiritualism was doing just the opposite; it caused science and religion "to travel together in the same direction." Hare felt that his work with spiritualism was absolutely critical because it alone could save Christianity from scientific annihilation. Given the way science was going, he felt it would eventually "consolidate all the matter in the universe into an inert lump" by systematically removing all ethereal presence in nature. He thus saw spiritualism as religion's last hope because its physical manifestations, such as the Fox sisters' raps, could be observed and measured and thus provide scientific proof of the existence of a spiritual realm. Without this proof, Hare was certain that religious belief would not survive the nineteenth century.[53]

University of Pennsylvania Professor Robert Hare developed this "spiritoscope" to detect and prove the existence of the spiritual realm. From *Frank Leslie's Illustrated Newspaper* (December 15, 1855).

Scientific proof, in a rather interesting logical twist, became one of spiritualism's greatest assets because many antebellum thinkers began arguing that spiritualism was "making an important contribution to empirical science."[54] Reverend Charles Hammond (one of the Foxes' earliest supporters) wrote of his research on the spirits and claimed that he had "found by actual experiment" that spirits could move his hand against his will.[55] More importantly, the first spiritualist book, Andrew Jackson Davis's 1847 *The Principles of Nature,* which predated the Fox sisters' fame, was laid out as a scientific treatise designed to prove spiritual revelation. The language of science dominated the literature of spiritualism, and many nineteenth-century men and women saw spiritualism as just another new branch of science. The Partridge & Brittan publishing company's advertisements attest to this fact. In 1853 they were selling at least twelve different works dealing with some aspect of the relationship between science and spiritualism.[56] Spirit raps hardly seemed outlandish; they didn't seem any more improbable than the amazing new telegraph that could transfer messages across vast spaces via seemingly magical raps, and, like electricity and magnetism, many people saw spiritual manifestations as just another phenomenon that could be measured and examined, but not yet fully explained.[57]

Even when scientific investigators' experiments proved spiritualism false, their findings still brought attention, and even support, to the movement. In February of 1851, three doctors in Buffalo, New York, investigated the Fox sisters and came to the conclusion that the spirit raps were actually made by the sisters popping their knee joints. These men, doctors Austin Flint, Charles A. Lee, and C. B. Coventry, published their findings in the *Buffalo Medical Journal* and in a local paper. Leah immediately challenged them to prove their findings publicly and the ensuing rounds of exhibitions only gained the Foxes more followers. Seeing this result, the doctors abandoned their efforts, which allowed Leah to declare the whole ordeal a victory for spiritualism.[58] Dr. Lee, bitter that the Foxes gained supporters from his work to disprove them, decided to take a different tack. He found a man who could pop his ankles and give "a more *striking* illustration of 'spiritual knockings' than the Foxes ever dreamed of." He then began touring through upstate New York, demonstrating that the raps had a logical explanation by having this man pop his ankles. To his surprise and disgust, he found that "several in the audience... became zealous converts to the doctrine of Spiritualism, and still refer to my exhibition as the strongest kind of demonstrative argument in its support." As he later wrote, he was shocked and horrified by this turn of events and, "abandoned the project, and begg[ed] my assistant to rap no more."[59]

Scientists and doctors were not the only skeptics who investigated the raps; religious zealots engaged and examined the Fox sisters as well. New York Supreme Court Justice John Worth Edmonds' investigations resulted in one of the first and most persuasive religious explanations of spiritualism. He attended one of the Fox sisters' early séances in Rochester and was immediately convinced of spiritualism's power and truth. After attending many more séances, and with the help of medical doctor George T. Dexter, he put together a two-volume work entitled *Spiritualism*. This work caused a huge sensation because Edmonds, a respected judge and community leader, declared that spiritualism was the most important religious event since the crucifixion of Jesus. He summed up spiritualism's importance by outlining the seven key theological points it proved:

1. The existence of man after life on earth is demonstrated beyond all peradventure....
2. That we are not by death separated from those whom we have loved on earth....
3. It has been demonstrated what death is, and thus it has been robbed of the undefined and mysterious terrors which have been thrown around it....
4. [T]hat our most secret thoughts can be known to and be revealed by the intelligence which is... surrounding us and communicating with us....
5. [T]hat our conduct in this life, in a great measure, elaborates our destiny hereafter, and that our happiness in the next stage of existence depends not upon our adherence to this or that sectarian faith....
6. We are taught the grand doctrine of Progression.... That man, neither here nor in any future existence, is governed by miracle, but only by universal laws which were from the beginning and have no end....
7. We are taught what is the state of existence into which man is ushered after the life on earth.[60]

Edmonds's work established the closest thing spiritualists had to a unified theology and it gained the movement support among mainstream Christian Americans. This spiritualist theology abandoned the idea of Hell and professed a happy afterlife. It also placed greater importance on one's actions than on any specific religious faith. This was a direct challenge to Calvinist doctrine because it denied any need for divine intervention or salvation through grace, and it took away the flaming brimstone pit of hell that had powered Calvinism's sermons since the time of Jonathan Edwards' "Sinners in the Hands of an Angry God." Many ministers, such as Charles Hammond, saw these new ideas as liberating and began writing books and preaching sermons on how spiritualism fit well into traditional Christianity and provided the next step toward the millennial kingdom. These ministers often became mediums themselves and would incorporate spirit-inspired ceremonies and rituals into their traditional religious services.[61]

Still, this was not the norm. Most clergy saw spiritualism as nothing less than the workings of the Antichrist. William R. Gordon was one such minister and his 1856 book, *A Three-fold Test of Modern Spiritualism,* is an excellent representation of how these men sought to expose the evils of spiritualism. Gordon studied Judge Edmonds' spirit theology and the articles in *Christian Spiritualism,* and then set up three tests to determine the movement's veracity. These tests were: 1. To visit several mediums and carefully observe them; 2. To study what different mediums said and to see if their messages were consistent; and 3. To see what the Bible said about the subject.[62] What Gordon found was Satan himself. After the first test, he was convinced that many mediums were truly communicating with spirits, but in his next test he found that the spirit voices were unreliable and tricky. His final test of careful Bible study revealed to him that the spirit voices were not the voices of deceased friends or relatives, as the mediums claimed, but the voices of Satan and his minions. Gordon did not hold mediums or their supporters culpable for this evil, but believed instead that they had been duped by the "Great Deceiver." He showed how Edmonds' message was surely a work of evil because it denied "the grand leading doctrine of atonement for sin by the merits of Christ, upon which the Bible suspends human salvation." He concluded that such a denial of the Bible "is the very thing that... we might expect from Satanic agency."[63] Unfortunately for Gordon, what had been true of the naysaying scientific investigators was also true of negative religious investigations—they only drew more curious people to séance tables, thus increasing spiritualism's influence. After all, even though Gordon concluded that the raps were evil, he did so by "scientifically" proving that they were from an otherworldly realm. Witnessing such a phenomenon was hard for many Americans to resist.

The final group that regularly attended the Fox sisters' private séances consisted of individuals experiencing spiritual and psychological pain from the loss of a loved one. Although this group did not gain spiritualism much press, they did gain it credibility as a healing force. Many of the most powerful and influential people of the nineteenth century turned to mediums in times of despair and found in them the reassurance and solace they needed. In this way, spiritualism in the antebellum period, like psychotherapy today, was seen as a healing practice that balanced somewhere between the physical world of science and the intangible world of the mind and soul.

Modern studies have shown that when people are under great emotional stress and traditional means of dealing with it fail, they began looking to alternative sources for relief. This relief often comes in strange and inexplicable forms, ranging from Jungian dreams and Reichian screams to copper armbands and healing crystals. What is ultimately important is not the logical, factual, or provable "truth" of the healing agent, but the patient's belief that the healer can bring them solace.[64] In the nineteenth century, spiritualism served as a fringe healing practice that many people turned to when their religious and medical professionals could not help them. The Fox sisters' work with Harriet Beecher Stowe is a clear example of this.

Raised under the strict Calvinist teachings of her father Lyman Beecher, Harriet Beecher Stowe experienced several periods of depression in her young adult years because she feared for her soul and felt trapped by the domestic life that was expected of her. Stowe's life changed dramatically in 1852 when she became an international celebrity after publishing *Uncle Tom's Cabin*. Success and fame did not bring happiness, however, and the death of her son, Henry, who drowned in a swimming accident at Dartmouth College in 1857, threw her into a deep state of depression.[65]

Stowe greatly feared for her son's soul because her Calvinist faith held that he was barred from entering heaven because he had never experienced conversion. A month after the accident, Stowe wrote to her sister Catharine Beecher, saying that "the most agonizing doubts of Henry's state were thrown into my mind—as if it had been said to me—You trusted in God did you?—you believed that he loved you—you had perfect confidence that he would never take your child till the work of grace was mature—& now he has hurried him out without warning without a moments preparation—& where is he[?]"[66]

Stowe's faith was in large part the cause of her distress. As the daughter of one of America's foremost Calvinist ministers and the wife of a respected Calvinist theologian, Stowe respected and admired this belief system; however, she also found its cold, intellectual God completely incapable of providing her the comfort she craved. In times of severe depression, Stowe often turned to many of the era's more common "cures." She spent several months in the Water Cure clinic in Brattleboro, Vermont, for both physical and mental ailments, and she also experimented with Dr. Taylor's Swedish Movement Cure.[67]

Though these treatments brought Stowe some relief, her greatest solace came from spiritualists. In the years following Henry's death, Stowe participated in at least four small-group séances with the Fox sisters.[68] Stowe explained these to her friend and fellow author Elizabeth Barrett Browning, noting that even though she was no "seeker after signs and wonders," spiritual evidence of her son Henry just kept appearing. She had received five definite messages from Henry, and "the news is always the same—of sadness and sorrow at first—of *increase* in improvement, joy, and peace at last reaching the beatific." When these revelations came to her, Stowe said she did "what Mary did—'Keep and ponder them in my heart,'" and she confessed that "I do at times have that vague shadowy sense of the presence of spirits beloved, especially in [times of] great trouble and perplexity which is at any rate a comfort to me."[69] Browning's response to this letter helps explain how and why people were willing to overlook the shadier aspects of spiritualism and accept it as legitimate. "I don't know how people can keep up their prejudices against spiritualism with tears in their eyes, how they are not at least thrown on the wish that it might be true... by the abrupt shutting in their faces of the door of death, which shuts them out from the sight of their beloved. My tendency is to beat up against it like a crying child."[70]

The use of spiritualism to bring relief from grief and depression became common in the 1850s, much like psychiatric counseling is today. In 1853, one month before his presidential inauguration, Franklin Pierce and his wife Jane witnessed their eleven-year-old son's death in a horrible train accident. In the coming months they sent for Maggie Fox several times, asking her to lead them in séances so they could say their last goodbyes.[71] New York *Tribune* editor Horace Greeley and his wife had Kate and Maggie stay with them for a month in the fall of 1850 to help them communicate with their dead son, Arthur. After the death of their son Willie, Abraham and Mary Lincoln invited each of the Fox sisters to visit the White House to hold séances to communicate with him.[72] Near the time of his death, James Fenimore Cooper wrote that he was "deep in the Rochester Knockings" and was reported to have sent a letter from his deathbed thanking the Fox sisters for "hav[ing] prepared me for this hour."[73] Each of these people sat at the Foxes' séance table for the same reasons that people sit on a psychiatrist's couch today—for relief from mental anguish. It is primarily the result of a changing culture that today psychotherapy and counseling are deemed legitimate healing practices and spiritualism a hoax. As Jerome Frank found in his study of psychology and healing, changes in "cultural norms and world views influence not only the definition of mental illness but also the nature of its treatment."[74] Rapping spirits make as much sense as the Id and Ego of Freudian thought, and they were equally capable of helping people deal with mental suffering. This is well illustrated in a 1931 biography of James Fenimore Cooper. Written at a time when spiritualism and Freudian psychoanalysis were viewed with equal skepticism, the biographer concluded his discussion of Cooper's involvement with spiritualism saying, "These things were a fad of the 1840s and 1850s as Freudism and psychoanalysis were in the 1920s. The later toys may seem quainter twenty years from now than the elder ones. Talk of inhibitions and repressions! Our grandfathers were at least free to dream of their grandams without shame."[75]

Taken together, the antebellum period's therapeutic use of spiritualism, combined with the intense investigation of the phenomenon on religious and scientific levels, explain why the Fox sisters became so well known in the 1850s. Their séances provided entertainment for many people while filling religious, scientific, and psychological needs for others. What is more difficult to understand, however, is how Maggie and Kate viewed themselves and their growing notoriety as spiritual mediums. Late in their lives they authorized a tell-all biography in which they insisted that they were innocent victims of Leah's aggressive agenda and spiritualists' naïve enthusiasm.[76] They left few letters, making it difficult to guess at their inner thoughts during these early years, and the sources that are available can easily be interpreted in conflicting ways. The two best biographies of Kate and Maggie, though both well-researched and argued, disagree about Kate and Maggie's thoughts and motivations during the early years of their popularity. Nancy Rubin Stuart's *The Reluctant Spiritualist: The Life of Maggie Fox* (2005) asserts that Maggie and Kate, despite their obvious charisma and unique money-making abilities, were ultimately young, unmarried women in an era that granted them little power and even fewer legal rights. This reality forced them to rely on their family or supporters for their economic and social well-being, leaving them little room for autonomy. Barbara Weisberg acknowledges this reality, but portrays the sisters in a different light in *Talking to the Dead: Kate and Maggie Fox and the Rise of Spiritualism* (2004). Influenced by Anne Braude's view of spiritualists as early feminists, Wiesberg portrays Maggie and Kate as assertive young women, calling attention to the occasions when they aggressively pushed their own agendas despite Leah's and others' objections. According to the sisters' own account written decades after their initial success, their meteoric rise as spiritual mediums caused them to struggle to define their own identities. Such a struggle would explain why their careers were marked by several vascillations between embracing and denying spiritualism. It also helps explain why Maggie, at the height of her fame in the early 1850s, would suddenly abandon her life as a spiritualist and allow her new love, Elisha Kent Kane, to re-create her as a "proper lady" suitable to be his wife.

As Maggie and Kate confessed late in their lives, the whole spirit-rapping phenomenon began when they, as young girls "full of petty devilment," tied apples to strings and bounced them on the floor to frighten their superstitious mother. When Mrs. Fox began to investigate the rappings, they hid the apples but continued their trickery by making similar noises by snapping their fingers. They soon discovered they could snap their toes as well, and, with a little practice, "got so we could do it with hardly an effort." Mrs. Fox began thinking the pops were made by spirits, which delighted the girls, and their ability to trick their neighbors as well only added to the fun. They claimed they never intended to do any harm, but as Maggie explained, "Soon it went so far, and so many persons had heard the 'rappings' that we could not confess the wrong without exciting very great anger on the part of those we had deceived. So we went right on."[77]

Just weeks after their first raps, E. E. Lewis assembled his pamphlet on the rappings and its publication attracted the notice of Leah. When Leah arrived in Hydesville she immediately realized what was causing the raps and made Maggie and Kate undress and show her exactly how it was done. She then took them back to Rochester and, according to Kate and Maggie, began planning ways to use this trick for profit. For the girls this was all great fun. Leah encouraged their mischievous antics by helping them expand their tricks to include poltergeist-like crashes that they used to terrorize Calvin Brown, Leah's superstitious friend (and later second husband), who was boarding with them at the time. Leah began inviting other people to the house, including the radical reformers Amy and Isaac Post, and helped the girls trick them as well. Leah and the girls developed a system of discreet signals that allowed Leah to provide Maggie and Kate with messages that they would then rap out to the amazement of their audiences. This continued for the next year, and during this time Leah slowly worked at convincing her younger sisters that what they were doing was not just a trick, but the spirits working through them for the betterment of humanity. She told them that their ability to rap was a God-given gift that they were obliged to use to help spirits make contact with humans and bring about a new era of Christianity. She reinforced this by asserting that, before either of them were born, she had "received messages warning her that they were destined to do great things."[78]

It is impossible to know exactly what Maggie and Kate thought of all this, but it is certain that they kept rapping as Leah instructed and enjoyed the excitement and travel of their lives as spiritual mediums. In a rare surviving letter from the period, Maggie wrote to Amy Post from Hydesville, complaining that she missed the "noise and Confusion of the city" and that she "had become so accustomed to the rattling of carriages and ringing of bells" that were a part of her nomadic, hotel-based life as a spiritual medium that the silence of the country kept her awake at night.[79] It is also clear that they were not nearly as artless and naïve about their abilities at this time as they would later claim. As noted earlier, in the spring of 1850 the *Rochester Daily American* wrote a bemused article, explaining that Kate and Maggie had revolted against Leah, refusing to participate in any further seances until she agreed to "fork over" more of the money their labors generated. Leah initially refused, but when she realized that neither spirits nor paying customers visited her home without them, she relented and Maggie and Kate returned.[80]

Though they enjoyed the economic gains of their rapid celebrity, the effect spiritualism had on Kate and Maggie's adolescent minds was considerable, and later in their lives both sisters agonized over their role in spiritualism. To some degree, both Maggie and Kate came to believe that their conscious trickery (which felt evil) did actually serve as a corridor to true spiritual communication for many people (which was good).[81] Though such self-deception seems odd, psychologist Jerome Frank found in his study of shamans and their power to heal that at a shift in the understanding of spiritual agency commonly occurs in faith healers. He discovered that although shamans know that much of their "magic" is merely a trick, they come to believe in their power because they repeatedly witness their followers benefiting from it. A shaman's knowledge of his own trickery "is not able to withstand his own successes and the belief of his group in his powers," and so eventually he too comes to believe.[82]

When the sisters traveled to New York and later to Philadelphia, Washington, D.C., Baltimore, Ohio, and as far west as St. Louis, they were struggling with these issues, but amazed by their successes and by the many important people who believed in their powers. Many other respectable people doubted and condemned them, however, and this too weighed on their minds. They thus alternated between enjoying their lives, thriving on the thrill of pushing their tricks further and further, and despising their lives and desperately seeking some sign to prove to themselves the truth of spiritualism. Their Ohio tour of 1851 is telling of this. Much of the trip was exhilarating. C. Chauncey Burr, a long-time lecturer and practitioner of such "sciences" as Electro-Biology and Animal Magnetism, had found he could draw larger crowds by popping his knees and thus debunking spiritualism generally and the Fox sisters specifically.[83] The girls enjoyed the competition this caused. Kate wrote to Amy Post, "Oh Amy the Spirits do such wonderful things. They ring the bells [and] move the tables all when our feet are held. We have convinced many skeptical people of the truthfulness of Spiritual communications."[84] By this time Maggie and Kate were seventeen and fourteen years old and were overtly challenging Leah's authority. Lemira Kedzie, a devout spiritualist and friend of the Post family, accompanied the girls to Cleveland and hoped to take them on an extensive tour of the West. Maggie and Kate initially refused, but by July they were playing Kedzie and Leah off each other. Leah knew she needed one of her younger sisters with her because crowds did not respond well when she ran séances alone, but managing them was increasingly difficult. They delighted in dreaming up new schemes for promoting the spirits, stirring up trouble among supporters, and then avoiding all responsibility for their actions by hiding behind their well-advertised innocent and childlike personas. How could they be blamed for anything? They were only naïve young girls who passively did the will of the spirits. By late July, Leah was exasperated. She wrote to Amy Post, exclaiming that "much of my trouble is caused by the girls, who are always planning out something and then if they fail in their calculations; they throw the whole thing on me." She noted that all the trouble between she and Kedzie stemmed from the girls' manipulative actions, which included writing letters to Kedzie's husband, trying to gain his favor. She concluded, "I can tell you truly if it had not been for them, I should never differ with Many—but they are always working so underhandedly that I am tired, tired of Life or in other words of so much deception."[85]

When Leah complained of "so much deception" she was specifically addressing her sisters' schemes that brought tension between her and Kedzie, but her statement was also true at a deeper level. Maggie and Kate enjoyed being celebrities and were energized by the challenge of baffling the skeptical and convincing the unsure, but this came at a price. As Maggie later confessed, she was often plagued with feelings of guilt, doubt, and confusion during this time. She knew the source of the raps and that she was willfully manipulating and misleading people with them.

Observing her own mother reminded her of this daily. Mrs. Fox had left her home to endure the sneers and jibes of crowds because she was a true believer, never doubting the veracity of her young daughters and the spirits that surrounded them. This devotion exasperated Maggie, whose feelings alternated between anger and pity toward her mother. She wrote, "I can well remember how my heart used to smite me at times when I looked upon her and knew that Katie and I were the cause of all her trouble."[86] Maggie began to question her perceived reality, wondering if she truly but unknowingly *was* a medium for the spirits. She began her own quest for spiritual manifestations, going to graveyards in the middle of the night and sitting on gravestones so "the spirits of those who slept underneath might come to me." When nothing happened she was left feeling dejected and fearful for her own salvation.[87] Despite her misgivings, however, her success continued to grow. She and Kate toured almost constantly for the next year and this firmly established them as the most visible and prominent practitioners among spiritualism's ever-growing numbers.

So it was that in October 1852, just days before her nineteenth birthday, Maggie Fox, accompanied by her mother, checked into the Bridal Suite of Philadelphia's Union Hotel to begin yet another series of séances.[88] In the three years that had passed since the spirit raps at Corinthian Hall, she had toured the nation and gained the support and respect of thousands. Her services were sought by the most influential people of the era and generated more than $100 per day—a shocking sum in an era when a laboring man made a dollar a day.[89] A daguerreotype from this time shows Maggie poised, attractive, and confident. She had the uncanny ability to read people, to perceive what they wanted to hear, and to deliver it in a way that made them believe it was true. Spirits or no spirits, this was the power of Maggie Fox.

In many ways, Elisha Kent Kane was in a very similar position in the fall of 1852. In the past three years he had moved from a wealthy but unknown member of Philadelphia society to a widely known explorer famous for his daring adventures. Like Fox, he had become an expert at understanding what people wanted to hear, and had learned to mold his persona to fit public expectations. Furthermore, he too had spent months living in hotels as he toured the nation, promoting the exploration of the Open Polar Sea, a mysterious place that was almost as otherworldly as the Fox sisters' spirit world. In these ways, Fox and Kane had a common motivation and drive in their lives. Both were self-made celebrities, both were the spokespersons for a cause many Americans viewed as important and noble, and both had learned how to carry and promote themselves in a way that instilled confidence in others, if not themselves. These similarities could account for the immediate attraction between them, or perhaps it was something much

Daguerreotype of Maggie and Kate Fox by Thomas M. Easterly (1852). Courtesy of the Missouri History Museum, St. Louis.

more basic—they were, after all, both attractive, charismatic young adults, which is in and of itself more than enough to explain the fickle blossoming of love.

Their relationship began in October 1852 when Elisha sought out the famed spirit-rapper for what were probably a variety of reasons. Primarily, he was curious. Kane never became a spiritualist and always publicly asserted that the whole thing was humbug, but he read the Fox sisters' ad in the penny papers and heard from friends that it was a good show, and so decided to attend.[90] This was not the Kane family's first contact with the Fox sisters. Tom met Kate in December 1850 when New York *Tribune* editor Horace Greeley invited him to his house saying, "Kate Fox is still with us, and may puzzle you with the 'Mysterious Rappings.' I think they are part humbug and can't find out the trick. Suppose you try?"[91] Kate was at the Greeley's to help them communicate with their beloved son who had recently passed away, and this points to another reason Elisha may have sought out Maggie—his brother Willie had died in August, just two months before Maggie's arrival in Philadelphia. The Kane family took Willie's death very hard; they sold their mansion and moved into the city because their house held too many memories of their lost loved one.[92] Elisha had stayed at Willie's side during the last weeks of his life, and when he died, Elisha became so depressed that his family worried that he too would collapse into illness and death. Trying to cheer him up, his mother wrote, "if we could only see [Willie] as he is, a glorified being, in the bosom of his Savior, our grief would be subdued"—a statement that could have easily prompted him to seek the services of a spiritualist.[93]

It is impossible to know whether Elisha discussed Willie's death with Maggie during his visits to her séance table, and if he did, whether he felt they helped him. It is certain, however, that something did happen during this time to improve Elisha's mental and physical state. By mid-October he had canceled his trip to the Brattleboro Water Cure Clinic and was back to his energetic self, seeking out support and supplies for his expedition and finishing his book for the Harper Brothers.[94] By December, Elisha was calling at the Union Hotel on a regular basis, not for the ethereal comfort of the spirits, but for the very corporeal pleasure of seeing their attractive young medium. Though Fox's busy séance schedule and Kane's travel and writing often kept them apart, they found time for frequent carriage rides. Notes from Elisha often reached Maggie between séances:

> My Dear Miss Fox:— The day is so beautiful that I feel tempted to repent my indoor imprisonment. If you will do me the kindness... and take a quiet drive, I will call for you at your own hour. With respect, very faithfully your servant, E. K. Kane[95]

Elisha also developed a friendly relationship with Mrs. Fox and got to know Kate and Leah because he carried letters to them for Maggie and Mrs. Fox when he went to New York on business. In all ways he behaved like a proper suitor. He sent letters and gifts to Maggie, but always through Mrs. Fox, whom he praised for being "carefully fastidious as to forms."[96] There is no hint that he thought this relationship inappropriate or in any way damaging to either of their reputations. He introduced Maggie to his friends and family in Philadelphia, and when he went to New York to lecture before the American Geographical Society—a very important meeting in which he laid out his plans for accessing the Open Polar Sea and officially announced the launching of the Second Grinnell Expedition—he gathered up several friends and took them to Leah's Twenty-Sixth Street home for a séance.[97]

Not long thereafter, however, Elisha's feelings about his relationship with Maggie changed. Though he still professed his love for her, almost overnight he switched from happily attending séances to demanding that she give up spiritu-alism. He began to scold her for a myriad of offences of propriety and refused to be seen with her in public. The root of this change appears to have been Elisha's realization that he was truly in love with her. If he simply saw her as a friend (as he publicly claimed) or as a fling (as many of his friends suspected), there would have been no need for him to demand changes in her behavior. As his previous life well illustrated, he was not opposed to illicit liaisons with less-than-respectable women; however, if Elisha truly wanted to marry Maggie, then it was essential that her public persona change.

Raised in a family that was constantly aware of social standing and governed by a strict sense of propriety, Elisha realized the host of problems that barred him—a socially elite, scientifically respected explorer—from marrying a girl who worked in the public sphere and participated in a movement that many consid-ered humbug at best and outright evil at worst. Thus, when Maggie returned to New York and he left for Washington in January 1853, Elisha became fanatical about wanting to know and control all of Maggie's actions.[98]

This was a difficult time for Elisha because many demands were pressing upon him. Though Henry Grinnell (his primary backer) and George Peabody (a wealthy American merchant living in London) had donated a ship and enough funds for basic supplies, he still needed funding from the government and an official release from the navy if his expedition was to go forward. To this end he spent several weeks in Washington to promote his cause with lectures and direct appeals to high-ranking officials, especially Secretary of the Navy John P. Kennedy, who was sym-pathetic to his cause.[99] Harpers was also pressuring him to complete the rest of his chapters and to make final arrangements for the printing of his illustrations, which they still felt were too expensive.[100] On top of all this, Elisha was also be-ginning to realize the ominous task that loomed before him. Since his return from the first expedition, he had promoted a second expedition to the Polar Sea with such bold speeches and detailed charts that the whole thing had come to seem simple—he would sail into the Open Polar Sea, find Sir John Franklin, and re-turn home a hero. Now that the expedition was coming together, however, the magnitude of his proposal came into terrifying focus. He, a thirty-three-year-old physician who had never commanded a ship, was about to lead a crew of men with almost no arctic experience to a location that had never been seen to rescue a man who was most likely dead. To get there, he would have to endure ship-crushing ice floes, bitter cold, months of darkness, hunger, scurvy, and conditions that had killed many far-more experienced explorers. Given these realities, it is hardly sur-prising that in the cold winter months of 1853 Elisha's letters to Maggie suddenly became desperately passionate. He demanded that she abandon her public life, work at becoming a "proper lady," and agree to faithfully await his return from the arctic—a location that seemed far more forlorn than the graves that divided her rapping spirits from the land of the living.

To this end, Elisha began attempting to transform Fox into a proper woman who would be acceptable in his social circles. This process often involved harsh, almost cruel reprimands. Despairing at her resistance to change, he wrote, "You are refined and loveable; and, with a different education, would have been inno- cent and artless; but you are not worthy of a permanent regard from me. You could never lift yourself up to my thoughts and my objects; *I* could never bring myself *down* to yours."[101] In the months that followed, Elisha actively tried to reform Mag- gie, who alternately embraced and resisted his efforts. Both his effort and her re- sistance are intriguing because they provide insights into the fundamental ideas and ideals of nineteenth-century gender relations.

As many scholars of nineteenth-century America have noted, the realities of in- dustrialization, urbanization, and mass immigration caused Americans to construct a strict division between the public sphere of business, commerce, and public af- fairs, and the domestic sphere of the home and family. As the public sphere was seen as a place of fierce competition that often necessitated force, violence, and even immoral behavior to succeed, it was deemed an improper place for women. Men would battle in this public sphere to provide for their families and, at the end of the day, would return home for solace and comfort—a protected space where morals never had to be compromised for the sake of survival. This protected home space was women's domain. There they tenaciously guarded the ideals of Christian generosity, selflessness, and compassion—the attributes of "civilized" society that were compromised and crushed in the public sphere of competition.

In many ways, Maggie Fox embodied the attributes of the private sphere per- fectly. She conducted her séances in the parlorlike setting of hotel suites, and, by passively submitting to the will of the spirits, she offered comfort and consolation to those battered by the harsh realities of life. In other revolutionary ways, how- ever, she was flying in the face of these conventions. She was clearly a public fig- ure. She dealt with dozens of people every day, embraced public attention, and essentially ran her own business. Her séance room had the appearance of the do- mestic sphere, but it was unquestionably public space. It was hired by the hour and she and her sisters engaged in intimate conversations with anyone who had a dol- lar to spend. They were publicly selling the private intimacy that the home was to guard. This was a direct threat to the division of public and private spheres, and the sale of such social intimacy seemed tantamount to prostitution to many of the era, Elisha certainly included.

Elisha based his reputation on attributes that Americans valued, such as sci- entific precision and a patriotic sense of honor and duty. He publicly justified all his adventures in these terms: He climbed into an active volcano to take scientific samples of its sulfuric lake; he scaled the monument in the Valley of the Kings to discover its hidden hieroglyphs; he fought renegade Mexican troops because of honor and duty; and he explained his trips to the arctic in terms of both scientific discovery and humanitarian relief. By justifying his daring feats in noble and scientific terms, Kane was able to project himself as a complete hero. He was famous not because he did sensational things, but because he did them for respectable purposes. The fame he achieved was thus different than the celebrity achieved by those who did not justify their fame via such terms. This difference between respectable fame and notorious celebrity is important and can be seen by comparing Kane's fame with the fame achieved by P. T. Barnum and his sideshow celebrities.

When Barnum presented a new sensation like the Fiji Mermaid or George Washington's one hundred sixty year-old nanny, Joyce Heth, he did so with a nudge and a wink, allowing the public to make up their own mind and to enjoy the show as purely entertainment. When Elisha displayed the pelt of a polar bear or lectured on the Open Polar Sea, he was in many ways little different from Barnum's shows. The public attended both events largely because they wanted to be amazed and fascinated, but though these events were consumed similarly, they were perceived differently. When people left Barnum's Museum, they felt amused and entertained, knowing, or at least suspecting, that they had been "humbugged." When they left Kane's lectures, however, they felt educated and enlightened—they believed that they were in some way now a part of his noble effort.[102]

Though spiritualists insisted that spirits were real and strove to provide scientific proof of their existence, most people attended their public séances for the same reasons they attended Barnum's Museum—to be entertained. The fact that New Yorkers had initially assumed (incorrectly) that the Fox sisters were employed by Barnum demonstrates this. They saw tables dance, instruments mysteriously played, and shadowy figures appear, and even though they were amazed, most assumed it was all a trick. Most séance goers attended primarily to be amused, not enlightened. Maggie was thus seen by most of the American public (herself sometimes included) as an attraction, not as a serious investigator of the spirits. If Elisha connected himself to such a person, he feared it would hurt his credibility.

In his study of antebellum America, David Chapin describes the emergence of a "culture of curiousity." The era's image-conscious public felt obliged to justify their entertainment choices and so public presentations began to advertise themselves "as both amusement and useful education." Examples include lyceum and lecture circuit speakers, who promised to entertain as well as edify, and panorama and magic lantern presentations (early forms of visual entertainment) that presented exciting images of foreign lands and mysterious forces designed to inform as well as awe. Chapin contends that Kane's lectures and books promoting arctic exploration, and Maggie and the Fox sisters "come and investigate" style of séances, each fed antebellum Americans' desire to be both enlightened and entertained. Although Kane was "coming from a world of Enlightenment and gentility" and Maggie from "a far more disordered and dynamic world of reformers, performers, and followers of popular pseudo-sciences," both were "headed in the same direction." As Kane promoted his arctic expeditions and Maggie her spiritualist séances, they were both "learning to tap into the antebellum American love of the unknown... learning how to perform, how to tell stories in a way that the American mass audience found interesting"[103]

Elisha's lectures were always seen as highly respectable and educational—if they were entertaining as well, that was just all the more to his credit. That the Fox sisters and other spiritualists constantly had to advertise and argue that they were engaged in scientific modes of investigation illustrates that the public did not see them in this way. Their séances were part of the popular quest for mind-spirit connections that also spawned experiments in mesmerism, animal magnetism, clairvoyance, and phrenology. These fields were much discussed and their presentations well attended, but they never gained the cultural cachet of a scientific lecture. Chapin explained that this discrepancy meant that Kane could gain "a level of cultural authority in America that Fox could never achieve." This cultural authority allowed him to become "a symbol of American moral and scientific progress," whereas Fox remained primarily an "antebellum curiosity... her spirit-rapping represented progress to some, to others it was a mark of moral and intellectual decline."[104]

That the public saw Kane's endeavors as respectable but viewed Fox's with skepticism also had some basis in monetary considerations. Kane was engaged in the scientific exchange of ideas in a way that Fox never was, and this was largely responsible for his superior credibility, but one of the other attributes that led the public to view him as noble and scientifically minded was that he was not lecturing for his own monetary gain. Elisha used some of the funds he raised to cover his expenses, but, as he continually reminded the public, the majority of the money he raised went directly toward funding his arctic expedition. This proved to the public that he was sincere and noble. Financial security allowed Elisha to do this; his basic expenses were covered partly by the U.S. Navy, and his family provided him with everything else.

This was a key difference between him and Maggie. The Fox sisters also presented themselves as professionals and appealed to scientific "proof," but they charged for their services and openly gained monetarily from them. They did this because they had to—it was how they made a living. The public saw this as a sign of insincerity, however, which was a fact that Leah recognized as she felt compelled to justify their fees, explaining that they often had expenses of $150 per week and were forced to rely on the fees for their basic needs.[105] In the cut-throat market economy of the antebellum period, the general perception was that if people were doing something for monetary gain, it was by definition more suspect than if they were doing it voluntarily. Elisha had the luxury of being able to work for little or no money. The Fox sisters did not. Thus, as one national magazine of the time noted, they were considered "cunning girls" who used their skills for "personal and pecuniary profit," not for the sake of science and humanity.[106]

The disparities in authority between Elisha and Maggie's cultural, financial, and gender roles largely explain Elisha's belief that Maggie had to be re-educated if their relationship was to continue. The program he set up for her betterment in many ways mirrored those outlined in the popular literature of the time. Susan Warner's hugely successful novel, *The Wide, Wide World* (1850)—which literary scholar Jane Tompkins describes as "the Ur-text of the nineteenth-century United States" because it "embodies, uncompromisingly, the values of the Victorian era"— is about an innocent but misguided girl, Ellen Montgomery, who is educated by, and eventually wedded to, the much older John Humphreys, after he taught her how to be a proper lady.[107] Though there is no evidence that Elisha asked Maggie to read this book, he did have her read many others like it. Early in their relationship he gave her a copy of the German fairytale *Undine* by Friedrich De La Motte Fouquée, which tells of a wayward water nymph who loved a far-traveling knight and, by marrying him, reformed herself and gained a soul.[108]

Commenting on the educational program that Elisha set up for her, Maggie noted that he was of "the old school, and held chivalrously sacred the delicacy of the fair sex."[109] He wanted her to study foreign languages, literature, music, and decorum; to learn how to act, what to wear, and how to present herself properly in public; in short, to become a "true lady" who would fit into his privileged society. This type of education was not the norm of the day; that Maggie labeled it "old school" is telling of this fact. As education became accessible to more women, its emphasis shifted from ornamental activities to practical skills. In his 1853 book, *The Young Lady's Book; or, Principles of Female Education,* William Hosmer argued on Christian grounds that women should be given an education based on moral and domestic duties. After chapters on women's moral, intellectual, physical, and domestic education, he concluded with a chapter on "Ornamental Education" in which he warned that educating women in music and art was not only "enormously and unreasonably expensive" but "of no real use." "It is admitted," he said of women educated in these arts, "that they serve a temporary purpose as embellishments, but it will hardly be contended that they contribute anything to the general welfare of the individual, or of society."[110]

This was the wisdom of the day for mainstream Americans, but it was not the education Elisha wanted for his wife. He was a member of an elite society and did not want or need a practical wife. What he needed was a woman who would be elegant and charming in proper society, who knew the right things and the right people, and who would do nothing to hurt, and many things to enhance, his reputation. He loved Maggie's quick wit, perceptive mind, and childlike sense of fun, but he wanted all of these to be refined "like gold purified from the furnace." When they began courting, Elisha presented Maggie with a delicate camellia flower and said, "Like you, it must not be breathed upon."[111] What he wanted was exactly what Hosmer warned against—an "ornamental" woman.

To this end Elisha went so far as to write his own instructional literature for Maggie. In a poem entitled, "The Prophecy," he wrote, "Weary! weary is the life / By cold deceit oppressed" and concluded noting that if she did not change her ways, "Thou shalt live and die forlorn." He also wrote a longer poem on the same theme entitled, "A Story: Thoughts which ought to be those of Maggie Fox." This second work was signed, "Preacher," Maggie's telling nickname for Elisha, and in it he cautioned against the "dangers of living so continually in the public eye" and insisted that a strict division must be drawn between the home and the world.[112] At home, one was to show love and affection, weakness and fear. In public, one was to show none of these things, but always a calm, well-polished exterior. This is what upset Elisha most about spiritualism—its discussion of private issues in a public setting.[113] Dress was also important and he demanded that Maggie wear her "undersleeves and spencer *always* when you have company," and he sent her a "rich ladylike set" of these for "morning wear" and another "for evening occasions." He also instructed her on conduct in the presence of the opposite sex, scolding her for such offenses as leaning against the back of a man's chair and for walking through a bedroom with a man.[114]

Elisha proposed to Maggie in late January 1853. She confessed her love, but turned him down. As she explained later in life, she did this because she was "not disposed to open her maiden heart unreservedly to one who despised her associates, condemned her calling, and often thought himself bound in self-respect to give her up for ever."[115] Though she admired Elisha and was tempted by the respectable and socially "higher" life he offered, spiritualism had allowed her to gain an unusual degree of power, and she did not want to be controlled. During the next four months their relationship swung back and forth between statements of everlasting devotion and tragic farewells, as they locked horns over what each expected of the other and what their families felt about their relationship. Much of this drama was played out via letters because Elisha was busy traveling—giving lectures and preparing for his voyage—while Maggie moved from Philadelphia to Washington to New York, setting up séances in each location.[116] Their on-again-off-again relationship, though more extreme than most, was not atypical for the times. In her study of the love lives of nineteenth-century Americans, Karen Lystra argued

that as arranged marriages gave way to marriages of romance during the early nineteenth century, one consequence was that a woman needed to make very sure that
her suitor was serious, because if she lost her reputation without gaining a husband, she was destined to a life of poverty. Lystra noted that this reality "resulted
in the dominant motif of nineteenth-century American courtship: women setting
and men passing tests of love."[117]

For Maggie and Elisha this process was a lively series of letters in which he
pleaded for her love while she, often under the instruction of her mother, alternated between accepting his advances and pulling away for the sake of her reputation. This made for a strange dance, because even though Elisha was trying to
teach Maggie to be a demure and proper woman, he was also constantly begging
her for more affectionate words in her letters and for small tokens of her love, such
as locks of her hair. His letters often began with frantic reassertions of his love and
desperate requests for her affection. "Dear, Dear Maggie:—Have you ceased to care
for me? *me* whose devotion you now can see, and of whose true, steadfast love
every fibre of your heart assures you!" They often ended equally dramatically. "I
am very sick, and it was only last night that I made the discovery of not possessing
your love.... I shall always be your friend, and perhaps you are glad to get rid of me
in the other relation! God bless you."[118]

Elisha's dual desires for a demure, proper woman but a more expressive lover
are an excellent example of what Lystra called the "public-private division" that
she argued was a "basic organizing principle of nineteenth-century middle-class
culture."[119] Raised in "proper society," Elisha understood that words and gestures
of affection, such as those expressed in love letters or stolen moments alone, were
acceptable parts of the private sphere. If other people were present, however, such
gestures were strictly taboo. As etiquette books of the times warned, "Make no public exhibition of your endearments," and, "above everything... avoid being personal" in society.[120]

It is important to note that the differences between public and private spheres
extended into the press as well. Elisha worked diligently to keep his public life—
his Open Polar Sea theory, his expedition plans, and his thoughts on Sir John
Franklin's whereabouts—in the press. If the press ever began to shift from covering his work to covering his life, however, he became indignant. When an article
about one of his lectures spent more time describing (positively) his appearance
and demeanor than his speech, he wrote to Maggie, saying, "How disgusting is this
life, to be discussed by the papers!" The fact that he shunned even positive personal press shows the extent to which privacy was essential to him and why he so
greatly feared his love life becoming public. In an effort to keep their relationship
private, Elisha insisted that they use the code names "Cousin Peter" and "F. Webster" for all telegraph messages, and, even when they were in the same city, Elisha

would not openly visit Maggie "for fear of talk."[121] Instead, he would send messages, usually via Cornelius Grinnell, who had become like a brother to him. Grinnell would visit the Fox residence, pretending to be interested in a séance. He would then slip Elisha's letters to Maggie when Leah and Mrs. Fox (both had come to disapprove of the relationship) were not looking. Grinnell bemusedly described one of these escapades to Kane, saying, "I did not see Miss Maggie, but her sister Kate came to the door, and I gave her the letters. She said she would hand them to her sister.... I had hard work to deliver the notes, as the old wretch [Leah] kept a sharp look out upon me. But when her back was turned I slipped them into Kate's hand."[122] Grinnell came to enjoy the company of Kate and Maggie, and even though Kane objected, he eventually attended one of their séances. He wrote Elisha, "I cannot refrain from telling you that in company with several gentlemen, we had a most satisfactory exhibition of the rappings last evening at 26th Street. Every question was answered correctly and we left the house bewildered with astonishment."[123]

Because Cornelius got to know Maggie, Kane asked him to keep an eye on both her and Kate when he was not in New York. Cornelius readily agreed. "You may be assured that I shall take much pleasure in looking after the young ladies, and shall be happy to have it in my power to be of any service to them." He then asked if he could take them out from time to time because he felt Elisha's demands of privacy, coupled with their long hours of séances, were most oppressive. "I think it would almost be an act of charity to show them some little attention. It is a pity that they should be penned up in that gloomy hotel... all day, and then be exposed to the sneers & jokes of a set of ignorant, unfeeling fellows in the evening."[124]

Although she too disliked the idea of having her name in the papers, Maggie did not want their relationship to be a secret. The more public their relationship became, the more difficult it would be for Elisha to deny it and abandon her if he ever changed his mind. Given the way he handled his relationship with Julia Reed a few years earlier, making the relationship public was a wise strategy for Maggie, especially given the fact that she knew his family felt she was a low-class social climber who was taking advantage of their son. Elisha feared at times that his family was right. He saw how Maggie could lead her clients "by the nose" and wondered if she was "only cheating me in a different way."[125] The result of this tension was a very strained relationship. For example, Elisha invited Maggie to Satler's Cosmorama (a touring panoramic art show), but asked her to walk there on her own so their meeting would appear coincidental and thus excite no public speculation. Maggie flatly refused, saying, "The idea seems to me so unbecoming. I do not care half as much for strangers, or the opinion of others, as I do for myself." She then laid down her own ultimatum: "If you will call here I will go."[126]

Several times the strain of the relationship became too much for Elisha and he would call the whole thing off. He desperately loved Maggie, but recognized that the only way their relationship could work would be for one of them to give up the cause that defined them, and neither was willing to do that. In a passionate and pointed letter he wrote:

> Maggie, darling, don't care for me any more. I love you too well to wish it, and you know now that I really am *sold* to different destinies; for just as you have your wearisome round of daily money-making, I have my own sad vanities to pursue. I am as devoted to my calling as you, poor child, can be to yours. Remember then, as a sort of dream, that Doctor Kane of the Arctic Seas loved Maggie Fox of the Spirit-rappings.[127]

Even though he broke off their relationship, he kept writing as they each continued pursuing their causes. In mid-February 1853, Maggie and Kate were in Washington, D.C., busily entertaining legislators with spirit-raps, while Elisha was in Boston, trying to drum up more support for his expedition. In an especially lucid moment, Elisha wrote Maggie, "When I think of you, dear darling, wasting your time and youth and conscience for a few paltry dollars, and think of the crowds who come nightly to hear of the wild stories of the frozen north, I sometimes feel that we are not so far removed after all. My brain and your body are each the sources of attraction, and I confess that there is not so much difference."[128]

Maggie was not enjoying her time in Washington. She and Kate were constantly busy because they became a popular attraction for politicians, many of whom came not to investigate the spirits, but to gawk at the attractive young mediums. Maggie wrote Elisha after one séance: "They looked at me so incessantly that I nearly fainted," and Kate reported that a dozen senators, "as drunk as they could well be," forced them to flee the room after making several "mean, low remarks."[129] Elisha replied quickly and suggested that Maggie leave her life and dedicate herself to "the one person in all the world who... leads you to better ways by the cords of *love*."[130] In a rare and telling letter, Fox opened up to Elisha and began to question her own life.

> I have been thinking over the very tiresome life I have been living.... What have I ever done that I should be denied the pleasures of quiet home, the blessings of love—the reward of virtue? I have given my whole time to this subject for six years. I think I have done my part. I feel that I have convinced this skeptical unfeeling world that I am innocent of making these sounds. I ask no more.
>
> And now my dear dear friend—for you are the only human being that has ever urged me to better things—what shall I do when you leave for your distant pilgrimage of danger? Who then will extend to me a helping hand? For you I would do anything yet you will be with me no longer. Is there nothing now that I can do?

Can I not educate myself and then live in a sphere of usefulness and refinement by my own effort? Do come and talk this over with me for I have one of my fits of low spirits.[131]

Elisha responded immediately: "Dear Maggie, I will do all in my power for you and it may be that some plan can be hit upon which will fulfill your object.... Your life is worse than bad, it is sinful, and that you have so long resisted its temptations shows me that you were born for better things than to entertain strangers at a dollar a head. Do dear Maggie stick to your good resolutions. I will not depart one jot from my promises." He then agreed to arrange for her education and advised her to "avoid your wretched sister as much as possible"—Leah was then demanding that Maggie break off the relationship because she feared Elisha would steal away her movement's biggest medium and moneymaker.[132] Maggie told her mother about Elisha's offer to educate her, and Mrs. Fox, after some time, consented, much to Leah's consternation.[133]

By the end of March the Fox sisters were all back in New York City, and Elisha was darting between Washington, Philadelphia, and New York, making final arrangements for his expedition. During this time he also made plans for Maggie's education. After inspecting several schools, he followed the advice of his favorite aunt, Eliza Leiper, and arranged to have Maggie live with the Turner family of Crookville, Pennsylvania, a rural community just outside of Philadelphia—an ideal location for a young woman hoping to remake herself away from public view. As Eliza explained to Elisha, Suzanna Turner would be a perfect teacher and role model because her family was "unexceptionable, Mother & Daughters well informed, tastes cultivated, cheerful dispositions & religious."[134]

After agreeing to his plan, Maggie expected that Elisha would again propose to her, however, it was now Elisha's turn to hesitate. Though he was pleased with her willingness to be educated, he explained that it was impossible for him to commit himself until she proved that she was truly reformed and had given up spiritualism forever. In early April he wrote that "the opposition of society, of education, and of conscience" all prohibited him from proposing to her at that time. "If you really can make up your mind to abjure the spirits, to study and improve your mental and moral nature, it may be that a career of brightness will be open to you; and upon this chance, slender as it is, I offer, like a true friend, to guard and educate you."[135] This was the agreement they came to. While Elisha was on his journey to the arctic, Maggie would transform herself into a proper lady, and, if upon his return Elisha found that she had truly reformed, he would renew their relationship. Maggie viewed this as a promise of marriage. Elisha did not disabuse her of this notion.

Elisha moved to New York City in mid-April to make final arrangements for his expedition and to spend time with Maggie. Though he was often ill and still had much work to do, these were golden moments for the young couple. He still tried to avoid publicity, but he was no longer so guarded about publicly spending time with her. As May came to a close, Maggie began living up to her "solemn promise" never to rap again. It appears that her last séance was done for the president's wife, Jane Appleton Pierce, whose eleven-year-old son had just died in a horrible train accident. Elisha scolded her for this transgression, but was so pleased with her generally that he could not help but show her off to his friends. He had her come to the Grinnells' house where he introduced her to his wealthy benefactor. He wrote to Maggie afterwards: "Mrs. Grinnell was much pleased with you. Every body who really knows you, *is*; for my Maggie is a *lady*; and by the time that she has had a course of Mrs. Turner's music and French, nobody will know her as the spirit-rapping original phenomenon."[136]

He hired the popular Italian portrait painter, Joseph Fagnani, to paint a portrait of Maggie for him to take to the arctic.[137] He also wrote a clever drama for her that portrayed him as the romantic and doting "Preacher" and her as a practical and unsentimental woman of good-sense and plain speech. "PREACHER. I've longed to make life's stream a fountain clear and bright. MAGGIE. How can I fix my hair, dear Ly, if you stand in the light?"[138]

On May 27, 1853, Maggie moved into the Turners' home. She wrote, "I looked anxiously at the pretty and unpretending dwelling my beloved had selected as my abode, and mentally I wondered whether its inhabitants were as tasteful and neat as their little home appeared to be."[139] The casual, domestic banter in the final letters Elisha wrote to Maggie shows a young couple very much in love. In Elisha's "farewell" letter he again talked marriage.

> And now, dear Maggie, my own dear Maggie, live a life of purity and goodness. Consecrate it to me.... Thus live, dear Maggie, until God brings me back to you; and then, meeting my eye with the proud consciousness of virtue, we will resign ourselves to a passion sanctified by love and marriage. Golden fields shall spread before us their summer harvest—silver lakes mirror your very breath. Let us live for each other.
>
> Farewell.
>
> E. K. Kane.[140]

The day before he left, Elisha made a final trip to Crookville to assure Maggie that all would be well and that he had made arrangements with Cornelius Grinnell to take care of her needs. With these last details taken care of, he returned to New York, and on May 31, 1853, set sail for the arctic. In a letter written as he left Newfoundland, Elisha imagined Maggie under the shade of a drooping chestnut tree, startling the birds with her "tokens of the spirit-world." He advised her to study German and asked that she "write naughty letters" to him in that "noble language." He promised to be true to his promises and asked her only to "exercise often, laugh when you can, grow as fat as you please; and when I return—God granting me that distant blessing—...let me have at least the rewarding consciousness of having done my duty."[141]

1. For examples of spiritualism's impact see: Ann Braude, *Radical Spirits: Spiritualism and Women's Rights in Nineteenth-Century America* (Boston: Beacon Press, 1989); Russell M. & Clare R. Goldfarb, *Spiritualism and Nineteenth-Century Letters* (Cranbury, NJ: Associated University Press, 1978); Howard Kerr, *Mediums, and Spirit-Rappers, and Roaring Radicals: Spiritualism in American Literature, 1850-1900* (Chicago: University of Illinois Press, 1972); R. Laurence Moore, *In Search of White Crows: Spiritualism, Parapsychology, and American Culture* (New York: Oxford University Press, 1977); Alex Owen, *The Darkened Room: Women Power and Spiritualism in Late Victorian England* (Philadelphia: University of Pennsylvania Press, 1990); and Robert S. Cox, *Body & Soul: A Sympathetic History of American Spiritualism* (Charlottesville: University of Virginia Press, 2003).

2. Fox family history is difficult to piece together because they left few letters and no known diaries. Also, because of the nature of their profession, they often lied about their ages and backgrounds to maintain an air of mystery. This scant evidence has not stopped several people from writing biographies of the Fox sisters. By far the best are Barbara Weisberg's *Talking to the Dead: Kate and Maggie Fox and the Rise of Spiritualism* (New York, Harper SanFrancisco, 2004) and Nancy Rubin Stuart's *The Reluctant Spiritualist: The Life of Maggie Fox* (New York: Harcourt Inc., 2005) which do a remarkable job of pulling together scant resources to piece together a picture of the Fox sisters' lives while correcting much of the erroneous information from earlier biographies and firmly grounding the sisters in the social, economic and cultural times in which they lived. Other biographies include Herbert Jackson Jr., *The Spirit-rappers* (Garden City, NY: Doubleday & Co. Inc., 1972), which provides an extensive survey of newspaper accounts (many quoted in their entirety) of the Fox sisters' activities. Earl Wesley Fornell, *The Unhappy Medium* (Austin: University of Texas Press, 1964) provides a similar but less thorough survey. The most interesting but least documented biography is Miriam Buckner Pond's, *Time is Kind: The Story of the Unfortunate Fox Family* (Clinton, CT: Centennial Press, 1947). Pond, a spiritualist who married a grandnephew of the Fox sisters, says she drew her biography from many "papers and letters never published" as well as the remembrances of friends and family. Margaret Fox told parts of her own story in *The Love-Life of Dr. Kane* (New York: Carleton, 1866) and in Reuben Briggs Davenport, *The Death-blow to Spiritualism: Being the True Story of the Fox Sisters, as revealed by authority of Margaret Fox Kane and Catherine Fox Jencken* (New York: Dillingham, 1888) but both of these books were

written for pointed purposes and thus must be used with caution. Maggie's eldest sister, Ann Leah [Fox Fish Brown] Underhill also wrote an account of their history in *The Missing Link In Modern Spiritualism* (New York: Thomas R. Knox & Co., 1885) which is helpful but hugely biased toward Leah and her work in the spiritualist movement.

3. Weisberg, 37. No known official records mark the Fox sisters' birth dates, and they lied about them often. Weisberg relies on the testimony of long-time Fox family friend, Titus Merrit, who testified that Maggie was born on October 7, 1833, and Kate on March 27, 1837.

4. Weisberg, 31-43. Pond, 5-8; Jackson, 2.

5. This story is told through sworn and signed statements by the neighbors and Fox family, which appeared a few months later in the pamphlet, E.E. Lewis, *A Report of the Mysterious Noises Heard in the House of Mr. John D. Fox* (Cananduaigua, NY: by the author, 1848).

6. Lyons, NY *Western Argus* (April 12, 1848), reprinted in Jackson, 13-14.

7. Newark, NY *Herald* (May 4, 1848), reprinted in Jackson, 15-18.

8. Lyons, NY *Western Argus* (May 17, 1848). See also the Livingston, NY *Union* (May 17, 1848); both reprinted in Jackson, 18-20.

9. See Charles Hambrick-Stowe, *Charles G. Finney and the Spirit of American Evangelicalism* (Grand Rapids, MI: William G. Erdmans Publishing Company, 1996); Jan Shipps, *Mormonism* (Chicago: University of Illinois Press, 1985); Robert Abzug, *Çosmos Crumbling* (New York: Oxford University Press, 1994); Nathan O. Hatch, *The Democratization of American Christianity* (New Haven, CT: Yale University Press, 1989); Robert Thomas, *The Man Who Would be Perfect: John Humphrey Noyes and the Utopian Impulse* (Philadelphia: University of Pennsylvania Press, 1977); and Paul Johnson, *A Shopkeeper's Millennium* (New York: Hill & Wang, 1978).

10. Underhill, 30-33; Weisberg, 44-47; Jackson, 21-23. Leah claimed three children later in her life, but Weisberg noted that several of these were probably nieces, nephews, and cousins she "adopted' informally.

11. Underhill, 48-49.

12. See Davenport, *The Death-blow to Spiritualism*, 102-20.

13. Thomas Hamm, *The Transformation of American Quakerism* (Indianapolis: Indiana University Press, 1988).

14. The Posts helped Elizabeth Cady Stanton organize the Seneca Falls conference at which she first presented her "Declaration of Women's Rights." The Posts also worked closely with Frederick Douglass, supporting him in his lecturing and publishing efforts. See Braude, 57-61; Maria Diedrich, *Love Across the Color Lines* (New York: Hill and Wang, 1999); and Philip S. Foner, ed., *The Life and Writings of Frederick Douglass* vol. 2 (New York: International Publishers, 1950).

15. Weisberg, 41-42.

16. Braude, 15-19.

17. Barbara Goldsmith, *Other Powers: The Age of Suffrage, Spiritualism, and the Scandalous Victoria Woodhull* (New York: Alfred A. Knopf, 1998), 38-39.

18. Underhill, 47-56; Pond, 31.

19. E.W. Capron, *Modern Spiritualism: Its Facts and Fanaticisms* (Boston: Bela Marsh, 1855, reprinted New York: Arno Press, 1976), 67; and Adelbert Cronise, "The Beginnings of Modern Spiritualism In and Near Rochester" *Rochester Historical Society Publication Fund Series*. ed Edward R. Foreman (Rochester: Rochester Historical Society, 1926), 5: 1-22. For detailed discussion of these early séances see Weisberg, 59-69; and Jackson, 40-44.

20. Andrew Jackson Davis, *The Stellar Key to the Summer Land* (Boston: William White, 1868), 72; and Andrew Jackson Davis, *The Principles of Nature, Her Divine Revelations, and a Voice to Mankind* (New York: S.S. Lyon and Wm. Fishbough, 1847). I am heavily indebted to Robert S. Cox for my understanding of the roots of the Spiritualist movement of the 1850s; the introduction to his *Body & Soul: A Sympathetic History of American Spiritualism* provides an excellent overview of this topic.

21. Weisberg, 73-74.

22. Capron, 88-89. Capron mistakenly puts these events in the fall of 1848 instead of 1849.

23. Capron, 89.

24. Capron, 89-90.

25. Underhill, 62.

26. Rochester *Daily Advertiser* (Nov. 13, 1849), 2. This ad continued to run throughout the week, the only change coming on Nov. 17 when it added, "Price Reduced"— admission dropped to 12.5¢ per person.

27. For more information on this movement toward popular religion see Ann Douglas, *The Feminization of American Culture* (New York: Alfred A. Knopf, Inc., 1977); Nathan O. Hatch, *The Democratization of American Christianity* (New Haven, CT: Yale University Press, 1989); and R. Lawrence More, *Selling God: American Religion in the Marketplace of Culture* (New York: Oxford University Press, 1994).

28. The events of the Corinthian Hall performances are recorded in the Rochester *Daily Advertiser* (Nov. 20, 1849), 2.

29. Weisberg, 82-83; Rochester *Daily Democrat* (Nov. 16 & 17, 1849), quoted in Jackson, 49-57.

30. Davenport, 119. Maggie asserted that Leah calculated the effect these meetings would have and was pleased with the results.

31. Rochester *Daily Advertiser* (Nov. 20, 1849), 2; Underhill, 70-73.

32. Cronise, "The Beginnings of Modern Spiritualism In and Near Rochester," 14.

33. Underhill, 103. Leah reported that November 28, 1849, was the first time they began accepting money for their séances.

34. Jackson, 61-65.

35. This article was widely reprinted across the nation. See *The Trenton State Gazette* (March 26, 1850), 4; *Milwakee Sentinel & Gazette* (April 6, 1850), 2; and the *New Hampshire Patriot and State Gazette* (April 4, 1850), 4.

36. Jackson, 76; Underhill, 121.

37. Jackson, 66-67. This was probably Professor Elias Loomis, a mathematician and physicist at New York University. If so, then, at the same time Loomis was explaining away the rappings of the Fox sisters he was helping Elisha prepare for his first voyage to the Arctic. See Corner, 83.

38. *New York Tribune* (Jan 1, 1850), 1; (Feb. 4, 1850), 1;

39. *New York Tribune* (Dec. 5, 1849), 1.

40. Underhill, 128. As Leah noted of Barnum's Hotel, "This proprietor must not be confounded with the great showman of that name."

41. E. W. Capron to Mrs. Fox (Feb. 10, 1850), Department of Rare Books and Special Collections, University of Rochester, as cited in Weisberg, 104-05.

42. Underhill, 128.

43. The events of this evening are described in detail thanks to Ripley and Willis who wrote up their accounts and published them shortly thereafter. See Ripley's "An Evening with the Spirits" *New York Tribune* (June 8, 1850), 4; and N.P. Willis, "Post-Mortuum Soiree" *Home Journal* (June 15, 1850), 2.

44. Willis, *Home Journal* (June 15, 1850), 2.

45. Scholarship on this separation of spheres is extensive. I have relied heavily on Ann Douglas, *The Feminization of American Culture*; Kathryn Kish Sklar, *Catharine Beecher: A Study in Domesticity* (New Haven, CT: Yale University Press, 1973); Mark C. Carnes, *The Secret Ritual of Manhood in Victorian America* (New Haven, CT: Yale University Press, 1989); and Mary P. Ryan, *Cradle of the Middle Class* (New York: Cambridge University Press, 1981).

46. Willis, *Home Journal* (June 15, 1850), 2; *New York Tribune* (June 8, 1850), 4. The *Tribune* article was reprinted in *The Spirit of The Times* (June 2, 1850), 209.

47. *New York Tribune* (June 8, 1850), 4.

48. Fornell, 25.

49. Underhill, 129.

50. Many accounts of these large public séances exist; several good descriptions appear in Dellon Dewey, *History of the Strange Sounds or Rappings* (Rochester: D.M. Dewey, 1850).

51. *Gleason's Pictorial Drawing Room Companion* (Aug. 30, 1851), 279.

52. A good example of this is Eliab W. Capron who was one of the spiritualism's most devoted followers but was still unwilling to advocate the book *Voices from the Spirit World*, "ghost written" by his friend Isaac Post and claiming to be spiritual communications from such notables as Washington, Jefferson, Franklin, William

Penn, Voltaire, and Emanuel Swedenborg. See Jackson, 115-18.

53. Robert Hare, *Experimental Investigations of the Spirit Manifestations* (New York: Partridge & Brittan, 1855), 2-3; Edgar Fahs Smith, *The Life of Robert Hare* (Philadelphia, J.B. Lippincott Co., 1917), 482-84.

54. Moore, *In Search of White Crows*, 14.

55. Charles Hammond, *Light from the Spirit World* (Rochester: D.M. Dewey, 1852), vii.

56. See the ads at the end of John W. Edmonds and George T. Dexter, *Spiritualism* vol. 1 (New York: Partridge & Brittan, 1853, 1855).

57. Moore, *In Search of White Crows*, 29-30.

58. "Discovery of the Source of the Rochester Knockings" *Buffalo Medical Journal* 6 (March, 1851), 628-42; Buffalo *Commercial Advertiser* (Feb. 18 & March 14, 1851), reprinted in Underhill, 168-71, 188-92.

59. *New York Tribune* (July 22, 1859), 5.

60. Edmonds & Dexter, vol. 1, 61-65.

61. Hammond; see also J.M. Brown and E.H. Baxter, *Spiritual Exposition of the Prophetic Scriptures of the New Testament* (Auburn, NY: Baxter & Benedict, 1850).

62. William R. Gordon, *A Three-fold Test of Modern Spiritualism* (New York: Charles Scribner, 1856).

63. Gordon, xii.

64. The literature on the interconnection of faith, science and healing is extensive. I have relied primarily on the seminal work in this field, Jerome Frank's, *Persuasion & Healing* 3rd edition (Baltimore: Johns Hopkins University Press, [1961] 1991).

65. Joan D. Hedrick, *Harriet Beecher Stowe, A Life* (New York: Oxford University Press, 1994). 45, 49, 64, 66, 227.

66. Hedrick, 227.

67. Hedrick, 173-85, 367.

68. Hedrick, 367.

69. Letter cited in Hazel Harrod, "Correspondence of Harriet Beecher Stowe and Elizabeth Barrett Browning," *Studies in English* (June, 1948), 30-32.

70. Constance Mayfield Rourke, *Trumpets of Jubilee* (New York: Harcourt, Brace & Co., 1927), 119.

71. *Love-Life*, 114. For further discussion of Pierce's use of spiritual mediums see, Russ Castronovo, "'The Half-Living Corpse': Hawthorne and the Occult Public Sphere," *Yearbook of Research in English and American Literature* 18 (2002), 231-258.

72. Rourke, 308; William Hale, *Horace Greeley, Voice of the People* (New York: Harpers, 1950), 122-24; Ishbel Ross, *The President's Wife* (New York: G.P. Putnam's Sons, 1973), 182-87; Jean H. Baker, *Mary Todd Lincoln* (New York: W.W. Norton, 1987), 221.

73. James F. Cooper, *The Letters and Journal of James Fenimore Cooper*, James Beard, ed., vol. 2 (Cambridge, MA: Harvard University Press, 1968), 193; Underhill, 141.

74. Frank, 11.

75. Henry Walcott Boynton, *James Fenimore Cooper* (New York: The Century Co., 1931), 373-74.

76. See Davenport, *The Death-Blow to Spiritualism*.

77. Davenport, 83-84, 90-92. Kate and Maggie were joined in this effort by Leah's daughter, Elizabeth, who was staying with them at the time. Davenport's book, though helpful, must be used with caution as it was written to promote Maggie and Kate's public denunciation of spiritualism and to get back at Leah who had just written a very pro-spiritualism account of their early lives, *The Missing Link in Modern Spiritualism* (1885), which Maggie and Kate hated.

78. Davenport, 103-05, 112-15, 127.

79. Maggie Fox to Amy Post (August 21, 1849), Amy & Isaac Post papers, Department of Rare Books & Special Collections, University of Rochester.

80. Article from the *Rochester Daily American* reprinted in the *Trenton State Gazette* (March 26, 1850), 4. Similar articles were repeated in the *New-Hampshire Patriot and State Gazette* (March 26, 1850), 4; and in the *Milwaukee Sentinel & Gazette* (April 6, 1850), 2.

81. Davenport, 32-38.

82. Frank, 57-58.

83. Burr launched his exposé on the Fox sisters with an article in the *New York Tribune* (Jan. 2, 1851) and soon thereafter began a lecture/demonstration tour. Burr and the Fox sisters would often follow each other from region to region, both gaining large audiences from the controversy they created. It is interesting to note that Burr and his display of "electro-Biology" was the act that appeared in Rochester's Corinthian Hall in the weeks before the Fox sisters debuted their rappings there. See Jackson, 45-46, 90-91.

84. Kate Fox to Amy Post (Oct. 30, 1851), Amy & Isaac Post papers, Department of Rare Books & Special Collections, University of Rochester.

85. Ann Leah Fox Fish Underhill to Amy Post (July 22, 1851), Amy & Isaac Post papers, Department of Rare Books & Special Collections, University of Rochester.

86. From an interview with Maggie, Davenport, 99.

87. Davenport, 37.

88. *Philadelphia Evening Bulletin* (Oct. 9, 1852).

89. Underhill, 120. They charged $1 per person for the public sittings, which could include up to 90 people per day (3 séances of 30 people each), and they usually did several private sittings, charging $5 each.

90. *Love-Life*, 237-38.

91. Horace Greeley to Thomas Leiper Kane (Dec. 1, 1850), BYU Thomas Leiper Kane papers.

92. Willie died on August 25, 1852, and the family moved in early 1853. Corner, 11, 104.

93. Jane Duval Leiper Kane to Elisha Kent Kane (Oct. 10, 1852), in folder Thomas Leiper

Kane , APS Elisha Kent Kane papers.

94. Jane Duval Leiper Kane to Elisha Kent Kane (Oct. 10, 1852), in folder Thomas Leiper Kane, APS Elisha Kent Kane papers; John K. Kane to Elisha Kent Kane (Oct. 13, 1852); W.M. Abbott to Elisha Kent Kane (Oct. 26, 1852); Alexander Dallas Bache to Elisha Kent Kane (Nov. 26, 1852); William Kennedy to Elisha Kent Kane (Dec. 3, 1852); and Samuel Colt to Elisha Kent Kane (Dec. 6, 1852), APS Elisha Kent Kane papers.

95. Elisha Kent Kane to Maggie Fox (Dec. 12, 1852), *Love-Life*, 28.

96. Elisha Kent Kane to Mrs. Fox (Dec. 18, 1852) *Love-Life*, 28-29.

97. "New-York Geographical Society. *Access to an Open Polar Sea Along a North American Meridian. A paper by Dr. E.K. Kane"* *New York Times* (Dec. 15, 1852), 4; *Love-Life*, 28-29.

98. Corner, 116-18; *Love-Life*, 50-51.

99. John P. Kennedy to R. Dunglison (secretary of the APS) (Jan. 2, 1853), reprinted in Henry T. Tuckerman, *The Life of John Pendelton Kennedy* (New York: G.P. Putnam, 1871), 229-30; Corner, 116-18; Henry Grinnell to Elisha Kent Kane (Jan. 2, 1853), APS Elisha Kent Kane papers. Kennedy's tenure ended in January of 1853. Not knowing if the next Secretary would support the expedition, Kane was in a race against time to ensure its funding.

100. Harper & Bros. to Elisha Kent Kane (Jan. 11, 1853), APS Elisha Kent Kane papers.

101. *Love-Life*, 48.

102. For a discussion of different perceptions of such similar "entertainments," see Christoph Irmsher, "Collecting Human Nature: P.T. Barnum," in *The Poetics of Natural History* (New Brunswick, NJ: Rutgers University Press, 1999), 101-48. That people feel a part of and in someway involved with the heroic person they associate themselves with is discussed at length in Leo Braudy, *The Frenzy of Renown* (New York: Oxford University Press, 1986).

103. David Chapin, *Exploring Other Worlds: Margaret Fox, Elisha Kane, and the Antebellum Culture of Curiosity* (Amherst: University of Massachusetts Press, 2004), 8, 53.

104. David Chapin "Exploring Other Worlds: Margaret Fox, Elisha Kane, and the Antebellum Culture of Curiosity," (Ph.D. diss., University of New Hampshire, 2000), 7.

105. Underhill, 120.

106. *National Magazine* 1 (Oct., 1852), 349.

107. Jane Tompkins, "Afterword," in *The Wide, Wide World* by Susan Warner (New York: The Feminist Press, 1987), 585.

108. *Love-Life*, 52. *Undine* was originally published in German in 1811 but was soon translated into English and became immensley popular; it was recast as both an opera and a ballet during the 19th century.

109. *Love-Life*, 39.

110. William Hosmer, *The Young Lady's Book* (Buffalo: Derby, Orton & Mulligan, 1853),

496-97.

111. *Love-Life*, 42, 66.

112. *Love-Life*, 26-30, 39-41.

113. *Love-Life*, 204-05. Kane wrote Fox a story about well-polished "crystal vases" regarding this interior/exterior relationship. On this topic, Elisha told Maggie, "you were born for better things than to entertain strangers at a dollar a head." See Elisha Kent Kane to Maggie Fox (March 15, 1853), APS Elisha Kent Kane papers.

114. *Love-Life*, 64, 50. Italics in the original. A spencer is a very short jacket worn over a gown.

115. *Love-Life*, 18.

116. *Love-Life*, 32-41.

117. Karen Lystra, *Searching the Heart* (New York: Oxford University Press, 1989), 9-10.

118. *Love-Life*, 50, 57, 65. Kane's reference to holding up his hand shows that, though he did not believe in spiritualism, he did have superstitions of his own. He believed he could tell the future by the quivering of his hands, a skill he had learned in China.

119. Lystra, 17.

120. Cited in Lystra, 17.

121. *Love-Life*, 43, 60, 84.

122. Cornelius Grinnell to Elisha Kent Kane (undated, c. Jan., 1853), APS Elisha Kent Kane papers.

123. Cornelius Grinnell to Elisha Kent Kane (undated #2, c. Jan., 1853), APS Elisha Kent Kane papers.

124. Cornelius Grinnell to Elisha Kent Kane (Jan. 19, 1853), APS Elisha Kent Kane papers.

125. *Love-Life*, 92.

126. *Love-Life*, 55-56. In her book, Maggie does not say whether Elisha came for her or not.

127. *Love-Life*, 49.

128. *Love-Life*, 62.

129. *Love-Life*, 68-69; Underhill, 270-71.

130. Elisha Kent Kane to Maggie Fox (March 10, 1853), *Love-Life*, 84.

131. Maggie Fox to Elisha Kent Kane (undated, c. March, 1853), APS Elisha Kent Kane papers.

132. Elisha Kent Kane to Maggie Fox (March 15, 1853), APS Elisha Kent Kane papers. This letter appears to be a copy Elisha made to prove to his family that he was not romantically involved with Fox. He sent a package of Fox's letters, along with what he said were copies of his letters (this one he marks "sent March 19, 1853, written March 15"), to his brother Patterson so Patterson could use them to put down any rumors that circulated while he was in the Arctic. See Elisha Kent Kane to Robert Patterson Kane (June 16, 1853), APS Elisha Kent Kane papers. Fox reprinted a letter dated March 17, 1853, that had the same content but is much more affectionately

written. See *Love-Life*, 87-89.

133. Maggie Fox to Elisha Kent Kane, and Mrs. Fox to Elisha Kent Kane (undated, c. March 1853), APS Elisha Kent Kane papers.

134. Eliza Leiper to Elisha Kent Kane (April 4, 1853), folder, "Fox to Elisha Kent Kane," APS Elisha Kent Kane papers; Elisha Kent Kane to Maggie Fox (April 11, 1853), reprinted in *Love-Life*, 100-101; Elisha Kent Kane to Eliza Leiper (May 1, 1853), APS Elisha Kent Kane papers.

135. *Love-Life*, 96.

136. *Love-Life*, 114, 117.

137. This painting survived Kane's Arctic adventure but has since been lost. A later portrait of Kane by Fagnani still survives in the collections of the Elisha Kent Kane Historical Society, New York City.

138. *Love-Life*, 146, 142-44. "Ly" was one of Maggie's petnames for Elisha.

139. *Love-Life*, 149.

140. *Love-Life*, 151.

141. *Love-Life*, 159-60.

CHAPTER

4

Absence Makes the
Heart Grow Fonder

On May 31, 1853, amid great fanfare and crowds of well-wishers, Elisha Kent Kane and his crew of seventeen men boarded the *Advance* and prepared to set sail on the Second U.S. Grinnell Expedition in search of Sir John Franklin. As a steam-tug pulled the small hermaphrodite brig from the Brooklyn Naval Battery out to sea, Elisha and his crew stood on deck and waved to the cheering masses that lined the shores. Cornelius and Henry Grinnell, along with Judge John Kane and his sons, Tom, Patterson, and John Jr., accompanied the *Advance* in the steamer *Union* to bid Elisha a final farewell. In a letter to Maggie Fox describing the events of the day, Cornelius wrote, "As the vessel passed along the wharves of the North River, she was saluted with cheers from the crowds assembled, and by guns from the shipping. Two steamers accompanied us to sea, filled with people. The Doctor was in good spirits."[1] Upon reaching open water, Elisha ordered the *Advance*'s sails set and a course laid for the one direction that mattered, north. The *New York Times* reported, "The *Advance* now turned her prow seaward, leaving the coastwise steamers at their wharfs, under a parting salute of bells, pealing from the craft at anchor. Every vessel passed in the Bay gave her a parting cheer, a ringing salute, and shouted good wishes."[2]

This parting moment was exquisite; it was all that a hero could desire. In the days leading up to this moment, P.T. Barnum's *Illustrated News* printed an engraving of Dr. Kane modeled from a daguerreotype of Elisha taken after he returned from the Mexican-American War. It showed him young, strong, and confident, dressed in a high-collared, brass-buttoned uniform, a sword clutched forcefully in his hand.[3] The weeks leading up to the departure had been far more harrowing than Elisha's poised image implied, however. His predeparture correspondence show that three issues weighed heavily on his mind: the completion of his book, his relationship with Margaret Fox, and questions about his own health and ability to lead.

A full six months before the expedition set sail, Elisha tried to separate himself from the day-to-day aspects of finishing his book. He assembled his journal notes from the first expedition, wrote a detailed outline, and then turned the project over to his father and Tom for editing, expansion, and completion. This done, he tried to turn his full attention to the expedition at hand, but the book project continued to make demands of his time. After months of negotiations and fre-

Portraits of Dr. Kane and Sir John Franklin from the New York *Illustrated News* (March 5, 1853); and the departure of the *Advance* from the *Illustrated London News* (June 12, 1853).

quent disagreements with Harpers, printing finally began on the illustrations. Even after all decisions were made, however, the process went slowly and continued to be a problem.[4] In March, difficulties arose over the appendices. The first expedition's captain, Edwin J. DeHaven, saw Elisha's growing fame and feared that he would be entirely eclipsed by the ever-growing persona of Dr. Kane. He thus urged Elisha to include his official captain's report in the book. To avoid conflict, Elisha agreed. He told his father to quote from DeHaven's report in the body of the book and to insert it in its entirety as an appendix: "Let him see the proofs after all done. He will not touch them and they will silence him hereafter."[5] About that same time, Elisha learned that even if he and his family were able to complete the book quickly, it would not be released until December 1853. Harpers decided to delay its publication to prevent it from cutting into the sales of Sir John Richardson's *Arctic Searching Expedition* that they published in 1852 and were still promoting heavily in 1853.[6]

Without pressure to finish quickly, work slowed, leaving portions of the book incomplete at the time of Elisha's departure. Before setting sail, Elisha scrambled to pull together the last bits of information his father would need to finish the work in his absence. He wrote to former Navy Secretary John P. Kennedy: "Would you do me the favor to loan me, for a few days, the 'Reports on Grinnell Land.' I am obliged to tax my father with the revision of my book, and he wants the notes as material for a chapter."[7] These final efforts on the book so vexed Elisha that he questioned whether he would ever write again. In a letter from sea he told his father: "I see two hundred and sixteen ice bergs floating in a sea as dead and oily as the Lake of Tiberias, yet I cannot warm my thoughts to talk about them. Time was when I could pile epithets upon such a scene, but that time has passed. I fear that there will not be a readable book unless that dear working Father does the didactic and Tom the attractive—Facts only are my aim now."[8]

Though he worried about his book, Maggie Fox occupied his thoughts to an even greater degree. He worried about her education, love and devotion, and the potential damage she could do to his much-celebrated heroic persona. In all the surviving letters between Elisha and his father there is no mention of Margaret Fox; nor does she appear in Elisha's letters to Tom. Elisha knew they would so disapprove of the relationship that he did not even discuss it with them. Thus, as he had done with Julia Reed seven years earlier, he turned to friends and his younger brother, Patterson, for aid in this delicate matter. Cornelius Grinnell agreed to take care of Maggie's needs in Elisha's absence—to keep track of her movements and educational efforts, send her monthly funds, and keep her up to date on the expedition's progress.[9] He also agreed to serve as the courier of their letters and to guard Elisha's reputation; in this last effort, Patterson agreed to help as well.

As the *Advance* left St. Johns for Greenland, Elisha sent Patterson specific instructions on how to guard his reputation. He gathered a series of letters regarding Fox's education and forwarded them to show his "position with regard to poor Maggie Fox—in my eyes a most worthy object for manly effort and charity."[10] These, he hoped, would provide Patterson with the power "documentarily to set me right in case of misrepresentation or false construction." He warned him to reveal these documents only if rumors arose; otherwise, Patterson was to "do <u>nothing</u>, stir nothing, agitate nothing. Let things alone... for it is bad to stir unnecessarily water already clear, it muddifies."[11] Elisha was quite sure that Maggie would not cause trouble and that he had adequately hidden their relationship—he had firmly instructed her to keep their agreement a secret and their correspondence strictly private.[12] He told Patterson that his biggest fear was his "friends volunteering explanations where it would be neither necessary nor dignified to vouchsafe them." Then, in response to Patterson's deep concerns about his intentions, Elisha wrote, "I would sooner die than injure a person to whom I stand in the relation which I do to this one, or injure myself by forgetting my own dignity by a misplaced marriage."[13]

When Elisha made his plans for Maggie's education, he consulted heavily with the Rev. Dr. Francis L. Hawks who was one of the cofounders of the American Geographical Society and a highly respected preacher and scholar. He was also one of the New York literati who had attended the Fox sisters' first high-profile séance in New York City in 1850. Maggie's wit and "simplicity" had impressed Hawk and the rest of the group at this event and had won her "the respect and liking of all present."[14] Hawk was thus delighted by the idea of "bettering" Maggie when Elisha asked for his help. When Elisha wrote to Patterson, he included his correspondence with Dr. Hawk as proof of his intention only to aid Maggie, whom he described in his letters to Hawk as "that poor victim of spirit-rapping delusion."[15] Elisha's manic attempts to head off rumors and his overly vehement denial of any ideas about "a misplaced marriage" only increased the suspicion of his friends and family that he had more than altruistic motives for aiding Maggie, and they had strong cause to be suspicious. Three days before Elisha sailed, he made a mad dash from New York to Crookville to see her one last time, and in the weeks before, he had hired one of New York's leading artists to paint her portrait so he could take it along to the arctic.[16] These were not the actions of a patron to his protégé and this more-than-friendly devotion was quite apparent to both the Kanes and the Grinnells.

There was little more Elisha could do about either his book or his relationship with Maggie once the *Advance* pulled away from New York; however, it was then that his third concern—his ability to lead such an ambitious and dangerous expedition—became very real. The precarious state of his health added to this concern because if he were ill it would diminish his ability to inspire and command his crew. A year earlier, in April 1852, the new U.S. Navy secretary, James C. Dobbin, had agreed to honor former Secretary John P. Kennedy's agreement to supply the expedition with a few navy volunteers and limited supplies, but he refused to provide any further funding. Elisha, backed by Henry Grinnell; Joseph Henry, secretary of the Smithsonian Institution; Alexander Dallas Bache, superintendent of the Coast Survey; and Matthew Fontaine Maury, superintendent of the Naval Observatory, pushed Congress for an additional $160,000. Despite such high-level backing, however, Congress refused. This meant that Elisha himself had to raise the funds and equipment for the expedition during the year leading up to his departure. Even with the help of Grinnell and George Peabody, who offered further contributions as well as strong support in soliciting scientific societies and agencies on the expedition's behalf, this was a daunting and tiring task. Elisha successfully courted the American Philosophical Society, Smithsonian Institution, Naval Observatory, Philadelphia Academy of Natural Sciences, and the American Geographical Society, and they provided funds and instruments as well as wages to hire one well-trained scientist for the mission, German astronomer Augustus Sonntag.[17] Elisha also procured daguerreotype equipment, a first in arctic history, but it failed to work in arctic conditions. He passed up another first by turning down a hot-air balloon that an enthusiast was sure would be a helpful piece of research equipment.[18]

Grinnell placed the *Advance* in dry dock in March 1853 and began preparing her for departure, and by April, Elisha arrived in New York to begin final preparations.[19] A few days after his arrival, however, his months of constant effort caught up with him and he was incapacitated by his life-long foe, rheumatic fever. Kane grew so ill that the Grinnells feared for his life and moved him from his hotel to their house, where Cornelius could run his errands and William Morton, Kane's personal assistant, could serve as his full-time sick nurse. The *New York Times* reported on April 15 that the expedition was ready to go, but discreetly omitted the fact that Kane was too ill to get out of bed, much less head the expedition.[20] Though Kane's illness persisted, after a few weeks Grinnell felt that he was on the mend and would soon be ready to sail. Elisha wrote Kennedy on April 17: "After a cruel attack of inflammatory rheumatism, and three weeks of complete helplessness on my beam ends, I find myself ready to start."[21]

Having just recovered from such a severe illness, Kane was still quite frail when the *Advance* set sail. To further add to his misery, upon leaving port he was hit by his other life-long ailment, seasickness. With a good deal of humor, Sailing Master John Wall Wilson noted the exacting toll "Father Neptune" took on Elisha and the other land-loving officers. "Pale faces would toddle now and then to the side of the vessel and gaze sentimentally after the <u>debris</u> of a breakfast or dinner as it floated away; [they were] literally 'casting their bread upon the water.'"[22] Elisha's shipmate and family friend, Henry Goodfellow, worried about him: "Instead

of the former restlessness and intense vitality, he had the subdued look of a broken-down invalid." Goodfellow's worries soon diminished, however, and he reported that Elisha "seemed stronger" and had "the alacrity of a well man."[23]

With his health on the mend, Elisha's concern turned fully to the enormity
of the task before him. He wrote Tom, "Now that the thing—the dream—has con-
centrated itself into a grim, practical reality, it is not egotism, but duty to talk of
myself and my plans. I represent other lives than my own."[24] Elisha certainly had
a hard job before him. As one arctic scholar has noted, his expedition may have
been the most poorly prepared in arctic history. Its "captain was a physician in poor
health, his chief officer a boatswain..., and his principal navigator a landsman astronomer."[25] To his credit, however, Elisha had done everything in his power to ensure the success of his expedition. Drawing from his medical background and
previous arctic experience, he supplemented the normal naval rations with a ton
of pemmican, a large quantity of Borden's meat-biscuit, and a "liberal quantity
of American dried fruits and vegetables."[26] He also secured several barrels of specially pickled cabbage as well as several barrels of malt extract and a small brewing apparatus for fresh beer, all to prevent scurvy.[27]

He had worked for nearly a year to gain the instruments he needed to perform
the scientific observations he hoped to conduct in the arctic. He consulted many
of the leading scientists of the day, and thanks to generous donations from the
American Philosophical Society, the Smithsonian, and the Naval Observatory he
was able to secure good thermometers, chronometers, and compasses for accurate
navigation and charting, as well as an apparatus for studying terrestrial magnetism. Elisha also tried to assemble a skilled crew, but because of slim funds he had
to rely largely on men willing to risk their lives for almost no monetary reward.
This in itself was not a problem. Many young men from across America wrote to
him to try to gain a position: a slim, young, Canadian teacher with "a promising
mustache"; a farm boy from Cincinnati who had never seen the ocean; a middle-
aged arctic enthusiast from New Orleans.[28] Finding qualified crewmembers was a
different matter, however. Two members of the First Grinnell Expedition—Henry
Brooks and William Morton—volunteered. Kane made Brooks (boatswain and second officer of the *Advance* under DeHaven) his first officer, after having him rein-
stated into the navy—he had been kicked out for excessive drunkenness. Morton,
an Irish-born sailor, came to play an important and ubiquitous role, serving Kane
as a man-servant for both the duration of the cruise and for the rest of Kane's life.[29]
Other crewmembers included Isaac Israel Hayes, a twenty-one-year-old surgeon
fresh out of medical school; Henry Goodfellow, a well-educated and at times
haughty friend of the Kane family; Amos Bonsall, a Pennsylvania farmer; and Jefferson Baker, Elisha's childhood hunting companion.[30] Other than Sonntag and
two wharf men of questionable character, William Godfrey and John Blake, the

rest of the crew—John Wall Wilson (sailing master), James McGary (second officer), Christian Ohlsen (carpenter), Peter Schubert (cook), George Riley, George Stephenson, George Whipple, and Tom Hickey—was supplied by the U.S. Navy and proved to be a mixed lot. Cornelius met them and reported to Elisha, "I think you will find Olsen [sic] an excellent man. McGreary [sic] will require to be kept in his place. Wilson is full of ambition & enthusiasm and is I think a person of some strength of character."[31]

There is no doubt that this crew was one of the greenest ever to attempt an arctic expedition, and they were doing so under a thirty-three-year-old surgeon who had never commanded a vessel. What he lacked in experience, however, Kane made up for through his sheer energy and his infectious love of adventure that epitomized this era of American exploration. Despite some initial doubts, Elisha quickly adapted to his role as captain. After a week at sea he wrote his family that "now, after years of apprentice and journey work, I am promoted to a master man seeking himself new oceans and new lands." He reported that most things were "quietly dropping into their places" and that when they did not, he was "learning to consider it as my legitimate junction to 'drop them.'" Elisha naturally adapted to his commanding status, but he still found "something repelling [about] the exercise of an artificial power." He noted that he fought "against this 'big Injun' feeling" but recognized the "necessary despotisms of authority" and confessed that "a conviction of their necessity comes over me as a sort of sober puzzle."[32]

Having witnessed the brutal beatings that were then a common part of naval discipline, Elisha worked hard to govern his men with a gentler hand. His goal was to "be exacting," but not oppressive.[33] Kane worked hard to maintain this disciplinary style, but he was soon tested when William Godfrey, a tough harborman from New York's East Side, and his friend, John Blake, assaulted First Officer Brooks with "insubordinate and disrespectful language." Because he was opposed to whippings and the use of the cat o' nine tails, Kane had them placed in a dark space between decks with bread and water, nailed down the hatch, and left them there for several days. "Since then," he wrote after their release, "they have been two of our best men," but the success of this disciplinary style was short lived. Godfrey erupted again a few days later. The officers recommended that he be sent home via a British whaler, but Elisha had a man-to-man talk with him, put him on two-weeks probation, and kept him aboard.[34]

Amid these disciplinary problems, Kane did manage to strengthen his crew by adding two valuable members. At the small harbor town of Fiskernaes in southern Greenland, Kane hired Hans Christian Hendrik, a nineteen-year-old "Esquimaux half-breed," to serve as the expedition's hunter. Kane was skeptical at first, but Hans quickly demonstrated his abilities with kayak, rifle, and javelin—Elisha was especially impressed when he casually speared a bird winging by overhead.[35]

Hans Hendrik from Kane's *Arctic Explorations* (Philadelphia: Childs & Peterson, 1856).

A few weeks later, at Upernavik, Kane added his nineteenth and final crewmember, Carl Christian Petersen. A Danish native, Petersen moved to the whaling port of Disco, Greenland, as a young man and there learned both English and the native Inuit language while becoming a skilled dog-team driver and outdoorsman. He had joined William Penny aboard the *Lady Franklin* in 1850, and he was offered a position aboard Edward Inglefield's expedition in 1852, but declined. Kane had acquired dogs in Newfoundland and Greenland and was excited to have such an experienced driver on his crew. In a letter telling of both his excitement about hiring Petersen and his reservations about his own health, Elisha wrote to Cornelius Grinnell: "This step I regard as the most fortunate for the success of the Expedition... [for] whatever may be my own strength or weakness, health or disease, I now feel as if some results [are] certain."[36]

The *Advance* left Upernavik on July 23, 1853, to head further up Greenland's coast to Melville Bay and the "Middle Ice"—the huge mass of crumbled sheet ice and icebergs that detach from Greenland's shore each spring and float treacherously in the middle of Baffin Bay throughout the summer, alternately blocking and making accessible the entrances to Smith and Lancaster Sounds. As they approached this intimidating obstacle, Elisha wrote home one last time, because no communication would be possible beyond the Middle Ice. In a letter dated "approaching Melville Island" he noted his disappointment of not reaching this point earlier in the season. This was important because an early entrance into Smith Sound would allow him more exploration time and a better chance to avoid being frozen in for the winter. It would also put him ahead of his would-be competitor, Edward Inglefield.[37]

A few months before Elisha departed, Lady Franklin had written to him that England had adopted his search plan and was sending Inglefield to Smith Sound aboard one of their best steam-powered ships.[38] This news greatly troubled Elisha because Inglefield's expedition was set to win for England the discoveries Elisha hoped to win for himself and the United States. In 1852, Inglefield had taken Lady Franklin's *Isabel* into Smith Sound, and upon his return he began diligently pushing for a chance to return to Smith Sound because, like Elisha, he believed it was the key to the Open Polar Sea and the fate of Sir John Franklin. Lady Jane's letter and Elisha's subsequent fears were unfounded, however. The Royal Admiralty did send Inglefield back to the arctic, but as the captain of a supply ship bound for Beechey Island with provisions for Edward Belcher's massive five-ship expedition.[39] This information did not reach the United States before the *Advance* left, however, and thus Elisha believed that he was in a race with Inglefield to unravel the mysteries of Smith Sound. Because of this, he decided to cross directly through the Middle Ice—a move that would either save him several days or quickly end the expedition by locking the *Advance* in an ice floe or crushing it with an iceberg. This risky maneuver was obviously on his mind when he wrote home, "Let none of my brothers join future 'Search Expeditions.' They would not add to the efficiency and one is quite enough out of a family."[40]

This letter, along with several others left at Upernavik, were the expedition's last communication home. Then came only silence. No further news of the Second Grinnell Expedition reached the United States for the next two years.

The summer of 1853 was difficult for Margaret Fox. The past five years had made her a celebrity. She traveled about the country, staying in the suites of the best

Map of the first Grinnell Expedition's route from *Harper's New Monthly Magazine* (December1851). This map shows all the territory known to Kane before he left for the arctic in 1853. He believed that the blank space that extended north from Smith Sound at the top of Baffin Bay held the key to the discovery of both the Open Polar Sea and Sir John Franklin's fate; it was also the void that people back home stared at, wondering what had become of their loved ones.

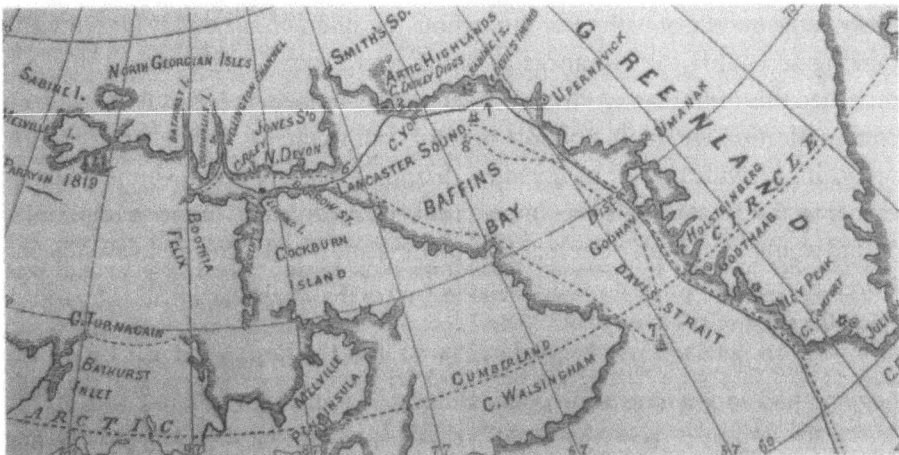

hotels and high-end boarding houses, and was visited daily by many of the nation's most-respected and intelligent citizens. Throughout her life she had always lived among either her tight-knit family or a devoted group of spiritualists who embraced her as their prophet. For the first time in her short life, Maggie was alone. The family she was with—the Turners—lived in Crookville, Pennsylvania, a now-forgotten spot in the road that even at that time was little more than a crossroads marked only by William T. Crook's cotton mill, a few houses, a Presbyterian church, and the Turners' farm, which lay on the outskirts of this small settlement.[41]

Maggie's decision to leave the séance table alienated her from many spiritualists as well as from her sister Leah, with whom she never fully made amends. Kate and Mrs. Fox maintained close ties with Maggie, but they saw little of her because Elisha had given Mrs. Turner strict instruction to keep her away from spiritualist influences. Kate reported in June 1853 that "Mother went to Philadelphia after Maggie, but her Teachers would not hear to her leaving school until the first of August. I was <u>very deeply</u> disappointed."[42] Elisha had planned for Maggie to stay with the Turners for the summer as "a temporary arrangement to exclude her from the pernicious influence of her clique." He then expected Cornelius and Dr. Hawks to help her find a women's school to attend in the fall.[43] In general, Maggie liked this arrangement. The Turner family was kind, and its matronly head, Suzanna Turner, treated her as one of her own daughters. Although their house was isolated, Maggie liked the location and found it "very tastefully laid out" with flowerbeds, handsome trees, and a "pretty piazza covered with honeysuckles and roses."[44] She worked diligently throughout the summer, but, as the months passed, she grew increasingly lonely. She received an encouraging letter from Elisha in July in which he insisted that fun was an "essential element" of her studies. He warned her not to "mope like a sickly cat" or to become "a strait-laced artificial automaton" that could only "grind out languages, and music, and long words." He also reminded her that in the fall she was free to "try another school-girl life."[45] Following up on this, Maggie told Cornelius that she would like to study in Troy, New York, that fall. Cornelius advised against this, however: "It appears to me that nothing could be better than the course you are now pursuing at Mrs. Turner's."[46]

Maggie became depressed to the point of physical illness shortly thereafter. Worried about her charge, Mrs. Turner consulted Dr. Edward Bayard, Maggie's friend and physician, and decided that a trip to New York would benefit her health. Mrs. Warner, a long-time friend of Maggie's, accompanied her from Crookville to New York, where Maggie stayed with Mrs. Ellen Cochrane Walter, a wealthy and well-placed widow.[47] Mrs. Turner assumed Maggie would just take a short break from her studies but Maggie seems to have had different intentions. More than a month after her departure, Mrs. Turner still had not heard from Maggie and so wrote a scolding letter. "I am feeling many anxieties on your account. If you were laid on a bed of sickness, surely you would get some friend to write a few lines to me mentioning your situation. If, on the other hand, your health is quite re-established, and you are merely remaining to indulge in the gaieties of the city, you should write to me yourself." She further warned that she had promised Elisha a full account of her studies when he returned and that she would now have to report this "cessation from well-doing—or, to use a harsher term, this lapse from duty!"[48]

Ellen Walter wrote back just two days later, apologizing that Maggie had not written and assuring her that Maggie had been quite sick, far too ill to have "partaken of the amusements and gaieties of the city." She further assured Mrs. Turner that Maggie's "associations have been of the most refined character, such as I know Dr. Kane and yourself would most highly approve." She concluded by noting that Maggie's health was on the mend and that she would return in two weeks.[49] Mrs. Turner immediately apologized for the accusatory letter, but noted that, "Being unaware of the real state of the case, and receiving no answers to my letters, I really began to fear that she had fallen under those influences from which it has been the aim and object of kind friends to shield her."[50]

It is clear that Mrs. Turner feared that the seductive influences in New York would cause Maggie to return to her former life. This was exactly what Elisha wanted to prevent and he had trusted Mrs. Turner to prevent it. He had also trusted Cornelius to help in this regard, but Cornelius had mixed feelings about the nature of this duty. Cornelius liked Maggie and found her an exciting and interesting person; however, he also believed that she was a liability to the public image of Elisha and his mission, a mission in which he and his father were hugely invested.[51] As a result, he followed an interesting tack in dealing with Fox, her education, and her relationship to spiritualism.

With regard to Maggie's education, Grinnell subtly used his influence to keep her from achieving the goals Elisha had set for her. He advised her not to seek formal schooling, but rather to remain at Mrs. Turner's for the duration of Elisha's absence. He reminded her that her situation at the Turners' was "comfortable and pleasant in all respects," warned that other places may not be as nice, and advised that she "think well of the matter before you decide to make a change."[52] By keeping her with the Turners, Grinnell accomplished two things. First, he kept her from expanding her social circles. Elisha had envisioned Mrs. Turner's as a "temporary arrangement" and assumed she would then go to a school in North Carolina headed by one of Dr. Hawk's friends.[53] This plan would have allowed her to start a new life away from spiritualism and to form friendships among respected young women from "good" families. Keeping her in Crookville prevented this. Second, knowing that the Turners' isolated home would prove far too dull for Maggie's cosmopolitan tastes, Grinnell predicted that she would want to return to the city and her spiritualist friends. This was what he wanted. If Maggie returned to spiritualism, it made her relationship to Elisha easy to explain—Elisha tried to help her reform and she failed him. The public would see Elisha as kind and benevolent and Maggie as a poor wretch beyond reform. If she shunned spiritualism and became a "lady," Elisha's devotion to her became much more complicated abd ptentially difficult to explain. Helping a "wretch" was a sign of benevolence; helping a young lady educate herself was a sign of commitment.

Grinnell knew that Elisha loved Maggie, but he feared their relationship could cast a bad light on both Elisha's image and the Grinnell Expedition in general. In his eyes, Maggie's past and low-class background were barriers too great to be surmounted. After years of effort, Elisha had achieved a well-respected and honorable fame, but his relationship with her threatened to destroy it all. Cornelius's fears were increased by the fact that Leah had began circulating rumors that Elisha was educating Maggie for the express purpose of making her his wife.[54]

This explains why in the fall of 1853 Cornelius advised Maggie against school, but readily consented to her going to New York. It also helps to explain the housing arrangements he made for her. While in New York he advised Maggie to stay with the wealthy widow, Mrs. Ellen Walter. At first glance, this appears to be a choice made to help Maggie. Walter was a friend of the Grinnell and Kane families and moved in socially elite circles—her brother was John Cochrane, surveyor of the Port of New York and later a U.S. Senator.[55] A closer look reveals something else, however. Having recently lost her husband, Mrs. Walter had sought out mediums and had come to believe in spiritualism.[56] The address of Mrs. Walter's house—60 Clinton Place (now Eighth Street)—is also of importance. As Cornelius well knew, this house was just a few blocks from the house on Tenth Street where Mrs. Fox and Kate were holding séances. If Maggie could be lured back to the séance table, Mrs. Walter's was a good place to make it happen.

Cornelius's letter to Patterson Kane in February 1854 makes his intentions absolutely clear. Maggie had returned to Crookville in January 1854 and shortly thereafter she wrote to Cornelius to request funds to cover her monthly board and education expenses. By this time, however, she had exhausted the funds Elisha had left for her. This provided an opportunity. Cornelius wrote to Patterson, bluntly noting that "it has occurred to me whether by withholding funds from [Ms. Fox] she could not be induced to return to her parents." He explained, "I am desirous of doing everything in my power to carry out your brother's wishes, and at the same time to promote his happiness.... A deep feeling of friendship for your brother alone prompts me to make this suggestion, and I shall be governed entirely by your views in the matter."[57]

Cornelius clearly felt there was a difference between Elisha's expressed wishes and what would ultimately "promote his happiness." This letter was a godsend for the Kane family. They never approved of Elisha's devotion to Maggie and saw this as a welcome opportunity to be rid of her. "It does strike me," Patterson wrote Cornelius, "that the opportunity presented of letting the young lady know your own impression of her position which she bears to the doctor, should not be lost." He explained that the family saw her "only as a dependent... a poor girl with a pretty face and an already disreputable association" whom Elisha, foolishly, was trying to help. "My dear brother resembles our very loveable Don Quixote; but then this resemblance must not be construed into anything affecting his reputation." He then stated bluntly, "Miss F is not his mistress and holds to him no other relation than that of the recipient of his charity and to you no other than that of a purely business correspondent. Do you take my drift!... I do think that at present there is offered a chance to effect something not for the purpose of saving money; but that which we both of us value much more."[58] It is unclear how or exactly when Maggie was informed of this decision, but in the months that followed she was put on a tight budget, restricted to either Crookville or friends in New York, and made to understand that her support could easily be cut off.[59]

Given this information, Maggie had to make a decision. The easiest choice would have been to abandon Elisha and return to the exciting and lucrative world of spiritualism—her services were still much in demand and she could easily have joined Leah and Kate at their séance tables in New York. This, however, was not the choice she made. Far more clever than the Kanes or Grinnells expected, Maggie understood what was at stake, what they were trying to do, and how she could best work the situation to her advantage. She knew they wanted her out of Elisha's life but she also knew they would continue to support her for fear she would go public with the relationship if they angered her. She also understood that if she put all her faith in Elisha both surviving the arctic and agreeing to marry her, she risked alienating her spiritualist friends and being cut off from the one method she had of supporting herself.

With these realities facing her, Maggie played both sides. She studied at Crookville, but also spent many months in New York, maintaining contacts with spiritualist friends and even performing private séances from time to time.[60] Even more importantly, she ensured that people knew who was supporting her and to what ends. Her friendships with Ellen Walter and Dr. Edward Bayard and his family were especially helpful for these purposes because they moved in the same social circles as the Kane and Grinnell families. Before sending a series of letters to Elisha, she first sent them to Walter for her perusal. Walter wrote Maggie that she found the letters "very sweet and touching from their sympathy and pure affection breathing throughout them" and referred to the relationship in romantic terms, addressing Elisha as "the noble friend... to whom you have given your heart's best love."[61] By confiding in these people about the relationship, Maggie ensured that he would face social consequences if he abandoned her.

It is not surprising that Maggie was cunning in her attempts to maintain a claim on Elisha's promised intentions and support. Their relationship and her subsequent abandonment of spiritualism put her in a dangerous situation. If Elisha refused to marry her, she ran the risk of being left destitute with little means of ever regaining financial or social stability. Her actions were thus careful and premeditated. These tactics did not mean she did not love him—her letters clearly show that she did—but love or no love, like all nineteenth-century women she had to be proactive in ensuring that an increasingly intimate relationship did not cost her both her reputation and her financial well-being.[62]

While Maggie remade herself as a "lady" and strove to maintain a hold on Elisha's promise of marriage, and while Cornelius Grinnell and Patterson Kane worked to keep the relationship a secret, Dr. Kane's celebrity continued to grow throughout the country. In many ways Elisha's absence was the best thing he could have done for his own promotion. As Leo Braudy noted in his study of fame, celebrities achieve the "highest realms of fame" after they die—when the actual person is no longer around to get in the way of the perfection of their projected image. As long as a hero is alive, they will do things the public sees as inappropriate, thus causing "innumerable irritations that plague the fan." This is no longer a problem once they are dead because the public can then construct and mold the object of their gaze without fear of having it contradicted by the person behind the image.[63] In terms of fame, going to the arctic in the 1850s was equivalent to dying. With no communication possible, no blunder or scandal could be reported. This meant that the only "news" about Dr. Kane came from those manufacturing it—Kane's family and publisher, and the public itself.

Once the initial fanfare of the expedition's departure subsided and the last letters from the *Advance* reached the United States from Greenland, the next news about Dr. Kane came from the Harper Brothers, and it was tragic. Soon after Elisha's departure, his father and Tom completed the manuscript of *The United States Grinnell Expedition in Search of Sir John Franklin* and submitted it to Harpers for final edits and publication. With an exciting narrative and more than one hundred engravings and mezzotints, the book promised to be an attractive item for the Christmas season. To this end, Harpers printed several thousand copies and had them ready to ship when disaster struck. On the evening of December 10, 1853, a fire broke out at Harper Brothers, destroying thousands of books, including all but a few copies of *The U.S. Grinnell Expedition*. The *New York Times* reported that all copies of Kane's book were destroyed and that, except for one advance copy given to Henry Grinnell, the book was lost because its plates had also burned.[64] Fortunately, this was not the case. On March 7, 1853, Judge Kane wrote Elisha that 4,000 bound copies of his book were destroyed in the fire, but that fifty copies survived, as well as one other that had been sent to England to secure copyright there. Although he had been concerned about how Harpers would handle things—especially since many of their contracts, including Elisha's, had burned in the fire—he happily reported that, "They went to work... like good fellows. The stereotype plates were luckily in a vault under the street & escaped. Harpers employed King & Baird of Philadelphia at once to print a new edition: and now it is again ready for publication."[65]

The Harper Brothers made Kane's book a priority and did a first run of three thousand copies which they released on March 9, 1854. Demand was so heavy that within a week they were preparing to print two thousand more.[66] Harper's, with the help of the Kane family, advertised the book heavily. Judge Kane sent advance copies to many well-known authors, scientists, and arctic explorers and gleaned highly complementary blurbs for the book from their letters of response.[67] During the week of the book's release, articles about Dr. Kane and his book appeared daily in the *New York Times*. The day before the book came out, an article entitled, "The Grinnell Searching Expedition," used the excitement regarding Elisha's second arctic expedition to promote his book about the first. It stated: "No one can read his narrative without a thrill of admiration for the generous spirit which led to this gallant crusade against the Polar ice. We do not hesitate to say that this beautiful volume, with its profuse illustrations, furnishes the most vivid and interesting account that has yet been given to the public, of the perils of Arctic navigation."[68] Two days later an ad by Harpers included the blurbs gathered by Judge Kane and cited "a distinguished English lady" (Lady Jane Franklin) who described the book as, "scientific, graphic, original, racy,— everything that is charming—superior to anything of the kind I have seen before." She then tied the book and Kane's arctic efforts directly to national prestige saying, "His country has reason to be proud of it. It is a national monument, worthy of the cause, and will be a standard work in your literature for ages to come."[69] This promotional effort worked well and copies sold rapidly. An article on the New York Trade Sale (a seasonal gathering of book publishers and buyers) from a few days later noted that, "The bidding for Kane's Grinnell expedition was remarkably spirited, and the number of copies ordered unusually large. Very few booksellers were present who did not secure copies."[70]

Harpers continued its promotional effort by making *The U.S. Grinnell Expedition* the cover story of the March 1854 edition of their popular periodical, *Harper's New Monthly Magazine*. This twelve-page article celebrated both Kane's book and his current expedition by noting that the narration of the first Grinnell Expedition "could not have fallen into better hands than those of the accomplished voyager to whom has been committed the charge of the Second Expedition." Its glowing prose and twenty-nine illustrations promoted the book as a monument to Kane's heroism and made its purchase seem almost a patriotic duty. Indeed, it is often difficult to tell what the article is promoting—Dr. Kane, his expedition, or his book.

For example, the last paragraph's use of many indefinite pronouns hides the signified with exclamatory signifiers, thus making the book, the expeditions, and Kane himself into a single entity in the reader's mind.

> It has shown that there are men to be found in every walk of life who are ready to expend their means and peril their lives for the sake of others. It was undertaken to subserve no private or selfish ends. Its sole design was to save those whose only claim upon the men who took part in it, was one growing out of common humanity. Peace has its triumphs, nobler than those of war; and this is of them.[71]

This initial promotion worked wonderfully, and publications from across the United States and England were soon singing the book's praises. New York's leading literary journal, *The Knickerbocker*, proclaimed: "The work has all the interest of a romance. We could not lay it aside, for half an hour at a time, until we had read every word of it, to the last page of the text." The *Southern Literary Messenger* agreed: "The Grinnell Expedition was an enterprise so honorable to the country that its record ought to be worthy of preservation both from its literary and artistic attractions; and such it is, thanks to the accomplished author and his excellent publishers." London's *Littell's Living Age* and *Atheneum* also both proclaimed that the book was "one of the most interesting of the kind that we have seen, and deserves a place by the side of our most cherished records of Arctic adventure."[72] Prominent New York lawyer and diarist George Templeton Strong, who was often skeptical of the

One of the dramatic illustrations from the cover story of the March 1854 *Harper's New Monthly Magazine* that heavily praised Kane's book, his bravery, and the prospects of his then-absent second expedition.

AURORA SEEN SOUTH OF CAPE FAREWELL.

literature of his day, noted that he was "most pleased with Dr. Kane's volume of Arctic experiences. It's far more attractive than any narrative of northern voyages and discovery that I've met. Franklin's first journey has a strong tragic interest, but this far surpasses it in clearness and picturesqueness of description and conveys a much more distinct image of the perils and marvels of the polar ice."[73]

As these accounts show, people praised Kane's book largely because of its powerful narrative force; it was a factual account that read like a novel. Elisha's ability to produce popular narratives accounted for much of his later popularity, and it is thus important to examine how he and his family worked to construct these narratives in a manner that would appeal to the American public. Elisha had an exciting story to tell, and this alone would have made the book popular, but Elisha and his family knew that careful editing and framing could enhance the story (and its sales) even more. They thus worked very conscientiously to enhance the power of his narrative by tapping into several of the popular literary trends of the day.

The first and most obvious way Elisha structured his narrative was to write it in the style of a scientifically precise exploration account. By including extensive maps, footnotes, and charts that recorded the changes in wind direction, tides, temperature, and barometric pressure, he ensured that his findings would be honored by the scientific community.[74] Unlike most scientifically respected exploring accounts, however, Elisha did not let precision restrict his prose. In the mid-nineteenth century much of the public was still skeptical of fiction—it was essentially lying after all. Because of this, well-written travel narratives were often "best sellers," embraced for their authenticity as well as adventure. Herman Melville's "true" books about his seafaring adventures, *Omoo* and *Typee*, sold far better than did his fictionalized *Moby Dick*. Other travel narratives, such as Bayard Taylor's *View's A-foot*, Richard Henry Dana's *Two Years Before the Mast*, John C. Frémont's Western exploration narratives, and George William Curtis's *Howadji* adventures were also among the bestselling books of the 1840-1850s.[75]

By providing scientific precision while embracing the framework of popular exploration narratives—a first-hand account of exciting adventures in an exotic land—Elisha tapped into the Romantic sentiment of the times in a new way. Americans' view of nature was shifting in this era. They saw nature as a vast array of minerals, plants, and animals to be catalogued and placed within the continuum of the Great Chain of Being, but also as a dynamic and sublime force that moved not only tides and glaciers, but emotions as well. They were fascinated "not with the image of man living in the state of nature, but with man in dramatic confrontation with a beautiful, ageless and often terrifying nature."[76] In this age of Romantic exploration, there was much talk of the "sublime power of nature." In his 1757 essay on "the sublime and the beautiful," Edmund Burke defined the sublime as a response instigated by ideas of pain, danger, and terror that resulted in "the strongest emotion which the mind is capable of feeling." Feelings of terror, he explained, produce far stronger emotions than pleasurable occurrences, and can, in the right circumstances, produce far greater feelings of delight.[77] The sublime is the powerful emotion people feel when they observe something immense and terrifying from a perspective that allows them to feel its power, but not an immediate physical threat. This is why people ride rollercoasters, climb mountains, and slow down at accident sites. It is also why they marvel at the vastness of the ocean, the magnitude of a skyscraper, or the power of a storm. In the mid-nineteenth century, feelings of the sublime went hand in hand with Romanticism's view of nature. It was a force too powerful to describe, too awe-inspiring to fathom, and thus the ultimate source of delight. Elisha addressed this Romantic sentiment by providing the sublime emotion that Americans wanted. As Strong noted in his diary, Kane's book proved to be better than previous arctic narratives because of its "clearness... of description" and its ability to convey a "much more distinct image of the perils and marvels" of the arctic.

The ability to invoke feelings of the sublime made Elisha's narrative powerful. He allowed people to feel the terrors and the awesome beauty of the arctic by writing in a style that read like an unfettered first-impression. This narrative style allowed readers to feel as though they too were there with him, experiencing everything he was experiencing. Creating this first-impression feeling was difficult and came only after a long and tedious writing process that was anything but spontaneous. Like almost all aspects of his success, this impressive writing style owed a large debt to his dedicated and skillful family. Weeks before Elisha ever started writing, Tom noted that the narrative would have to be "perfectly unartificial" to be successful, and he urged Elisha to "write fresh from your notes of first impressions."[78] Judge Kane agreed with Tom, but he also recognized the difficulty of this task: How does one deliberately write a spontaneous narrative? After what must have been much thought, he wrote his son a letter of advice on this matter. He began, "Few of us can afford to take very long journeys (nowadays) and few to read very long book travels, but... many are glad to read the best plain narrative of one." To create a "plain" narrative, he suggested imitating the style Horace Greeley used in the *New York Tribune*, explaining that Greeley's reports "tell us all he saw or thought he saw and what were his really contemporaneous cogitations thereon,—but nothing more; they present us with no occasional sermons, writing desk improvisations or ex post facto raptures." By using this style, Judge Kane believed "nothing is allowed to assume an importance out of its due proportion, the reader is persuaded that [the author] has transferred to him the same impressions he would have received had he made the same journey under the same auspices as the author, and which if he were a man of as good sense and famous memory he would have best liked to remember for his friends at home."[79] This advice was quite perceptive and it identified a trend that scholars have since recognized in the writing of this era. Kristie Hamilton has noted that this first-impression, impromptu, "sketchbook" style developed in nineteenth-century newspaper and magazine writing, and that by the middle of the century it had spread to books as well. This is seen in the many titles of the era that advertise themselves as "dashes," "jottings," "peeps," "glances," and "glimpses."[80]

Elisha followed his family's advice, writing a descriptive, free-flowing narrative with much of his text taken straight from his journal. Once done, his father and Tom spent several months carefully editing his text to create, paradoxically, an "unedited" feeling.[81] The detailed appendix provided the exact statistics of the journey, whereas the text itself flowed easily, providing "glimpses" of all varieties of arctic life and scenery. The result was a book that gave readers both the spontaneous view of the arctic they wanted and the precise information they expected. In one scene typical of this style, the book quotes from Elisha's journal of August 28, 1850, right after they had discovered the graves of Franklin's men:

> The sun is traveling rapidly to the south, so that our recently glaring midnight is now a twilight gloom. The coloring over the hills at Point Innes this evening was somber, but in deep reds; and the sky had an inhospitable coldness. It made me thoughtful to see the long shadows stretching out upon the snow toward the isthmus of the Graves. The wind is from the north and westward, and the ice is so driven in around us as to grate and groan against the sides of our little vessel. The masses, though small, are very thick, and by the surging of the sea have been rubbed as round as pebbles. They make an abominable noise.[82]

The book's many illustrations also contributed to this combined feeling of spontaneity and accuracy. Some are detailed woodcuts of flora and fauna done in the style of a scientific guidebook, while others are dramatic scenes of ships and icebergs—man and nature—locked in a struggle for dominance. These latter were the scenes Elisha had James Hamilton depict in dramatic watercolor paintings and which Cornelius Grinnell felt had to be printed as color mezzotints because it was the only medium capable of "rendering the peculiar characteristics of the Arctic scenery."[83] In the book, the reader is assured of the authenticity of these dramatic, blue-tinted images, as each one is labeled, "From an original sketch by Dr. Kane." Reviews of the book also called attention to the power and authenticity of the illustrations: "Being made from sketches by the author, they are equally authentic with the text, and give, even better than words could do, an idea of the perils of Arctic navigation."[84]

Along with a sketchbook style and dramatic illustrations, Elisha used another literary tactic to evoke an emotional response to his narrative—authenticity. In her cultural study of nineteenth-century America, Karen Haltunnen found that as people moved from small towns to urban areas they became increasingly worried

Another stunning example of John Sartain's engraving of a James Hamilton painting that was taken from one of Elisha's arctic sketches. From Kane's *U.S. Grinnell Expedition* (New York: Harper Bros., 1854).

about being able to determine a person's trustworthiness. In a society of strangers, it was easy for "confidence men" and "painted women" to sneak into proper society by appearing true while being false. The result was what Haltunnen called a "cult of sincerity" and what other scholars have described as rituals of authenticity and virtue—efforts to ensure that one's exterior resembles one's interior. It was a code of etiquette and style that helped people to identify other proper and up-standing people by their dress and manners. Rituals of determination were conducted in the parlor—the meeting ground that bridged the public and private spheres where a family could investigate new people and judge their true character by their actions and attire.[85]

In many ways, a new book was much like a new acquaintance. It too was brought into the parlor and judged for its veracity and moral character. Parents, especially fathers, often insisted on previewing all reading material before allowing their families to read them. In Susan Warner's extremely popular and didactic novel, *The Wide, Wide World* (1850), this process is explicitly expressed as the fatherly figure John Humphreys carefully monitors the reading material of his young pupil (and later wife) Ellen Montgomery. He allowed histories, biographies of noble characters, hymn books, and moral magazines with "no fiction in them," but he forbade all mainstream magazines and novels—with the exception of *Pilgrim's Progress* (and we can assume *The Wide, Wide Word* itself).[86] These reading recommendations resonated with the American public. Warner's novel went through fourteen editions and sparked such spin-offs as "Ellen Montgomery's Book Shelf," which provided Americans with further examples of "good" reading material for their children. Women did not always like this censorship, but Barbara Sicherman, in her study of women's reading habits in nineteenth-century America, found that they did usually agree with it—as one woman commented, her father's literary tastes were "probably a wholesome factor in a household of women."[87]

Though Kane's narrative was a true tale of exploration, it still had to pass muster in the parlor, and this was potentially tricky because the book dealt with such gruesome topics as starvation, scurvy, polar bear hunting, and the "barbaric" rituals of Greenland's natives.[88] Furthermore, such a book could be seen as too proud—a man bragging of his achievements. As evidenced by the strict rules of propriety he enforced with Maggie, Elisha was a strong adherent to the rules of nineteenth-century decorum. It is thus not surprising that he began his book by placing its narrative firmly in the context of the home and parlor. In his introduction, he began with a note of humility and explained that, as the expedition's medical officer, he "had no claim to be considered its historian." He wrote the book only because he was "invited to prepare a history of the cruise" after DeHaven, the captain and rightful historian, declined the job.[89] With this established, Elisha humbly explained and apologized for his text:

> I had promised my brother at parting, that I would keep a journal, to furnish topics, perhaps, for a fireside conversation; and I have chosen to draw most of my materials from this record. I might have done more wisely, if I had been content to substitute sometimes the educated opinions of others for those which impressed me at the moment. My apology must be, that I do not profess to be accurate, only truthful.[90]

This explanation is telling in several ways. First, by noting that the text was originally written as material for a fireside chat with his brother, Elisha placed the book firmly within the physical context of the parlor. The narrative was surely safe for family reading because it was written not for a public audience, nor out of personal pride, but simply to facilitate conversation around the family hearth. Second, though the book contained charts and maps meticulously prepared to meet scientific standards, Elisha also drew from a different type of authenticity— simple truthfulness. The last line of his introduction states this bluntly: "I do not profess to be accurate, only truthful." He admitted that he may be fallible in his observations, he admitted that he had not always followed the advice of "educated opinions," and he apologized for both these faults. In doing this he demonstrated that he was no confidence man pretending to be something he was not; rather, he was simply a man providing the public with the honest, unedited impressions recorded in his journal. This professed dedication to first impressions assured authenticity. He did not claim to be right; he was only reporting what he saw. Elisha maintained this appeal to authenticity throughout the book by placing large portions of the text in quotes and by reminding the readers continually that, "I have thought it best to quote literally from my journal."

A final feature of Elisha's narrative style worthy of mention is his constant use of local analogies to explain exotic phenomenon. In some ways, this style is related to sincerity because it allowed readers to judge foreign material by comparing it with things they knew and understood. He described the first iceberg he saw as "about twice as large as Girard College," and later he compared an enormous ice floe to the Delaware River in midwinter: "There was the same crackling, and grinding, and splashing, but the indefinite extent—an ocean instead of a river—multiplied it to a din unspeakable."[91] These descriptions allowed American readers to relate to the exotic arctic landscape in a personal way. As Frank Rasky noted in his analysis of arctic narratives, Kane's book was unique because it "humanized the Arctic in terms that Americans could appreciate; it introduced genuine Yankee idiom to polar folklore. His narrative brims with freshly minted phrases: some overstrained, some whimsical, some delightfully extravagant, like the early Mark Twain."[92] Such writing can be seen in Elisha's description of an "Esquimaux kayack":

> While we were standing on deck... something like a large Newfoundland dog was seen moving rapidly through the water. As it approached, we could see a horn-like prolongation bulging from its chest, and every now and then a queer movement, as of two flapping wings, which, acting alternately on either side, seemed to urge it through the water.... It was a canoe-shaped frame-work,... graceful as the nautilus, to which it has been compared.... Indeed, even for a careful observer, it was hard to say where the boat ended or the man commenced; the rider seemed one with his frail craft, an amphibious realization of the centaur, or a practical improvement upon the merman.[93]

As the *Knickerbocker* noted in its review, "The work has all the interest of a romance."[94] Grinnell's financial backing and the artistic skills of James Hamilton and John Sartain further enhanced the book by providing visual examples of the Romantic era's view of nature's sublime beauty. In addition, and perhaps most importantly, Harper Brothers promoted the book and its author in a glowing style, gaining both nationwide exposure. As a result, by the end of 1854 the American public celebrated Dr. Kane as both a daring explorer and as one of the country's most skilled authors. Judge Kane proudly wrote to his son that his book had been praised by many American men of science as well as by Lady Jane Franklin and John Barrow of the Royal Admiralty, and that glowing reviews had appeared "in the London *Athenaeum & Morning Post, & Sharp's Miscellany* &c., &c." He told Elisha that he had recently had lunch with General Winfield Scott (the chief commander of the Mexican-American War) and that Scott had "talked flatteringly of you." He also noted that Park Benjamin, the prominent editor and poet, had been "rhyming about you in his lectures." "Indeed," Judge Kane concluded, "you are something of a celebrity just at this present."[95]

As fortune would have it, in the same month that Harpers released *The U.S. Grinnell Expedition* newspapers announced an opportunity to send mail to the Expedition via Captain Edward Inglefield, who planned to leave England for the arctic in early April. Many people took advantage of this opportunity and their letters show that Dr. Kane was becoming a popular hero. Friend and supporter George R. Russell wrote Elisha that he found his book "most excellent," and was sure it would "awaken great interest in your present undertaking" and "be sought for & read with avidity." His letter illustrates Kane's growing fame as he noted: "My wife often speaks of you &... my children rank you among the heroes & feel great interest to know where you are & what you are doing."[96] In Baltimore, George Peabody, a wealthy merchant and substantial backer of the expedition, also sang Elisha's praises. In a public speech he proclaimed, "In what story, ancient or modern, written to celebrate brave adventure, may you find courage and humanity so beautifully united, or danger more cheerfully embraced or generously pursued, than in that expedition which has recently left our shores under the conduct of Kane, our young countryman"[97]

Keenly aware of Elisha's growing fame, Tom wrote to his brother: "Father has probably told you of your reputation. It was not suffered to sink before your Book came out; and now this is a complete success. So far I see but one opinion in the journals that are reviewing it all over the country, and the best proof of the pudding is that it is selling off rapidly.... This is the best of puffs for a man; it is, and it will remain. So you must be prepared to come home and find yourself famous." Here, amidst his praise, Tom subtley reminded his brother that fame can cut both ways and that Elisha now needed to be more careful than ever with his reputation. He told Elisha that he hoped the arctic "has elevated your soul," and explained that, upon return, it was essential "that you will keep your bright name unsullied for us all till you die."[98]

Tom's comments that Elisha's reputation "was not suffered to sink," and his warning to keep his name "unsullied" suggests that the Kane family was worried about his reputation. Though not clearly articulated, these worries were based on his relationship with Margaret Fox because nothing else in his life at that time was cause for alarm. It is clear from this letter that Tom felt that his life and identity were tied to Elisha and his success. He wrote: "Dear Elisha, in the obscure life I lead, my ambition and my pride exist chiefly if not altogether through you. And I have no greater source of happiness than my ability to keep unimpaired my early love for you. I cannot trust this paper with the thoughts that crowd upon me, saying this. I am a mere calf when I allow myself to... wish you were home."[99]

Tom and Elisha's relationship went beyond usual brotherly bonds. They worked together on many projects and, most importantly, on the creation of "Dr. Kane." In fact, in many ways "Dr. Kane" was as much a result of Tom's efforts as it was of Elisha's. Elisha was Dr. Kane incarnate, the daring hero that provided the physical body and the actual adventures of Dr. Kane, but it was Tom who took this raw material and molded it into the adventures of the heroic figure that the public knew and adored. Elisha traveled the globe gathering exciting tales and adventures. Back at home in Philadelphia, Tom edited Elisha's adventures and turned them into the press releases, newspaper articles and books that turned Elisha the man into Dr. Kane the hero. Furthermore, what was true of Tom was in many ways true of the whole Kane family. Patterson worked diligently to keep Elisha's relationship with Maggie from hurting Dr. Kane's image and, far more than Elisha, Judge Kane spent hours editing and polishing the narrative of Dr. Kane's first arctic adventure. This explains why Tom implored Elisha to "keep your bright name unsullied for *us all* till you die." Tom's letter here hints at a reality that Elisha would soon painfully realize. Elisha Kent Kane the man and Dr. Kane the hero were becoming two different entities.

The summer months of 1854 brought with them heightened interest in the expedition as the American public began to look forward to the return of Dr. Kane and his gallant crew. This excitement increased when whaling ships began to return, one bringing with it letters from the American expedition. Written a full year before, just before the *Advance* was to cross the treacherous Middle Ice and enter Smith Sound, the letters were happily received but carried with them an ominous tone.

Among these letters was one to Maggie from Elisha. Apparently unaware that Maggie was then in New York, Cornelius forwarded this letter to Crookville. Mrs. Turner wrote Maggie of its arrival and Maggie quickly returned to retrieve it. Elisha began, "In the midst of ice and desolation I still think of you," and he then reassured her that he understood the difficulties of their relationship and asked her only to be "all that I have advised you to be, and thus reward me for an act which the harsh world could neither understand nor appreciate." Although this must have been somewhat comforting, it was not the promise of devotion Maggie was hoping for. The only assurance he gave for the future was, "Trust in my honor."[100]

In his letters to his family Elisha was optimistic and cheerful but openly addressed the dangers of the journey and his fear of suffering the same fate as Franklin. To Tom he noted his exact plans for travel in case he did not return after a second winter and a rescue party was organized.[101] And to his father he also addressed the possibility of a prolonged absence: "Should we remain out then a Second Winter—<u>Keep Hope alive in your hearts, Cheer Dear Mother and await the results of time</u>."[102]

Although these letters took nearly a year to reach the United States, the Grinnells believed that if the expedition was going well and arctic weather conditions were not unusually harsh, further news from the *Advance*, if not the *Advance* itself, would soon follow. Cornelius told Maggie: "I sincerely trust that we may again see our good friend the Doctor back again in October."[103] Later in July and again in August he restated this opinion and felt that exact news of the *Advance*'s arrival would soon reach them.[104] As summer turned to fall, however, anxiousness turned to anxiety. No further news of the expedition arrived and, to add to the apprehension, articles began appearing in national periodicals demanding that arctic searches be ended because they were far too costly and dangerous.[105] By mid-October, Cornelius wrote Maggie, "We have no tidings yet of the Doctor; nor do we look for him until the latter end of the month. My father says that if he is not at home by the end of November, that he will conclude that he intends to remain another winter in the Arctic regions." He noted more ominously, "You will perceive by the papers that Sir Edward Belcher has abandoned his squadron, and has returned to England, leaving Dr. Kane alone in the field."[106] This was bad news indeed. Belcher's expedition was a massive British effort that placed five ships under his command, captained by such seasoned arctic veterans as Henry Kellett and Leopold M'Clintock. After one winter in the arctic, Belcher, fearing he couldn't survive a second, packed all crewmembers aboard one ship, abandoned the rest, and sailed for England—this constituted the biggest failure in a long series of British arctic blunders. When news of these events reached America, fear for Kane and his men grew. Newspaper articles reflected this somber mood as they turned to biblical, prayerful prose when addressing their missing hero: "Verily, Dr. Kane and his bold comrades will have their reward.... That their return may be safe and speedy we earnestly pray, and thousands upon thousands would breathe the deepfelt 'Amen' to such an orison."[107]

After another month with no sign of Elisha's return, Maggie was a wreck. Edward Bayard's daughter wrote her a consoling letter, trying to brace her resolve and faith saying, "But dear Maggie, if he is only spared to return to you after his perilous journey, that is all you can ask. I pray that he may be guarded safely."[108] Maggie tried to stay focused on her studies, but with her future on hold and a growing fear that Elisha would never return, she left Crookville and went to stay with her

Mother and Mrs. Walter in New York, where she could seek solace among her friends and family.[109] Though Mrs. Turner did not feel that this was best for Maggie's education, she did not stop her. She wrote Mrs. Walter, "I really pitied her from my inmost heart, and felt that she required a change of scene to dissipate the sickness of the heart which arises from hope deferred."[110] Despite Mrs. Turner's constant pleas for her to return to her studies, Maggie remained in New York for the remainder of the winter. No letters from this period record her actions and her later narrative only notes that this was a "dreary interval when no tidings came, and gloom rested on the future."[111]

This was a dark time for the Kane family as well. The chilly fall winds from the arctic brought with it ominous news as late-returning whalers reported an especially cold summer and heavy ice blocking the northern portions of Baffin Bay. On September 30, Tom's wife Bessie recorded in her diary, "This day four years ago Elisha returned from his first Arctic Voyage. Where is he now!" The family gathered to mark this date, but it brought little cheer. Bessie reported, "There was a forlorn attempt to drink the health of the absent ones that broke down completely." Adding to their pain, the family also felt somewhat responsible for the hardships endured by the families of those men Elisha had taken with him to the arctic. "Thank God," Bessie wrote upon hearing that the wife of sailing master John Wall Wilson was being provided for, "we need not fancy her suffering from the want of our employment this winter."[112] By November, Judge Kane was pushing for a relief expedition. He gave a passionate speech before the American Philosophical Society and inspired them to pressure Congress for the speedy funding of an expedition. Henry Grinnell took up similar efforts in New York and Boston, former navy secretary John P. Kennedy followed suit in Baltimore, and the Smithsonian's Joseph Henry and the Coast Survey's head, Alexander Dallas Bache, began pushing for the cause in Washington.[113] These efforts were successful. The American public was soon calling for a relief expedition and the Senate was actively discussing the issue by mid-December.[114] Judge Kane lobbied the Senate and put pressure on the House to move quickly in their deliberations. He made it very clear that the rescue mission would have to leave by early summer if it were to be successful. In mid-January he wrote to an influential friend, "We passed the Senate today, but cannot get before the House till next Monday. In the mean time, if the legislatures of New York and New Jersey can be moved, they will help us much."[115] His efforts were a success. Both houses quickly passed a resolution for an expedition, and President Franklin Pierce signed it on February 5, 1855. Though encouraged, Judge Kane knew the battle was only half over; Congress still had to fund the expedition if it was to become a reality. As Congress debated, Henry Grinnell began planning the logistics of the rescue mission and consulted with Sir Edward Inglefield, the British commander who had been to Smith Sound in 1852.[116] Finally, after nearly a month of wrangling, both houses agreed to fund the expedition by tacking an additional $150,000 onto the annual Navy Appropriation Bill.[117]

Despite the fact that there were now funds to send out a rescue mission, Kane's safety was still anything but sure. After seven years of searching, Sir John Franklin's grim fate had just been learned the summer before when John Rae, while exploring King William Land for Hudson's Bay Company, discovered local tribes who had seen Franklin and his men abandon their ships in 1848 and then perish while trying to cross to the Canadian mainland. Even though this was second-hand information, few people doubted Rae's findings because he brought back several pieces of silverware that bore the crests of some of the expedition's officers, including Sir John himself.[118] Lady Jane continued to hope, but few others believed that any of Franklin's crew still survived. In the face of this news, Cornelius Grinnell, who had been so optimistic the year before, was now reserved in his hope for a speedy rescue of Elisha. He wrote Maggie, "If the Doctor returns this year, he will probably be here in October next; but if he is not home by that time, he cannot get here before October, 1856."[119] For the Kane family the relief expedition was greeted with mixed feelings. It offered a chance for the rescue of their eldest son, but their youngest living son, John, Jr., just weeks after earning his M.D. from the University of Pennsylvania, went against Elisha and his family's wishes and volunteered as the expedition's assistant surgeon.[120] The family now faced the possibility of losing another member to the icy arctic north.

With preparations for the relief expedition underway, Dr. Kane's fame grew as his persona began to take on a tragic hue. Rae's discovery of artifacts from the *Erebus* and *Terror* brought the search for Franklin essentially to an end and allowed the world to focus instead on the fate of Dr. Kane.[121] This became an issue of national pride for many Americans. They would not allow their native son to suffer Franklin's fate. "Doctor Kane is a gallant officer, conducting a hazardous and meritorious enterprise, with the consent and under the orders of the government," *The Pennsylvanian* noted, "and hence it becomes the duty of a generous government, representing a generous people, to take measures for his rescue or relief."[122] Another paper noted that "so great is the desire to afford relief to the Doctor and his men, that enough persons in and out of the Navy would volunteer to man and officer a very respectable fleet."[123] Taking advantage of the popularity of the relief expedition, the *North American Review* ran a thirty-five-page article on Kane's *U.S. Grinnell Expedition* that also called attention to the danger that now threatened its valiant author.[124] The search for Kane became so popular that even England briefly contemplated a rescue effort; Lieutenant Sherard Osborn of the Royal Navy asked Lady Franklin to help him push the Admiralty to send an English steamer to Smith Sound in search of Kane.[125]

As winter turned to spring and the ice that locked Baffin Bay slowly thawed, Kane's family and friends had nothing to do but wait. To help relieve their anxiety many of them occupied themselves by turning to the optimistic effort of preparing for Elisha's return. Horace Greeley had one of his reporters compile a detailed report for Elisha and entitled it, an "epitome of the World's progress during a portion of the period of your estrangement from civilization and newspapers."[126] Judge Kane also assembled a report for his son, informing him of Rae's discovery of Franklin's fate and other arctic news, as well as of the success of his first book. He wrote, "Your book, Franklin's fate, and the action of Congress in consequence of your failure to return have given you quite a historical notoriety." But his letter contained bad news as well:

> Your book has earned for you much fame; but as yet no profit. The Harpers were burnt out at the close of 1853, and the first edition of some 4,000 or 5,000 copies totally destroyed. In their account as sent to me they charge these as part of the edition, making you lose 1/2, and they make you debtor besides for the cost of all the illustrations save only one half of the wood cuts. The result is that they leave you in debt on an edition of some 9,000 copies in all. It is a rascally account.[127]

Cornelius Grinnell also wrote Elisha to prepare him for his return and he too began by noting Kane's popularity. "You are now the Lion of the Arctic Regions, and I pray to God that the present Expedition will bring you and your Companions safe honor where hearty welcome awaits you from, I may say, Every body." Cornelius then noted, "the eyes of the world are now all turned towards you and I am sure that your exertions will fully equal their expectations." Cornelius certainly meant this as praise—he wanted Elisha to be adored by the nation—but he also recognized that adoration brought scrutiny and Elisha had things that needed to remain hidden from the eyes of the world. He wrote, "I have sent you under separate cover several notes from Miss Fox since your departure. She has not written by this opportunity... as she appears to have received all impression from the newspapers that you are already on the way home." He told Elisha that Maggie was still at Crookville and that "she certainly deserves a great deal of credit for her steadiness and perseverance." He then noted that, though he had "carried out your wishes regarding her in every particular," it had not always been easy to keep the relationship quiet. He explained that Leah had "endeavored to spread about a report that you were educating Miss F. with the intention of marrying her on your return," and that this had stirred some speculation. These rumors first appeared in eastern newspapers in the spring of 1854 and spread quickly; by May a San Francisco newspaper ran on its front page a notice that, "One of the Fox girls" was "being educated at Philadelphia, as the *affianced* of the famous Dr. Kane, now in search of Sir John Franklin."[128] But Cornelius assured Elisha, saying, "I have done everything in my power to contradict such insinuations, and as I have heard nothing of them of late I trust they have 'died out.'" He mentioned no further details, but said, "Your brother will write to you on this subject."[129]

Though several members of the Grinnell and Kane family wrote Elisha to prepare him for his homecoming, the most important letter was the one written by his devoted brother Tom. In the weeks before the relief expedition left, Tom dedicated himself to figuring out how Elisha's image should be managed to assure that "Dr. Kane" met all the expectations the nation had for their arctic hero. On the day of its departure, Tom traveled aboard the rescue expedition's steamer *Arctic* to wish his brother John a final goodbye and to write Elisha a letter that would provide him with any pertinent, last-minute information. As the steamer made its way toward Staten Island, Tom began his letter, and after a brief but emotional salutatory paragraph, he got to the heart of the matter—how Elisha should conduct himself upon his return. He began, "fortune has made you the child of your whole country, and not of any part of it; a fact to be remembered when you draw near New York."[130]

At this time, the United States was anything but united as the North, South, and West each had distinct interests and were often at odds to protect them. The Kane family itself was intensely involved in these sectional disputes: Tom served as Brigham Young's advisor on national issues affecting the Utah Territory, and Judge Kane was in the middle of the struggle between Northern and Southern relations thanks to his rulings in several of the most important legal tests of the 1850 Fugitive Slave Act.[131] Given the heated relations between sections of the country, Tom knew that it was important for Elisha to remain neutral on all controversial issues if Dr. Kane was to maintain his popularity in all regions. To make this point, Tom noted that the rescue expedition for Dr. Kane received support from across the divided nation. "We used to think together how much more... the North had done for the Franklin Search than the rest of the Union. In the search after you, it has not been so. If there has been any difference among the States it has been in favor of those lying West & South of Jersey. Our Philadelphia press led in the discussion of the question... and, when the thing came into Congress, it owed its success to the earnest Southern influence brought to bear upon it."[132]

Sectional differences were not Tom's only concern. He informed Elisha that during his absence Dr. Kane had become the hero of many "different classes of persons." He explained, "You have had the misses of the Northern Young Ladies Seminaries with you, but you have also carried the most ugly gritty of your own naval men." He further noted that among military men, all ranks "have been y[ou]r backers," and that when a crew for the rescue effort formed, "all, and the best of them... volunteered from the first." Elisha and the Kane family often doubted the sincerity—not to mention competency—of career military men, but Tom addressed this prejudice with a warning. "You may reply that they [volunteered] with a view to their own interests, &c. Granted, but this is not the version of it which the country adopts, and which they w[oul]d have their brethren to receive. They assert that they must rescue you as a brother officer—a gallant friend—an honor to their own corps. This has become the accepted statement of the affair, and [by it]... you thereby must hereafter stand."

Tom made it very clear that, in order to create the optimum heroic persona for Dr. Kane, Elisha needed to put his own thoughts and feelings aside and to behave as the public expected. Elisha Kent Kane the man had many prejudices. As a member of an elite Philadelphia family, he held many of that society's biases regarding class and regional differences; these are seen in his class-conscious re-education of Maggie Fox as well as in his condemnation of both the South's "perversion" of the Democratic party, and the North's "chizzling" Yankee ways.[133] Though these prejudices existed in Elisha, they could not appear in Dr. Kane if this image was to maintain the heroic status it had gained during Elisha's absence. While Elisha was gone, Dr. Kane had been able to become all things to all people because he was, in essence, fictional. He was the tragic and heroic lost explorer who, like Ulysses in the contemporary poem by Alfred Lord Tennyson, sought "To strive, to seek, to find, and not to yield"—a similarity that was lost on neither the public nor Elisha himself.[134] Once Elisha returned, however, Dr. Kane would be mortal again—a real man whose actions could alienate Dr. Kane's adoring public. How was this to be avoided? Tom knew and he explained it to Elisha.

> When a nation makes a pet of a man, all it requires of him is to take his petting gracefully.... Your tack will be the official Scientifics—Science with the brevet of sword spunk and gentlemanly savior faire—Hurrah Horse and head of Bureau... or American Humboldt—and so forth. You have the chance of pushing this thing to its very farthest—a worthy aim for the ambition of any man. But a little study of a concise sham modesty of speech in public, and a composed and courteous demeanor universally, will compass more than all the geodetic schemes & computations your head will ever master.[135]

Here Tom showed that he understood the nature of celebrity. When and if Elisha returned from the Arctic, he would be a hero—a person who had accomplished great and amazing deeds. Dr. Kane, however, was more than a hero, he was a celebrity. As Tom noted, "The last piece of <u>furnishing</u> done on y[ou]r account was a column of anecdotes for the lecturer of an Arctic Panorama which you may laugh at yourself some day."[136] Few Americans had ever met Elisha Kent Kane the physician from Philadelphia, but thousands knew the larger-than-life character "Dr. Kane"—the star of the latest panorama show and the hero of newspaper poems and soliloquies. Tom understood this. He recognized what scholars have since labeled "celebrity"—the idea that fame comes not from great deeds, but from the public knowing and celebrating those deeds. Fame is a product not of heroism, but of journalism—of having one's image constantly before the public eye. This explains why Tom ended his comments to Elisha saying, "remember your newspaper friends. Respect *ou l'adieu!* — It is they who <u>made us and not we ourselves</u>."[137]

Having finished his instructions for Elisha, Tom returned to New York while his letter continued on to the unknown North. Several months later, this letter would be opened at a far-northern port and there give Elisha his first tidings of the duality that would mark the rest of his life. Two and a half years in the far north would make Elisha "master of the Arctic," but it would also make him the slave of "Dr. Kane."

The Relief Expedition left New York on May 31, 1855, two years to the day after the *Advance* had departed from the same location. The rescue effort consisted of two ships, a 327-ton clipper bark and a 558-ton propeller steamer, both refitted for Arctic conditions and renamed the *Release* and the *Arctic*, respectively. Finding commanders for these vessels had been difficult only because so many qualified men volunteered for the positions. DeHaven, the obvious choice, was unwilling to go because of ill health, but other officers from the first Grinnell Expedition were more than willing to command. The *Advance*'s first officer, William Murdaugh, and second officer, William I. Lovell, both volunteered, as did the *Rescue*'s captain, Samuel P. Griffin. After considering each of these men, Secretary of the Navy John C. Dobbin chose not to give the command to any of them, but to Henry J. Hartstene, a lieutenant with twenty-seven years of naval experience and, as a veteran of the Wilkes Expedition to the south polar seas, familiarity with polar conditions. As commander of the expedition, Hartstene captained the smaller and faster *Release*, with Lovell as his sailing master, while Lieutenant Charles C. Simms served as acting captain of the steamer *Arctic*.[138]

The expedition departed from New York and headed directly for Newfoundland on stormy seas that left John Kane, Jr. extremely seasick—apparently a family trait. They left Newfoundland bound for Greenland but soon had their first mishap when the *Release* hit an iceberg and was then rammed by the *Arctic*, which she was towing.[139] Though this collision startled both crews, no serious damage was done and the ships soon reached Greenland's coast and headed on to the northern whaling port of Upernavik. There they were greeted with ominous tidings. The governor asked the expedition's doctors to examine Carl Petersen's wife because she was ill with grieving, convinced that her husband had perished along with the rest of the long-absent Grinnell Expedition. The whalers returning from the far north also brought bad news, reporting that Melville Bay was completely choked with ice and practically impassable. Undaunted, Hartstene pushed on. After several bad nips and a few fearful days locked in pack ice, the two vessels emerged from the Middle Ice and passed into the open North Water that led to Smith Sound. They continued still further north and entered Smith Sound but were soon blocked by solid pack ice. Unable to go any further, Hartstene and his crew rowed small boats along the shore, looking for any sign of the *Advance*. Searching together aboard the same boat, Hartstene and John Kane were surprised by a most welcome sound, human voices. They rushed ashore and found that the men they heard were not the men they sought, but rather several members of the far-northern Inuit village of Etah. Using a phrase book and sign language, they learned that these Inuit had been in frequent contact with "Kayen" and his men, a fact proved by the many articles from the *Advance* they had among them. One of the Inuit who greeted them was Myouk, who had spent enough time with the crew of the *Advance* to have learned some English. With his help and drawings, Hartstene learned that Kane and his men had abandoned their ship several months before and gone south into Baffin Bay aboard two small boats.[140]

With this news, Hartstene turned south and searched the nearby islands off Cape Alexander at the entrance to Smith Sound. Then, ignoring Myouk's statement that Kane and his men had headed southeast toward Melville Bay, Hartstene turned his ships to the southwest and the opening of Lancaster Sound. He did this because, before Elisha departed for the Arctic, this was the direction he said he would go if he ran into trouble. Fortunately Hartstene soon ran into heavy pack ice that completely blocked Lancaster Sound. Far more quickly than most Arctic explorers before him, Hartstene made the wise decision to rely on the wisdom of the natice people instead of his official orders, and thus he turned back toward Melville Bay and the direction Myouk originally indicated. He had to again cross the Middle Ice to accomplish this, which proved to be a harrowing experience when the *Release* hit an iceberg and was nearly capsized in heavy seas. They made it across, but only after powerful winds had pushed them south of both Melville Bay and Upernavik and forced them to dock at the port of Godhavn on the southern side of Disco Island.[141]

So it was that on September 11, 1855, as they came into sight of Godhavn, they saw the Danish brig *Mariane* about to set sail. As the American vessels came into view of the port, there was a sudden commotion aboard the *Mariane*—two small boats were quickly lowered from her deck and began rowing fiercely toward the *Release*. As John Kane, Jr. wrote later: "The men in the boats were long-bearded and weather beaten; they had strange, wild costumes; there was no possibility of recognition." But as the small boats grew closer, John did recognize one familiar figure—a small man "standing upright in the stern of the first boat, with his spy-glass slung around his neck."[142] Shocked by this sight, Captain Hartstene hailed the boat asking, "Is that Dr. Kane?" As Elisha remembered later, "with the 'Yes!' that followed, the rigging was manned by our countrymen, and cheers welcomed us back to the social world of love they represented."[143]

New-York Daily Times.

DR. KANE HOME AGAIN.

The Second and Third Arctic Expeditions Safely Ended.

Arrival of Propeller Arctic and Bark Release at New-York.

THE ADVANCE LEFT IN THE ICE.

NEW LANDS FOUND.

A Bridge of Ice from Greenland to the Continent.

AN OPEN SEA FOUND.

NO TRACES OF SIR JOHN FRANKLIN.

LATITUDE 82° 30' N. REACHED.

LIFE IN THE FROZEN REGIONS.

ON SLEDGES FOR THIRTY DAYS.

Detailed and Interesting Account of the Two Expeditions.

DR. KANE'S OWN ACCOUNT.

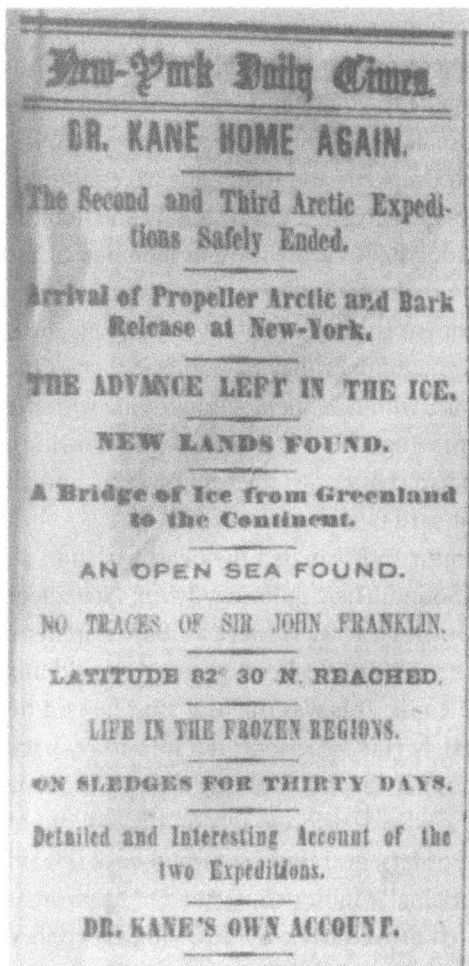

The stacked headlines of the October 12, 1855, edition of the *New York Times* that proclaimed the return of Dr. Kane and his discovery of an Open Polar Sea.

A few days later the *Release* and *Arctic* sailed directly from Godhavn to New York and thus the nation learned no news of Dr. Kane's rescue until the two boats appeared off Sandy Hook, New Jersey, in the early afternoon of Thursday, October 11. According to the *Times*, as the ships headed up the bay to quarantine, "Every tongue did its best to circulate the gladdening intelligence" and the news "spread throughout the City with the rapidity of scandal in a country town." They reported that in their excitement, "Merchants forgot the dignity of their positions, and stood familiarly with their clerks; the clerks rubbed shoulders with the porters, and all joined in conversation on the subject.... Old women looked out from their parlor windows and asked their neighbors if they'd heard the news... and cartmen leaned upon their rungs, regardless of a job, and, for once, with pleasant countenance, told their co-workers that Dr. Kane was coming up the bay."[144] Flags flew and cannons roared from Governor's Island, the Battery, and several of the city's shipping ports. The *Tribune* reported the next day: "From the decks and rigging of ships, from the forts, and, in fact, from every available position, three cheers were swelled and prolonged until the vessels neared the Battery, abreast of which they moored."[145] When Kane and his men disembarked, they were greeted by throngs of reporters and well-wishers. New York papers rushed to print Kane's story. The day after their arrival the *Times* dedicated its entire front page to Kane's homecoming. The first of their thirteen block headlines announced what every paper within reach of the telegraph proclaimed as well, "DR. KANE HOME AGAIN."[146]

1. Cornelius Grinnell to Maggie Fox (undated, c. June, 1853), reprinted in [Margaret Fox] *The Love-Life of Dr. Kane* (New York: Carleton Publisher, 1866), 155.
2. *New York Times* (June 1, 1853), 5.
3. *Illustrated News* (March 5, 1853), 148.
4. W.L. Duval to Elisha Kent Kane (Dec. 22, 1852), APS Elisha Kent Kane papers. This letter from Duval, a printer, notes that the cost of each tinted illustration would be $8.00 for set-up costs, 50¢ per tint color and 25¢ for paper for each hundred prints. Elisha accepted these terms and used Duval for the ten tinted (blue & black) illustrations in his book. He was still inspecting and critiquing these illustrations in April 1853. See Thomas Leiper Kane to Elisha Kent Kane (undated, c. April, 1853), APS Elisha Kent Kane papers.
5. Elisha Kent Kane to John K. Kane (undated, c. March, 1853) in folder, "Kane, E.K. to Mrs. J.D.L. Kane," APS Elisha Kent Kane papers.
6. Cornelius Grinnell to Elisha Kent Kane (undated, c. March, 1853), APS Elisha Kent Kane papers. Grinnell refers to "Kennedy's narrative" but he appears to have confused William Kennedy with John Richardson; both Arctic explorers had books circulating at that time. Harpers was then strongly promoting Richardson's *Arctic Searching Expedition*, which they published in 1852 and reprinted in 1854; Kennedy's book, *A Short Narrative of the Second Voyage of the Prince Albert, in Search of Sir John Franklin* was printed in London by W.H. Dalton in 1853 and was not being promoted by Harpers.
7. Elisha Kent Kane to John P. Kennedy (May 17, 1853), reprinted in Henry T. Tuckerman, *The Life of John Pendleton Kennedy* (New York: G.P. Putnam, 1871), 227-28.
8. Elisha Kent Kane to John K. Kane (July 23, 1853), APS Elisha Kent Kane papers.
9. Cornelius Grinnell to Elisha Kent Kane (Jan. 19, 1853) and Cornelius Grinnell to Robert Patterson Kane (Feb. 4, 1854), APS Elisha Kent Kane papers; Elisha Kent Kane to Maggie Fox (undated, c. April, 1853), *Love-Life*, 104-06; and multiple letters from Cornelius Grinnell to Maggie Fox, *Love-Life*, 161-62, 170-73, & 182-83.
10. Elisha Kent Kane to Robert Patterson Kane (undated, c. June, 1853), APS Elisha Kent Kane papers. This packet of letters still survives, bound together by a pink ribbon and in the folder, "Kane, E.K to Margaret Fox," APS Elisha Kent Kane papers.

11. Elisha Kent Kane to Robert Patterson Kane (undated, c. June, 1853), APS Elisha Kent Kane papers. Emphasis in original.

12. Elisha Kent Kane to Maggie Fox (undated, c. June, 1853), *Love-Life*, 157.

13. Elisha Kent Kane to Robert Patterson Kane (undated, c. June, 1853), APS Elisha Kent Kane papers.

14. This event is described in N.P. Willis, "The Post-Mortuum Soiree," *The Home Journal* (June 15, 1850), 2.

15. Elisha Kent Kane to Dr. Hawks (July 19, 1853), APS Elisha Kent Kane papers.

16. *Love-Life*, 146-150; George Corner, *Dr. Kane of the Arctic Seas* (Philadelphia: Temple University Press, 1972), 123-24.

17. Corner, 118-21. It should be noted that Kane spelled "Sontag"' with one "n" but Sonntag himself signed it with two.

18. R.F. Lewis to Elisha Kent Kane (March 28, 1853), APS Elisha Kent Kane papers.

19. R.F. Lewis to Elisha Kent Kane (March 28, 1853), APS Elisha Kent Kane papers.

20. *New York Times* (April 15, 1853), 4.

21. Lady Jane Franklin to John P. Kennedy (May 7, 1853), and Elisha Kent Kane to John P. Kennedy (May 17, 1853), in Tuckerman, 226-28.

22. John Wall Wilson, "Narrative of the Second Grinnell Expedition in Search of Sir John Franklin," National Archives, Washington, D.C.

23. From a letter from Henry Goodfellow, reprinted in William Elder, *Biography of Elisha Kent Kane* (Philadelphia: Childs & Peterson, 1858), 276-77. Elisha's improved health was probably the result of the largely germ- and allergy-free environment of the Arctic. For a full discussion of Elisha's health see George W. Corner, "Hero with a Damaged Heart: The Clinical History of Elisha Kent Kane, M.D.," in *Medicine, Science, and Culture: Historical Essays in Honor of Owsei Temkin* (Baltimore: Johns Hopkins Press, 1968), 249-63.

24. Elisha Kent Kane to Thomas Leiper Kane (July 14, 1853), reprinted in Elder, 188-89.

25. L. H. Neatby, *Conquest of the Last Frontier* (Athens: Ohio University Press, 1966), 5-6.

26. Elisha Kent Kane, *Arctic Explorations* (Philadelphia: Childs & Peterson, 1856), I, 19.

27. Corner, 121.

28. James R. Percy to Elisha Kent Kane (Feb. 21. 1853); S.W. Ludlow to Henry Grinnell (Jan. 17, 1853); D. Macaulay to Henry Grinnell (Jan. 19, 1853), APS Elisha Kent Kane papers.

29. Kane hired Morton as his personal valet and assistant shortly before the first Grinnell Expedition, a position Morton never relinquished. Fox noted that Morton often served as their go-between and it was Morton who in later years would accompany Elisha to England and then on to Havana where Elisha died.

30. Corner, 120.

31. Cornelius Grinnell to Elisha Kent Kane (undated, March, 1853), APS Elisha Kent Kane papers.

32. Elisha Kent Kane to Kane Family (June 8, 1853), APS Elisha Kent Kane papers. At this

point it seems Elisha expected his family to immediately turn his letters into press releases because in this one he asks them not to, saying, "Don't let any of [this] peculiar letter find its way into the newspapers but send an extract to Mr. Grinnell."

33. Elisha Kent Kane to Spencer F. Baird (undated, c. May 12, 1853), Baird papers, Smithsonian Institution.

34. Corner, 130-31. In this instance, as in many others during the Second Grinnell Expedition, Corner's biography of Kane in invaluable. Corner provides a balanced and accurate account of what truly occurred on the expedition by comparing the popular account of this expedition, Kane's *Arctic Explorations*, with Kane's private journal and the other crewmembers' accounts. Having read these sources myself, I have come to trust Corner's interpretation and I rely heavily on his scholarship in my analysis of the Second Grinnell Expedition.

35. Kane, *Arctic Explorations*, I, 23-24. In this period, all northern tribes were generally referred to as "Esquimaux" or "Eskimos." Today, while northern tribes in Alaska and the northern Pacific region still refer to themselves largely as Eskimos, the tribes of northern Canada and Greenland prefer Inuit, which is how I will address them.

36. Elisha Kent Kane to Cornelius Grinnell (July 20, 1853), Historical Society of Pennsylvania, John Kane papers.

37. Elisha Kent Kane to John K. Kane (undated, c. July 25, 1853), APS Elisha Kent Kane papers.

38. Elisha Kent Kane to Henry Grinnell (May 17, 1853); and Elisha Kent Kane to John P. Kennedy (May 19, 1853), quoted in Elder, 178.

39. See Pierre Berton, *The Arctic Grail* (New York: Viking Penguin Inc., 1988), 235-36, 241.

40. Elisha Kent Kane to John K. Kane (undated, c. July 27, 1853), APS Elisha Kent Kane papers. It is uncertain how or when this letter reached the Kane family. Most likely, Elisha sent it back to Upernavik via contact with the far-northern Inuit villages of Kingatok, Kettle, and Yotlik that stretch up Melville Bay and into Smith Sound.

41. Corner, 123. According to Corner, Crookville, now completely non-existent, was "about four miles north of Chester, on Ridley Creek, just above the bridge by which Providence Road crosses the stream."

42. Kate Fox to Amy Post (June 19, 1853), Amy and Isaac Post papers, Department of Rare Books and Special Collections, University of Rochester.

43. Elisha Kent Kane to Dr. Francis Hawks (July 19, 1853), APS Elisha Kent Kane papers.

44. *Love-Life*, 149-50.

45. Elisha Kent Kane to Maggie Fox (June 13, 1853), *Love-Life*, 159-61.

46. Cornelius Grinnell to Maggie Fox (Aug. 23, 1853), *Love-Life*, 162. For Maggie's general mood, see folder, "Margaret Fox to Cornelius Grinnell," APS Elisha Kent Kane papers. These letters are all undated but show that Fox was continually asking Grinnell for funds and complaining of her loneliness.

47. *Love-Life*, 163. It is difficult to determine who "Mrs. Warner" was, as she is never

addressed by her full name and her letters provide little personal information. Both Maggie and Elisha knew her, and Maggie would often confide in her. Her letters show her to be a friend of the Fox family but also sympathetic to Kane and his reputation because, in later years, she tried to talk Maggie out of publishing Elisha's love letters. One strong possibility is that she was Abby Warner, a contemporary spirit-rapper from Ohio who rose to fame in December of 1851 when she was arrested after disrupting the Christmas Eve sevice at the Episcople Church of Massillon, OH, when rapping noises emanated from around her. She was taken to court for disrupting a religious service and represented by Dr. Abel Underhill, a long-time supporter of spiritualism and the eventual husband of Leah Fox. See Frank Podmore, *Modern Spiritualism: A History and Criticism* (London: Methuen & Co., 1902) vol 1, 304.

48. Suzanna Turner to Maggie Fox (Dec. 12, 1853), *Love-Life*, 165-66.
49. Ellen Walter to Suzanna Turner (Dec. 14, 1853), *Love-Life*, 166-68.
50. Suzanna Turner to Ellen Walter (Dec. 15, 1853), *Love-Life*, 168-69.
51. For Cornelius's positive feelings about Maggie, see Cornelius Grinnell to Elisha Kent Kane (Jan. 19, 31 & Feb. 2, 1853), APS Elisha Kent Kane papers. The Grinnells had donated the *Advance* and large sums of time and money to the expedition, which was officially called, "The Second U.S. Grinnell Expedition."
52. Cornelius Grinnell to Maggie Fox (Aug. 23. 1853), *Love-Life*, 162-63.
53. Elisha Kent Kane to Dr. Francis Hawks (July 19, 1853), APS Elisha Kent Kane papers.
54. Cornelius Grinnell to Elisha Kent Kane (June 2, 1855), APS Elisha Kent Kane papers. Here Grinnell tells Elisha about Leah's efforts, noting that he was largely able to discredit them.
55. Corner, 227.
56. *Love-Life*, 170-71.
57. Cornelius Grinnell to Robert Patterson Kane (Feb. 4, 1854), APS Elisha Kent Kane papers.
58. Robert Patterson Kane to Cornelius Grinnell (Feb. 13, 1854), APS Elisha Kent Kane papers.
59. Implied in multiple letters in folder, "Margaret Fox to Cornelius Grinnell," in the APS Elisha Kent Kane papers; and *Love-Life*, 170-73.
60. Maggie's movements between New York and Crookville are noted in *Love-Life*. Several undated letters in folders, "Margaret Fox to Cornelius Grinnell," and "Margaret Fox to E.K. Kane," APS Elisha Kent Kane papers, also note these movements and mention her involvement with several séances.
61. Ellen Walter to Maggie Fox (March 7, 1854), *Love-Life*, 170-71. Note also letters to Maggie from Bayard's wife and daughter regarding her relationship with Elisha, *Love-Life*, 179-81, 186-87.
62. Maggie's deep affection for Elisha is seen in her surviving letters to him. The price this love could cost her was not unique to her, nor were the means she went through to ensure his support. See Karen Lystra, *Searching the Heart* (New York: Oxford

University Press, 1989).

63. Leo Braudy, *The Frenzy of Renown: Fame and Its History* (New York: Oxford University Press, 1986), 6.

64. *New York Times* (Dec. 12, 1853), 1.

65. John K. Kane to Elisha Kent Kane (March 7, 1854), John Kane papers, folder "letters to E.K. Kane," Historical Society of Pennsylvania. Most of the engravings had been printed in Philadelphia under the direction of Sartain and Hamilton and so were not threatened by the fire. Inexplicably, a few wood-block illustrations differ between the reprinted "First Edition" and the few surviving copies of the original edition that survived the fire. There is a copy of the original edition at the Historical Society of Pennsylvania.

66. Eugene Exman, *The Brothers Harpers* (New York: Harper & Row, 1965), 359-60. Thomas Leiper Kane to Elisha Kent Kane (March 15, 1854), APS Elisha Kent Kane papers. In this letter Tom notes that Sartain told him that after an initial run of 3000, Harpers ordered another 2000 copies of the engravings.

67. John K. Kane to Elisha Kent Kane (March 7, 1854), Historical Society of Pennsylvania, John K. Kane papers.

68. *New York Times* (March 8, 1854), 4.

69. *New York Times* (March 10, 1854), 5.

70. *New York Times* (March 15, 1854), 2.

71. *Harper's New Monthly Magazine* 8 (March, 1854), 446.

72. *The Knickerbocker* 48 (April, 1854), 410-12; *Southern Literary Messenger* 20 (April, 1854), 256; *Littell's Living Age* 40 (March 11, 1854), 516-17; *Athenaeum* (Dec. 3, 1853), 1583-84.

73. *Diary of George Templeton Strong*, Allan Nevins & Milton Halsey Thomas eds. (Seattle: University of Washington Press, 1988), 70. The editors incorrectly note that Strong was addressing Kane's later book, *Arctic Explorations*.

74. Elisha Kent Kane's *The U.S. Grinnell Expedition* (New York: Harper & Brothers, 1854) included a fold out map and a 63-page appendix, including charts on currents, winds, air and water temperatures, barometric pressure, and meteorological abstracts.

75. For a good discussion of the popularity of travel narratives, see Carl Bode, *The Anatomy of Popular Culture, 1840-61* (Berkeley: University of California Press, 1960), 221-35; William Goetzmann, *New Lands, New Men* (New York: Viking Penguin Inc., 1986) and *Exploration and Empire* (New York: W.W. Norton Co., 1966); and Larzer Ziff, *Return Passages: Great American Travel Writing, 1780-1910* (New Haven: Yale University Press, 2000).

76. William H. Goetzmann & William N. Goetzmann, *The West of the Imagination* (New York: W.W. Norton & Co., 1986), 148.

77. Edmund Burke, *A Philosophical Enquiry into the Origin of our Ideas of the Sublime and Beautiful* (South Bend, IN: University of Notre Dame Press, 1986), 39-40.

78. Thomas Leiper Kane to Elisha Kent Kane (Jan. 1, 1851), APS Elisha Kent Kane papers.

79. John K. Kane to Elisha Kent Kane (undated), folder "Kane-Arctic Exp. Notes-Miscellaneous," APS Elisha Kent Kane papers. It is a bit odd that John K. Kane chose Greeley as an example of this style because Greeley was infamous for his sermonizing and moralizing on issues.

80. For a discussion of this literary phenomenon see Kristie Hamilton, *America's Sketchbook: the Cultural Life of a Nineteenth-Century Literary Genre* (Athens: Ohio University Press, 1998).

81. Judging from their letters, Elisha turned his text over to his father and Tom for editing in December 1852 and they continued to work on it until at least July 1853.

82. Kane, *The U.S. Grinnell Expedition*, 172.

83. Cornelius Grinnell to Elisha Kent Kane (Aug. 18, 1852), APS Elisha Kent Kane papers.

84. *New York Times* (March 8, 1854), 4.

85. Karen Halttunen, *Confidence Men and Painted Women* (New Haven, CT: Yale University Press, 1982). See also, Paul Boyer, *Urban Masses and Moral Order in Urban America, 1820-1920* (Cambridge, MA: Harvard University Press, 1978).

86. Susan Warner, *The Wide, Wide World* (New York: Feminist Press, 1987, 1850), 350, 464, 477, 506.

87. Barbara Sicherman, "Sense and Sensibility: A Case Study of Women's Reading in Late-Victorian America" in *Reading in America*, Cathy N. Davidson, ed. (Baltimore: Johns Hopkins University Press, 1989), 201-25.

88. That exploration narratives could be seen as inappropriate is evidenced by the fact that Lady Jane Franklin feared that Kane's second book, *Arctic Explorations*, was too descriptive of the sufferings of arctic exploration and would offend people and prejudice them against future arctic explorations.

89. Kane, *U.S. Grinnell Expedition*, 15-16.

90. Kane, *U.S. Grinnell Expedition*, 16.

91. Kane, *U.S. Grinnell Expedition*, 27, 52.

92. Frank Rasky, *The North Pole or Bust* (New York: McGraw-Hill Ryerson Limited, 1977), 166-67.

93. Kane, *U.S. Grinnell Expedition*, 37-38.

94. *The Knickerbocker* 48 (April, 1854), 410-12.

95. John K. Kane to Elisha Kent Kane (March 7, 1854), folder "letters to E.K. Kane," John Kane papers, Historical Society of Pennsylvania.

96. G.R. Russell to Elisha Kent Kane (March 11, 1854), APS Elisha Kent Kane papers. Russell's letter was directed to Cornelius Grinnell and notes, "I saw a few days since a notice in the newspapers that there would be an opportunity to send letters to you by way of England if forwarded to Mr. Cornelius Grinnell of New York before the 15 inst." Russell was a significant supporter of the expedition, and Elisha named a cape in Kane Basin in his honor.

97. Baltimore *Sun* (Dec. 5, 1855), clipping in the Dow papers, Stefansson Arctic Collection, Dartmouth College. This article addresses Peabody's long dedication to

Kane's efforts and notes that he made this speech shortly after Elisha's departure for the Arctic.

98. Thomas Leiper Kane to Elisha Kent Kane (March 15, 1854), APS Elisha Kent Kane papers.

99. Thomas Leiper Kane to Elisha Kent Kane (March 15, 1854), APS Elisha Kent Kane papers.

100. Elisha Kent Kane to Maggie Fox (undated, c. July 23, 1853), *Love-Life*, 175-76.

101. Elisha Kent Kane to Thomas Leiper Kane (July 14, 1853), reprinted in Elder, 188-89.

102. Elisha Kent Kane to John K. Kane (undated, c. July 20, 1853), APS Elisha Kent Kane papers. Emphasis in original.

103. Cornelius Grinnell to Maggie Fox (July 17, 1854), *Love-Life*, 173.

104. Cornelius Grinnell to Maggie Fox (July 29 & Aug. 17, 1854), *Love-Life*, 176-77.

105. See for example *The Guardian* 11 (Oct., 1854), 158-59; *National Magazine* 6 (Jan., 1855), 24-31; *New York Times* (Oct. 28, 1854), 4.

106. Cornelius Grinnell to Maggie Fox (Oct. 17, 1854), *Love-Life*, 178. Belcher's massive five-ship expedition was the greatest blunder of English Arctic exploration. Belcher abandoned all but one of his ships and returned home having made no new discoveries.

107. *New York Times* (Oct. 31, 1854), 4.

108. [Miss Bayard] to Maggie Fox (Oct. 12, 1854), *Love-Life*, 179-80.

109. Maggie Fox to Cornelius Grinnell (Nov. 7, 1854), APS Elisha Kent Kane papers.

110. Suzanna Turner to Ellen Walter (Dec. 7, 1854), *Love-Life*, 182.

111. *Love-Life*, 178.

112. Elizabeth Wood Kane Journal, 1854-57 (Sept. 30, 1855), BYU Thomas Leiper Kane papers. Thanks to Matthew Grow for calling my attention to this entry.

113. Corner, 220.

114. See articles on the Senate debates in the *New York Times* (Dec. 12, 15, 20 & 27, 1854).

115. John K. Kane to J.D. Dinker (Jan. 15, 1855), Kane family papers, Clements Library, University of Michigan.

116. E.A. Inglefield to Henry Grinnell (Jan. 17, 1855), APS Elisha Kent Kane papers. In the summer of 1852, Inglefield took Lady Franklin's steamer, *Isabel*, to the head of Baffin Bay and entered Smith Sound, pushing 80 miles further into it than any previous expedition. See Edward A. Inglefield, *A Summer Search for Sir John Franklin, with a Peek into the Polar Basin* (London, T. Harrison, 1853). He recommended that the rescue operation use a small, strong steamer manned by a crew no larger than 25 men.

117. Corner, 221.

118. The search for Sir John Franklin began in 1848 and by the time of Rae's discovery no fewer than 27 ships had been sent in search of him. For the complete story of Sir John Franklin's fate, see Scott Cookman, *Ice Blink: The Tragic Fate of Sir John Franklin's Lost Polar Expedition* (New York: John Wiley & Sons, Inc., 2000).

119. Cornelius Grinnell to Maggie Fox (April 20, 1855), *Love-Life*, 182-83.

120. *New York Times* (May 25, 1855), 4; and John K. Kane, Jr. to J.C. Dobbin, Secretary of the Navy (March 2, 1855), cited in Corner, 222.

121. After Rae's discoveries, the British Admiralty called off all searches for Franklin and continued the effort only by asking the Hudson's Bay Company to do a brief search of the area Rae described. Lady Jane continued to promote missions and her persistence sparked a few more expeditions, most notably F.L. M'Clintock's 1859 journey to King William's Island aboard the *Fox* and his discovery of the record of the Franklin Expedition.

122. *The Pennsylvanian* (Dec. 21, 1854), 1.

123. Unlabeled clipping in the Dow papers, Stefansson Arctic Collection, Dartmouth College. Several other articles expressing similar sentiments regarding Kane's rescue appear in this collection as well.

124. *North American Review* 80 (April, 1855), 307-42.

125. Sherard Osborn to Lady Franklin (Feb. 10, 1855), transcript in Dow papers, Stefansson Arctic Collection, Dartmouth College. Osborn knew Elisha from their meeting at Beechy Island in 1850. Nothing came of this effort.

126. J.W. England (marine reporter for the *New York Tribune*) to Elisha Kent Kane (May 28, 1855), APS Elisha Kent Kane papers.

127. John K. Kane to Elisha Kent Kane (May 29, 1855), John Kane papers, Historical Society of Pennsylvania. Elisha's contract with Harper & Brothers was destroyed in the fire of December 1853. The only documentation of this publication in the Harpers' papers are two letters disputing what the contract said. See letters between Cornelius Grinnell and the Harpers in *The Archives of Harper and Brothers, 1817-1914* (Teaneck, NJ: Chadwyck-Healey Microfilm Edition, 1980), reels 1 and 51.

128. San Francisco *Daily Placer Times & Transcript* (May 22, 1854), 1.

129. Cornelius Grinnell to Elisha Kent Kane (June 2, 1855), APS Elisha Kent Kane papers. Presumably the brother he is referring to is Patterson, with whom he often discussed Maggie and Elisha's relationship. If Patterson wrote Elisha regarding the relationship, the letter has been lost.

130. Thomas Leiper Kane to Elisha Kent Kane (May 31, 1855), APS Elisha Kent Kane papers.

131. For Tom's involvement with Mormon political issues see Matthew Grow "'Liberty to the Downtrodden': Thomas L. Kane, Romantic Reformer" (PhD diss., University of Notre Dame, 2006) forthcoming from Yale University Press. Judge Kane vigorously upheld the Fugitive Slave Act in the controversial *Christiana* case of 1850, and just a month after the expedition left, he would become embroiled in the *Passmore Williamson* case, in which his ruling would directly address states' rights to regulate slavery and the slave trade.

132. Thomas Leiper Kane to Elisha Kent Kane (May 31, 1855), APS Elisha Kent Kane papers. David Chapin also notes the national unity that Kane inspired (especially at the time of his funeral) in his article "'Science Weeps, Humanity Weeps, the World Weeps':

America Mourns Elisha Kent Kane," *The Pennsylvania Magazine of History and Biography* 123 (Oct., 1999), 275-301.

133. Elisha Kent Kane to William Weaver (March 20, 1850); Elisha Kent Kane to John K. Kane (c. Feb. 16, 1852), APS Elisha Kent Kane papers. During this era, the Mid-Atlantic states (specifically New York and Pennsylvania) experienced massive industrialization and immigration, which created huge disparities in wealth and a marked class consciousness. Also, in the heated disputes between the North and South the Mid-Atlantic states tended to take a middle ground as geographically and socially they were neither fully Northern nor Southern.

134. Charles W. Shields, "The Arctic Monument Named for Tennyson by Dr. Kane," *Century Magazine* 34 (1898), 483-92.

135. Thomas Leiper Kane to Elisha Kent Kane (May 31, 1855), APS Elisha Kent Kane papers.

136. Thomas Leiper Kane to Elisha Kent Kane (May 31, 1855), APS Elisha Kent Kane papers. Several Arctic panorama shows were touring in 1855, and when the search for Kane became popular, his story became the driving narrative of at least some of them. For example, a panorama show explicitly about Kane (painted by George Heilge and promoted by "Dr. E. Beale") debuted in Washington, D.C., in September 1855. See Russell A. Potter & Douglas W. Wamsley, "The Sublime yet Awful Grandeur: the Arctic Panoramas of Elisha Kent Kane," *Polar Record* 35 (Jan., 1999), 193-206.

137. Thomas Leiper Kane to Elisha Kent Kane (May 31, 1855), APS Elisha Kent Kane papers. Emphasis in original. For good discussions of "celebrity" see Braudy, 3-18; and Daniel Boorstin, *The Image* (New York: Macmillan Publishing Co., 1961, 1987).

138. Corner, 220-22.

139. John Kane Jr., "The Kane Relief Expedition," *Putnam's Monthly Magazine* 7 (July, 1856), 451-63. Though John K. Kane, Jr.'s account of the relief expedition was the most publicized—appearing in a national magazine—three other accounts exist. See Hartstene's official report to the Secretary of the Navy and the diaries of William Lovell and head surgeon James Laws, both housed in the Stefansson Arctic Collection, Dartmouth College.

140. John K. Kane Jr. "The Kane Relief Expedition"; and Corner, 222.

141. John K. Kane Jr. "The Kane Relief Expedition."

142. John K. Kane Jr. "The Kane Relief Expedition."

143. Kane, *Arctic Explorations*, II, 297.

144. *New York Times* (Oct. 12, 1855), 8.

145. *New York Tribune* (Oct. 12, 1855), 4.

146. *New York Times* (Oct. 12, 1855), 1.

5

The Cold Reality of Heroism:
The Second Grinnell Expedition

W hen the *Release* and *Arctic* appeared off Sandy Hook, New Jersey, as they entered New York Harbor on October 11, 1855, they sparked a frenzy of excitement and activity. By the time they reached New York City, an eager and ever-growing mob had thronged to the Naval Battery to hear the tale of their long-lost hero. The last solid information regarding the expedition had been the letters the crew left at Upernavik in late July 1853, just before they attempted to cross the dreaded Middle Ice of Melville Bay. More than two years of worried silence followed these last epistles, and America and the world were now anxious to hear the exciting discoveries and sublime horrors that had undoubtedly transpired.

The public eye was now firmly fixed on Dr. Kane's expedition, and it was up to Elisha to tell the tale. He had begun preparing for this moment even before the expedition set sail, forcing each of his crewmembers to relinquish their rights to publish their own accounts of the journey. Elisha took this so seriously that he removed the expedition's naturalist when he refused to comply with this demand.[1] Judge Kane had been intimately involved in the struggle that raged after the return of the U.S. Exploring Expedition in 1842, when Captain Charles Wilkes, fearing what his disgruntled crew would say about him, had confiscated all their journals to ensure that he alone would write the expedition's narrative. This act caused many bitter feelings and years of litigation. To prevent such an incident from happening to his son, Judge Kane advised Elisha to make his exclusive authorship of the narrative clear before the expedition ever sailed.[2] Because of this agreement, as well as his claim to the story as the expedition's commander, Elisha had complete control of the presentation of the expedition to the public. He needed to be cautious and calculated with the story he told, however, because the tensions of the expedition had been far greater than either the clamoring newspaper reporters or the anxious public suspected. There had been many instances of heroism, discovery, fortitude, and loving brotherhood that Elisha was excited to tell, but there was also a dark side that had to be handled carefully. Mutiny, death, poor leadership, and, as one crewmember would later claim, attempted murder had marred this harrowing expedition. As Elisha well knew, these facets of the story had to be obscured or recast if Dr. Kane was to maintain his reputation.

❧

When the eighteen men aboard the *Advance* left port on the last day of May 1853, they were all anxious for adventure, but each had vastly different expectations and backgrounds. The crew was made up of ten navy volunteers and seven men gathered by Kane and Grinnell. The most trusted and loyal to Elisha were his powerfully built first officer, Henry Brooks, and his Steward and personal assistant, William Morton. Both of these men had been aboard the First Grinnell Expedition and had eagerly volunteered to serve again under Elisha's command. As noted earlier, German astronomer August Sonntag was the best-paid member of the crew because Kane had gathered funds from several scientific agencies for his hire. Henry Goodfellow, a friend of the Kane family, volunteered; so too did Amos Bonsall and Jefferson Baker, both from Pennsylvania and acquainted with Elisha before the expedition began. Goodfellow and Bonsall had specific tasks aboard the expedition—Goodfellow was a naturalist, and Bonsall was in charge of the expedition's photographic equipment. Of the navy men, Kane handpicked the recently graduated surgeon Isaac Hayes, likely because he reminded him much of himself. He also had a hand in picking their cook, Peter (Pierre) Schubert, who worked at the famous Delmonico's restaurant, which Elisha frequented when in New York. John Wall Wilson and James McGary were both signed from the navy volunteer list as sailing master and second officer. Wilson was ambitious and amiable, but he was largely inexperienced. McGary had some arctic experience, as did the ship's carpenter, Christian Ohlsen—both had worked aboard whaling ships as far north as Davis Strait. In addition to the other Navy men—George Riley, George Stephenson, George Whipple, and cabin boy Thomas Hickey—the two final crewmembers were William Godfrey and John Blake, whom Grinnell hired from the New York wharves to fill out the crew.[3]

With such a small crew, Elisha hoped that he could command without resorting to harsh naval discipline. To this end, he informed the crew that there would be only three rules governing the ship: "First, absolute subordination to the officer in command or his delegate; second, abstinence from all intoxicating liquors, except when dispensed by special order; third, the habitual disuse of profane language."[4] These rules were soon put to the test. Before the *Advance* even reached arctic waters, Elisha severely disciplined both Godfrey and Blake for insubordination, having both these warfmen bound and placed below deck for several days. Even more distressing, Elisha found that Wilson, who as sailing master was officially second in command, was often indecisive and unable to gain the respect of the crew. After a blunt talk with him, Elisha made Brooks his superior, an act that left Wilson with an ambiguous place in the chain of command and bad feelings toward his commander.[5]

Kane added two more crewmembers in Greenland: the Inuit hunter Hans Christian Hendrik, and the Danish sledge-driver and Inuit interpreter Carl Petersen. Thus, by the time the *Advance* prepared to cross the Middle Ice, Elisha had come to recognize that commanding this group of nineteen men from six different countries was not to be as easy as he had originally hoped.[6] In one of the letters he left at Upernavik he told his father of these difficulties, but remained optimistic. "[E]very thing connected with the <u>personnel</u> of our little party is encouraging.... I put the dark side towards you as a matter of sober duty—I neither anticipate nor fear extremes."[7] This was the last news the Kanes or anyone else in America heard from the expedition for the next two years.

On July 29, 1853, Elisha left the thin channel of clear water along Greenland's coast and cut westward through Melville Bay and the Middle Ice. This decision, based on his observation of the narrowing waterway and the thinning of the shore ice, appeared to be the best option. DeHaven had stuck to the waterway two years earlier and was blocked by ice, whereas the *Prince Albert* had set off to the west and made it through. Furthermore, Kane thought British explorer Edward Inglefield was also on his way to Smith Sound, and Elisha wanted to get there well ahead of him. The next days were harrowing. Moving ice constantly slammed against the *Advance*, and the crew worked almost without rest to cut, pull, and pry their ship through the broken and fast-moving drift-ice. At one point, the *Advance* collided head-on with a large berg that broke her jib boom and destroyed one of her lifeboats. Petersen, critical of Elisha and the rest of the crew, was horrified by this and later asserted that he and Ohlsen saved the ship by taking temporary command while Elisha and Brooks argued about who was at fault for the near disaster.[8] Whether foolish or wise, Elisha's gamble to cross the Middle Ice paid off handsomely. The *Advance* broke free of the pack and into the relatively ice-free North Waters in just six days. Thanks to a fine northwest wind, they made good time, and the awe-inspiring headlands of Cape Alexander and Cape Isabella that marked the entrance to Smith Sound were in sight by August 6. As they passed these enormous, eight-hundred-foot cliffs, Elisha noted poetically that these "Arctic pillars of Hercules... look down on us as if they challenged our right to pass," and that even the usually stoic sailors were impressed by their grandeur.[9] This is just one of several instances in which Elisha called attention to the disparity between his romantic view of nature and the sailors' practical, prosaic views.

The next day they arrived at the final point outlined by Inglefield's earlier exploration of the mouth of Smith Sound, the tiny Littleton Island, where they left a cairn noting their arrival. They then went ashore to stow a small lifeboat and some provisions in case of a future disaster. After naming the spot Lifeboat Cove, raising a proprietary flag, and then giving three cheers to the United States, they discovered that they were not the first people to claim this desolate shore as a place of rest. The ruined stone structures of several small houses and graves marked what had once been a small Inuit settlement. Elisha was fascinated by the graves' simple elegance— stones piled over cross-legged corpses that sat among all the tools they had used in life. In his journal he noted admiringly that, despite the graves' valuable contents (tools were hard to come by in a land with little wood or metal), "Esquimaux never disturb a grave." In a telling juxtaposition, he followed this sentence by noting that "from one of the graves I took several perforated and rudely fashioned pieces of walrus ivory." He also removed several skulls.[10]

These statements and actions bring up the difficult issue of this and all nineteenth-century expeditions' relationships to native peoples. In his examination of the Wilkes and Kane expeditions, Barry Allen Joyce argued that American explorers always viewed natives as inferior to assure themselves of their superiority, especially in circumstances where they felt out of place and powerless. This feeling of superiority, he argued, caused explorers to see native populations as objects to study, collect, and do with as they pleased and not as human. Of Kane and the Second Grinnell expedition he noted, "both during and after the two year journey into the Arctic, Kane could give no more than grudging acknowledgement to the people to whom he and his party owed their lives."[11] Joyce certainly has a point. Kane and his men often survived only because of the aid of far-northern Inuit tribes, yet Kane maintained an attitude of superiority that is shocking to modern readers albeit not unusual for his time. As Joyce asserted, it is likely that this attitude came largely from his need to maintain a feeling of control when he was rendered powerless by arctic conditions; but Joyce overstated his argument.

Unlike most of the expeditions preceding his own, from the outset of his journey Kane embraced and credited natives and native ingenuity for much of the expedition's success. Kane's plan to use dog sleds and to clothe his men in fur garments of native construction demonstrates this. So too does his inclusion of both Inuit Hans Hendrik and interpreter Carl Petersen as members of his crew. Even more telling, when Elisha outlined the five things that he felt were absolutely necessary for the success of his expedition, he specifically named "the co-opera-tion of the Esquimaux."[12] Elisha certainly held many of the prejudices toward na-tive peoples that marked his era and thus did many insensitive and cruel things; this is not surprising. What is surprising is the extent to which he broke with the attitudes of his own era—by the end of the expedition he had adopted Inuit ways of survival and had come to acknowledge and even admire their culture. This was extraordinary for the day and, perhaps more than anything else, explains the vastly different outcomes of Kane's and Franklin's arctic entrapments.

Elisha pushed northward after leaving Littleton Island, but the expedition soon hit dense pack ice and was forced to seek shelter in a small cove. The *Advance* remained stuck in this cove for several days, during which time the fifty-seven ca-nine members of their crew, having been tightly confined for weeks on end, erupted in mutinous behavior. Elisha brought along the sled dogs to help him with later travels but did not recognize the full burden of housing these creatures. In early August he noted that they were more like "ravening wolves" than dogs, and that keeping them fed was "a difficult matter." Things had grown worse within a few more weeks: "These wretched dogs!... the unruly, thieving, wild-beast pack! Not a bear's paw, or an Esquimaux cranium, or basket of mosses, or any speci-men whatever, can leave your hands for a moment without their making a rush at it, and, after a yelping scramble, swallowing it at a gulp." Furthermore, if the dogs were allowed off the ship, they immediately scattered "like a drove of hogs in an Illinois oak-opening," and it took hours to recapture them.[13] The crew shot two polar bears, but their enormous carcasses lasted the dogs only eight days. It was soon apparent that keeping the dogs fed and from destroying the ship was to be a constant struggle.

The dogs were not the only rowdy members of the crew. On August 11 William Godfrey again acted up, this time physically assaulting John Wilson. As he had done before, Kane had Godfrey tied hand and foot and locked in the booby hatch with only bread and water. On August 13 the weather cleared and Elisha again set out into the ice-clogged sea, but hours of hard work pushed the *Advance* only three quarters of a mile further north. The crew worked late into the night, and, after only a few hours of sleep, Elisha roused them again. A storm was coming and they had to secure the ship or face being placed at the mercy of the fast-moving ice. After twenty-one more hours of hard labor (Godfrey was temporarily freed to help with this effort), they finally managed to secure the *Advance* to a small rocky island via three strong whale lines. The weather calmed over the next few days, and Elisha sent small boats forward to scout out possible avenues for further north-ern advancement, but storms began again on August 18, and two days later "it blew a perfect hurricane." The crew watched helplessly as the whale lines popped one-by-one and the *Advance* was cast off into the rushing sea. For the next two days the crew was in constant peril. They narrowly escaped being crushed between two enormous bergs, and later an ice floe forced the ship up a long, sloping berg and completely out of the water. Several members of the crew had to be temporarily abandoned when they attempted to attach the *Advance* to a large iceberg and were cut off by fast-moving ice. The storm finally subsided, and once the lost crewmembers were retrieved, the men jumped overboard onto the ground ice, strapped themselves into harnesses, and pulled the ship three miles further north along the shore. A careful measurement that night showed that they were at latitude 78°41', further north than any other expedition had ever reached via the American route.[14]

Elisha had his men attempt to pull the *Advance* further north through the ice, but after several days of this arduous labor, one crewmember openly stated that he felt their effort was useless and proposed they return to more southerly waters for the winter. Elisha immediately called his officers together and found that, with the exception of Brooks, they all agreed. "Not being able conscientiously to take the same view," Elisha determined to remain in the sheltered inlet they had reached that day and to send a team further north to investigate other possibilities, a decision his crew took "in a manner that was most gratifying, and entered zealously upon the hard and cheerless duty it involved."[15] Elisha took seven men with him, left Ohlsen in charge of the *Advance*, and set off on a ten-day journey to scout the northern coastline. On their third day he found that the slender lead of open water he had hoped to follow was blocked by a ten foot wall of ice attached to an enormous limestone cliff a thousand feet high. Elisha climbed the wall of ice and pushed on with three volunteers. From a headland well north of 78°50', he was able to see that the entire basin was solid ice to well beyond 80° North.

Upon returning to the *Advance*, Elisha announced that they would remain where they were for the winter. The crew received this news gratefully and set to work securing the ship and preparing for the long, dark months ahead. A few days later, on September 10, the temperature fell to fourteen degrees and the tiny harbor froze solidly, allowing the men to easily walk from ship to shore. During the next weeks the crew transferred the content of the hold to supply houses built on shore and constructed a wooden housing over the ship's deck to shelter this area from the ravages of the coming winter. They also happily built a dog kennel on the shore, but were disappointed when the dogs refused to use it, returning instead to the ship each night. On a small islet a hundred yards from the ship, Kane and Sonntag built a small observation hut in which they set up their thermometers, barometers, and magnetic instruments. These small efforts gave the barren harbor a nominal feeling of civilization. To add to this feeling, Elisha dubbed their arctic abode Rensselaer Harbor, reminiscent of his family's warm and secure country estate nearly two thousand miles to the south. Neither he nor his crew then

The *Advance* lodged in the ice of Rensselaer Harbor, the place Kane's expedition called home from the fall of 1853 through the summer of 1855. From Kane's *Arctic Explorations* (Philadelphia: Childs & Peterson, 1856).

knew that this was to be the final resting place for three of their number and that the *Advance* would depart only years later, unceremoniously crushed and sunk by the arctic ice that would force her crew to abandon her stripped and worn hull.[16]

In preparation for the winter and the sled journeys he hoped to make in the spring, Elisha kept the crew busy throughout most of October. Seven men, led by Second Officer McGary, traveled far up the northern coast to deposit food and supplies at three points to facilitate spring excursions. While they were gone, the rest of the crew worked to make the ship as comfortable as possible for the winter. While they built a shelter over her decks, Hayes and Elisha used their combined chemistry skills to concoct a way of driving out the rats that were rapidly multiplying below deck. Their first attempt involved "the vilest imaginable compound of vapors—brimstone, burnt leather, and arsenic." This had no effect on the rats, but it nearly killed Schubert, who passed out when he went below deck to season his soup. They then attempted to asphyxiate the pests by stoking up the ships' three stoves and filling her with carbon monoxide. This effort killed twenty-eight rats, but nearly ended in disaster when the super-heated stoves set the deck on fire. While putting out the blaze, both Elisha and Brooks were rendered unconscious from the fumes.[17]

By mid-October the sun completely left the sky, leaving only a twilight glow during afternoon hours. Elisha kept himself busy practicing with his dog team, trying to master its steering mechanism, a twenty-foot whip; however, the bitter cold and twenty-four-hour darkness of the arctic winter soon forced him and the rest of the men below deck. By the first week of November it was difficult to read a thermometer at noon and even faint stars were visible all day. On November 7, Elisha wrote in his journal: "Our darkness has ninety days to run before we shall get back again even to the contested twilight of today. Altogether, our winter will have been sunless for one hundred and forty days."[18] With the coming of winter, already frigid temperatures plummeted; by the end of October they had fallen to minus twenty-five and continued to drop until early February when they were often more than one hundred degrees below freezing. Though Elisha tried to keep the crew's spirits up by having a dress-up ball and beginning a newspaper, *The Ice-Blink*, by late-December conditions were miserable. Nervous and deranged by the continual darkness and harsh conditions, the dogs howled constantly and died in large numbers—only six survived the winter. Scurvy began to take its toll as fresh meat supplies dwindled, affecting all crewmembers to one degree or another. Confined to tight quarters lit only by smoky lanterns and the cook stove, the men struggled to maintain their sanity. Blake snapped in January and had to be confined when he refused to obey any orders and threatened to kill all the dogs. Elisha himself was struggling; he recorded in his journal, "I am so afflicted with the insomnium of this eternal night, that I rise at any time between midnight and noon."[19] Even Hans, who had always lived in the arctic and was familiar with the darkness of winter, found this more northerly winter insanely oppressive. He recalled later, "Never in my life had I seen the dark season like this.... I thought we should have no daylight any more. I was seized with fright and fell a-weeping."[20]

The incredible harshness of the arctic winter reduced the crew to near desperation, but it did not end Elisha's dedication to science. Twice every day, despite the excruciatingly cold temperatures and complete darkness, Elisha, Hayes, Bonsall, and Sonntag took turns trudging the hundred meters out to their little observatory to record the temperature, currents, wind direction, and barometric pressure. In addition to this, they observed and carefully documented several occultations of Saturn and Mars, and once a week they would alternate watches for a full twenty-four hours, manning a magnetometer, chronometer, and telescope to record general magnetic and astronomical data. The extreme cold made this difficult; their skin instantly froze to the metal instruments, and the thermometers had to be read from a distance with a telescope because the mere approach of a person, so dramatically warmer than the outside temperature, changed its reading. In March 1854 Elisha noted that even with their small stove glowing red hot, the temperature in the observatory would often be "twenty degrees above zero at the instrument, twenty degrees below zero at two feet above the floor, and minus forty-three degrees at the floor itself."[21] This dedication to a strict and regular observation schedule in such extreme circumstances, along with his careful collection of hundreds of plant, animal, and mineral samples, is testimony to Elisha's commitment to science. No matter what else one may say of his expedition, the pages and pages of meticulously recorded numbers, recorded with mittened hands in temperatures one hundred degrees below freezing, are testimony to the scientific spirit of the age and Elisha's dedication to fulfilling his duty as a student of nature.[22]

By late February the sun again rose high enough in the sky to cast a few rays of light across the *Advance*'s deck. At first sign of light, Elisha climbed to the top of a nearby crag and there, alone, welcomed back the sun. When the few faint rays hit his face after more than ninety days of darkness, he said it "was like bathing in perfumed water."[23] But the return of the sun did not bring much relief from the bitter cold; average temperatures remained below negative forty degrees. Despite these temperatures, Elisha was determined to begin preparations for the summer's northern excursions. In the fall, while laying out the food depots, McGary and his party discovered an enormous glacier, which Elisha named for the world-renowned German scientist, Alexander Humboldt. Elisha was determined to reach this glacier and to push beyond it to what he was sure would be the warmer waters of the Open Polar Sea.

Excited by the prospects of new discoveries, by March 19, despite loud protests from Petersen, Elisha equipped eight of his men for another depot mission aboard a newly constructed sled—its wider runners were designed to slide easily through the sand-like snow that exists in such extreme cold. Just a week after their departure, however, Sonntag, Ohlsen, and Petersen came stumbling back to the ship bearing terrifying news. Brooks, Baker, Wilson, and Schubert were incapacitated and freezing to death; Hickey was with them as well, the only one strong enough

The observatory from Kane's
Arctic Explorations
(Philadelphia: Childs &
Peterson, 1856).

to care for them. Elisha and eight others immediately loaded up a sled and headed back out into the cold with Ohlsen, the only one of the three returning members still coherent after their fifty-hour trek in negative forty degree weather, strapped to the sled to guide them. After a brutal march without food or water and in temperatures that dropped to nearly negative fifty degrees, they found their lost comrades. Exhausted and relieved, Elisha almost burst into tears when he entered their tent and found them grateful but not surprised to see him. He exclaimed later, "They had expected me: they were sure I would come!"[24] During the fifty hours it took them to return to the ship, all men reached a point of exhaustion and cold that left them babbling and senseless. They stopped only twice for water, fearing that any lack of movement would cause them to freeze to death. At one point Elisha and Godfrey pushed ahead alone to set up a shelter and prepare food for the others. Both men nearly perished because of this effort, but Godfrey's steadfastness in this difficult time impressed Elisha and led him to respect his delinquent crewmember for his stamina and persistence. By April 4, all members made it back to the ship alive, but not all survived the ordeal. Before the end of the month both Jefferson Baker and Pierre Schubert died from injuries incurred during the trip.[25] Elisha's enthusiasm had proved disastrous. Petersen, a man with years of arctic experience, had strongly warned that travel so early in the season could lead to disaster, but Elisha had ignored him. Now half the crew lay incapacitated and two dying because of his poor judgment. Elisha expressed neither regret nor self-doubt in his journal, but this incident shook his confidence and damaged his credibility with his crew. They would remember this event that fall when Elisha would once again go against Petersen's advice and adopt a plan that many of them thought unwise.

With two of their number dying, reminding all crewmembers of the tenuous nature of their lives in the arctic, they were distracted from their gloomy thoughts by a new group of men who hardly seemed to notice the harshness of the climate. On April 4, several Inuit appeared on the horizon. Elisha, unarmed and holding his arms wide in a gesture of welcome, went out to meet them. Metek, the elder member of the Inuit group, did not hesitate to come forward and, with the help of Petersen's translation, introduced himself to Elisha. In his journal, Elisha described these men as "wild and uncouth, but evidently human beings," but he also noted that they looked at his crew in an equally questioning manner, "laughing heartily at our ignorance in not understanding them."[26] Metek, who was powerfully built, healthy, and nearly a head taller than Elisha's pale, weak frame, nonchalantly accompanied Elisha onboard the *Advance* to look around. Tom Hickey took bread, corned pork, and lumps of sugar to their guests, but they shunned these foods and instead settled down to their own fare of raw walrus. Soon all members of the Inuit group were aboard the small ship and the crew had

Two views of the first meeting of the Inuit of Etah. The top image from Kane's *Arctic Explorations* (Philadelphia: Childs & Peterson, 1856) is odd because, in Kane's own description of the event, he notes that he was unarmed at this first meeting. That the image in his book shows him standing confidently with a rifle slung nonchalantly over his shoulder while he calmly observes frantic looking Inuit implies much more confidence than the text of his narrative suggests he felt. The second image, from *Godfrey's Narrative*, reverses the implied power of this encounter, portraying the Inuit as relaxed, confident, and even playful as they fearlessly take items from the *Advance*'s cache and wave welcomingly at Kane and another crewmember, both of whom appear small and timid. The differences between these two images illustrate the complex and varying attitudes the members of the expedition felt toward their new neighbors and hint at the complicated ideas of "savage" and "civilized" that marked all nineteenth-century exploration.

to keep moving to keep them from taking everything that was not nailed down.

Elisha's description of this first meeting potrays a clash of cultures where both sides were alternately amused, fascinated, and horrified by the ingenuity and barbarous actions of the other. Elisha clearly recognized that he and his men were physically far weaker than the Inuit, and he was amazed to find that they lived only seventy miles to the south in the village of Etah, and hardly seemed to notice the brutal winter that had reduced his men to invalids. Fearing that they would discover that two of his men were dying, and not wanting them to think him intimidated, Elisha had his men conduct a "gentle laying on of hands" to remove the curious Inuit from the forecastle of the ship, where the dying men lay. He then did his best "to make them understand what a powerful Prospero" he was. He flaunted mirrors, compasses, clocks, and other gadgets, and showed them "my hand terrible with blazing ether, while it lifted nails with a magnet."[27] Elisha reported that the Inuit enjoyed these tricks, alternately laughing and grimacing at them. They spent the night aboard the *Advance* and, before they left in the morning, they promised to return soon with fresh meat and more dogs.

Elisha ended his commentary of this first meeting by noting that he gave them gifts and "then gave them leave to go." This is clearly an example of the confident superiority projected by explorers, trying to buoy themselves up in uncertain circumstances. Elisha recognized that he and his men were far more at the mercy of the Inuit than the other way around. This caused him to feel he had to reassert his superiority by using force, but despite his best efforts to impress and control them, the Inuit came and went as they pleased, making off with an axe, a saw, and several knives. Five other Inuit returned the next day, and after being denied access to the ship, they ripped apart the India rubber boat for its wooden frame and then robbed the storehouse on the shore. Supplies of wood and metal were all Elisha had to bargain with, but these were only useful if he could prevent them from being stolen. Thus, when the youth Myouk appeared a few days later, Elisha seized, questioned, and then imprisoned him in the hold overnight. This was clearly a demonstration of power, not designed to harm Myouk (Elisha confessed that he was glad he escaped in the morning), but to show his kinsmen that "Kayen" and his crew were not powerless. Elisha's instructions to his men regarding firearms is telling of this plan; he told them never to raise a gun unless attacked but, if firearms became necessary, they were to shoot to kill. He explained, "The prestige of the gun with a savage is in his notion of its infallibility," and thus firing in the air "is neither politic nor humane" because it would not impress the Inuit and thus lead to greater future problems.[28]

Despite these policies, it is important to recognize that the dichotomy between "civilized" expedition and "savage" Inuit was not as clear as Elisha and most scholars have expressed it. Both Hans, an Inuit, and Petersen, a Dane raised in Greenland, were members of the "American" expedition. Thus, whereas Elisha and other members of the crew found the Inuit exotic and shocking, these two saw them as friends and family. Petersen noted in his journal that the visiting Inuit included "one of my former friends from Cape York" as well as another familiar face from an earlier adventure. And though they spoke a slightly different language and wore different clothing than his family in southern Greenland, Hans certainly felt at home with these northern Inuit—he later married one of their daughters.[29] The idea of a uniform "civilized" response to the Inuit was further complicated by the fact that this "American" expedition was made up of a Dane and a Greenland native, as well as members from Germany, France, and Ireland. In addition, the Inuit tribe they met, although remote, was not as completely isolated as Kane portrayed them. According to Petersen, these people had visited Danish trading posts as well as whaling and exploring expeditions, had objects of European and American origin in their possession, and did not find the sight of a ship at all strange.[30] The relationship, then, between the crew of the *Advance* and their Inuit visitors, although one of contrast and adjustment, was not as completely foreign as it has been typically presented. With occasional shows of force, accompanied by more frequent acts of good will, Elisha and the residents of Etah soon came to a respectful understanding. Both had skills and goods that the other desired and both maintained the belief that they were the superior group, but each recognized the potential to benefit from the other, and so adapted to each other's idiosyncrasies.

Reinvigorated by the return of the sun and the knowledge that the village of Etah could potentially supply them with dogs for travel and fresh meat for their scurvy-ridden bodies, Elisha began preparing for a spring expedition. His goal was to head north to Humboldt Glacier on Greenland's coast, and to then cross the ice-filled channel to the American side. There they could chart the edge of the ice to the north and look for openings to the Open Polar Sea. It was important to execute this expedition before the warming temperatures melted the ice-covered basin and rendered their sleds useless. On April 25 he sent McGary, Morton, Riley, Hickey, Stephenson, and Hans off on foot and he and Godfrey, now the best dog-driver of the crew, followed the next day with a sled full of provisions. Both groups made good time, even with Elisha pausing to sketch the amazing rock towers formed by the erosion of the coast's sandstone cliffs. He named one especially dramatic tower "Tennyson's Monument" in honor of Alfred Lord Tennyson, whose heroic poetry he often read to his crew.[31] After a week of easy travel the now-unified group ran into trouble. On May 3 they encountered heavy snowdrifts and, in the effort to press on, several of the men began to fade, suffering from scurvy and snow blindness. To make matters worse, they discovered that the food cache they deposited the year before had been emptied by polar bears. Elisha himself collapsed the next day. He had himself strapped to the sled and ordered his men to push on. They made it within view of Humboldt Glacier, which Elisha managed to sketch before he fell into a stupor. Taking command of themselves, the men immediately turned around and, by a series of forced marches, made it back to the ship by May 14. Once again Elisha's ambitious efforts had failed.

After a week of incoherence, Elisha recovered enough to retake command by the end of May. He immediately sent McGary south to Lifeboat Cove to check on their cache and to report on the condition of the ice. McGary made this trip of roughly one hundred miles in just four days and happily reported that the cache was undisturbed and that navigable water lay only thirty miles away. The twenty-four-hour summer sun was certain to break up the remaining ice by August.

With this good news Elisha set in motion an aggressive series of expeditions because after nearly a year in the arctic he had yet to discover any evidence of either Sir John Franklin or the Open Polar Sea. Both the March and April expeditions had ended disastrously; this inspired Elisha to change his methods. Instead of sending out heavily laden, eight-member parties, he decided to use two-man teams that could travel lightly aboard a dog sled. This decision was based on both observation and necessity. Even if he had wanted to, Elisha could not have safely sent out another eight-man team because very few of his men were in traveling condition.

For the first mission, Elisha wanted a team to cross the still-frozen basin to the American side and to accurately chart the exact dimensions of

From Kane's *Arctic Explorations* (Philadelphia: Childs & Peterson, 1856). Kane named this grand formation "Tennyson's Monument," partly because of Tennyson's connection to Sir John Franklin (Franklin was his wife's uncle), but primarily because of his love of Tennyson's poetry; he frequently read to his crew from Tennyson's works and found inspiration and solace in his poem, "Ulysses."

what was to be known as Kane Basin. Because both he and Sonntag were still too ill to travel, Elisha put Hayes (the only other member able to make geodetic observations) in charge of the mission, and selected Godfrey as his companion. They set off on May 20, a beautifully sunny day, but soon ran into nearly impossible conditions. Warm weather and drifting icebergs had caused the icy surface of the Basin to break into a series of sharp hummocks (ice ridges). Hayes suffered horribly from snow blindness and Godfrey began to panic, insisting that they head back. Godfrey became so desperate by May 26 that he grabbed their rifle and demanded a return, but Hayes talked him out of his revolt, and by the next day they made it to the other shore. Hayes pushed north as far as 79°45' and was able to see and chart an additional thirty miles further north. He then traveled south to Cape Sabine, the most northerly point Inglefield had charted in 1852. With supplies running low and his snow blindness almost complete, Hayes had Godfrey set off again across Kane Basin. They made it back to Rensselaer Harbor on June 1. The trip was a huge success because they added nearly two hundred miles of coastline to the arctic map and located several new landmarks, but it left Hayes blinded for nearly six weeks. Although he did not mention Godfrey's mutinous conduct in his official report—instead praising him for his excellent skill with the dogs—he undoubtedly discussed it privately with Elisha.[32]

Elisha sent out a second mission just four days after Hayes and Godfrey's return, that was designed to follow Greenland's coast beyond Humboldt Glacier. This was a critical mission because it would determine if the basin had an outlet, and if so, if it led to the Open Polar Sea. Elisha thus gambled heavily, opting to dedicate all six of his still-healthy crewmembers to a multistage push to the north. McGary, Bonsall, Hickey, and Riley would accompany Morton on foot to Humboldt Glacier; Hans would follow them some days later by dog sled. After reaching the glacier, Morton and Hans would push on to the north while the other four men would set up a base camp and attempt to ascend the massive glacier. This multiple stage mission, using base camps and a series of caches, was the system Elisha had planned the year before. Robert E. Peary, following Kane's example, used this same system fifty-five years later in his successful ascent to the north pole.[33]

McGary, Morton, and the other men set off on June 5 and Hans followed five days later, meeting up with them on June 16. After a day to rest the dogs, Hans and Morton set off while McGary and the others attempted to scale the sheer face of the glacier. They found this an impossible task and, fearing it would result in serious injury, they set off back for the ship, leaving behind a store of goods for Hans and Morton's return. They met no serious obstacles on their return trip and reached the *Advance* by June 27. They reported, however, that the warm weather was quickly melting the ice belt along the shore, which would make sled travel dif-

This engraving of Morton triumphantly gazing out over the vast Open Polar Sea became *the* image of Kane's expedition, so much so that in the following years people came to associate the exuberant figure in the image as Kane himself, not Morton. From Kane's *Arctic Explorations* (Philadelphia: Childs & Peterson, 1856).

ficult. For the next two weeks Elisha worried what this meant for Hans and Morton, but his fears were allayed when the sound of baying dogs announced their return in the early morning hours of July 3.[34]

After a hearty welcome, Morton reported the one thing Elisha most wanted to hear. He explained that he and Hans had pushed well beyond Humboldt Glacier and found that Kane Basin narrowed, forming a channel just thirty miles in width (Elisha named this Kennedy Channel in honor of ex-secretary of the navy John Pendleton Kennedy). They followed this channel north and were amazed to find thinning ice and swarms of birds. At latitude 81°22', further north than any Western explorer had ever achieved, they were stopped by a jagged cape. Climbing it to a height of 480 feet, Morton looked to the north and, even though the day was clear and he could see for forty miles, he could see nothing but open, iceless water. Reporting this event, Elisha poetically wrote that, while staring out at this iceless water, Morton's "ears were gladdened with the novel music of crashing waves; and a surf, breaking in among the rocks at his feet."[35]

To back up his discovery, Morton brought back samples of several forms of vegetation he gathered along the mysterious shore. He also reported that he saw many birds, including the arctic petrel, which lives only in the vicinity of open water. The discovery of the Open Polar Sea, if it could be proved, would be the biggest event in the history of arctic exploration. It is not surprising, then, that Morton's announcement aroused "emotions of the highest order" among the crew. Elisha noted, "I do not believe there was a man among us who did not long for the means of embarking upon its bright and lonely waters."[36] Though a lack of absolute proof of this discovery would prevent Elisha from conclusively declaring his discovery of the Open Polar Sea, in his heart he firmly believed that he had found it. In an uninhibited note to his brother Tom he exclaimed, "The great North Sea, the Polynia, has been reached." [37]

With this momentous discovery made, Elisha and the entire crew turned their attention to one thing and one thing alone—getting home. Though pools of water now stood all about the *Advance*, the basin remained a solid, unmoving mass of ice. Elisha feared the worst and could tell that his crew was thinking the same thing. In a heartfelt letter that he feared would never make it back home, he wrote to Tom: "Never dear brother can poor Elish go through all this again—Fresh trials are ahead, for the ice is unbroken around me—and I am well aged and worn. Yet the brig and my comrades must get back to tell their story and I must get them back at the risk of what remains to me."[38] With Hans accompanying him, Elisha again went to inspect the ice to the south, where he found that open water had advanced only four miles since May. This confirmed his fear that the *Advance* would not be freed that summer. At this discovery, Elisha decided that he must follow a frantic but necessary plan. He would sail one of their small boats to Beechey Island (six hundred miles to the south and west) and try to find Edward Belcher's expedition. He would then borrow one of Belcher's five ships and return to Smith Sound to pick up the rest of his crew. Elisha knew this was a desperate plan, but he felt it was the best option.

The next day he called his officers and crew together to announce his plan and to call for volunteers for this dangerous trip. He reported later, "It was the pleasantest interview I ever had with my associates. I believe every man on board would have volunteered."[39] From the crew he picked McGary, Morton, Riley, Hickey, and Hans to accompany him, leaving Brooks, now recovered from the March excursion, in charge of the brig. They mounted their twenty-three-foot long whaleboat, "Forlorn Hope," on a sled and the six men set off on July 14. After three days of heavy labor, dragging the boat across the ice, they finally reached open water. For the next weeks they rowed, pulled, and sailed their small craft along the ice-clogged water of Smith Sound, only to discover that their way was blocked by a massive ice floe. Heartbroken, they were forced to turn back. They reached the *Advance* two weeks later. The one consolation of the failed journey was that it strengthened the men who had undertaken it. They discovered a huge flock of

Members of the crew of the *Advance*. This engraving, made from a daguerreotype by Matthew Brady (see page 261), was modified, giving Kane a stern, troubled expression that reflected the challenges he faced as nearly half his crew broke from his command and attempted to escape the arctic on their own. From Kane's *Arctic Explorations* (Philadelphia: Childs & Peterson, 1856).

birds on Littleton Island and feasted on them; the fresh meat refreshed their bodies and helped rid them of scurvy.[40]

The only hope left was that July had been very warm and constant winds were helping to break up the surrounding ice floe. By the time Elisha and the other five men made it back, the rest of the crew had prepared the *Advance* for departure, hopeful that a sudden storm would unlock her from the ice that had encased her for the past eleven months. The day after his return, Elisha had the men saw through a few yards of ice, which put the brig afloat. They then warped her toward a break in the floe that they hoped would become an open lead. On August 11, however, Elisha again inspected the floe and found that new ice was already forming and that leads were shrinking instead of expanding. With this information, he reduced food and fuel allowances to just enough for coffee twice a day and soup once. He wrote in his journal, "Bad! bad! I must look another winter in the face... another year of disease and darkness—a year to be met without fresh food and without fuel—but I can look forward like a man, without fear but with tempered sadness, to the du-

THE GRAVES BY MOONLIGHT.

From Kane's *Arctic Explorations* (Philadelphia: Childs & Peterson, 1856)

ties of providing for my comrades."[41] Still hoping they could break free of the ice, Elisha had the words, "ADVANCE, A.D. 1853-54," painted in huge letters on a nearby stone cliff that was easily visible from the basin. Below it he placed an account of the expedition in a bottle, but before sealing it with lead, he added a second note explaining that their hoped-for departure was almost certainly blocked by new ice. Tellingly, Elisha altered his daily prayer at this time, changing it from "Lord, accept our gratitude and bless our undertaking," to "Lord, accept our gratitude and restore us to our homes."[42]

As the days progressed, members of the crew became gravely concerned about their situation and began to plot their own escape, with or without their captain. On August 21, Elisha's faithful steward, Morton, reported to him that there was an organized agitation to leave the ship and that several of the men were going to make this proposal publicly within a few days. Elisha was hurt but not surprised by this intelligence. Fully aware of the dangers of a second winter, he questioned his right to demand that his crew stay with him aboard the ship. To gain perspective he consulted McGary, a seasoned whaler, and learned that in such situations whaling crews were given the right to abandon ship if they wanted. In his journal he noted that, among his men, "There was no mutiny, no disturbance, but a simple wish to exercise a natural right connected with their personal safety." In an effort to determine his duty, he continued, "I differ with them as to the policy and soundness of the step & I think it a gross violation of their agreement & a violation of everything gallant and honorable. Very good! but have I the moral right to detain them? Can I look forward to the horrible contingencies of the coming long dark winter and see myself and the faithful, surrounded by men... whose inclinations I had forced and whose sufferings were upon my head?"[43]

With this on his mind, he made another journey to inspect the ice and came back certain that the *Advance* was trapped for another winter. Although he felt an attempt to escape via small boats would be suicidal, he decided to let each man chose his own fate. On August 23 he called all hands together and explained the situation. He told them that he felt that their best chance for survival was to stay on the brig, but, if they wanted to go against his advice and attempt to flee, he would not stop them and would supply them with a fair share of the provisions. He made it clear, however, that he considered abandoning the ship and its captain a dishonorable act, and would thus demand that all departing members sign a note, exempting him of all responsibility for their actions. With this said, he dismissed them. They were to return the next day at noon to give their replies. In his journal that evening he recorded the events of the day and "wondered if it occurred to those who may meditate a departure that there is something of a sin in abandoning sick comrades."[44]

Tensions were high the next day. The men assembled and Elisha calmly read through the roll, asking each man to speak out for themselves: "yes" if they intended to leave, "no" if they intended to stay. Elisha reported that he "read the roll with grave deliberation, showing no change of manner" as each man responded. But behind this cool exterior, he was seething. Only five men—William Morton, Thomas Hickey, Henry Goodfellow, Henry Brooks, and Hans Hendrik— said they would stay, and Hans was not firm in his decision. Elisha expected Ohlsen and Petersen to leave; they had been critical of his leadership throughout the expedition. Nor was it a surprise that Godfrey and Blake announced their departure; they had been insubordinate from the beginning. He had assumed that a few of the other navy men would join these men, but he was shocked when most of his officers also announced their intention to leave. Of the German astronomer who outwardly supported him, even in his speech to the crew the day before, Elisha wrote, "Sonntag's course seemed to me indefensible, adding deceit to treachery." Bonsall, a friend of the Kane family, so surprised him with his decision that Elisha pulled him aside and "pointed out the grave errors of his course, the loss of respect and standing at home, and so fourth," but though Bonsall wept bitterly, he "adhered to his selfish inclinations."[45]

To Elisha's pleasant surprise (and likely because of his direct pressure), a few men changed their minds over the following days.[46] On the August 25, McGary, who did not originally voice his decision, announced his intention to stay—"He is a most cheerful addition to our little party of 'faithfuls,'" Elisha noted. The next day Sailing Master John Wall Wilson also approached Elisha and asked if he could change his mind as he "had not been happy since he decided to leave." Wanting him to feel the full weight of his decision, Elisha made him get permission from the departing party, pointing out that he was now guilty of "double desertion." With this done, however, Elisha happily took him back, noting in his journal that Wilson "had gentlemanly instincts and has been reared a gentleman but is very weak. I comforted the poor fellow as well as I could."[47]

That Elisha demanded all departing members to sign a statement, officially terminating their connection with the expedition and exempting him of responsibility for them, intimidated many of the crewmembers, especially those with little education. Written in an elevated and complex style, this document was difficult to read, a fact attested to within its text as it noted that it was "read... aloud and handed round for separate perusal."[48] Wilson and McGary, when faced with this document, decided not to sign it for fear of what might happen if they did. It is also telling that the only members who readily signed it were Hayes, Bonsall, and Sonntag—all educated and relatively affluent men who were accustomed to legal documents. The document proved confounding for Ohlsen, one of the leaders of the departing group, and Elisha used this to his advantage. He noted in his journal that, after refusing to sign the document, Ohlsen "gravely requested that he might be considered as in the expedition and yet accompany the withdrawal party.... He said that his ignorance of our language (he is a Dane) prevented his understanding." Given this request, Elisha noted that, "My course was now very clear." He then used this opportunity to tell the whole crew that "all who did not distinctly and understandingly comply with the letter just signed" could stay with the expedition. At this, Ohlsen "argued, urged, entreated," and "behaved like a madman, declining either to sign or remain." Elisha thus removed the contract, said he was no longer eligible to sign it, and explained that "if he left the brig, it would now be at his own peril, that signature or no signature, I now withdrew my permission." Ohlsen came back a few days later, "offering to sign any paper" if Elisha would let him go. Elisha refused and told him that he would shoot him as a deserter if he attempted to leave. He noted in his journal, "[Ohlsen] went away crying like a woman.... He is weak, vacillating, and insidious, but full of valuable qualities.... [A]s I was delicately intimating his chance of a bullet should he attempt to follow his party, he exclaimed with an almost ludicrous association of ideas—'Thank you, Captain Kane; you have saved me.' 'Oh god, what shall I do?' 'I must go.' 'I must go.'"[49]

On August 28, only a week after he first learned of the plans of secession, Elisha watched half his men abandon his mission and leave his command. The departure happened peacefully and even gracefully as Elisha brought out champagne from his private stores and all men drank to the health of both parties. But in his journal that night, Elisha poured out his emotions.

> This trial has developed the characters of my company, confirmed the worthless and transformed some false gold. Bonsall, Hayes and Sonntag had never the associative gallantry and right-mindedness of Goodfellow or the whaler McGary, or the man-of-war's man Brooks. Petersen was always a cold-blooded sneak, Ohlsen double-faced and fawning and insincere. Their associates number all the crew except Morton and the Irish cabin boy Hickey. These two stand out as natural gentlemen when compared with any of the officers or men who are leaving their posts.
>
> Sad as I feel at the dismal prospect ahead, anxious as I may be for the future of those thus severing connection, I feel that it is a relief, a purgation, relieving me of condemned material, worthy heretofore but rotten now.
>
> I have washed my hands of them as a man and a Christian.... They have left the expedition and God's blessings go with them, for they carry not the respect of good men.[50]

It took the departing party more than a week to sled their two boats over the ice to open water, and there was frequent contact and tension between the two groups during this time. Elisha sent Hans to help the departing party and to then bring back the sled, but Petersen persuaded him to stay, forcing Elisha to send McGary and Goodfellow to retrieve him, forcefully if necessary. One of the sleds fell through the water, inspiring Riley and Blake to return to the ship. They declared that they no longer wanted to leave. Elisha readily took Riley back, but gave the troublesome Blake a very cool reception and Blake rejoined the evacuating party once again. By the time Petersen (the elected leader of the departing party) and his men reached open water on September 5, the two parties stood as follows: Elisha, Brooks, McGary, Wilson, Goodfellow, Morton, Hickey, Riley, Ohlsen, and Hans aboard the *Advance*; heading south in two small whale boats were Petersen, Hayes, Bonsall, Sonntag, Stephenson, Whipple, Godfrey, and Blake. With the separation complete, Elisha again railed in his journal. He noted that those who left him were "deserters in act and in spirit—in all but the title" but that even so, he would take them back if they returned, sharing with them "to the halving of our last chip." "[B]ut—but—but," he exclaimed in an entry addressed to his family, "If I ever live to get home—home! and should meet Dr. <u>Hayes</u> or Mr. <u>Bonsall</u>, or <u>Master</u> Sonntag, let them look out for their skins. If I don't live to thrash them, which I'll try very hard to do (to live I mean) why then, dear brother John, seek a solitary orchard and maul them for me."[51]

Though Elisha let his men choose their own path, he viewed the departing company as deserters. The men who left, however, did not see their actions as inappropriate. Dr. Hayes reported later that, because Elisha "threw the responsibility upon his men [and] pretended to come to no decision for them," he and others came to the conclusion that "the chances of safety were enhanced by separations... since all could not live on board the winter through." Hayes thus saw the departing company as contributing to "the public good... one of the means under heaven of our salvation."[52] In Petersen's account of the departure, he too saw it as a tense but amiable agreement made in the face of harsh circumstances. "Dr. Kane called together a ship-council... [and] imparted to us that since there appeared no hope of getting away and since we, moreover, were in want of fuel and provisions, he would permit every one of us, who might have the desire and courage, to abandon the ship and to save ourselves as best we could." Petersen did note that Elisha expressed some bitter feelings, but said those arose only after "twelve men out of the eighteen that composed the crew demanded to leave the ship."[53] This, he noted, was when Elisha demanded that all officers and ranking men sign the paper stating their decision to leave. Godfrey wrote a similar account of the separation: "Dr. Kane, in a formal speech, announced that such of the men as wished to leave the brig for the purpose of traveling homeward, had full permission to do so." He felt that only the "scarcity of provisions led to this generous offer," and explained that he readily accepted it because "I had never enjoyed much comfort, or experienced much kindness, on board... the *Advance*."[54]

The circumstances facing the men of the *Advance* in the fall of 1854 were extreme and would have challenged any leader. Elisha's decision to let the men decide for themselves was certainly rooted in notions of democracy and self-determination; however, it was also a cop-out—a decision made by a leader who feared that he did not have the force of character necessary to control his men in such extreme circumstances. Years later, Elisha's sister Bessie asked Henry Goodfellow to write an account of the division of the crew. This account showed that Elisha—a young and inexperienced leader—questioned his right to determine other men's fortunes and feared that if he tried to, he would face outright mutiny. Goodfellow noted that, on the day after the men voted to leave, Elisha called him in for a confidential meeting and explained his actions. Elisha knew he could order his men to stay and could enforce this to the point of executing anyone who deserted, but he felt "it would never do to deny my permission and to have a spirit of bitter discontent or smothered mutiny on board." He then confided to Good-fellow his bigger fear—with all men on board he felt he would be lucky to "get through the winter with half the Ship's company alive," and he added ominously, "and the most danger is for you and me."[55] Elisha feared his men would mutiny if he forced them to stay on board.

By letting his men choose their own destinies, Elisha avoided being culpable for their suffering and prevented what he believed could become outright mutiny. A more powerful and skilled leader may have taken a different tack, but Elisha's decision—whether cowardly, noble, or necessary—proved to be "successful" in the most basic sense. All crewmembers survived the winter.

Once the departing company launched their small boats and were finally gone, Elisha calmly and decisively directed the winter preparations for his men aboard the *Advance*. He had learned much from the winter before and had come to respect the survival tactics of the Inuit. His first goal was to turn his ship into an igloo. To this end, he blocked off all the below-deck space except for an eighteen by eighteen-foot square chamber, which he sealed with paste and plaster of paris, lined with a two-inch layer of oakum, and then covered completely with thick layers of moss and turf. This chamber could be entered only by crawling along a long, moss-lined tun-nel, thus further insulating it from the frigid outside air. He then stripped the ship of all unnecessary wood and stacked it for fuel and, to supplement their stores of flour, salt-pork, beans, and dried apples, he and Hans went out to hunt seals.

Though this hunt produced nothing and nearly ended in tragedy—the sled fell through the ice, pulling the dogs and Elisha into near-freezing water—three men from Etah appeared a few days later, inspiring hope for fresh meat through trade. Elisha fed and housed his guests and gave them generous gifts in the hope he could arrange a trade agreement. When he awoke the next day, however, the three men were gone along with two buffalo robes, several cooking utensils, and their best sled dog. This was a desperate situation. Despite his attempt to appear a "power-ful Prospero," the people of Etah had no fear of Elisha and his men, especially since half of them were now gone. To trade successfully with the Inuit he had to be able to show that he too could master arctic conditions and back up his state-ments with force. With this in mind, Elisha immediately sent Morton and Riley after the three men, hoping to encounter them at Anoatok, a small shelter half way between the *Advance* and Etah. When Morton and Riley arrived, the three men were not there, but two women and the boy Myouk were; they had the cooking utensils and had cut up the buffalo robes and turned them into jackets, which they were already wearing. Morton and Riley bound the women and marched them back to the *Advance*, sending Myouk back to Etah to report this event.

Metek, leader of the Etah Inuit From
Kane's *Arctic Explorations* (Philadelphia:
Childs & Peterson, 1856).

Though harsh, this tactic proved successful. Two men, including Metek and
the husband of one of the prisoners, came to the *Advance* a few days later, bringing with them many items they had taken from the ship in previous visits. With
Hans interpreting, the two parties again negotiated a treaty. The people of Etah
agreed to sell or lend them dogs and to guide them in their hunting; Kane and
his men promised not to harm them, to hunt with them using their guns for the
mutual gain of both groups, and to always welcome them aboard the ship. The
most important result, though, was that they established a set system of trade:
metal and wooden objects for fresh meat. In honor of the treaty Elisha gave the
men of Etah several gifts and Morton and Riley accompanied them back to Etah,
where they were greeted warmly and given a forty-pound walrus flipper. Once
made, this treaty was never broken by either side, and it proved to be the founding relationship for many subsequent encounters between exploring expeditions
and Inuit of the far-north. Elisha noted that in the months that followed, "We went
to and fro between the villages and the brig, paid our visits of courtesy and necessity on both sides, met each other in hunting parties,... organized a general community of interests, and really established some personal attachments deserving
of the name."[56] Though the argument that Kane and later explorers exploited the
Inuit and treated them as inferiors is true in some senses, it is important to recognize that the Inuit too had their own interests in mind and were not the self-sacrificing and exploited natives that some scholars have suggested. The relationship
that resulted between these two groups is most accurately seen not as one-sided
exploitation, but as mutual, competitive cooperation and trade.

Although the months of November and December were difficult and scurvy
again threatened many of the crewmembers, the men aboard the *Advance*, thanks

to Elisha's careful planning and trade agreement with Etah, were relatively secure. Elisha went on an extended hunting expedition with the men of Etah and spent several days living with them. Hans was impressed. He noted that Elisha did quite well and readily adapted to Inuit cuisine and lifestyle.[57] Unlike his men, Elisha was willing to eat anything, and thus remained quite healthy by supplementing his diet with rat soup, dog meat, and raw walrus blubber. Even with adequate provisions to physically survive the winter, however, the men of the *Advance* still faced the extreme psychological trauma of months of darkness and confinement. The forced gaiety of a mock ball or a newspaper were not even attempted this second winter. They read, played games, and talked, but most of their time was spent in stoic silence as they waited for the sun's return. This waiting was mentally excruciating, especially for Elisha, who felt personally responsible for their circumstances. He wrote one Sunday afternoon:

> My thoughts, my diseased craving for love and caressment, everything that unbends, I crush, strangle, before they take shape.... Every energy of my nature—a vile nature, too—is bent to bear myself and those who lean on me out of a severe trial. If I let weakness come over me now, we—I mean all of us—are gone.[58]

With the darkest days of winter approaching, the nine men aboard the *Advance* received distressing news—the departing party had failed in their effort to reach Upernavik and were now stranded two hundred miles to the south. This intelligence reached Elisha on December 7 when five Inuit sleds appeared, bringing with them Carl Petersen and Amos Bonsall. Before they left, Elisha had promised to take back the party if they failed in their efforts. Now Petersen, who had loudly declared that he would rather spend the winter on the rocks than under Elisha's command, was back and asking for help.[59] Elisha gave it without hesitation. He packed a sled full of their precious provisions and, though he did not fully trust the Inuit sled drivers (they were from an unfamiliar village), he had no choice but to accept their offer to deliver the goods; he could not afford to send any of his own men. He fed them a huge meal, gave them several gifts, and requested that leave "one of their company as hostage for safe delivery of the provisions."[60] They then left, promptly returning to their own village and keeping the provisions for themselves. Fortunately, just four days later, the rest of the seceding party returned, thanks to a desperate scheme and the help of the Inuit villages of Netlik, Peteravik, and Etah.

The returning men's tale was harrowing.[61] Despite quarreling and outright insubordination by Godfrey and Blake, things went relatively well in the beginning. They left Cape Alexander and crossed Whale Sound easily, but then their luck ran out. They hit dense pack ice and were forced to construct a makeshift shelter on Greenland's rocky shore, just west of the Carey Islands. The next two months were excruciating. They had no fuel and often had only moss to eat. Inuit from the

Netlik settlement just to their north visited and traded food for goods, but were unwilling to provide any transportation. Petersen and Godfrey traveled often with members of this tribe and attempted to establish a better trade relationship, but they were in no position to negotiate, a fact made very clear when Petersen over-heard a plot to kill them and simply take their goods.[62] Despite this fear of hostil-ity, the leader of of the Netlik Inuit, Kalutunah, remained relatively friendly and kept providing them with some food, but never enough to sustain them.

By November 20, Petersen finally agreed with the rest of the men that return-ing to the *Advance* was their only option. Despite this, his spirit of dissent remained strong and he proposed that upon return they should "form a separate society in-dependent of the command of Dr. Kane and to demand of him only that hospi-tality which is granted a crew having suffered shipwreck at sea."[63] On November 29 all eight men set out, seven of them dragging Stephenson, who was unable to walk, but they turned back after only twelve miles—they were too weak and ill-equipped to survive the journey. Petersen and Bonsall set out again the next day and made it to the brig after a week of hard travel, facilitated by an Inuit hunting party they met along the way.[64] In the mean time, Hayes and the other men were visited by Kalutunah and two of his men. Desperate to escape, several of the men proposed that they kill Kalutunah and his men and make their escape on their sleds. Trying to avoid such a violent solution, Hayes launched a less gruesome but equally devious plan. He prepared soup for the visitors and spiked it with a heavy dose of laudanum, an opiate that quickly put them to sleep. He then stripped them of their coats and, with the rest of the men, set off on their sleds. One of the dog teams escaped, however, so when Kalutunah and his men awoke

Kalutunah, leader of the Netlik Inuit.
From Kane's *Arctic Explorations*
(Philadelphia: Childs & Peterson,
1856).

they recaptured this team, wrapped themselves in blankets, and soon overtook the scurvy ridden men. Kalutunah treated the incident as a joke—probably because Hayes readily brandished his rifle—and agreed to help them reach the *Advance*. With stops at Netlik, Peteravik, and Etah, Hayes and the rest of the men, accompanied by Kalutunah, arrived at Rensselaer Harbor on December 12.[65]

As he had promised, Elisha took back the prodigal members of his crew, but not without ill feelings. Two days after Petersen and Bonsall's return he wrote in his journal: "God of heaven, it makes my blood boil to think that men who have so leaned on me, trusted me, and like little children taught by me their very walk, should at last in the midst of a coming winter, set up their juvenile opinions against my own drearily earned judgements of Arctic Ice.... And here is the result. They send to me, imploring succour and claiming my aid and direction as their only hope."[66] Despite his anger, however, this was also vindication for Elisha. He had been right and he was now, once again, clearly the commander of the expedition. This helped warm him a bit toward his wayward men. When the last of them reached the *Advance* he wrote, "Poor fellows! I could only grasp their hands and give them a brother's welcome.... One by one they all came in and were housed... how they relished the scanty luxuries which we had to offer them!"[67]

The day after the seceding party's return, Kalutunah and five men from Netlik and Etah came to Elisha. They charged that Hayes and his men had stolen clothing from them during the journey. Elisha took this matter very seriously because he had punished the Inuit for their thievery earlier and knew that if he did not now punish his own men, it could result in damage to their essential trade agreement. He thus conducted a trial of sorts, and though he concluded that his men were not thieves—they had only temporarily borrowed objects necessary for their survival— he agreed that they had done so wrongly. He thus returned all the items they had taken and then presented each of the six Inuit men with five needles, a file, and a stick of wood for compensation. He also gave knives and a few other small gifts to Kalutunah and Shanghu, the leaders of the group. The Inuit accepted this as a fair judgment and happily participated in a dinner celebrating their continued friendship. They left the next day "with apparent confidence and good humor," but, as Elisha noted amusedly, not before "they prigged a few knives and forks."[68]

With his Inuit neighbors gone and his eight wayward men returned, Elisha had a hard task ahead of him. He had planned his "igloo" to accommodate ten men, but now had to house eighteen. This allowed each man a space of just three by six feet, roughly the size of a coffin. More critically, his carefully planned food rations now had to be halved from their already near-starvation levels, and the Inuit would be of no help. The fall had been especially harsh and they too faced starvation in the months of January and February. To make matters even worse, there was great tension among the men. Though Elisha allowed the seceding party back aboard the *Advance*, he refused to consider them as members of the crew and so dismissed them from all duties and had them dine in a different corner of the small cabin. Blake and Godfrey, whose belligerence had estranged them from both groups, dined alone in a third corner. Thus three separate groups tried to avoid each other, all in a space of less than 325 square feet.

The psychological pressure of this situation was excruciating to all parties, and things finally exploded just before Christmas, when Blake and Godfrey, along with George Whipple, became aggressively insubordinate. Elisha felt he had to crush this spirit before it infected the whole crew. He called each of the three men up to the deck one at a time, and, after a short interview, bashed them in the side of the head with a heavy metal belaying pin. He recorded in his journal, "John had a concussion of the brain from the belaying pin. I confess I tried to kill him—but Godfrey fell again after a short scuffle and was not hurt.... [Whipple's] nerves gave way and he fell at my feet begging mercy. He got up, after a short cuffing with my mittened hands and went below thanking me." Elisha noted that "the gross worthlessness and depravity of the subjects" alone justified such harsh treatment and that such violence was the only thing that could keep them under control.[69]

This drastic discipline, along with the growing scurvy that left most of the crewmembers unfit for duty, slowly pulled the group back together.[70] All members came to recognize that if they were to survive they had to work together. After a Christmas dinner that included all members of the crew, Elisha determined to set off for help. On December 30 he and Petersen left for Etah, but weather forced them to return the next day. In the next days things became desperate as the outside temperature dropped to 101 degrees below freezing and their reduced fuel

Kane's favorite member of the Etah community, the precocious boy Myouk. From Kane's *Arctic Explorations* (Philadelphia: Childs & Peterson, 1856).

allowed them to maintain a cabin temperature of only eight degrees. On January 18 Elisha and Hans set off for Etah, but weather again stopped their efforts and forced them to return empty handed. The rest of January and February dragged on miserably. By the time the sun again peaked above the horizon in late February, only Elisha, Bonsall, Hans, and Petersen were still able to do any work. In a disparaging journal entry Elisha confessed that the arctic winter had finally frozen away even his warm feelings of romance. "Yes, Elish' Kane—dream away all dreams of youth, think no longer of a married home. Bless God if you carry your gray head and wrinkles to the dear old one and then earn back old loves."[71]

On March 6 Elisha again sent Hans and the sled to Etah for food. This mission was necessary because they desperately needed food, but also because Elisha learned the day before that Godfrey and Blake were planning on stealing the sled and going to live with the Inuit of Etah. This news again heightened tensions. Hans returned on the tenth with news that the people of Etah were starving, they had only the skin of a narwhal left, and had already eaten all but four of their thirty dogs. Hans offered to help them hunt and with his gun and with their additional manpower they were able to kill a medium-sized walrus. This animal saved both the people of Etah and the men of the *Advance* and further cemented their already close ties. Hans also brought back the energetic boy Myouk, who would help him hunt. Elisha took a special shine to the energetic young Inuit boy he had once imprisoned, noting, "I think we understand one another better than our incongruities would imply."[72]

By mid-March the men of the *Advance* were completely out of fuel. This forced Elisha to order the removal of essential planks from the ship, thus rendering her unseaworthy. He again sent Hans to Etah, this time with supplies that would help them hunt walrus more efficiently.[73] On the day Hans was to leave, Elisha learned that Godfrey and Blake were plotting to follow him, overtake the sled, and flee to the Inuit village of Netlik. With Bonsall and Morton's help, he caught the two men in their act of desertion and then, after beating Godfrey with "a leaden fist which I had secretly manufactured and concealed for the purpose," he dragged the two men before the entire crew and charged them with their crime. He explained that, had they succeeded, it would have meant the death of them all. Unable to confine the men in such close quarters, he put them both to hard labor. Godfrey fled an hour later alone on foot.[74]

Unable to pursue him, Elisha could only hope that Godfrey would be unable to catch up to Hans and take the sled. The two weeks that followed were tense because Hans failed to return and, with no fresh meat, scurvy ravaged the whole crew. Only Elisha, Bonsall, and Petersen remained capable of caring for the rest. On April 2, while on watch, Bonsall called down into the cabin that a man was approaching the brig. Hoping it was Hans, Elisha rushed above deck, but it soon became

William Godfrey from *Godfrey's Narrative of the Last Grinnell Arctic Exploring Expedition, in Search of Sir John Franklin, 1853-4-5* (Philadelphia, J.T. Lloyd & Co., 1857).

WM. C. GODFREY.

apparent that the returning figure was not Hans, but Godfrey, and he had the sled. With a pistol in his pocket and covered by Bonsall's rifle, Elisha walked out to meet Godfrey. Godfrey told Elisha that he had been to Etah and had found Hans there, laid up with illness. He had thus taken the sled, filled it with 450 pounds of seal meat, and returned with it to his comrades. He now planned to head south and to spend the rest of his life living among the Inuit of Netlik. Elisha listened silently and then ordered him to come on board. Godfrey refused. Elisha drew his pistol and repeated his demand. Under such duress, Godfrey accompanied him to the ship's side, but he still refused to go on board. Elisha and Bonsall were both barely able to walk and certainly unable to resist Godfrey if he decided to struggle, so Elisha went aboard to get ankle irons. He instructed Bonsall to shoot Godfrey if he attempted to flee. As soon as Elisha left, Godfrey headed back to the sled. Bonsall shouted a firm warning and then pulled his trigger, but the rifle misfired. Elisha returned to see Godfrey running. He grabbed another rifle, which also misfired, and then another that worked but he missed Godfrey. Running for his life, Godfrey left the sled behind. Once again he walked the ninety miles to Etah, carrying with him neither food nor fuel.

This incident became the most controversial of the expedition and it is difficult to tease out exactly what happened given the multiple conflicting accounts. It is true that Godfrey abandoned his crewmembers and left without permission, both grave offenses, but he was not malicious, because even though he successfully made his escape, he voluntarily returned with much-needed food for his fellow crewmembers. In his account of his actions, Godfrey claimed that he left the *Advance* only because he wanted to help the other men, but knew that Elisha would not give him permission to go look for food. He did not see his departure as abandonment because, as he rightly noted, "I had once been dismissed from the brig, and had never entered into any new contract with the Commander."[75] Kane was certain that Godfrey's motives were not altruistic, but his return did show that he was not a complete scoundrel either. In his journal Kane wondered at Godfrey's behavior. "The past conduct of Godfrey on board, and his mutinous desertion, make me aware that he is capable of daring wrong as well as deception.... Yet he came back to our neighborhood voluntarily, with sledge and dogs and walrus meat!" Kane wondered if he had returned to regain the company of "his former partner in the plot," John Blake, or to use the meat as a bargaining chip to regain admittance to the expedition. Even with such dark suspicions, however, he did admit that "one may forgive the man in consideration of the good which [the meat] has done us all."[76]

And the meat certainly did help. Within days, the signs of scurvy left the men and many were back on their feet. By April 10, the crew was healthy enough that Elisha set off on the sled for Etah to find Hans. Halfway there, they met. Although he was still weak from his illness, Hans had left Etah to hunt for seal and to return to the *Advance*. On their trip back, Hans told Elisha that during his illness he had fallen in love with Mersuk, the daughter of Peteravik's leader, Shanghu. This had further delayed his return. He also noted that before his illness he and three men from Etah killed several seals. This was the meat Godfrey had taken them. Elisha returned to the ship and then a few days later set off again for Etah, where he hoped to trade for some new dogs and to capture Godfrey. Armed with a pistol and ankle irons and disguised as an Inuit boy (he was far smaller than the average Inuit man) Elisha easily sneaked up on Godfrey, who immediately surrendered. As Etah had no dogs to spare, Elisha marched Godfrey back to the *Advance*, sending Hans on to Peteravik to see if they had any dogs.

As April wore on, the men of the *Advance* continued to improve in both health and spirit as the fresh meat aided their bodies, and their preparations for heading home brightened their moods. Two long sleds were made to carry their small whaleboats to open water—these small boats the crew renamed *Faith* and *Hope*. Hans soon returned from Peteravik with Netlik headman, Kalutunah, who had been at Peteravik to hunt. He was willing to supply Elisha with two fine dog teams. Elisha was thrilled and he grew even more excited when he learned that Kalutunah and his men were heading north to hunt bear and were willing to let him join them. Elisha was sure that traveling north with these experienced Inuit was his best chance of seeing the Open Polar Sea for himself, but unfortunately for Elisha, the hunt was far too successful. The company killed several bears just south of Humboldt Glacier and thus prepared to return home. Though Kane was happy to again see this enormous mountain of ice—he filled seven pages of his journal with observations of it—he was unable to convince Kalutunah to travel any further north. With feelings of longing and regret, Elisha climbed a high peak and stared off at the distant range from which Morton had seen the fabled waters crash.[77]

Upon return to the brig, Elisha found preparations for their escape progressing well. Hans, saying that he needed new walrus hide to mend his boots, asked if he could go to Peteravik. Though he was sure Han's motives for the trip revolved more around his new-found love than his boots, Elisha needed a message delivered at Etah and so let Hans go. Hans faithfully delivered the message, but never again returned to the *Advance*. He stayed at Mersuk's side in Peteravik, and though these two would be active members of many later expeditions, Kane never again saw the young Inuit man to whom he had grown so attached.[78]

On May 1, to the shock of the whole crew, Elisha announced that he was going to make one final excursion. He wanted to explore the western side of the basin to look for any traces of Franklin and to try and connect Hayes's northernmost point of observation from the year before with the point on Kennedy Channel that Morton had sighted from his most northerly point. Taking only Morton with him, Elisha left on this excursion. He wrote, in what would be his last private journal entry of the expedition, that his officers were "with one accord impressed" by this ambitious plan—stunned would probably have been a more accurate description.[79] Exactly when they left and returned is uncertain, but it was a difficult journey that left Morton "broken down anew" and Elisha's energies "just adequate to the duty of supervising our final departure." In his later book, Elisha noted that from this time forward he had "neither time nor strength to expend on my diary."[80]

On Sunday, May 20, all hands assembled. Elisha led them in prayers, read a chapter from the Bible, and then ceremoniously removed the portrait of Sir John Franklin from its frame and placed it in a waterproof bag. He then gave a heartfelt speech in which he said that he was sure they could all make it to Upernavik if they would commit themselves to each other and the mutual care of all. This done, he presented a paper which all the men solemnly signed:

SECOND GRINNELL EXPEDITION,
BRIG ADVANCE, MAY 20, 1855.

The undersigned, being convinced of the impossibility of the liberation of the brig, and equally convinced of the impossibility of remaining in the ice a third winter, do fervently concur with the commander in his attempt to reach the South by means of boats.

Knowing the trials and hardships which are before us, and feeling the necessity of union, harmony, and discipline, we have determined to abide faithfully by the expedition and our sick comrades, and to do all that we can, as true men, to advance the objects in view.[81]

This engraving of the private lives of Inuit women suggests that the men of the *Advance* knew the people of Etah very well; Hans would later marry a woman he met during the expedition, and Kane implies that both Godfrey and Blake took on Inuit lovers. Kane also included images of more than a dozen specific Etah residents, and his candid pictures of their lives show a close, personal connection. From Kane's *Arctic Explorations* (Philadelphia: Childs & Peterson, 1856).

For the first time since the August before, Elisha and his crew were again officially united. Elisha nailed a notice to the stanchion near the gangway that explained the events of the expedition, and then he and the men lowered the flags and left behind the harbor that had been their home for nearly two years.[82]

The task of dragging the boats eighty-one miles to open water was arduous; all the men had to pull one boat and then go back and pull the other, thus walking three miles for every mile gained. Elisha was constantly busy on the dog sled, transporting the injured and the needed supplies from station to station. If there were any disgruntled feelings during this process, they were not recorded by any of the six members who later wrote of their escape from the arctic.[83] Two mishaps oc-curred along the way, one fatal and the other nearly so. On June 5 the *Hope* fell through the ice, dragging six men with her. Though it was very difficult, the men managed to pull her back out and no lives were lost. Two days later the *Hope*'s front end again broke through, but Ohlsen managed to hold her up while the others pulled her out. This extreme effort ruptured something within Ohlsen's body, how-ever, and four days later he died.[84]

The men finally made it to open water on June 16 and there were joined in a celebration by their friends from Etah. Viewing these two groups of people at that time, it would have been hard to tell them apart. Elisha and his men were dressed entirely in Inuit garb—fur trousers, jumpers with hoods, and slotted wooden goggles to prevent snow blindness. When they reached the waters edge, twenty-five citizens of Etah (all except an old blind man and two women) came out to bid their neighbors farewell. Elisha looked over the group and noted, "I can name them every one, and they know us as well. We have found brothers in a strange land.... My heart warms to these poor, dirty, miserable, yet happy beings, so long our neighbors, and of late so staunchly our friends. Theirs is no affectation of regret."[85] A storm prevented their leaving for two days, and the people of Etah remained with the men of the *Advance* until the end. Then, after dispersing many

From Kane's *Arctic Explorations*
(Philadelphia: Childs &
Peterson, 1856).

parting gifts and more parting words of affection, Elisha and his men set off into the ice filled sea for the harrowing five-hundred-mile trip to Upernavik.[86]

The evacuation Kane led, moving his crew from the entrance of Smith Sound to Upernavik, is one of the most amazing feats in all of arctic exploration. The men were crowded aboard three small boats (the *Faith, Hope,* and much smaller *Red Erik*), which were constantly tossed by rough seas. On several occasions they had to unload the boats, remount them to sleds, and pull them across large ice floes. They were nearly crushed between large masses of ice, and at one point, heavy winds forced them to take shelter on Greenland's rocky shore for three days. This forced stop at a seemingly barren shelter proved to be fortunate because the cliffs were full of nesting eider ducks; thus the men were able to rest and gorge themselves on fresh meat and eggs. They again took to the water on July 3, but after a week of relatively uneventful sailing, they hit a long ice floe that again forced them to take to pulling their sled-mounted boats. Elisha climbed a high berg and discovered that Melville Bay was still solidly frozen. There was nothing to do but go ashore and wait for the summer to progress. He did not tell his men that their way was blocked, but said only that he felt they needed a rest. He named the location "Providence Halt" and had the men make camp at the mouth of a small cave at the base of an eleven hundred foot cliff. Once again the rocks were full of nesting birds—this time auks and tridactyl gulls—and among the mosses they found several plants growing, including duckweed and scurvy grass, which the men greedily consumed.

After two weeks of waiting Elisha decided to push on again, but three days later hit another solid mass of ice at the base of Cape York. After consulting with his officers, Elisha decided to risk moving out into Melville Bay instead of waiting for the ice along the shore to recede. Elisha ordered the *Red Erik* chopped up for fuel; all the men then boarded the *Hope* and *Faith* and set off into the ice-clogged bay. The next days were frantic. The men's strength began to fail from the hard effort of forcing the boats through slush ice, and, fearing they could be on open water for many days, Elisha cut food rations to just five ounces of bread dust, four ounces of tallow, and three ounces of bird meat per day. At one point, all the men had to gather to push the *Hope* over a tongue of ice and during this effort the *Faith* broke free and nearly drifted away; she was saved only by Elisha and McGary scrambling onto a passing cake of ice and manipulating it over to the *Hope*'s side. By this point the punishing conditions had rendered each of the boats so leaky that they had to be bailed day and night to stay afloat. The men were showing clear signs of starvation and Elisha began to fear that they would all perish before reaching shore. Just as conditions were becoming excruciatingly desperate, the men spotted a large seal resting on a nearby patch of ice. They maneuvered the boats as close as they could

Map of the Second Grinnell Expedition from Kane's *Arctic Explorations* (Philadelphia: Childs & Peterson, 1856).

and tensely waited for Petersen, their best hunter, to get off a shot. He fired and the seal fell dead. Franticly, the men rushed onto the ice patch and, after dragging the seal a safe distance from its edge, set into it "crying and laughing and brandishing their knives." Kane noted, "It was not five minutes before every man was sucking his bloody fingers or eating long strips of raw blubber.... The cartilaginous parts of the fore-flippers were cut off in the *mêlée*, and passed round to be chewed upon; and even the liver, warm and raw as it was, bade fair to be eaten before it had seen the pot."[87] These "civilized" men now clearly knew the ways of the "savages."

Things went smoothly for the remainder of the trip; seal were abundant and the waters relatively ice free. They reached Devil's Thumb by August 1, and soon thereafter encountered a Greenlander in his kayak. Petersen recognized the man and greeted him with almost insane happiness, which the man regarded with hesitation, calling out to him that Carl Petersen's "wife says he's dead."[88] Two days later, in the midst of a dense fog, they were greeted by the sound of the voices of the men of an Upernavik oil boat. They had made it. After eighty-four days of travel in open boats they had completed the five-hundred-mile trip to Upernavik and the northern limits of Western settlement.

After a few days at Upernavik they left aboard the Danish bark *Mariane*, which took them to Godhavn by August 11. There, just as they were about to again set sail, a lookout spotted a steamer and, as Elisha reported, a few minutes later the "stars and stripes of our own country" were seen flying from Captain Hartstene's ships. Elisha, the battered leader of a rag-tag group of men that often questioned his leadership, launched the *Faith* for the final time and rowed out to meet Hartstene and the men the American people had sent in search of the intrepid Dr. Kane.[89]

❧

The month that passed between September 11, 1855, when the crew of the *Advance* met the relief expedition at Godhavn, and October 11, when they arrived in New York, was a time of strange transition for Elisha Kent Kane. For the past two years his world had been confined to the company of a few dozen Inuit and his nineteen men, who had come to know him intimately. His men knew him to be a brave and heroic man, who risked his own life to save others, and as a wise and thoughtful man, who successfully planned their survival of a second winter and escape from the arctic. But they also knew him as a driven and stubborn man, whose Ahab-like quest for Franklin and the Open Polar Sea had caused them tremendous suffering. He had brutally punished some of them with leaden fists and belaying pins; others he had skillfully nursed back to health. Of the fourteen crewmembers traveling back to New York with him, all but five had at one time voted to leave his command, and two of them, Blake and Godfrey, saw him as nothing short of a tyrant.[90] After all that they had been through together, these men *knew* Elisha Kent Kane—his skills, talents, idiosyncrasies, faults, and failings.

With these men surrounding him, Elisha met the relief expedition's crewmembers. Like most Americans, these men did not know Elisha, but his persona, "Dr. Kane." To these men, he was a hero. For the past two years they had consumed the stories of his amazing adventures via newspapers, magazines, panorama shows, and his own book. Now he was there before them in the flesh, having just maneuvered two small, leaking boats through five hundred miles of the same waters that had confounded their steam-powered expedition. Wrapped in furs and wearing a huge wooly beard, he appeared the incarnate amalgamation of the great fictional heroes of the sea—Robinson Crusoe, Ulysses, and Sinbad the Sailor.[91] To them he was a larger-than-life hero—he was "Dr. Kane," a man of such great importance that they had volunteered to risk their lives to go in search of him.

When Elisha climbed aboard the *Arctic* with his men, he came face to face with the duality that would mark the rest of his life. He was now both the man, Elisha Kent Kane, and the hero, Dr. Kane of the Arctic Seas. During the month-long voyage back to New York, Elisha had to learn to manage this dual identity—a task far different from, but equally difficult to, any he had faced in the arctic. Fortunately for him, he had help. His family had foreseen this difficulty and had worked to prepare him for it. His brother, John, was the first person to greet him when he stepped aboard the *Arctic*, and he had with him letters from Tom, Pat, Judge Kane, and Cornelius Grinnell, each trying to help Elisha prepare for his arrival in New York. As the *Arctic*'s steam engine chugged him toward a nation eagerly awaiting his return, Elisha read over his letters and began to prepare himself. Thus, when he stepped off the ship in New York, he was ready. He played the part of Dr. Kane to a nation that greeted him with overwhelming enthusiasm.

As his brother Tom's letter had instructed him, he was now a hero, and his biggest job was simply to "take his petting gracefully." Tom suggested that Elisha's tack should be "the official Scientifics—Science with the brevet of sword spunk and gentlemanly savior faire" accompanied by "a concise sham modesty of speech in public, and a composed and courteous demeanor universally."[92] This is exactly how Elisha presented himself. He greeted the throngs of newspaper reporters gratefully and provided them with a detailed account of the expedition, which he had prepared during the voyage home.[93] He profusely thanked Hartstene and the men of the rescue expedition, and the nation at large for the effort on his behalf; and when he announced the discovery of the Open Polar Sea, he humbly (and rightly) gave the credit to the members of his crew with the lowest social status, Morton, his faithful steward, and Hans, an Inuit boy. No hint of discord among the crew was reported, nor any mention of the schism that had divided the crew into two parties. In fact, the *Tribune* noted that, "Between the doctor and his men an almost fatherly feeling seemed to exist, they looking up to him with pride and veneration, feelings which he returned by an affection for them that was truly paternal."⁹⁴ Whether "sham modesty" or not, Elisha followed Tom's suggestions precisely, offering constant thanks and praise, and making sure not to upset anyone. The press noted that "well as [Dr. Kane] has earned his laurels, he wears them with a meekness that adds redoubled luster to his fame, for in his own heart he says, 'I did no more than my duty.'"⁹⁵ In his homecoming, Elisha lived up to what the country expected of Dr. Kane and it embraced him as its hero. The *Tribune* proclaimed that, "through the country the glad tidings of his safety, and the story of his struggles, were borne on the swift steam breath and throbbed through the telegraph, till every hamlet and home throughout the length and breadth of the land was greeted with the good news, and one universal aspiration of gratitude arose from the heart of the nation." With editorial flourish it added, "No warrior returning from victory ever excited half the exultation which burst spontaneously forth at the almost unhoped-for return of Dr. Kane from his mission of mercy."⁹⁶ The *Times* also reported the egalitarian nature of the celebration, noting that newsboys "shouted loud and long, for they knew they had an extra that would sell"; Old drunks "called for another drink to the safe return of Dr. Kane"; Wall Street men "introduced their applications for a loan on call, by the remark that Dr. Kane and party were just off Sandy Hook"; and "The clergy, of every sect and denomination, thanked Providence and fell to work immediately on an eloquent sentence for Sunday morning sermon."⁹⁷

After disembarking, Elisha went first to Astor House, where many of New York's finest had organized an impromptu party to welcome him back. The papers noted that "for some hours he was fully occupied in receiving their congratulations."⁹⁸ The press followed him from Astor House to Grinnell's mansion at 17 Bond Street, where he was to spend the night. Henry Grinnell greeted Elisha with a fatherly welcome and for the next several hours they entertained reporters in the parlor. Elisha's family arrived that evening and they spent the night with him there.⁹⁹

The Kane family had much to discuss because Elisha was not their only member receiving national attention. That same day (October 12, 1855), Judge Kane ruled in the highly publicized Passmore Williamson case and, in a foreshadowing of the *Dred Scott* case that would shake the country two years later, asserted that Constitutional laws protecting property rights called into question any state's right to restrict slave ownership. This ruling outraged many in the North and a storm of harsh editorials were condemning Judge Kane. The next day, the same issue of the *Tribune* that praised Elisha's homecoming raged against Judge Kane, mockingly comparing him to his son by noting that Dr. Kane was the Columbus of the arctic, whereas his father was "the Columbus of the new world of slave-whips and shackles."¹⁰⁰ Later that week the Portsmouth *Morning Chronicle* refused to see a connection between the tyrannical judge and the noble Dr. Kane and wondered if Judge Kane was not instead "related to that other Cain who killed his brother Abel?"[101]

The family ignored the attacts against Judge Kane and celebrated Elisha's return by praising and even contributing to the press's celebration of Dr. Kane. They wanted him to be portrayed as a hero who had led his grateful men through a harrowing but triumphant expedition, and this is exactly what the papers reported. Elisha must have feared that some of his crewmembers would refute the unified, conflict-free face he put on the expedition—that he made all members agree before departure that he alone would be the narrator of the mission foresaw this fear—but in the months following the expedition's return, this fear proved unfounded. The crew remained silent.[102]

This silence is not surprising given the circumstances of the Second Grinnell Expedition's homecoming. The last months of the journey had beenmarked by unity and triumph, and this helped pull the men together behind their commander. More importantly, by the time they reached New York, it was abundantly clear that Elisha was the nation's hero. Flying in the face of the public's adoration of Dr. Kane would have been disastrous to any of the crewmembers' reputations, whereas embracing and supporting him could do nothing but bring them fame as well. That many of them had broken from his command and chose to leave the *Advance* in the winter months of 1854 was an event they too were anxious to ignore. Their effort had failed, after all, and they were forced to come back under Elisha's command. Protesting that he ignored this part of the story would have been drawing attention to their own stupidity and lack of faith. Hayes, Bonsall, and Sonntag, the three members of the seceding party with significant social standing, had nothing to gain by bringing up this schism, and the other separating crewmembers, especially Godfrey and Blake, would have been afraid to say anything, for in the darkest hours of the expedition, Elisha had threatened to seek courts-martial for their behavior. The only member of the expedition bitter and independent enough to contradict Elisha was Carl Petersen, but he had remained in Upernavik, far from the immediate reach of the American press. Even though in later years he, Godfrey, and Wilson would each publish or threaten to publish negative accounts of Elisha's leadership, in the months immediately following the expedition's return, the crew remained united behind their commander and his sanitized version of their journey.[103]

When the Kane family gathered at Grinnell's house on the night of October 12, it was a time of great joy. Two of their sons had returned from the arctic and the family was again united. In a short but telling note, Judge Kane wrote to their pastor and future son-in-law, Rev. Charles W. Shields, "My dear Sir, Will you be kind enough to invite the thanksgivings of our church tomorrow for the happy return of my two sons?—They have been exposed to perils, especially the elder, from which deliverance was almost miraculous."[104] But though the family was again together, they still feared for their eldest son. Elisha had escaped the arctic's cold, hard grip, but he had not freed himself from the warmer, gentler ties of a much closer threat—Margaret Fox was sitting just a few blocks from the Grinnell's house, waiting for the return of her lover and the fulfillment of his promise.

After the disappointment of Elisha failing to return in the fall of 1854, and the heartbreaking winter that followed, which included several well-publicized but baseless rumors of Dr. Kane's discovery of Sir John Franklin, the spring of 1855 brought Margaret Fox renewed hope. At the end of April, Cornelius wrote her that the search expedition would leave by the first of June, and this news, along with several editorials that predicted Dr. Kane's imminent return, cheered her considerably.[105] In a letter written for delivery via the search expedition, and which still survives among Kane's papers, her flirtatious happiness and enthusiasm for the future is clearly evident. After a warm greeting she teased, "Ly what do you think I have done?—I have made a proposal—to Mrs. Walter. There: you thought I meant some gentleman." She then playfully noted that people were asking Mrs. Walter "if she thought that you had any idea of marrying me," and asked, "If any one should ask me that question what shall I say[?] You say and I know it very wrong to tell stories." On a more serious note, she planned out the logistics of the day of his return: "As soon as you arrive at New York call on Mrs. Walter and bring her with you when you come after me." She explained that she would rather then go back to Mrs. Walter's instead of directly to his parents' house because she was "not at all acquainted with your father and mother."[106]

This letter makes Maggie's expectations about Elisha's homecoming clear. She assumed he would rush to her arms, embrace her at last as his betrothed, and whisk her off to meet his friends and family. She wrote frankly about his "Sacred Promise" and was sure she would live up to his expectations because she was "getting along finely with all my Studies." She wrote of her friendships with Mrs. Walter, the Grinnells, Elizabeth Leiper (Elisha's favorite aunt), and other members of the Leiper family, showing that she had gained in social respectability. Although she had done no more public séances, she unashamedly confessed her continued involvement with spiritualism, noting that she and Kate had spiritually cured Dr. Edward Bayard's chronic headaches and that she had recently asked the spirits "a number of questions about you." Here Maggie addressed Elisha as both her lover and her equal. She demonstrated her acquiescence to his wishes but also justified her own past; she noted, "some of the greatest men in the world have become believers in the Spirits." She even began acting as a spouse, stating only half-jokingly, "I will not let you go on another expedition very soon."[107] Maggie clearly had assumed that she was soon to be Mrs. Elisha Kent Kane.

In the summer months of 1855, Maggie continued to travel between Mrs. Walter's in New York and the Turner's Crookville home, all the while continuing her studies. Complying with Mrs. Turner's letters reminding her that Elisha's eminent return made every moment "doubly precious," Maggie spent all of August and September in Crookville engaged in "severe study" and perfecting "some pretty new songs."[108] Her New York friends encouraged her in these last-minute preparations. Mrs. Bayard wrote, "I am sure your are deeply engaged, and are making rapid progress, so that when your long absent one returns, he will have great pleasure in finding you all he could desire.... I want you to greet the stranger with a sweet blooming face; such a one as he has not seen during his two years' absence, only in his dreams!"[109]

On September 29, Maggie left Crookville and, by early October, she was again staying with Mrs. Walter at Clinton Place. There, on October 1, she and the rest of the city learned that Elisha's ship had passed Sandy Hook; the next day, her heart thrilled when she heard the cannons announcing his arrival. In Crookville Mrs. Turner also heard the news and excitedly wrote her pupil of the past two years, "And now, dear Margaret,... I hope the remembrance of those hours we have spent in conversation or reading, will long continue to afford you happy thoughts.... Present my kindest regards to Mrs. W[alter], and by all means kind *love* to the Doctor."[110] After two and a half years, Elisha was finally home, but his arrival would not go as Maggie had hoped. As her later ghostwritten account of that day notes, "All that evening, when it was known that Dr. Kane was in the city, [Maggie and Mrs. Walter] waited for the ring of the bell that should herald his visit. Till midnight they listened every moment for his familiar step. He did not come."[111]

When Elisha returned from the arctic he embraced his role as "Dr. Kane" and readily went along with his family's advice on how he should conduct himself. With the exception of his initial report on the expedition and a brief letter to John P. Kennedy proclaiming, "My health is almost absurd: I have grown like a Walrus," there is no record of Elisha's thoughts at the time of his arrival.[112] On his trip back from the arctic he would have read both Maggie's excited letter about their impending wedding as well as Cornelius Grinnell's letter warning him that rumors of the same had circulated in the press. In addition, if Cornelius's letter can be believed, Elisha also had before him a letter (now lost) from his brother Pat, outlining the family's fears regarding Miss Fox. His brother, John, would have also emphasized this during the journey home.[113] Elisha spent the night after his arrival at the Grinnells' house, surrounded by his family. The next day he received a letter from Mrs. Walter explicitly stating that Maggie was at her house and anxiously awaiting him.[114]

The only surviving record of Maggie and Elisha's reunion is *The Love-Life of Dr. Kane,* the ghostwritten book Maggie published in 1866 to justify her claim to part of Elisha's estate.[115] Created for such specific ends, the work is obviously problematic as a source. Given this, however, it appears to be largely accurate; its dates and events coincide perfectly with all surviving letters and documentation of their relationship. It also explains the rumors that appeared in both the press and in friends' and family members' journals far more convincingly than any other source. Perhaps the most convincing statement about its validity, however, is that the Kane family spent years trying to keep it from being printed, and when it finally did come out, the women of the family quietly admitted to each other that its basic details were neither shocking nor inaccurate. After reading an advance copy of the book, Bessie Wood Kane (Tom's wife), wrote to Elisha's sister, Bessie Kane Shields, "I confess that the description touched me."[116]

According to Maggie's account, on the evening of October 13, exhausted and utterly discouraged from having waited two days for Elisha's visit, Maggie left Mrs. Walter's and went to stay with her mother and Kate at their Tenth Street residence. A few hours later Dr. Edward Bayard brought word that a carriage had arrived at Mrs. Walter's door. He hurriedly escorted Maggie back to Clinton Place, but upon arrival, Mrs. Walter sadly announced that the visitor was not Elisha, but another caller. Her hopes again crushed, Maggie went upstairs to spend the night. What Mrs. Walter had not mentioned was that the visitor was Cornelius Grinnell and that he had come to explain that Elisha was delayed because of "great trouble in his family" over the relationship. He also requested that Mrs. Walter give him all the letters Elisha had ever written to Maggie. She refused. The next morning, dressed in naval uniform, Elisha finally arrived at Clinton Place. Maggie initially refused to see him, but eventually she came down to the parlor where she found Elisha "walking the room in a fearful state of excitement." When he saw her he rushed to her, kissed her brow, and held her "for some minutes closely pressed to his breast." He then told her "in broken words" that he still loved her, but that their marriage had to be indefinitely postponed because of the violent opposition of his family. To her horror, he then pleaded that she sign a note stating that their relationship had always been "merely friendly and fraternal" and that "no matrimonial engagement had subsisted" between them. He insisted that he had to obtain such a letter to appease his mother. He wrote out the note and asked her to copy it into her own hand and sign it. Tearfully she complied. Elisha then showed the note to Mrs. Walter and asked Maggie to state verbally that it was true, but at this point she broke down and exclaimed, "No—no—it is not so! Doctor Kane knows it is not!" Frightened and embarrassed, Elisha grabbed the note and left despite Mrs. Walter's protest. He returned that evening, ashamed and broken. He begged Maggie "to stand firm, and to be true to him, till the storm had blown over," and he promised that he would not abandon her. A few days later, he returned again with the note. He handed it back to her and apologized that he had been "compelled by his persecutors to act a part unworthy of a gentleman." She immediately tore it to bits. He then showed her a letter from his aunt Elizabeth Leiper that scolded him for his actions and banished him from her house until he fulfilled his duty to Maggie. Despite this, however, he made it clear that for the foreseeable future, he could not acknowledge any romantic interest in her. To Maggie's surprise and disgust, he came back a few days later with a newspaperman and "bade her tell him the engagement had been kindly broken off."[117]

If he had not realized it before, Elisha now understood that he was no longer in control of his life. For the past decade he had dedicated himself to achieving fame, and now he had it. He was "Dr. Kane," the nation's hero. This was a grand achievement and one that Elisha doubtlessly relished. He, the small, sickly doctor from Philadelphia was now one of the nation's greatest men. Such fame was intoxicating and not something he wanted to lose, but it came at a heavy price. To maintain the praise of the world, Elisha needed to make a Faustian bargain, trading his private desires for the immortality of fame. After his heroic return from the arctic, he began both reaping the benefits and paying the price of this bargain. After two years of suffering and toil, he had unprecedented fame, but this fame necessitated his avoiding the woman he loved. He was now Dr. Kane the hero, and as such, he had to live not as he wished, but as his public demanded. As his brother Tom warned, to maintain his fame, Elisha had to respect the fame-creating voice of the nation's media: "Respect au Adieu! —It is they who made us and not we ourselves."[118] Even if he wanted to, Elisha could not refuse the role of Dr. Kane because he alone was not its creator. The long and difficult task of creating Dr. Kane had been a group effort, one in which the Kane family and many others had heavily invested. These people did not want to see their creation destroyed just as it was realizing its full potential. Elisha's debt to them was deep and binding. They had funded his expedition, published his book, promoted him, and were now financially supporting him because he himself was penniless.[119] Furthermore, Dr. Kane was now beyond even their control. Dr. Kane was the property of the nation. The people of the United States purchased his book, consumed his exploits in the popular media, and funded his rescue with $150,000 of their own money. They had granted him the fame he desired; he now had to give them the hero he had promised.

1. Elisha Kent Kane to John K. Kane (undated, c. Aug., 1856) in folder, "EK Kane to Mother & Father," APS Elisha Kent Kane papers. This naturalist was probably 21-year-old W.H.B. Thomas, who was recommended by Spencer F. Baird of the Smithsonian Institute. Elisha hired him just a few weeks before the expedition set sail but, for unspecified reasons, Thomas did not ultimately join the crew. See S.F. Baird to Elisha Kent Kane (May 11 & May 13, 1853), APS Elisha Kent Kane papers.

2. Wilkes was afraid of what his crew would write because many saw him as an erratic and unjust commander. The expedition and its aftermath resulted in several court cases which Wilkes ultimately won, but not without severely hurting his reputation.

J.K. Kane was at this time in charge of what was left of Peale's Philadelphia Museum and worked diligently to claim the specimens from the expedition for the Museum and the American Philosophical Society (the Smithsonian was not yet established as the national museum). See William Stanton, *The Great United States Exploring Expedition of 1838-1842* (Berkeley: University of California Press, 1975).

3. George Corner, *Dr. Kane of the Arctic Seas* (Philadelphia: Temple University Press, 1972), 120, 126.

4. Elisha Kent Kane, *Arctic Explorations* (Philadelphia: Childs & Peterson, 1856), I, 16.

5. Corner, 126. Wilson's feelings are seen clearly in his unpublished narrative of the expedition, *Narrative of the Second Grinnell Expedition in Search of Sir John Franklin*, National Archives.

6. Sonntag was German, Petersen & Ohlsen were Danish, and Hans was Inuit/Greenlander. At the time of the expedition, Ohlsen and the rest of the crew were living in the United States, but Hickey and Morton were Irish born and Peter (Pierre) Schubert was from France.

7. Elisha Kent Kane to John K. Kane (undated, c. July 23, 1853), APS Elisha Kent Kane papers.

8. Oscar M. Villarejo, *Dr. Kane's Voyage to the Polar Lands* (Philadelphia: University of Pennsylvania Press, 1965), 60-62. This book is a translation with introduction and commentary taken from Carl Petersen's account of the Second Grinnell Expedition, published in Danish in 1857. See Carl J. Petersen, *Erindringer fra Polarlandene opegnede af Carl Petersen, tolk ve Pennys og Kanes nordexpeditioner, 1850-55* (Copenhagen: P. G. Philipsen, 1857).

9. *Arctic Explorations*, I, 47. Another good example of this comes when Elisha sings the praises of one of their sturdy little boats and names it "Eric the Red," while noting that "the crew have named [it], less poetically, the 'Red Boat.'" See *Arctic Explorations*, I, 67.

10. *Arctic Explorations*, I, 51-52.

11. Barry Allen Joyce, "As the Wolf from the Dog"; American Overseas Exploration & the Compartmentalization of Humankind: *1838-1859* (PhD diss., University of California, Riverside, 1995), 343.

12. *Arctic Explorations*, I, 18.

13. *Arctic Explorations*, I, 56, 64-65.

14. These exciting few days are described vividly in chapter seven of *Arctic Explorations*. Explorers had pushed to further northern latitudes via a European route north from Scandanavia and Russia.

15. *Arctic Explorations*, I, 83-84.

16. The final resting place of the *Advance* is still a mystery. When Hayes returned to Rensselaer Harbor in 1861, no sign of her remained. See Isaac I. Hayes, *The Open Polar Sea* (New York: Hurd and Houghton, 1867), 288.

17. *Arctic Explorations*, I, 118-21.

18. *Arctic Explorations*, I, 143.

19. *Arctic Explorations*, I, 156.

20. Hans Christian Hendrik, *Memoirs of Hans, the Arctic Traveller Serving under Kane, Hayes, Hall, and Nares, 1853-1876*, Henry Rink trans., George Stephens ed. (London, Trübner & Co., 1878), 24.

21. An occultation is the complete or partial disappearance of a celestial body when another passes between it and the observer. This occurrence can help astronomers measure the size and speed of objects, as well as the distance between Earth and the object. *Arctic Explorations*, I, 167.

22. *Arctic Explorations*, I, 152-55, 165-69; see also the extensive tables of data in the appendixes 5-18 , II, 363-467.

23. *Arctic Explorations*, I, 162.

24. *Arctic Explorations*, I, 192.

25. This exciting rescue effort is told in wonderful detail in chapter sixteen of *Arctic Explorations*. Another reason they stopped so rarely for water was that it took great effort to heat ice to a point that it would not freeze instantly upon contact with their lips.

26. Corner, 155; *Arctic Explorations*, I, 201-07.

27. *Arctic Explorations*, I, 208-09, II, 251; Wilson, *Narrative*, 113.

28. *Arctic Explorations*, I, 216. Elisha suggested that an alternative to spilling human blood was to shoot and kill their dogs as a warning.

29. Villarejo, 81-82. Even before the Second Grinnell Expedition was complete, Hans left it and married Mersuk of the small northern Inuit village of Peteravik. The two of them continued to accompany American and British exploring expeditions, further blurring the savage/civilized barrier. See Hans Hendrik, *Memoir of Hans*; and "The Wifely Heroism of Mersuk, the Daughter of Shang-hu" in Augustus W. Greely, *True Tales of Arctic Heroism* (New York: Scribner, 1912), 367-85.

30. Villarejo, 81-82.

31. Elisha supplied the ship's library with Tennyson's two-volume poetry work of 1842, which included his favorite poem, "Ulysses." Tennyson also had another connection to the expedition in that his wife was a niece of Sir John Franklin. See Charles W. Shields, "The Arctic Monument Named for Tennyson by Dr. Kane," *Century Magazine* 34 (August, 1898), 482-93.

32. *Arctic Explorations*, II, 365-73. That he discussed this with Elisha is apparent from Elisha's comments toward Godfrey when he later exhibited similar mutinous inclinations. Hayes addressed Godfrey's behavior years later, but still judged him gently, blaming his behavior on the fear that develops in "uninstructed minds" during difficult hardships. See Isaac I. Hayes, *Arctic Boat Journey* 2nd enlarged ed. (Boston: Ticknor & Fields, 1868), 379-80n7. Godfrey himself mentions nothing of this incident in his account of their journey. See William Godfrey, *Godfrey's Narrative of the Last Grinnell Arctic Exploring Expedition* (Philadelphia: J.T. Lloyd & Co., 1857), 147-54.

33. Though Peary's reaching the north pole has been a matter of great debate, it is generally accepted that he reached 90° North, or a point very near to it, on April 6, 1909. See William H. Goetzmann, "Re-Thinking *New Lands, New Men*," *New Lands, New Men* 2nd ed. (Austin: Texas State Historical Association, 1995), xviii-xxi. For Peary's account see Robert Edwin Peary, *The North Pole* (New York: J.B. Lippincott, 1910).

34. Note that Corner mistakes their date of return as July 10, 1854. See Corner, 166.

35. *Arctic Explorations*, I, 305.

36. *Arctic Explorations*, I, 306.

37. Quoted in Corner, 167.

38. Elisha Kent Kane to Thomas Leiper Kane (July 7, 1854), John Kane papers, Historical Society of Pennsylvania.

39. *Arctic Explorations*, I, 315.

40. *Arctic Explorations*, I, 315-36. Had they been able to reach Beechey Island, they would likely not have gained the help they needed for Belcher's expedition had gone horribly; four of his five ships were icebound in Melville Sound and Wellington Channel. Belcher abandoned these ships and, with all crews aboard his final ship, set sail for England on August 26, 1854. See George M. McDougal, *The Eventful Voyage of H.M. Discovery Ship "Resolute" in Search of Sir John Franklin* (London: Longman, 1857).

41. "Warping" is to move a ship by pulling it with ropes. Private Journal of Elisha Kent Kane (Aug. 12, 1854), Special Collections, Stanford University Libraries, reprinted in Corner, 173-74. An edited version of this statement (without the sentiment that all rested on him) appears in *Arctic Explorations*, I, 343.

42. *Arctic Explorations*, I, 343.

43. Private Journal of Elisha Kent Kane (Aug. 21, 1854), Special Collections, Stanford University Libraries. Much of this journal is reprinted in Villarejo.

44. Private Journal of Elisha Kent Kane (Aug. 23, 1854), Special Collections, Stanford University Libraries.

45. Private Journal of Elisha Kent Kane (Aug. 25, 1854), Special Collections, Stanford University Libraries.

46. Elisha held that Hans, McGary, and Wilson all decided on their own to remain with him, but Petersen noted in regard to Hans and Wilson (as well as Ohlsen) that Elisha "contrived to keep [them] on board partly by persuasion and not without some menace." See Villarejo, 86.

47. Private Journal of Elisha Kent Kane (Aug. 25 & 26, 1854), Special Collections, Stanford University Libraries.

48. Elisha recorded this document in his journal, see Private Journal of Elisha Kent Kane, Special Collections, Stanford University Libraries, 75.

49. Private Journal of Elisha Kent Kane (Aug. 26 & 28, 1854), Special Collections, Stanford University Libraries.

50. Private Journal of Elisha Kent Kane (Aug. 28, 1854), Special Collections, Stanford University Libraries.

51. Private Journal of Elisha Kent Kane (Sept. 5, 1854), Special Collections, Stanford University Libraries.

52. Isaac Hayes to William Elder (Dec. 5, 1857), Steward Collection, Glassboro (NJ) State College, reprinted as Appendix A in Villarejo, 183-86. In 1857 Hayes was lecturing and trying to drum up support for his own expedition to prove the existence of the Open Polar Sea—he returned to Kane Basin in 1860-61. What appears to be his lecture manuscript still survives in the Hayes papers of the Chester County (Pennsylvania) Historical Society. On this manuscript are signed endorsements of its veracity by John Wall Wilson and Amos Bonsall. Hayes expanded this work into a full-length book a few years later. See Isaac Israel Hayes, *An Arctic Boat Journey in the Autumn of 1854* (Boston: Brown, Taggard, & Chase, 1860). A second edition with added notes and illustrations was published later, see (Boston: Ticknor & Fields, 1868).

53. Villarejo, 86.

54. Godfrey, *Godfrey's Narrative*, 157.

55. This unpublished manuscript is titled, *The Facts Relating to the Separation of the Ship's Company of the Brig "Advance" in the Fall of 1854. Written out by Henry Goodfellow. By command of Miss Bessie Kane.* According to Corner, the original, as of 1957, was in possession of Mrs. E. Paul DuPont of Montchanin, Delaware. Typed copies are in the APS Elisha Kent Kane papers; the Dow papers, Stefansson Collection of Dartmouth College; and the archives of the National Geographical Society (Washington DC) No. 330, Greely MS collection. Large portions of it are also reprinted in Villarejo, 100n46-47, 170-72

56. *Arctic Explorations*, I, 369-70.

57. Hendrik, *Memoirs of Hans*, 30. Hans noted that Elisha was "very clever in not despising native food."

58. Private Journal of Elisha Kent Kane (Dec., 1854), Special Collections, Stanford University Libraries.

59. According to Goodfellow, before his departure from the *Advance*, Petersen "indulged in quite a little harangue in which he declared his intention to pass the winter on the rocks rather than return to the Ship." See Goodfellow manuscript.

60. In all the accounts of this event, only Godfrey mentions the hostage, and it is unclear under what circumstances this arrangement was made. It is clear, however, that the men never returned nor did they deliver the provisions. Godfrey, 171-72.

61. The adventure of this party is told in three different narratives. Hayes's *Arctic Boat Journey* is the most detailed, but Petersen's (translated in Villarejo) is probably the most accurate as it is simply the compilation of the daily notes that Petersen had Sonntag keep during the journey. *Godfrey's Narrative* provides many interesting and exciting details but was written primarily to show that he was not the rascal Kane portrayed him to be, and is thus quite skewed.

62. Hayes, *An Arctic Boat Journey*, 224-25.

63. Villarejo, 142. Neither Hayes nor Godfrey mentioned this idea in their account.

64. Villarejo, 146-48.

65. See Hayes, *Arctic Boat Journey*, 287-326; and *Godfrey's Narrative*, 170-78.

66. Private Journal of Elisha Kent Kane (Dec. 9, 1854), Special Collections, Stanford University Libraries.

67. *Arctic Explorations*, I, 439.

68. *Arctic Explorations*, I, 441-43.

69. Private Journal of Elisha Kent Kane (Dec., 1854), Special Collections, Stanford University Libraries.

70. Elisha, having dismissed the seceding men from their duties, actually re-appointed them under new agreements. See Corner, 197-98.

71. Private Journal of Elisha Kent Kane (Feb., 1854), Dreer Collection, Historical Society of Pennsylvania.

72. *Arctic Explorations*, II, 66.

73. Elisha knew that the citizens of Etah had lost or been forced to eat their walrus lines, the seal-skin ropes they attached to the barbed spears they used to hunt walrus. He thus sent the ship's sounding lines, the ropes used to gather sea-depth measurements for Mathew Maury's charts, for them to use instead. This, among other gestures, show that at this point, the men of the *Advance* and the people of Etah were working together to ensure their mutual survival. See *Arctic Explorations*, II, 71-72.

74. Private Journal of Elisha Kent Kane (March 20, 1855), Special Collections, Stanford University Libraries.

75. *Godfrey's Narrative*, 182.

76. *Arctic Explorations*, II, 89-90.

77. *Arctic Explorations*, II, chapter 14.

78. For the further adventures of Hans and Mersuk with the expeditions of Hayes (1860-61), Charles Francis Hall (1870-71), and George Nares (1875-76) see Hendrik, *Memoirs of Hans*; and Augustus W. Greely "The Marvelous Drift of Captain Tyson" and "The Wifely Heroism of Mersuk" in *True Tales of Arctic Heroism* (New York: Scribner, 1912).

79. Private Journal of Elisha Kent Kane (May, 1855), Special Collections, Stanford University Libraries.

80. *Arctic Explorations*, II, 165-66.

81. *Arctic Explorations*, II, 178-79.

82. This was a ceremonial leaving, the men continued to sleep on the brig for several more days and the sick remained there for several weeks.

83. See Kane, *Arctic Explorations*; Hayes, *An Arctic Boat Journey*; Petersen in Villarejo; Bonsall's letter to Elder in William Elder, *The Biography of Elisha Kent Kane* (Philadelphia: Childs & Peterson, 1858); Goodfellow in his letter to Bessie Kane (see note above); and *Godfrey's Narrative*.

84. Examining the scant evidence, George Corner (a Kane biographer and Medical Doctor) believed that the "injury was probably collapse of the lumbar vertebra, weakened by loss of calcium due to malnutrition, with resultant crushing of the spinal cord." See Corner, 292n2.

85. *Arctic Explorations*, II, 248.

86. In the *Faith* were Elisha, McGary, Petersen, Hickey, Stephenson, & Whipple; in the *Hope*, Brooks, Hayes, Sonntag, Morton, Goodfellow & Blake; and in the little "Red Erik"—the small boat they also decided to take—were Bonsall, Riley and Godfrey. For some reason, Elisha fails to mention where Wilson was.

87. *Arctic Explorations*, II, 288.

88. *Arctic Explorations*, II, 290.

89. *Arctic Explorations*, II 296-97.

90. Of the nineteen crewmembers, Baker and Schubert died in April of 1854, Ohlsen in August of 1855, Hans stayed among the far-northern Inuit villages, and Petersen at his home in Upernavik thus leaving fourteen to return to New York. Hayes, Sonntag, Bonsall, Stephenson, Whipple, Godfrey, & Blake were members of the seceding party and Wilson and Riley had voted to leave but later changed their minds and stayed aboard the *Advance*.

91. In the following months Elisha was publicly compared to each of these characters. See *United States Magazine* 3 (Dec. 1856), 538-43; and James G. Wilson, *Thackeray in the United States* (New York: Dodd, Mead, & Co., 1904), 66-67.

92. Thomas Leiper Kane to Elisha Kent Kane (May 31, 1855), APS Elisha Kent Kane papers.

93. Though all the major New York papers ran extensive stories of the expedition and Elisha's homecoming, the *New York Times'* story was by far the longest and most complete and its headline proclaimed, "Dr. Kane's Own Account." *New York Times* (Dec. 12, 1855), 1. As noted in chapter two, the Kane family chose to privilege the *Times* because its editor, Henry J. Raymond, was very well connected in publishing circles and could help them with later book projects.

94. *New York Tribune* (Oct. 12, 1855), 4.

95. *New York Tribune* (Oct. 13, 1855), 5.

96. *New York Tribune* (Oct. 13, 1855), 5.

97. *New York Times* (Oct. 12, 1855), 8.

98. *New York Tribune* (Oct. 13, 1855), 5.

99. *New York Tribune* (Oct. 13, 1855), 5; *New York Herald* (Dec. 13, 1855).

100. *New York Tribune* (Oct. 13, 1855), 4. This case began in July of 1855 when abolitionists helped several slaves escape while traveling with their master through Pennsylvania. Kane demanded that Passmore Williamson—who represented the abolitionists but was not directly involved in the escape—bring the slaves to court. When he could not, Kane put him in jail for contempt of court. The case continued for months and on October 12, Kane ruled that slaves were still slaves when they were

being transported through free states. He then went further and stunningly suggested that Constitutional rights regarding property forbade any state from outlawing slavery—the same argument Supreme Court Chief Justice Roger Taney would use in his ruling on the landmark *Dred Scott* case of 1857.

101. Portsmouth, New Hampshire *Morning Chronicle* (Oct. 15, 1855).

102. Several members of Hartstene's crew published their accounts in newspapers and magazines in the months following the expedition's return, which makes the silence of the men of the *Advance* stand in sharp contrast.

103. For these later conflicting accounts see: *Godfrey's Narrative of the Second Grinnell Expedition*; Petersen's *Erindringer fra Polarlandene opegnede af Carl Petersen* translated in Villarejo; and John Wall Wilson's unpublished *Narrative of the Second Grinnell Expedition*.

104. John K. Kane to Rev. Charles W. Shields (Oct. 13, 1855), in pamphlet "Letters to B.K.," 24. This rare, undated pamphlet is a compilation of letters to Elizabeth "Bessie" Kane, the Kane family's only daughter, who later married Rev. Shields. A copy of this pamphlet is in the folder, "Kane Family Information," Kane family papers, Clements Library, University of Michigan.

105. In December 1854 papers across the country reported that Kane had found Franklin and was on his way home, but these were soon proved false, see the San Francisco *Daily Placer Times and Transcript* (Jan. 1, 1855), 2. Cornelius Grinnell to Maggie Fox (April 30, 1855), *Love-Life*, 182-83; and Cornelius Grinnell to Elisha Kent Kane (June 2, 1855), APS Elisha Kent Kane papers. In the latter letter, Cornelius noted that Margaret had "received all impression from the newspapers that you are already on the way home, and she appears to think that you will be here very shortly in spite of what I have written her."

106. Maggie Fox to Elisha Kent Kane (undated, c. May 1, 1855), APS Elisha Kent Kane papers.

107. Maggie Fox to Elisha Kent Kane (undated, c. May 1, 1855), APS Elisha Kent Kane papers.

108. Suzanna Turner to Maggie Fox (July 3, 16, & 20, 1855), *Love-Life*, 183-85.

109. T. Bayard to Maggie Fox (Sept. 3, 1855), *Love-Life*, 186-87.

110. Suzanna Turner to Maggie Fox (Oct. 12, 1855), *Love-Life*, 188-89.

111. *Love-Life*, 190-91.

112. Elisha Kent Kane to John P. Kennedy (Oct. 11, 1855), quoted in Elder, 215.

113. Cornelius Grinnell to Elisha Kent Kane (June 2, 1855), APS Elisha Kent Kane papers. Cornelius's letters states, "Your brother will write to you on this subject."

114. *Love-Life*, 192.

115. In 1858 Maggie began negotiating with the author/publisher Elizabeth Lummis Ellet about the publication of her biography that would include the love letters Elisha had sent her. This project progressed rapidly as Joseph La Fumée of the *Brooklyn Eagle* strung the letters together into a narrative, working as Fox's ghostwriter. In the fall

of 1858, Maggie pulled the manuscript, and instead of publishing it, used it as a bargaining tool with the Kane family for the next eight years. See multiple letters between Maggie Fox and Robert Patterson Kane, APS Elisha Kent Kane and Robert Patterson Kane papers; *Love-Life*, vii-x; and Miriam Buckner Pond, *Time is Kind: The Story of the Unfortunate Fox Family* (New York: Centennial Press, 1947), 219.

116. Elizabeth "Bessie" Wood Kane to Elizabeth "Bessie" Kane Shields (undated, c. Nov., 1865), Kane family papers, Clements Library, University of Michigan.

117. *Love-Life*, 192-99.

118. Thomas Leiper Kane to Elisha Kent Kane (May 31, 1855), APS Elisha Kent Kane papers. Emphasis in the original.

119. Fox asserted that Elisha told her that he was completely dependent on his family for funds, *Love-Life*, 200. This is supported by the fact that Elisha asked his publisher for an $800 advance for personal expenses immediately after signing on. See George Childs to Elisha Kent Kane, "Mem: of Cash advanced on Acct. of Copy Right to Dr. E.K. Kane," APS Elisha Kent Kane papers.

6

A Man Divided: The Two Lives of Elisha Kent Kane

❧

Within days of his arrival from the arctic in October 1855, Elisha Kent Kane realized that he was no longer in control of his life. He was, in fact, no longer just one man, but two. He was Elisha Kent Kane, a physician from Philadelphia who had explored the world, made mistakes, fallen in love, and fully realized his faults and failings as well as accomplishments and triumphs. He was a skilled scientist, artist, and writer, a talented speaker and promoter, and a charismatic and driven leader. He was also a frail and at times petty man, whose men had abandoned his leadership; a son who desperately wanted to maintain the respect of his powerful father; and a lover trying to maintain the favor of a woman he had scorned. Elisha Kent Kane was a complicated person. He was also the physical embodiment of a very uncomplicated hero, Dr. Kane. As Americans across the nation knew from their newspapers and magazines, Dr. Kane was faultless—a "true hero" who possessed "a daring that never quailed, endurance that knew no yielding, a devotion to duty that nothing could shake, a fidelity to friends as sacred as life, inextinguishable hope, undying energy, and the crowning virtue of all, a modesty that makes no pretensions, and instinctively shrank from all public display."[1]

Elisha Kent Kane was both a man and a superman, and while he struggled to maintain balance within his human life of confusion and turmoil, he also tried to live up to the expectations the nation had for Dr. Kane. This duality of existence was the direct consequence of fame. As Elisha learned, fame can be sought, but not controlled; it is not a product or attribute possessed by the famous, but a quality placed on them by their admirers.[2] Although the effort of becoming famous is active, necessitating some deed or quality that attracts public notice, fame itself is passive. It does not come from any particular action or attribute, but from public recognition. If a tree falls in a forest but no one hears it, did it make a sound? Fame answers this old question emphatically: No. With regard to fame, for something to exist it has to attract public notice. Descartes philosophically asserted individual existence, stating, "I think, therefore I am." The existence of fame is somewhat different: "They think I am, therefore I am." Attracting public attention is the first step toward achieving fame, but it is public recognition that allows an individual to become and remain famous. This has terrifying consequences because, as people become famous and begin to embrace and define themselves by their fame, they come to recognize that the public has more control over their fame than they do. The public can destroy fame just as easily as it can create it: "If they cease to think I am, then I am not." Tom expressed such ideas when he warned Elisha that he must respect the newspapermen because "it is they who made us and not we ourselves," and it is embedded in the press reports surrounding Elisha's return. As one *Tribune* article concluded, "Of this we may be certain—the fame of Dr. Kane is in the sacred keeping *of his country.*"[3]

The only way a person can maintain fame is to remain in the public eye. This is not a problem if one is famous for sustainable reasons. For example, in this era P. T. Barnum was famous for providing curiosities that entertained the public. He did not have to be perfect or even honest because he fulfilled the public's expectations whether he was "humbugging" them with the Fiji Mermaid or dazzling them with the sweet voice of singing sensation Jenny Lind. Elisha did not have this luxury. He was famous for being Dr. Kane, a faultless hero. The public's expectation of Dr. Kane was a perfection no human could maintain. To complicate matters further, part of the reason people celebrated him was because they believed he did *not* pursue fame—as papers noted, he wore his honors with "meekness" and "instinctually shrank from all public display."[4] His only hope to maintain fame was to remove himself physically from the day-to-day encounters of the public sphere and allow his public persona to passively reflect the heroic attributes the public projected onto Dr. Kane. Elisha had the skills and means to do this, but it necessitated an extraordinarily sharp division between his private and public life. Scholars of nineteenth-century America find such divisions common in this era, noting that antebellum society assumed "separate spheres" of existence—one the public, male-dominated, ruthlessly competitive work-a-day world; the other the private, female-dominated, self-sacrificing, virtuous, and domesticated world of the home. Proper, middle-class virtue thus expected men to have two identities: a public persona that was confident, powerful, and capable of bold and even ruthless behavior that would ensure economic survival; and a private persona that existed only in the intimacy of the home sphere, which was kind, compassionate, and even vulnerable.[5] As a celebrity constantly in the public gaze, Elisha was forced to live an extreme form of this separation of spheres. He had to embrace a dual existence and learn to live as both the private man Elisha Kent Kane, and the public superman Dr. Kane, recognizing that too much devotion to either could destroy the other.

In the days immediately following his return from the Arctic, Elisha worked to hide all aspects of his life that he felt would detract from the public's image of Dr. Kane. He glossed over his conflicts with his crew and disassociated himself from Margaret Fox while working to present an image that reflected the public's expectations of Dr. Kane. To this end, he harnessed the power of a booming new medium, the illustrated newspaper. Thanks to massive increases in both population and education, the American reading public increased from roughly six million to well over fifteen million between 1840 and 1860. This addition of more than nine million readers allowed publishers to create specialized papers for target audiences and still sell enough copies to stay solvent; this can be seen in the huge jump in the number of weekly newspapers, which rose from 1,266 in 1840 to 2,971 by 1860.[6] The illustrated newspaper boomed in this environment. *Harper's New Monthly Magazine* (1850) was the first American illustrated paper, but this rather highbrow monthly was soon followed by several weekly illustrated newspapers aimed at more general audiences, including *Gleason's* (later *Ballou's*) *Pictorial Drawingroom Companion* (1851); *The Illustrated News* (1853, partially funded by P. T. Barnum and later purchased by *Gleason's*); *Frank Leslie's Illustrated Newspaper* (1855); and Harpers own effort to compete in the weekly illustrated market, *Harper's Weekly* (1857). Because of the high cost of engraving images, these papers sold for the relatively large sum of six cents per issue. Though they were expensive for most Americans, these eight-page papers were popular because, for the first time, they offered the public timely images of current events.[7]

Given the boom in illustrated periodicals, it is easy to understand why the Kane family found it essential to create a graphic image of Dr. Kane for the public to consume. At the time of his return in 1855, the public had few actual images of Dr. Kane. Before he left on his second expedition, only one portrait appeared in the press and it was based on a daguerreotype from six years earlier. After that time, his physical attributes were not addressed much beyond noting his small but energetic frame and intense eyes.[8] This description was modified upon his return when newspapers noted that he "wore a beard of patriarchal proportions" and that he appeared more robust—"His little body was wrapped in multitudinous layers of flannels and skins, and over all was drawn a tight worsted shirt, so that his person was of almost Falstaffian proportions."[9]

Judging from the changes in his description in the months following his return, it is clear that Elisha and his family carefully structured his physical appearance to match the public's image of a heroic arctic explorer. The first and most obvious evidence of this is that when he arrived in New York, Elisha was not in military garb; rather, he was in the fur jumper and long beard of his expedition. A full month passed between the time of his rescue and his arrival back in the United States, yet when he stepped off the ship in New York he was still dressed as if he had been in the arctic that morning. This was intentional. The trip home provided ample time for Elisha to shave his beard and abandon his Inuit-style fur clothing for proper naval garb, but by maintaining this "natural" appearance, he better resembled the hero the American public expected. He was Ulysses just returned after years of battle and adventure; he was Robinson Crusoe just back from his exotic entrapment.

The newspapers described Elisha just as he and his family desired, but an actual image was also necessary in this new era of illustrated papers. Just a few days after Elisha's return, Tom was already planning how this image should look. He wrote to his brother John and asked him to "think out the grouping of Elisha's party in the Photograph" to ensure that there would be "some artistic character in it." He insisted that the crew should not all be standing—Elisha's small frame would be dwarfed by his larger companions—and instead suggested a pyramid type arrangement, "I should think the little fellows would prefer dropping on one knee, with rifle in hand e.g., & generally dory attitudes." Tom was also very conscious of symbolism and wanted to "get in all the properties" that would best promote Elisha. He told John to include the Masonic sign and Toodles (one of the sled dogs they brought back), and, most importantly, "The American Flag—a big one will be invaluable for falling drapery." He also felt the photo should, in a stylized way, portray an event from the expedition. He recommended having the men sitting, as though they had "paused from pushing the Whale Boat," while Elisha stood above them, reading from a book. "This would admirably attract attention without affectation to the central figure, the Doctor, holding the book while the others listened."[10]

Tom's staging of this photograph was designed to make Elisha reflect the public's multifaceted image of Dr. Kane. Dressed in furs and standing above his armed and attentive men, he was the fearless explorer who, like Ulysses' and his voyage to Hades, had led his men in and out of a mysterious and dangerous world that consumed most mortals. The book in his hand demonstrated that he was a dedicated man of science who, like Prometheus, unraveled the godly mysteries of nature and made them accessible to all humankind. Finally, with a large American flag hanging behind him, he would personify a patriotic hero who transcended the sectional divisions that were then plaguing the nation—as one New Yorker put it in an editorial of the time, "You, and I, and every other American, reap honor from the discoveries lately made in the Arctic ocean by Dr. Kane."[11]

Tom planned to reproduce this picture and to distribute it widely; he instructed John to, "Only take the Daguerreotype in N. York.... We will get the pho-

Records suggest that Matthew Brady took a series of
photographs of Kane and his men in early 1856, although
none of them seem to have survived to the present. This image
comes from a copy of one of the pictures from this now lost
series. From left to right: Amos Bonsall, Henry Brooks, Elisha
Kent Kane, William Morton, Isaac I. Hayes. This image became
the basis for many engravings, including the image of the crew
in Kane's own *Arctic Explorations* (see page 221).

tographs from it so much cheaper in Philadelphia."[12] John took Tom's suggestions,
modified them slightly, and hired the nation's most celebrated photographer,
Matthew Brady, to take the picture.[13] Brady did his job well. The portrait included
Bonsall, Brooks, Kane, Morton, and Hayes, all dressed in full Inuit garb. Bonsall
and Hayes were on the far left and right, respectively. Like Elisha they were standing, but they were a step back from the camera, making Elisha (standing in the center and wearing a tall fur cap) appear the tallest. Brooks and Morton sat next to
Kane. None of the men had anything in their hands except Elisha, who cradled a
large telescope in his arm. Like the images of St. Peter holding the keys to heaven,
in the months and years that followed, the telescope became the iconographic
prop of Dr. Kane. In his article about the rescue expedition that appeared a few
months later, John Kane, Jr. justified and further perpetuated this iconography by
noting that the rescue squadron first saw Elisha "standing upright in the stern of
the first boat, with his spy-glass slung around his neck."[14]

　　This image became *the* image of Dr. Kane for the next year as multiple publications used some form of it to ornament their pages. Although most papers took

Note that the cover of the first edition of *Frank Leslie's Illustrated Newspaper* (December 15, 1855) is taken directly from the photograph made for Dr. Kane's promotion. The London *Illustrated Times* (November 8, 1856) then reprinted a mirror image of Frank Leslie's engraving, but with a few additions, such as a bottle in Henry Brooks hand—perhaps a jab at his earlier expulsion from the navy for drunkenness.

just Elisha's head from the photo, reproducing it as an engraved portrait of Dr. Kane, the image first appeared in its entirety as the front-page illustration of the first issue of *Frank Leslie's Illustrated Newspaper*. Leslie (born Henry Carter) was one of the nation's most celebrated engravers who, after turning down a lucrative position with *Gleason's Illustrated*, began his own paper. Wanting to start with a splash, he dedicated most of his December 15, 1855, first edition to the new national hero, Dr. Kane. He filled four pages with stories and illustrations from the Second Grinnell Expedition. In addition to the cover image, Leslie also included a stunning full-page etching of "Dr. Kane and his comrades abandoning the 'Advance.' From a sketch made on the spot."[15] This image was full of sublime power, showing the *Advance* held fast by immovable ice and dwarfed by massive mountains and bergs. In this desolate scene, Dr. Kane and his men are steadfastly pulling their sleds south, none of them looking back at either their trapped vessel or the cold polar sun looming above.

Albert W. Berg's "The Polar Bear Polka" (New York: Firth, Pond & Co., 1856). Courtesy of Keffer Collection of Sheet Music, University of Pennsylvania Library.

Though very popular, these visual representations were by no means the only way the American public could consume their hero. Promoters of many entertainment genres sought to capitalize on Dr. Kane's popularity throughout the winter of 1855-1856. Just hours after his return, leading New York theater entrepreneur James Wallack commissioned a play for immediate production entitled "Dangers of an Expedition to the Arctic Sea and Safe Arrival of Dr. Kane."[16] Two light-hearted songs, "Dr. Kane's Arctic Polka" and "The Polar Bear Polka," also quickly appeared, the latter composed, appropriately enough, by "Mr. Berg." The cover of "The Polar Bear Polka" included a humorous sketch of two polar bears dancing and a small, crudely done portrait of Dr. Kane taken from another Mathew Brady image of Kane.[17] In September 1855, a month before Elisha's return, Dr. Edmund Beale debuted his panorama, *Arctic Regions!*, in Washington, D.C. Panorama shows (enormous canvases with multiple images that were displayed in-the-round or scrolled across a stage) were very popular in this era. *Arctic Regions!* was no exception. It traveled from Washington to Richmond, Virginia, and then on to Philadelphia, receiving rave

From *Frank Leslie's Illustrated Newspaper* (December 15, 1855).

reviews in each location. Surviving handbills show that it was advertised as a complete history of the English, American, and Danish searches for Sir John Franklin, but that it focused primarily on the first Grinnell Expedition, "Embracing a complete Voyage from New York to the North Pole." The images in the panorama drew primarily from the illustrations in Elisha's *U.S. Grinnell Expedition*, and once Elisha returned, it became much more explicitly advertised as the story of Dr. Kane. In their study of arctic panoramas, Russell Potter and Douglas Wamsley investigated Dr. Beale's panorama and found that fifty-seven of its images came directly from Kane's book and that, "from the beginning... Kane was the big draw. Indeed, in the text of the programme, Kane completely supplanted his commanding officers [of the first Grinnell Expedition]; both *Advance* and *Rescue* were referred to as 'Dr. Kane's Vessels.'"[18] In the winter of 1855, Dr. Beale's young nephew, Joseph Boggs Beale (later a celebrated artist himself), was so impressed with his uncle's show that he began painting his own arctic panorama in his parents' attic—a telling example of the popular influence of Dr. Kane's story.[19]

Having had his portrait taken by Brady and controlling (he thought) the public's fascination with his relationship to Fox, Elisha left New York just three days after his return. On October 15 he arrived in Washington to present his official report of the expedition. This report, although written in a formal manner, was thrilling because it officially noted the expedition's discovery of open water in extreme northern latitudes. As Elisha and most others believed, this was the fabled Open Polar Sea, and as the first "civilized" man to tread on its shores, Morton had taken a giant step for American interests and prestige. Printing the report in its entirety, the *New York Times* made public Elisha's observation that Kennedy Channel "expands to the northward into an open and iceless area, abounding in animal life, and presenting every character of an *open Polar* sea."[20]

This announcement had a profound effect on the U.S. public—it was a source of pride similar to the United States' moon landing of a century later. Like the space race of the 1950-1960s, the quest for arctic discoveries was one of intense international competition in the 1840s-1850s. Russia, England, Denmark, France and the United States all battled to be the first to discover and explore the Northwest Passage, the north pole, and the Open Polar Sea. Elisha's announcement put America at the forefront of the arctic race. It is thus hardly surprising that no American ever even questioned the validity of the discovery during Elisha's lifetime— the only debate was over why there was an Open Polar Sea. One Englishman, Charles R. Weld, a scholar and relative of Sir John Franklin, did publicly question Kane's discovery, but when he did, both British and American scientific societies roundly criticized him. Upon hearing of Weld's assertion, Elisha demanded a public apology. Weld complied and printed a retraction in the *London Times*, where he had first published his disagreement. This satisfied Elisha, who told his father: "Under the above circumstances I think it best as soon as the *Times* appears to write a kind letter to Mr. W[eld]. His position is most lamentable and I feel for him."[21]

In America, the public thrilled at Dr. Kane's discovery and began to debate their own theories to explain the existence of this "polar paradise." An editorial to the *Times* noted, "Dr. Kane has settled the fact of the *existence* of the Sea, but it is reserved for scientific research to ascertain the cause of the apparent anomaly." It then suggested that "the *centrifugal force* and the *internal heating* power of the earth" were responsible for the phenomenon. A few days later, the *Times* printed another theory from an anonymous editorialist who was sure that "the spheroidical shape of our earth" explained the open sea; his calculations showed that the poles were thirteen miles closer to the earth's hot center and were thus also covered by thirteen more miles of insulating atmosphere.[22] John C. Symmes's "holes at the poles" hollow-earth theory still had its adherents as well; a person from Carlisle, Pennsylvania, insisted that, "This theory alone can account for the 'open polar sea.'"[23] Armchair scientists were not the only ones caught up in the excitement of the discovery. One of the United States' greatest scientists and the father of modern oceanography, Matthew F. Maury, was thrilled by the "proof" of this mysterious ocean. In the 1857 revised edition of his monumental work, *The Physical Geography of the Sea*, amid his exact charts constructed from thousands of meticulously recorded measurements, Maury could not keep from waxing poetic about Kane's discovery:

> Seals were sporting and water-fowl feeding in this open sea of Dr. Kane's. Its waves came rolling in at his feet, and dashed with measured tread, like the majestic billows of old ocean, against the shore. Solitude, the cold and boundless expanse, and the mysterious heavings of its green waters, lent their charm to the scene. They suggested fancied myths, and kindled in the ardent imagination of the daring mariners many longings.[24]

Images of the Open Polar Sea soon appeared as well. The "official" image, that would later appear in Kane's narrative of the journey, showed Morton (or Dr. Kane as most people preferred to believe) standing at the edge of a beautiful, foaming sea. Other images were far more dramatic, however, such as one that showed a gi-

NORTH POLE—THEORETICALLY.

This "theoretical" image matched the sensational nature of the unauthorized, narrative that an overzealous publisher wrote and attributed to the Kane's naturalist, Augustus Sonntag. From [August Sonntag], *Professor Sonntag's Thrilling Narrative of the Grinnell Exploring Expedition to the Arctic Ocean* (Philadelphia: James T. Lloyd & Co., 1857). For Kane's image of the Open Polar Sea see page 219.

gantic whirlpool at the top of the world. Public excitement over this discovery was so great that just eight days after Elisha's return, advertisements for maps of his discoveries appeared on the front page of the *Tribune* next to ads for such other goods as Maria Ward's shocking and popular novel, *Female Life Among the Mormons*, and a newly released book of poetry, Walt Whitman's *Leaves of Grass*.[25] Even farming journals were discussing the mythic sea; between articles on crop production and new horseshoe technology *The Cincinnatus* (published by the Farmer's College of College Hill, Ohio) reported that "our readers doubtless perused the narrative of the Kane Expedition with a breathless attention" in which "he stood upon the shores of, to his eyes, a limitless sea."[26] All this excitement took on a strongly nationalistic sentiment in a New York newspaper article that was repeated across the nation. It exclaimed that, thanks to Dr. Kane's discoveries, the American Flag "may some day be floated on the point known to tradition as the pole; *that in fact the North pole shall one day become the flagstaff of our country's banner!*"[27]

While the nation was celebrating Dr. Kane's discovery of the Open Polar Sea, they were also beginning to pry into the details of his personal life. On the same day that the map of his discoveries was first advertised in New York's major newspapers, a small paper from upstate New York ran a much different story about Dr. Kane that would cause Elisha and his family months of panic:

> A gentleman of this city informs us that Dr. Kane, of the Arctic Expedition is soon to be married to Miss Margaretta Fox, the second sister of the "Fox girls" at whose residence... the spirit rappings were first manifested. Dr. K became acquainted with the Fox family in New York. During his absence Miss Fox, his said-to-be-affianced, has been attending a young ladies' school at Philadelphia.[28]

Within two weeks, this small article in the *Troy Daily Whig* was reprinted in papers across the nation, from New Hampshire to Wisconsin, New Jersey to Missouri.[29] As this first article appeared with no notice of source other than "a gentleman of this city," it is impossible to know who provided the information, but given its appearance in a paper in Troy, a hotbed of spiritualism, it is likely that one of Maggie's spiritualist friends or family members was behind it.[30]

Denials of this story immediately appeared, most notably in the New York *Evening Post*, but this only expanded public interest. The papers hummed with the story during the last week of October, and then, in its heavily read Saturday edition, the *New York Times* fanned the flames further, reporting: "We are confidently assured that the editor of the *Evening Post* has no reason to contradict the report of the engagement of Dr. Kane to Miss Margaretta Fox. This young lady is said to have retired long since from all association with spiritualists, and spent the time of Dr. Kane's absence with his aunt, near Philadelphia, from whom she has received instruction. She is said to be a beautiful, pure-minded and amiable girl." This article thrilled Maggie, but then on Monday, the *Times* retracted its story, noting that, "The parties who so 'confidently assured' us that the *Post* was in error, have announced to us that they themselves were mistaken," and insisted that they now found "the rumor concerning the Doctor utterly unfounded."[31] Such a flat denial of the engagement angered both Maggie and her friends, who were horrified that Elisha did not defend her honor by publicly addressing the issue; they were sure that the reversal in the *Times* was the result of "some party furious in the Kane interest." Maggie clipped several articles denying their engagement and sent them to Elisha with a note reading, "Many of my friends have called (and you are aware of the position my friends hold) and requested permission to answer the articles in the newspapers. My mother has had much difficulty in preventing them from doing so." Directly addressing the horror she felt about such a public discussion of personal matters, she continued, "I cannot tell you how unhappy it makes me to think of my affairs being in the mouths of so many strange persons, and the subject of newspaper comment." She reminded him that such publicity "cannot fail to injure you, as well as myself," and directly noted the impact it would have on his new-found celebrity status saying, "you are... widely known, and a stain on your honor would be hard to efface. I should not think of such things, believe me, but they are forced upon my mind by what I *know* many persons say." She concluded pointedly, "I have implicit confidence in you, and trust that you will think of some right and proper means to silence all this disturbance and meddling. I believe the newspaper writers make it their business to pry... but neither of us should give sanction to any statement not strictly true. If we depart from this straight path, we shall be sure to suffer for it in one way or another."[32]

Maggie's wish did not land on deaf ears. The day after the second *Times* story ran, Horace Greeley, editor of the *New York Tribune* and a friend of both the Fox and Kane families, wagged his editorial pen at the *Times* and *Evening Post*. Calling attention to their multiple reports concerning "Dr. Kane's prospects," he fumed:

> We wish the several journals which have originated reports, pro and con, respecting the persons above named would consider whether they have or have not therein perverted their columns to the gratification of an impertinent curiosity. What right has the public to know anything about an 'engagement' or non-engagement between these young people?... Whether they have been, are, may be, are not, or will not be, 'engaged,' can be nobody's business but their own and that of their near relatives.[33]

It is unclear whether Elisha or Maggie had any direct part in Greeley's reprimand, but it certainly benefited them both. A few days later, however, a much more explicate statement appeared in several Philadelphia newspapers that bluntly denied any romantic involvement between Fox and Kane, and called the report of their engagement a "foolish story" that originated from a simple misunderstanding. It explained that before Dr. Kane left for the arctic, he was moved by "pure motives of humanity" to donate money to help educate "one of the Fox sisters—a remarkably bright, intelligent girl, and worthy of a better employment than 'spirit rapping.'" Upon return, he went to check on her progress, and "from this simple incident has arisen the engagement story." The story then closed by noting that Dr. Kane's generous support of a less-fortunate member of humanity was just another example of "the noble liberality" of the Kane family.[34]

This story, almost certainly placed by the Kane family, in combination with Greeley's stern editorial, worked well; Elisha clipped the one from the *Pennsylvanian* and read it to Maggie "with chuckling fun, pinching her arm mischievously as 'the noble liberality' of his family was mentioned."[35] These two statements largely stopped the rumors in the press, but the denial of their engagement was a direct affront to Maggie and her family. Mrs. Fox and many of Maggie's friends confronted her and insisted that she break off all contact with Elisha. They were certain he was only playing with her affection and would ultimately break her heart and destroy her reputation. Maggie had little reason to disagree given Elisha's behavior since his return. Explaining that her duty ultimately lay to herself and her family, she wrote him: "I would be willing to sacrifice my life for you but not my honor. To lose my home and reputation would be far far far worse than to lose my life."[36] In another letter she flatly stated: "Dear Doctor Kane:—I have seen you for the last time. I have been deceived.... I must either give you up from this moment and forever, or give up those who are very dear to me, and who hold my name and reputation as sacred." She confessed that "you still have my love" and assured him that "I believe in your honor and truth," but she concluded by directly questioning his devotion to public opinion. "There is one who knows my heart; why should he think so much of this world and so little of the other? Why try to please the eyes of mortals, and overlook those eyes which are continually watching us? for the time is not distant when we will have to hear our doom; either happiness awaits us or eternal misery. And it is our privilege now to take which we please."[37] Although it was couched in terms of Christian judgment, this statement had double meaning. By devoting himself to the whims of public opinion, Maggie suggested that Elisha had forsaken both his Christian duty and their potential future as husband and wife. Mrs. Fox also wrote to Elisha and told him to end the relationship, "My child is as pure as an angel and if you are seen coming here the world will consume her."[38]

Maggie threatened to burn any further letters he sent, but she did not break off communication, and for the next several months they engaged in a strained but heartfelt correspondence, often signing their letters "Sister" and "Brother." They worried about public opinion, social status, loyalty to family, loyalty to each other, and personal reputation. Faced with losing Maggie, Elisha began having serious doubts about the sacrifices he had to make to maintain the image of Dr. Kane. He wrote, "Sometimes I am tempted to give up friends, name, position, honor—all for you, Maggie!" He also acknowledged that the effort to maintain such an impossibly perfect image of fame was in itself dishonest— "As for myself, I'm only half a *gentleman*; for they make me tell so many *stories*."[39]

The "they" Elisha addressed is telling of how he had come to view his life. He was no longer being Dr. Kane because he wanted to, but because he felt he *had* to. In other letters from this time he wrote, "I long for a holiday where I can cease to play great man, and play the fool instead," and he told Maggie, "Don't think of me as the wicked person that I have learned to be since I came to this uncharitable land... but as dear Lye, the friend of old times, who never advised you in all his life to do wrong, or did wrong himself, if he could help it."[40] Elisha wanted his life back, but "they" would not let him forsake Dr. Kane.

This ambiguous "they" was Elisha's hazy personification of the forces that bound him to Dr. Kane. His family was certainly part of this. His brother Tom counted on him to be Dr. Kane because for years he had helped create and promote Elisha, doing so because he believed their mutual goal was "to stick together, share luck and make of life generally a sort of joint stock concern."[41] Now they had "the chance of pushing this thing to its very farthest," and as he had always done, Tom was skillfully directing the promotional work necessary to achieve this goal. Elisha simply had to "take his petting gracefully."[42]

Pleasing his parents was also one of the major factors that drove Elisha to maintain his image. He sought desperately to keep from doing anything that would distress his mother, which is especially evident in his attempts to keep her from knowing of his relationship with Maggie.[43] Far more importantly, however, Elisha was driven to live up to the expectations of his powerful father. As a twenty-one year old medical student he wrote his father, saying of his life, "if dear Father, after a quiet supervision, you can consistently express an opinion in any way that of satisfaction—you have no idea of the real satisfaction it would afford."[44] During his first globetrotting adventure to China he exalted in being free from his father's judgmental eye, only to discover that he had internalized this gaze, making it inescapable. Thus, throughout all of his subsequent travels and trials he continued to long for his father's approval. As a thirty-four-year-old commander of an arctic expedition, when he contemplated his discovery of the Open Polar Sea and the important scientific data he had to contribute to the study of polar regions, he wrote in his private journal: "If I can only get home again to report to Father and Grinnell the results of all this, my satisfaction and gratitude will surpass my hopes.... I may advance myself in my father's eyes."[45]

Elisha certainly sought to please his family, but they were not the only "they" that drove him to be Dr. Kane. He had gained the support of such wealthy backers as Henry Grinnell and George Peabody, and he felt indebted to them personally, but even more importantly, he felt he had to live up to what they believed he was—a "man of science."[46] The Smithsonian, the American Philosophical Society, the American Geographical Society, the Philadelphia Academy of Natural Sciences, and the Naval Observatory had all supported him. So too had such famous men of science as Alexander von Humboldt, Louis Aggasiz, Spencer F. Baird, and Matthew F. Maury. Dr. Kane had lived up to their expectations—he was now one of them—but would this still be true if they learned that he was involved with a spirit-rapping medium?

Each of these groups was certainly part of the "they" Elisha felt pushing him into Dr. Kane's shoes, but there were still bigger forces he had to address. The first of these was the American public that celebrated Dr. Kane. To them, there was no Elisha Kent Kane outside of Dr. Kane. They knew nothing about the man from Philadelphia whose face lent its image to their hero. In fact, as fate would soon prove, they would love Dr. Kane far more once Elisha ceased to exist. The only way Elisha the man could appear in public and not be a disappointment was to be the Dr. Kane of the panorama shows, magazine articles, and celebratory poems that the American public adored.

Even more powerful than the public at large, however, was the "they" in Elisha's own head. Elisha wanted fame and Dr. Kane provided it; ultimately, this was the force that guided his actions. Elisha felt he had to be Dr. Kane because he had come to see himself as Dr. Kane. To destroy Dr. Kane would be to destroy himself. In a letter he wrote Maggie a few months before he left for the arctic, Elisha rhetorically asked, "Who am I?" He explained that when he investigated his "worldly wealth, intellectual character, public estimation, and family name," he found that, "I am better, nobler in moral tone than I have seemed.... My conscience urges me to a crusade of rescue for our lost men... and for it and them I am about to sacrifice the thousand dear things of life, home, luxury, and love." He told Maggie that his feelings for her had been a betrayal of the person he hoped to become: "I forgot my high calling and let myself down to love."[47]

This self-motivated drive for fame caused Elisha to abandon the life of a respected Philadelphia physician and to pursue a life of adventure—it was the one impulse that marked his entire life. In this sense, Elisha was Dr. Kane through and through; however, the optimistic and energetic twenty-three-year-old man who set off for China to achieve respect and fame was a far different man than the thirty-five-year-old who returned from the arctic, having survived two intense years of mental, emotional, and physical punishment. By 1855, Elisha had become everything he had hoped for as a young man. This was certainly satisfying. Having achieved fame, however, the more mature Elisha recognized its hollowness. In this sense, Elisha's emotional devotion to Maggie becomes clear. She was one of the few women in the nation who also understood the thrilling allure and haunting hollowness of fame, and this commonality united them at their cores. At one point Maggie wrote Elisha, "I have been thinking over the very tiresome life I am living. Tiresome because I have to meet with all kinds of people. These things oppress me—indeed dear Doctor they nearly drive me crazy. What have I ever done that I should be denied the pleasures of quiet home, the blessings of love—the reward of virtue? I have given my whole time to this subject for six years. I think I have done my part."[48] By the time he returned from the Second Grinnell Expedition, Elisha felt much the same. In the final months of 1855 he wrote Maggie a fairytale describing their lives:

> Once upon a time there were certain crystal vases in Fairy Land, kept bright by the hands of "little spirits." When burnished they shone like the stars of heaven, and served as beacon lights to weary pilgrims afar off; but when soiled they lost their lustre and never knew brightness more.
>
> You would suppose that each of these fairy crystals contained some pure and beautiful object, such as young flowers kissed by dewdrops, or golden fruit just ripened on the bough. But this was not the case. In the centre of each vase, surrounded by mould and rust and mildew, was a *loathsome toad*.
>
> Yet in spite of this forbidding interior, so long as the "little spirits" kept up their daily polish, so long they shone on as before; and to the weary pilgrims from afar off lost none of their brightness.[49]

For Elisha and Maggie, this parable explained their lives as celebrities. They had both become "crystal vases" that thousands of "weary pilgrims" celebrated and longed to be near. As long as the "little spirits" of publicity kept them polished, they continued to shine and provide inspiration for the public, but as they well knew, their shining brilliance was a lie. They were at heart just the same as everyone else, the "loathsome toad" of humanity, complete with their own unsightly warts and surrounded by the "mould and rust and mildew" of real life hurts, pains, and complications. They were both dynamic and talented people, but fame had made them appear to be more. In them, people saw the perfection that they could not achieve in their own lives. As Leo Braudy explained in his study of fame, the famous—those "who court public appreciation (and possible disapproval) on a grand scale"—gain and maintain their fame by representing extreme "extensions of what is normal, extensions of everyone's culturally fostered desire to be given his or her due."[50] Everyone wants to believe that they are uniquely talented and perfect in some special way. Celebrities allow this public dream to stay alive by providing examples of such perfection. In this way, when the public makes an indi-

BALLOU'S PICTORIAL DRAWING-ROOM COMPANION.

THE SISTERS FOX, THE ORIGINAL SPIRIT RAPPERS

Elisha was constantly in the public eye after his return, which was to be expected given his celebrity status. Maggie, however, tried to stay out of the public eye after 1853, yet she continued to appear in publications (e.g., this image from a very sympathetic article that appeared in the June 14, 1856, edition of *Ballou's Pictorial Drawing-Room Companion*). The accompanying article attributes the engraving to a recent daguerreotype by the Meade Brothers of New York. Note the ring very conspicuously displayed on Maggie's left-hand ring finger—like today, this was a symbol of engagement or marriage in mid-nineteenth century America.

vidual a celebrity, they are not celebrating that person so much as an ideal that they wish to achieve. The successful celebrity, then, is the person most able to keep this hope alive.

Elisha and Maggie understood this. They knew that to maintain their fame they had to shine so brilliantly that it obscured the mundane normalcy of their real lives. In the lines following his story, Elisha wrote, "The world knows nothing of that which we all carry in our own vases; but we go on with the daily brightening, and trust to the 'little spirits' that we may always shine as beacon lights to weary pilgrims."[51] In a letter a few days later he encouraged her saying, "Rub hard, 'little spirit,' at your crystal vase, and dear Ly will help you to brighten it."[52] But this "polishing" had its price. They loved each other and wanted to marry, but such a union would destroy their fame because it did not match the ideals they embodied for the public. Heroic men of science did not marry humbugging spiritualists; otherworldly spiritual prophets did not engage in such earthly pleasures as secret love affairs, especially with staunch nonbelievers. The glimmering luster of their fame allowed them to hide the warts of their humanity, but at the price of imprisoning them both.

In an effort to balance and sustain both their romance and fame, Elisha and Maggie agreed to a plan. Maggie would remain with her family where she would maintain close and friendly relationships with the spiritualist community, but not actually engage in séances. To this end, she moved with her mother and sister Kate to a three-story house on Twenty-Second Street in New York. She had the third floor as her own apartment, where she could retreat during the daily séances that Kate conducted in the first floor parlor. For his part, Elisha would continue to play the part of Dr. Kane, but with the idea that his new book would secure his fame and finances to such a point that within a year or so after its publication, he would be able to set up his own household and quietly marry Maggie.[53] Maggie's family still questioned Elisha's motives and periodically forbade him from seeing her, and Elisha's family continued to insist that he abandon the relationship, but despite these challenges, Maggie and Elisha remained committed to each other.

To be able to go against his family's wishes and marry Margaret Fox, Elisha had to become financially independent. From the time he first left for the arctic in 1850 he had dedicated all his energy and income to arctic exploration. At the time of his return from his second expedition in 1855 he was world famous but dead broke, and thus completely economically dependent on his family, Elisha knew this could quickly change, however, because fame is a saleable commodity. His narrative of the Second Grinnell Expedition was a gold mine, and once it was published, its royalties would give him a handsome income. He set to work on this project immediately.

During his trip to Washington to deliver the official record of his trip, Elisha was already thinking of the monetary possibilities of a popular account of the expedition. It was thus quite a scare when Navy Secretary James C. Dobbin suggested that the government should be its publisher. Elisha wrote his father, "There will have to be... a quiet confidential letter from you to that Frump Mr. Dobbin—stating your wishes as to the publication of the narrative. I cannot afford to lose the prospects of a private publication and the secretary talks on a grand scale of governmental folios."[54] If the government published his narrative, they would do so in a basic manner with little or no promotion of the book. Furthermore, as a public employee (he was still a navy officer), it was within the government's power to order him to write the book and then give him no royalties because it would technically belong to them. This had to be avoided if he was to gain monetarily from his book. During the next month he and his father lobbied everyone from Secretary Dobbin to First Lady Jane Pierce, and their efforts were successful. Elisha met with Dobbin in November, and the secretary granted him everything he wanted: copyright to the public narrative, permission to publish it with the company of his choice, and special duty wages for the time it took him to write it. All Dobbin asked in return was an official report including charts and projections from the expedition, and acknowledgment that the narrative was published under navy auspices.[55] Dobbin's generosity came from pressure, not kindness. As reports of the hardships of the expedition became known, the navy came under fire for skimping on food and other necessary supplies. Dobbin hoped that granting Elisha generous publication rights would encourage him to be less critical of these hardships and thus help the navy save face.

Even before he had Dobbin's permission to do so, Elisha began to court commercial publishers. Still angry with Harpers for their handling of his first book, Elisha was not about to work with them again. Using the hype surrounding his return, Harpers advertised his first book with renewed vigor, noting that "There can be no doubt that this volume is the most interesting which has yet been produced by any voyagers in the Arctic regions."[56] This effort did not impress Elisha or his family. Although his first book had sold well, Harpers claimed that Kane still owed them money because his expensive engravings had to be done twice because the first run had burned in their fire. Cornelius Grinnell tried to straighten out this problem, but Harpers would not budge. There was no way to prove that Harpers was cheating them because their contract with Elisha had also been destroyed in the fire. As Judge Kane had told Elisha, "it is a rascally account."[57] On the recommendation of George W. Curtis (a popular travel-writer and an editor for *Harper's Monthly*), Elisha threatened litigation against Harpers. Elisha noted to his father, "[Curtis] declares that the charge for the loss of the first edition is an outrage and that for the sake of my brother authors it should not be tolerated. By his request I have allowed him to make known (informally) his views to the Harpers—and to obtain from them an outline of their intentions."[58]

When Elisha wrote this letter at the end of October he was already considering a bold move—to put his narrative in the hands of an ambitious young Philadelphia publisher named George W. Childs. He got bids from other publishing firms in Boston and New York, but Childs' offer was the most appealing. He offered the huge royalty of one dollar per edition sold and agreed to print the massive two-volume edition in a timely and stylish manner, complete with the more than three hundred engravings and the multiple maps and charts Elisha insisted upon. This offer was too good to pass up. After just a few meetings, Elisha deemed Childs an "honorable gentleman" and a "sound advisor" and by mid-November he officially named Childs' company—Childs & Peterson—as his publisher.[59]

Elisha's family continued to help him manage his image, but once he signed with Childs & Peterson, George W. Childs took a very active hand in the promotion of Dr. Kane. Publicity agents were not an acknowledged part of U.S. culture in antebellum America, but that is exactly the role Childs played in the following years. From 1855 through the mid-1860s Childs was the primary force that

George W. Childs. From his *Recollections*
(Philadelphia: J.B. Lippincott Co., 1890).

enhanced and maintained Dr. Kane's celebrity status—a process that ultimately severed almost all connections between the carefully constructed image of Dr. Kane and its frail human counterpart, Elisha Kent Kane.

To understand how Dr. Kane became the heroic icon of antebellum America it is necessary to understand George W. Childs. This is difficult, however, for just as he helped create the flawless character, Dr. Kane, Childs also created a public image for himself that obscured much of his true past. Not surprisingly, as a successful publisher who eventually ran Philadelphia's largest newspaper, the *Public Ledger*, Childs modeled his image after that other brilliant self-promoter who portrayed himself (more or less correctly) as the rags-to-riches hero of Philadelphia's publishing world, Benjamin Franklin.[60]

According to his own account, Childs was born in Baltimore on May 12, 1829, the unacknowledged son of a man from a "prominent family." At the age of thirteen he entered the navy and apprenticed on board the *Pennsylvania*, stationed out of Norfolk, Virginia. In 1844, he quit the navy after just fifteen months and went to Philadelphia to work as clerk and errand boy for Peter Thomson, owner of a book and stationary shop on the northwest corner of Sixth and Mulberry Streets. Thomson specialized in inexpensive books, and Childs, a quick and eager apprentice, soon began attending the city's book auctions for him. Thomson was so impressed with Childs' sales and negotiation skills that he sent him to the major book trade sales in New York and Boston, where the vivacious young Childs became acquainted with many of the nation's leading publishers.[61]

In 1848, after four years with Thomson, Childs had saved enough money to begin a business of his own. He rented a small shop at 320 Market Street and, under the name of George W. Childs & Company, opened a small confectionery business. He soon changed his focus to toiletries and patent medicines; his advertisements at this time proclaim that he was the sole dealer of Dr. Wiley's Celebrated Cough Candy, which was "the great remedy for coughs, colds, hoarseness, and in fact all diseases likely to terminate in confirmed consumption."[62] During this time he honed his advertising skills, promoting other products such as Gouraud's Italian Medicated Soap and Asiatic Golden Life Drops, but despite his best efforts, his business flopped. By 1849 he went back to the book business, accepting a position as clerk with the R. E. Peterson Company.

Robert E. Peterson was an estranged cousin of the powerful Peterson publishing family of Philadelphia. The Petersons ran the publishing house T. B. Peterson & Brothers and their members included both Charles Jacobs Peterson and Henry Peterson. Charles was editor of several magazines and newspapers and was the founder of *Lady's World* (later *Lady's National Magazine*) and *Peterson's Magazine*. Henry helped edit the *Saturday Gazette* and *Saturday Evening Post* and was one of Philadelphia's most celebrated poets.[63] After working unsuccessfully as a merchant and an attorney, R. E. Peterson used his family name and connections to get into the publishing business. He became a partner of booksellers Daniels and Smith, but soon broke with them to begin his own self-titled publishing company, R. E. Peterson. Apparently bitter about the split, Daniels and Smith accused him of being an "infidel"—a harsh charge against a publisher who specialized in theological works. To improve business, Peterson began to diversify his line, which is the reason he hired Childs. R. E. Peterson was truly a family firm as Peterson relied heavily on immediate family members to expand his catalog. His father-in-law, John Bouvier, wrote a four-volume law text, *Institutes of American Law*. The "Lady of Philadelphia," who wrote his popular kitchen reference work, *The National Cook Book*, was his own wife, Hannah M. Bouvier Peterson. Petersen himself provided the firm's most successful work, *Familiar Science*, which was a condensation of a British text that Peterson re-edited for American audiences.[64] The company's advertisements in the early 1850s show that it was publishing religious and school texts, as well as popular celebrity and political biographies.

Childs entered this family firm whole-heartedly, eventually marrying Peterson's daughter, Emma Bouvier Peterson. On January 1, 1852, he became a partner in the firm and the company changed its name first to R. E. Peterson & Company, and then, in November 1854, to Childs & Peterson.[65] Between 1852 and 1854, under Childs' guidance, the company stopped directly dealing books, moved to new offices at 602 Arch Street, and redefined themselves as exclusively a publishing company, not a book dealer.[66] During this time they focused their efforts primarily on reference works, adding *The National Portrait Gallery of Distinguished Americans, The Constitutional Text-Book, A New Medical Dictionary*, and *Year Book of Agriculture* to their catalog. They also published two new popular science books, *Familiar Botany* and *Familiar Astronomy*, for which Childs collected endorsements from important scientists including Sir John Herschel and Mathew F. Maury—an advertising tactic he would continue to use with great success.

These books provided Childs & Peterson with a solid income, but they did not represent the kind of publishing Childs longed to do. He saw himself as a scholar and a promoter of American *belles-lettres*. As early as 1851 he was corresponding with Nathaniel Hawthorne about the symbolism and historical context of his new novel, *The Scarlet Letter*—Hawthorne wrote Childs that his critique of the book "gratifies me much."[67] He was also trading and discussing items with one of Philadelphia's biggest collectors of American literary memorabilia, Ferdinand J. Dreer.[68] With these aspirations, Childs longed to move Childs & Peterson in a more popular and literary direction. When rumors began circulating that the heroic Elisha Kent Kane was seeking a new publisher, Childs saw an opportunity to make his mark in the literary world while also turning a hefty profit. Childs must have contacted Elisha almost immediately after the expedition's return because he and Elisha were already negotiating the final details of their contract by the end of October 1855.

Once Elisha signed with Childs & Peterson, Childs wasted no time in beginning his promotional efforts. Citing an earlier article in the *Philadelphia Ledger*, the *American Publishers' Circular & Literary Gazette* (the primary periodical for publishers and book sellers) announced that Childs & Peterson would bring out Dr. Kane's narrative in a lavish two-volume large octavo format. "It will include a variety of scientific papers, and be illustrated with maps and several hundred engravings, from Daguerreotypes of Arctic scenery, taken on the spot, and also from original sketches made by the author." The article named no exact dates, but it did note that the manuscript was "in a very forward state, the greatest portion having been prepared while hemmed in by the ice, and during the voyage home."[69] In a later issue of the *Circular & Literary Gazette*, Childs & Peterson again received major notice. A correspondent reported that the firm was "sparing no expense to make the book worthy of the subject, and judging from the fact that the estimated cost of its production is upward of $20,000, we have every reason to believe that it will be one of the most magnificent and elaborate works ever issued from the American press."[70]

With more than a decade of experience in promoting and selling books as well as patent medicines, Childs had a good sense of what would sell and how to sell it. To ensure that he would have a good product to market, Childs worked closely with Elisha, giving him specific instructions about the text. They agreed on most matters. As Elisha had done with his first book (under the instruction of Tom and his father), he again created a volume written in a journal-like style and accompanied by elaborate illustrations that would give readers the impression that they were witnessing the events with the author. He included all the graphic and brutal details of the voyage, but he made sure that the book was appropriate for all readers. He wrote Childs, "My wish is to make a centre-table book, fit as well for the eyes of children as of refined women." To ensure this, Elisha had Miss Emma Peterson (Peterson's daughter and later Childs' wife) read over his entire work and to comment, especially in "reference to the inclusion of certain passages describing the social habits of the Esquimaux."[71] Childs fully supported these ideas because he too believed that a lavishly illustrated book, written in a style suggesting the immediacy of an on-the-spot journal, would appeal to the public. These were the attributes of the book Childs first publicized: that it would include hundreds of engravings, cost $20,000 to produce, and that it was not the work of a Philadelphia editor but an arctic explorer who wrote up his narrative "while hemmed in by the ice, and during the voyage home."

Elisha agreed with these aspects of the narrative and threw himself into the project. As with his first book, Tom did much of the editorial work, and all the text went past Judge Kane before going on to Childs. Elisha again hired James Hamilton to turn his sketches into romantic watercolor scenes, and to assure their quick and satisfactory completion, he had Hamilton stay at Fern Rock (the Kane family's new country estate) for a month so they could work side by side.[72] By the end of 1855, just a month and a half after signing with Childs, Elisha had more than three hundred pages of his journal marked for printing. After another six weeks of hard work the narrative was almost complete; Elisha wrote Childs in mid-February that he was "anxious to write 'Finis,'" which he felt he could do in the next few days.[73]

There were some problems, however, for though they agreed on issues of style, Elisha and Childs disagreed on other aspects of the book. One of Elisha's primary concerns was to make it scientifically respectable. He had dedicated huge amounts of time and energy during his expedition to scientific observation, and he wanted these findings to be clearly presented to the scientific community. To this end, he insisted that his narrative include nearly one hundred pages of appendices. These would include charts on winds, currents, tides, geographical position, and magnetic readings; abstracts on meteorological and astronomical observations; official reports on findings; and a detailed essay on arctic flora written by Philadelphia botanist Elias Durand.[74] Furthermore, these time-consuming and expensive appendices would not be edited and published by Childs alone, they would all be reviewed by Alexander Dallas Bache, superintendent of the U.S. Coast

Survey, and would be printed as official government documents for distribution to the scientific community.[75]

Childs agreed to these demands, but he also made one of his own. If the book was to include dense scientific information that the average reader would not understand, he wanted to ensure that the story of the expedition was fast-paced and exciting. Most of the narrative would come from the direct journal abstracts Elisha had already provided, but Childs wanted these entries tied together and reworked in a way that would further enhance the excitement, danger, and action of the narrative. The book would essentially have to operate on two levels: as a scientific work, backed up by charts, graphs and data; and as a popular travel narrative, complete with stunning scenery, exotic natives, and spine-tingling adventure. Elisha agreed to these demands, but not without reservations. He wrote Childs: "I attempt to be more popular and gaseous: this latter inflated quality in excess. Most certainly my effort to make this book readable will destroy its permanency and injure me. It is a sacrifice."[76]

These re-edits, along with the compilation of the appendices, pulled the whole Kane family together on the project. In June, Elisha's sister Bessie wrote her sister-in-law (Tom's wife, who was also Bessie Kane): "The second volume is at its hundredth page; and this is good reason why I cannot spare time to write to you, however much I may wish it"; she then warned that these "book troubles" would continue to disrupt the whole Kane household for at least another two weeks.[77] This was not happy news for Tom's wife. Elisha's book was disrupting her family and especially the life of her husband. Bessie Wood was only sixteen when she married Tom in 1853, an event that took place on a hurried schedule because Elisha made Tom promise that the ceremony would occur before he left for the arctic. She did not complain at the time, but she later pointedly noted in her journal that despite their accommodation to his schedule, "rheumatism had prevented him from being present." A keen observer of the Kane family, Bessie quickly came to understand that Elisha was the shining star and Tom and the rest of the family served as his support staff. She liked and respected Elisha, but resented Tom playing second fiddle to his fame. In March 1856, in the midst of the push to complete Elisha's book, she wrote in her journal, "We are losing a large portion of our income, and are slipping behindhand in our board... we are really in need of ready money." She then addressed the problem and her anger specifically. "Tom is so busy on Elisha's book that <u>he</u> can't do anything else. Elisha will probably be renowned in the story of this generation, while Tom will not be known." She noted that Tom was "perfectly unselfish, never requiring a service from any one, but always working for others," and that as "a model of complete self denial [and] self abnegation—is as superior to Elisha as light to darkness." She concluded emphatically, "All is not gold that glitters!"[78]

Elisha, often ill and seemingly unaware of the stress he was putting on his larger family, kept pushing the project at a furious pace, determined to get the book out quickly. In mid-June he wrote Childs, "My health is nothing extraordinary under this extreme heat; but I think that I have accumulated enough of nerve-force to carry me through to that ominously pleasant word, 'Finis.'"[79] Two weeks later his mother wrote Tom and Bessie to update them on the "subject most on Tom's mind," and explained that Elisha and Judge Kane were still "hard at it—the latter writing and rewriting, the former with a bad head ache furnishing material."[80] Everything was complete by July 4 except the appendices. Elisha wrote Childs: "With little spirit of congratulation, and much weariness, I send you the preface, which completes my text." With a statement reflective of both the writing process and his life generally, he concluded: "There is a sort of moral conveyed by this ending of my labors. Now that the holy day is at hand, I am ungrateful enough to complain that it finds me without the capacity to enjoy it."[81]

While Elisha and the Kane family were rewriting the narrative, Childs was equally busy promoting the book that Elisha had entitled *Arctic Explorations: The Second Grinnell Expedition In Search of Sir John Franklin, 1853, '54, '55*.[82] With his background in book sales, Childs was well versed in the standard promotional tactics of antebellum publishers, but unlike most publishers, he also embraced the more aggressive promotional tactics he had learned during his time peddling patent medicines. Childs understood that whether the product was a book or a cough drop, what was really being sold was an ideal. When he was hawking Dr. Wiley's Celebrated Cough Candy, he was really selling an ideal of health. Likewise, when he was selling Dr. Kane's book, he was really selling national pride and an ideal of heroism. With this understanding, Childs went about marketing *Arctic Explorations* in a unique manner. Instead of marketing the book, he marketed its author—the great American hero, Dr. Kane.

In 1856, most publishers promoted their new books by simply placing ads in a wide variety of newspapers. In January 1856, for example, Harpers spent over $300 to place ads for their books in seventy three papers and magazines across the country, including major publications in New York, Philadelphia, Boston and Washington, as well as in religious periodicals (e.g., the *Puritan Recorder*, *Zion's Herald*, *Christian Advocate*), and in more far-flung papers in New Orleans, Louisville, Indianapolis, Chicago, Pittsburgh, Milwaukee, Detroit, St. Louis, and San Francisco.[83] This tactic allowed them to inform a large portion of the population about their wares, but to questionable effect.

In a series of articles addressing the book business in 1856, the *United States Magazine* noted that the American public's huge demand for books had caused publishers to produce vast quantities of works "gross in construction, crude in material, poor in English and worse in morality." To sell these works publishers resorted to the "inordinate puffing" that appeared in ads and reviews. These ads irked the American public; the article noted "that a wholesome distrust has been engendered which will be felt for some time to come—a distrust not partial but pervading the whole reading community." It concluded, "The very fact that a book needs so much laudation creates a doubt as to its merits."[84] There was good reason for such skepticism about book reviews. Newspapers and publishers both understood that good reviews were less dependent on the content of the book than on the publisher's willingness to buy high-dollar advertising space in a given periodical—a system that publishers rightly saw as nothing short of bribery.[85]

George Childs understood both this system and the public's frustration with it. If the public had grown disillusioned with these traditional advertising techniques, then new promotional methods had to be found. Childs thus turned to more innovative ideas. As one book historian has noted, in the mid-nineteenth century a publisher needed to sense or create "the common denominators in the literary taste of the whole country."[86] But how did one do this? Scholars often note P. T. Barnum's 1850 promotion of soprano Jenny Lind, "the Swedish Nightingale," as the beginning of modern mass advertising. Barnum's energetic use of handbills, broadsides, and newspaper ads and articles worked so effectively that, after six months of promotion, thirty thousand Americans flooded to see and celebrate Jenny Lind upon her arrival in New York, though not one of them had ever heard her sing.[87] An 1852 article entitled "The Philosophy of Advertising" shows that Barnum's techniques caught on quickly. Innovative retailers were beginning to use new advertising techniques—such as testimonials, celebrity endorsements, and "scientific testing"—to promote their products, and Childs was at the forefront of this trend.[88]

Soon after the announcements of Elisha signing with Childs & Peterson, *Frank Leslie's Illustrated Newspaper* published its first edition and dedicated it primarily to Dr. Kane, which, as noted earlier, included an engraving of Brady's portrait of Elisha and his men as well as several heavily detailed, full-page re-cretions of Elisha's sketches from the arctic, images that Childs was already preparing for the book. Leslie was thrilled to have this hot topic grace the pages of the first edition of his magazine and thus promoted Dr. Kane whole-heartedly, referring to the expedition members as "our heroes" and praising their "noble traits" as a profound example of the sort of manly action that "redeems human nature."[89] Within a few more months, Childs had his own engravings ready for the book and began to send them, along with exciting excerpts from the text, to editors across the increasingly divided country, North, South and West. This worked well. The *Southern Literary Messenger* noted, "The few pages of Dr. Kane's forthcoming work, which have been sent us, make us very impatient for the appearance of the whole." The New York-based *Knickerbocker* wrote, "What an appetising lunch is to a delicious dinner at a late hour in the day, these 'Specimen Pages' are to Dr. Kane's magnificent work, soon to be forthcoming."[90]

Another method Childs used to promote Kane was one he borrowed from partisan politics—the campaign biography. In an era before nationwide mass media, the far-flung population of the United States needed a way to "get to know" the candidates for national political offices, and candidates were happy to comply. The campaign biography genre emerged during the heated elections of 1824 and 1828 between Andrew Jackson and John Quincy Adams. Just as today, candidates then wanted to paint themselves as virtuous, self-made individuals with an abundance of that all important but difficult to define quality, "character." To this end they hired biographers to tell (and often invent) the story of their heroic strivings and persistent strength of character that allowed them to overcome adversity and end up in a position where they felt duty-bound to serve their country for the country's sake. These heavy-handed hagiographies, such as the pro-Jackson biographical pamphlet that Judge Kane wrote for the 1828 election, matured as the century progressed, becoming more nuanced and subtle in their pointed effusions. In his study of nineteenth-century biographies, Scott E. Casper found that by midcentury critics and the reading public alike were tired of biographies that "replaced individualism with formulaic bundles of characteristics, labeled 'individualism' or 'piety,'" and began to embrace biographies that instead portrayed their subjects' "true selves." Such works still presented a polished and highly moral character, but they became less prescriptive in their morality and worked toward influencing "a reader's character through inspiration, not imitation" on the assumption that "a truly individual subject could encourage the reader to develop his or her own 'genius.'"[91]

By midcentury this campaign biography style also began to be used in other public arenas. One of the ways Barnum promoted Jenny Lind was to have N. P. Willis, one of the nation's most celebrated authors, write a biography of her, noting her almost superhuman beauty, talent, and virtue. As he began working with Elisha on his book, Childs was keenly aware of this promotional tactic as he had helped guide the Lind biography through R. E. Peterson Co., which had been its primary publisher.[92] Thus, Childs did much the same thing when he took on Kane's project. Instead of directly promoting Kane's book, *Arctic Explorations*, he commissioned a biographical sketch of Dr. Kane. This personality piece was designed to introduce the public to the "real" Dr. Kane. It began with tales of his heroic childhood in which young "Elish'" battled bullies and defended young ladies. It then described his triumph over rheumatic fever and his subsequent adventures in the Orient, Africa, and Mexico. It justified this long story saying, "When a man's life is heroic, and his name has passed into history, the world wants to know him personally, intimately." This sketch, written by Kane family friend Dr. William Elder, first ap-

Illustrated newspapers picked up images from *Arctic Explorations* and used them to enhance their own pages while promoting Kane's book. From *Ballou's Pictorial Drawing-Room Companion* (December 18, 1856).

peared in the February 1856 edition of *Graham's Illustrated Magazine* and was quickly reprinted in a wide variety of publications across the nation and England.[93]

Elder's sketch shows the sophistication of Childs' marketing. It made almost no mention of Dr. Kane's book or its publisher (only one brief mention in the final paragraph) and thus had little in common with the normal book advertisements of the day. Because it did not read like a typical book "puff," it sparked public interest while avoiding the disingenuous appearance of an advertisement. This was Childs' plan. He was selling his book by celebrating the ideal heroic qualities of its author. He understood that if the public saw Dr. Kane as a noble hero they would view the purchase of his book differently—it would become an act of patriotism, national pride, and self-improvement.

This indirect method of advertising became Childs' primary strategy for *Arctic Explorations*. Instead of running ads, he would write pieces celebrating Dr. Kane and then circulate them to newspapers and magazines hungry for text to fill their columns. To further entice editors to run these articles, Childs offered engraving plates so periodicals could inexpensively illustrate their pages. Illustrations sold papers and editors were thus more than happy to print these stunning images and their accompanying articles. The success of this marketing tactic is readily evident as reproductions of illustrations from *Arctic Explorations* appeared in a variety of publications, ranging from the mainstream *Graham's Illustrated* to such specialized publications as the *American Phrenological Journal*.[94]

Elisha recognized the importance and benefit of Childs' publicity methods, but he did not always like them. After Elder's sketch ran in *Graham's*, Childs began another publicity effort—he had a man ("Mr. Morris") push the Pennsylvania house and senate to officially honor Dr. Kane. This effort, along with further praising commentary about Dr. Kane, quickly appeared in newspapers. Childs proudly clipped these stories and sent them to Elisha. Shocked by the hugely flattering articles, Elisha replied, "My dear Mr. Childs, I regret to have to say that I conceive it to be indelicate to connect [myself to] or even read the manuscript which you have enclosed. The remarks of Mr. Morris as contained in the public journals are most kindly meant and gratefully appreciated by me, but they contain distorted views of fact, as well as a tone of undeserved praise for which I desire in no wise to be responsible." He noted that Elder's sketch also had "the same unfortunate tone of exclusive eulogism and perverted incidents" and that he was disturbed that these articles gave him all the praise for the arctic expedition's successes while never mentioning his associates. He explained, "I will never consent to have an officer under my command feel that I am absorbing the merit due to his own position." To remedy the situation he planned to write an article "correcting publicly a paragraph in the article... which assumes for me the duties of astronomer, surgeon, and indeed every thing."[95] It is telling, however, that such an article never appeared.

Elisha feared that such eulogizing would backfire and make Dr. Kane appear to be a braggart. He also feared the biographical tone of these articles, for though they were flattering, they delved into his already too-public private life. To help restrain Childs, Elisha made him agree to pass all further "puffs" past George M. Dallas, who had been vice-president under James Polk, and was a major player in the Democratic Party as well as a close friend of the Kane family. Dallas's years of political experience made him a keen judge of the effects of publicity—what would help and what would damage a reputation. Elisha told Childs to refer to Dallas "for the adjustment of my views which may on my part conflict with your own" and to "consider me as guided entirely by such opinions as he may express." Elisha acknowledged that he was obligated to help Childs promote the book and that their interests were "in nearly all respects conjoint," but he also had to protect his personal life from his public persona. "All that I desire is not to blend my private relations with those which connect themselves with my position as an author."[96]

More than these publicity pieces, the effort that bothered Elisha most was Childs' unorthodox political scheme to have Congress buy enough copies of the book to cover its production costs. As soon as Elisha signed with Childs & Peterson, Childs began lobbying Congress to buy twenty-five thousand copies of the book for distribution to government agencies and schools. He argued that this $125,000 expenditure was justified because the expedition had been partially funded by the government and thus, as the government was then doing with Wilkes's expedition, they should support the publication of its findings. Although he had his doubts about the propriety of such an effort, Elisha initially supported it. As a political feeler, he wrote to Senator Thomas Hart Benton, saying, "Being undecided as to the propriety of the step, I have taken the liberty of desiring Mr. Childs to confer with you. I feel that if there be any indelicacy you will at once advise me against it, and that if there be none that your kind interest in the Expedition, and I hope in myself, will lead you to favour me with the practical suggestions of your valuable experience."[97] Benton's son-in-law was John C. Frémont, the celebrated Western explorer and soon-to-be presidential candidate, who, like Elisha, published popular narratives of his adventures. In fact, at that time, Frémont was negotiating the publication of his next book with Childs & Peterson.[98] It is thus not surprising that Benton found nothing wrong with Childs' plan. On this advice, Elisha agreed to Childs' lobbying effort and even recruited prominent friends to help. In the next months, both Henry Grinnell and Alexander Dallas Bache backed the proposal. As superintendent of the U.S. Coast Survey, Bache wrote congressmen and told them that they should "feel at liberty to give this manner of remunerating the great explorer your support."[99]

Less than a month later, however, Elisha began to question this decision. Childs embraced the project wholeheartedly and, to Elisha's shock, a letter soon appeared in Philadelphia's *Public Ledger* criticizing Congress for not officially recognizing Dr. Kane's efforts or supporting his book.[100] As the letter was signed with a pseudonym, "Potomac," Elisha feared people would think he was behind it and was lobbying Congress for his own economic gain. He wrote Childs that he was "exceedingly pained" by this letter and reminded him that any promotional matter had to be reviewed by Mr. Dallas before being executed.[101] His fears proved well founded; a few days later Pennsylvania Senator Richard Brodhead—who had earlier headed Senate efforts for Kane's rescue expedition—publicly questioned the proposed bill to fund Kane's book and accused Elisha of using his family's political power for his own monetary gain.[102] Horrified by this accusation (though it was largely true), Elisha quickly wrote to his father, noting that even though he valued Childs for his "sympathy, his efficiency, his friendship and the other good qualities connected with these," he also recognized that Childs was ultimately working not for him, but for himself. "Depend upon it, I understand Mr. Childs—and he is <u>using</u> me for his own ends.... Were our interests disconnected there would be none of all this activity."[103]

A few weeks after making this observation, he wrote his enthusiastic publisher a frank letter. "I had—like a fool—looked upon my approaching narrative as that of a voyage of discovery under taken by orders of government and it seemed to me under the circumstances open to purchase or adoption by our national legislature.... But my views upon this matter have undergone a mortifying change." He noted Brodhead's letter and its implication that "I am acting with you to carry out a congressional act of pecuniary reward" and insisted that this was "in every respect repugnant to my instincts as a gentleman and an officer." He thus demanded that Childs completely remove his name from any further solicitations and informed him that he was sending his brother Tom to Washington to ensure that this was done. He understood the ill effects this could have on the sale of the book, and thus their profits, and he apologized, saying, "Nothing but a rigid sense of duty impels me to seem unmindful of your kind exertions or to seem counter to your views."[104]

Childs stopped his lobbying for several months, but in July, as the book was nearing completion and Congress was again considering the matter, he renewed his efforts. Upon seeing several articles in newspapers, Elisha wrote him another stern letter: "[T]his coupling of my name with the book will interfere with any expression of <u>disinterested</u> feeling on the part of the Senate and thus stand in the way of that which I value far beyond either books or money, viz. an honorary testimonial in recognition of our party."[105] The issue was entirely laid to rest a few days later when it finally came before Congress. The house readily approved $75,000 for the purchase of fifteen thousand copies of the book, but the Senate, led by Senator Brodhead, killed the bill, noting that such a purchase would ne-

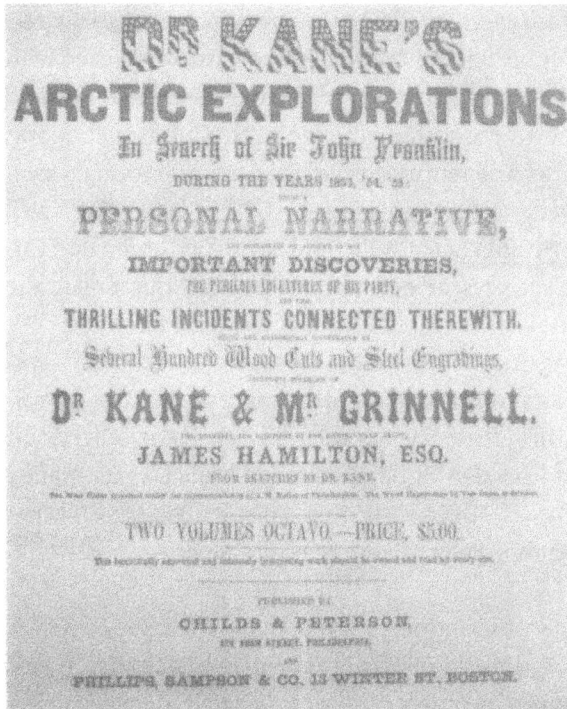

Part of a prospectus that Childs' sent out with sales agents who peddled *Arctic Explorations* door to door. Courtesy of the American Antiquarian Society.

cessitate the "establishment of a new precedent" and that there were "no adequate reasons" to do so.[106]

This was disappointing for Childs, but it was not devastating. He had used several other methods to insure sales of the book and these were going well. At this time, most books were sold in one of two manners: at trade sales or by subscription. Trade sales were the most common method. At these semi-annual events in New York, Philadelphia and Cincinnati (and less frequently in other U.S. cities), publishers and booksellers from across the nation came together for a week of auctions and trading. Here booksellers would buy sizeable quantities of different publishers' works at discounted prices and then take them back to their stores to sell. This system allowed publishers to reach large portions of the U.S. population with relatively little effort, and it gave booksellers the ability to carry a wide variety of works from multiple publishers and to select the specific books that best matched their patrons. Subscription sales operated quite differently. In this sales system, publishers would by-pass the bookseller by sending their own agents out to peddle their works. This had the potential to cut losses and increase profits because publishers would only publish a work once a sufficient amount of sales had been confirmed, preventing them from being stuck with an unpopular book, and because there was no bookseller, they kept a larger share of the books' sale price. The drawback was that this method forced publishers to expend time and money on sales, shipping, and bill-collection, which took resources away from their publishing efforts. By the mid-1850s, most publishers preferred to stay focused on publishing and to leave sales and collection to booksellers.[107]

Childs opted to use both these methods for *Arctic Explorations*. Trade sales were obviously the best method to reach the far-flung small town and rural book buyers of the nation, so Childs happily promoted *Arctic Explorations* at the major trade sales. Before the New York sale, he personally took copies to the major New York booksellers to solicit orders directly.[108] Surviving records, however, show that Childs also had agents sell the book door to door in affluent, densely populated areas. Childs recognized that such well-targeted subscription sales would give him many sales with little effort and at a greater profit by eliminating the bookseller as middleman. In this way, Childs both used and competed with the booksellers. He captured the easy sales for himself, while having booksellers stock and promote the book to harder-to-reach populations.[109] His subscription efforts went well, and by the time the book was released in September 1856, Childs claimed he had thirty thousand advanced subscription orders, a number that was certainly exaggerated, but still suggestive of the subscription sales' success. This is especially impressive because the two-volume narrative was expensive, ranging from the five-dollar cloth-bound edition, to the ten-dollar full-leather and gilt edition.[110]

Though he condemned Childs' solicitation of Congress, Elisha helped him promote the book in other ways. Despite his busy schedule and ill health, he made a few public appearances to help keep his name in the press. He lectured on the Open Polar Sea before the American Geographical Society in New York in February 1856, and in March he attended a lecture at Baltimore's Maryland Institute with President Pierce—after the lecture the two men greeted the public and were "heartily received."[111] As the book neared completion, he gladly helped Childs get endorsements, directing him to send advance copies to many of the most prominent scientists and literary figures in the world.[112] He rapidly received many replies. Oceanographer Mathew F. Maury wrote, "The story is told in the most agreeable way, and the reader identifies himself with the party and becomes as much interested as though he himself were one of them. I waked this morning singing 'Amna Ayah' and wishing that Hans would come back." The flamboyant editor and writer, N. P. Willis—who was as excited about receiving Elisha's autograph as his book— noted the growing cult of personality surrounding Dr. Kane. "I have watched your career as almost the only liv'd romance of these unromantic times, & to meet you (at Judge Daly's) was like shaking hands with the hero of a ballad.... I shall take time, of course, to read your book critically, & help the 'Dull Many' to a knowledge of it."[113] Childs also sent out advanced copies, and minced no words about what he wanted done with them. He enclosed a note with the copy he sent New York editor Rufus Griswold, bluntly asking him to write a favorable notice of the book

Title page of Elisha Kent Kane's
Arctic Explorations (Philadelphia;
Childs & Peterson, 1856).

"after the Election." He explained that before the election, "your columns are over crowded and people haven't time to think of books."[114]

Remembering Elisha's lecturing success of 1852, Childs wanted him to again go on the circuit, this time to promote his book. Elisha wanted to comply, but feared he was simply too ill to take up the task. In September of 1856 he wrote Childs, "My lecturing invitations are becoming so numerous and pressing that I can no longer avoid a decided answer." Regretfully, he reported that he was "unable to announce any improvement in my health," and thus he declined all offers.[115] But even without an accompanying lecture series, when *Arctic Explorations* came out in September 1856, it received an overwhelming response from critics and the public alike. Childs noted that one New York bookseller—who originally bought only a few copies and told him that the book "won't sell more than a thousand altogether"—wrote him back a few weeks later with an order for five thousand copies to meet the demand.[116]

It is only a slight exaggeration to say that every periodical in the nation sang the book's praises. Such disparate publications as the art journal *Crayon*, Cincinnati's *Lady's Repository*, New Orleans's *DeBow's Review*, the *Ohio Cultivator*, and the *American Phrenological Journal* were all united in their high estimation of Dr. Kane's new book.[117] Not even the inability to spell "arctic" kept publications from praising the book—the Rochester *Genesee Farmer* proclaimed, "His Artic expedition, as lately published, is one of the most stirring narratives of Artic research and discovery yet published."[118]

As many of the major U.S. literary magazines noted, *Arctic Explorations* was important for many different reasons. *The Knickerbocker* reviewed the book in its October, November and December issues, and proclaimed that the book was exceptional first because of Dr. Kane's literary talent. "His descriptions are exceedingly *graphic*. He gives you a complete picture in a few strokes of the pen, and bores you with no merely dry detail."[119] It compared his literary impact to the prose of James Fenimore Cooper and concluded that Kane's writing "is equal to any thing we remember to have read." More important than style, however, was the content of the book. It was a factual narrative of a real journey that represented what *The Knickerbocker* felt was best about "the Anglo-Saxon race." It explained that, like Sir John Franklin before him, Dr. Kane had an "unceasing yearning after conquest;... to plant the symbol of nationality on unfructifying points of eternal desolation," and that this was "characteristic of the *Picked People of the World*."[120] *Graham's* echoed these sentiments, but with a stronger nationalist sentiment. Separating Americans from the English, it noted that it was a "peculiarity of the Anglo-American character to be extravagantly fond of bold exploits, to be daring and reckless in the pursuit of any object, whether of fame, riches, adventure, or discovery." It explained that there was "a national longing for the heroic" and that Americans were thus "the most fearless and undaunted of explorers... men of rare penetration and sagacity, who go where others have never gone and who see what others never saw before." It then exclaimed that "the latest and most brilliant example" of this Anglo-American character was "undoubtedly Dr. Kane, whose conduct of the American expeditions in search of Sir John Franklin, had won for himself and his country such a noble fame."[121] Further perpetuating this nationalist spirit, the *North American Review*—always interested in promoting American literature over the literature of England—also found *Arctic Explorations* a reason to celebrate. Comparing it to British explorer Edward Belchers's recently published book, *The Last of the Arctic Voyages*, it proclaimed, "In manner and matter, the American book far surpasses its English companion. We can be justly proud of it, as in all respects a worthy specimen of American literature."[122]

Childs & Peterson also gained from this nationalistic sentiment. Their technical execution of the book gained them the nation's gratitude while also drawing more people to the book. The *Knickerbocker* congratulated Childs & Peterson, noting that "the enterprising publishers have succeeded in making these volumes in respect of typography, illustrations, and general getting-up, perhaps superior to any work which has ever issued from the American press." They felt that its physical execution left "absolutely nothing to be desired," and concluded, "It is a work, reader, when we are dust, which will be read and cherished by thousands upon thousands of our countrymen."[123] The art journal *Crayon* agreed. Noting their general dismay with American illustrated works, they admitted that *Arctic Explorations* stunned them. They found the book's illustrations so informative that they could "read it hieroglyphically." They exclaimed, "by merely looking at the plates and wood cuts... we find them sufficiently attractive to lead us into the text, when time permits, instead of repelling us from it."[124]

Beyond its artistic and literary merit, the book did well because its central character, Dr. Kane, embodied the era's ideal of American manhood. Reviewers strongly recommended it to the young men of the nation. The *United States Magazine* compared Dr. Kane with Robinson Crusoe, but noted that the perils he encountered were "tenfold more terrible than the sentimental struggles of [that] great hero of boydom." It was sure that "every youth should read this book for the sake of its noble simplicity and its promptings to untiring effort and wholesome manliness; our Young America will be made better by the reading. It should be in the hands of parents and school children."[125] While being an inspirational and didactic book for boys, however, the book was also seen as appropriate reading material for women because it provided graphic realism without offense. The *Ladies' Repository* noted in its review, "The style of narration is very chaste, and the observations evince a high order of scientific acquirement on the part of its author." It strongly approved of the book, but recognized that such approval was really a moot point—"We scarcely need recommend the work; our readers will feel that they must have it."[126]

The book's virtures provided for much of its success, but as fate would have it, nature herself, the powerful antagonist in Dr. Kane's narrative, contributed to his book's massive sales. The winter of 1856 was one of the coldest in history for the northern United States, and these arctic conditions prompted a further interest in *Arctic Explorations*.[127] The *Knickerbocker* recommended that readers, "Fill up the grate this raw October night and close the doors and windows; draw up the cushioned chair, and listen to the wind torturing the rheumatic sign-boards in the metropolis, or the trees which surround your country cottage, and then read of Dr. Kane and his small band, in their huts of snow."[128] Some readers embraced the arctic narrative in even more substantial ways. Henry David Thoreau, back from his own "expe-

An ambrotype of Elisha Kent Kane by an unknown artist, c. 1856. Courtesy of the National Portrait Gallery, Smithsonian Institution.

dition" to Walden Pond, was so inspired by *Arctic Explorations* that he filled five pages of his journal with information from the book. Then, according to Thoreau scholar John Christie, he took to examining the world around him through Kane's eyes and compared the Inuit's isolation to his own. "January 20 [1857] found him on his hands and knees inspecting Eddy Emerson's snowhouse and later recording in his Journal with unfeigned excitement his realization of a 'good deal of Esquimau life.'"[129] On a more humorous note, one Maine newspaper reversed the cause and effect of that winter, noting that "the query has arisen, whether the immense sale of Dr. Kane's work all over the States, poring from the press like an avalanche, and containing so many sketches of icebergs, glaciers, and frozen seas, may not have introduced this arctic weather to us in its present unusual familiarity."[130]

While the nation was voraciously consuming his narrative and celebrating Dr. Kane in all his heroic glory, Elisha was ill, despondent, and longing for something more. He had fame, and a book that would bring him fortune, but he was miserable. A few days after the book was out and the critics were showering him with praise, Elisha wrote to Childs: "The book, poor as it is, has been my coffin." All during 1856, Elisha struggled to balance his dual existence as both himself and Dr. Kane. His book had been for the promotion of Dr. Kane. For himself, he wrote poetry. More than any other surviving objects from his life, these poems show the internal workings of his mind at this time:

A Question

What shall man do when his heart has gone
When his soul is old and his Carcass worn
When Care is joy and joy is Care
And a sameness soundeth every where?

What shall he do when the echoes long
Say self same things in an endless song
Sending memory cursed from heart to brain
And brain to heart straight back again?

What shall he do when his hopes are gray
As the hair which moltes the wrinkle's way
No prayer of love no breath of strife
But an only breath in the breath of life?

When he says to his soul and he says to his Clod
You're a curse to the image made after your God.
You're a curse to your God, if God there be,
And if there be none you're a curse to me?

❦

Why? Why? Am I sad when my day dreams are dawning,
And the world opens wide, for a wanderer's rest,
While my heart is yet steeped in the dews of the morning,
While youth may yet ripen, and manhood be blest?

Why fear I the world, its false gilding and sorrow,
Why am I unable its sneering to brave? —
Life — dims with the morning, and dies with the morrow;
Its sunrise is sadness, its sunset the grave.

Then why swells my heart with such fearful commotion,
Has reason no power a crushed spirit to save?
Oh! Why am I tossed like the bird of the ocean
Now bright, in the heavens now dark, in the wave.

For better, far better, than Fathers below—
The hearts, dreary wanderings to guard and control,
Is that Father, from whom all our blessings must flow,
That Father, who gives us the pride of the Soul.

Then rouse thee my soul, and Earth's pride forgetting,
Low trample beneath you the trammels of Earth;
Place your trust in yourself, and cease, cease, regretting
The false pride of station, the false pride of <u>birth</u>.[131]

These are not the poems of a triumphant hero; they are the poems of a tormented man. He had achieved fame and renown, but these were only aspects of Earthly pride. He was in love with a woman who also loved him, but he could not go to her because he could not brave the world's sneering gaze. Rationally, he knew what he had to do. He had to break from the demands of the world and his family (that "Father below" who guarded and controlled his heart's wandering) and to place his trust in himself and God "and cease, cease, regretting." He could not do this, however, and thus, he was his own greatest enemy. He raged at his own soul, "You're a curse to your God, if God there be, / And if there be none you're a curse to me." This inner battle, combined with his weak constitution, took a heavy toll. In July Henry Grinnell said of Elisha: "I never saw him look so bad; he is but a skeleton or the shadow of one."[132]

Elisha became hugely popular because Dr. Kane projected everything Americans thought a hero should be. He bravely led his men out of the frozen arctic, discovered the mythical Open Polar Sea, single-handedly bested a platoon of Mexican soldiers, dared the depths of a volcano to bring back its secrets, and wrote and illustrated an entertaining and scientifically important book. Elisha had truly done all these things, but what he thought of himself seems to have been quite different. In other writings he used the biblical image of the "Whited Sepulcher"—a beautiful tomb that is appealing to the eye but contains only the dry bones of death—to describe his and Margaret Fox's lives. They were "loathsome toads" hiding within their public personas that shown like crystal.

By 1856, Dr. Kane was the hero of the nation and a role model for its youth, and yet Elisha was in actuality a coward, unable to live up to his promises to Maggie. Instead of bravely embracing her, he was cowed by his own fears and reduced to sneaking around to be with the one he loved. Maggie also acted fearfully because she too had her own loathsome toad to hide. An entire movement recognized her as its founder and "high priestess," but she knew that all that they saw in her was built on a hoax. In this way, both Fox and Kane knew that large groups of Americans looked to them as strong, confident "beacon lights," and they both enjoyed this attention, but neither of them were able to reconcile this fame with the fact that at center they were both as fragile, scared, and human as everyone else. The more the press and their followers celebrated them, the more keenly they felt the "loathsome toad" that dwelled within them. Elisha's poems and private writings to Maggie clearly illustrate that though Dr. Kane was a hero to the nation, Elisha was never more than a celebrity in his own eyes. Heroes are made of substance; their actions and accomplishments shine from the interior of their very being. Celebrities must continually polish their exteriors for fear that the world will see their toadlike center. If Elisha had viewed himself as a hero, he would not have cared about the press or his family's opposition, but would have simply declared his love for Fox and gone on with his life fearing no press account or familial outcry. He would have behaved like a hero.

In the midst of his depression, two new issues began to press on Elisha in 1856: one concerning his crewmembers, the other his duty to his nation and Lady Jane Franklin. In the midst of writing his book, Elisha learned that his long-silent crewmembers were beginning to grumble. The primary threat came from John Wall Wilson. Wilson had been hurt when, early in the expedition, Elisha removed him from his place as second in command and put Brooks above him. Furthermore, as Elisha had feared, Wilson read Childs' puffs and was upset that Elisha was getting credit for things he had done. In response to this, Wilson began to prepare his own narrative of the expedition. Elisha got news of this in August 1856 and immediately took steps to prevent its publication. As noted earlier, in 1853, well before the expedition left, Elisha had required all his crewmembers to agree that he alone would publish the narrative of their trip. To stop Wilson, Elisha instructed his father to collect affidavits from the expedition's officers to enforce this verbal agreement. He told his father to first get Goodfellow's statement because "He remembers the agreement... and his memory will strengthen that of the rest." Once Goodfellow's statement was secured, he was sure that Bonsall and Hayes would also sign because, "They fear [Wilson's] account of the withdrawal of Aug '54 and this will influence them."[133] Fortunately for Elisha, this effort was successful and Wilson withdrew his narrative.[134]

The other issue pressing on Elisha was more daunting because it came from one of the most persuasive and determined people of the era: Sir John Franklin's wife, Lady Jane. After the disappearance of her husband in 1845, Lady Jane began a tireless campaign for his rescue. She sponsored private expeditions, influenced the sending of multiple British rescue efforts, and it was her letter to President Zachary Taylor that first began the efforts that became the First Grinnell Expedition. She was the Helen of Troy of her era; multiple countries launched dozens of ships because of her persuasiveness. In 1856, two years after John Rae brought back evidence of her husband's demise, Lady Jane was still determined to definitively learn his fate. The British Admiralty was no longer willing to entertain her pleas because they felt Rae's evidence, combined with the nine years that had passed since Franklin's disappearance, made any further searches pointless. Lady Jane thus turned to the United States, hoping that Henry Grinnell's generosity and Kane's popular influence would be enough to pull together a final expedition.

Fate was working in her favor. In 1856 tensions were running high between England and the United States because Cuba was pushing for its independence from Spain and the United States was showing signs of using the situation to claim the island for itself. England had just gone to war with Russia over its occupation of Turkey and was making rumblings that it would do the same if the United States moved to take Cuba. Though there was much high-level saber rattling, the people of both nations strongly opposed any conflict. English papers ran articles noting that any such action against "Brother Jonathan" would be foolish because "neither the population of the U.S. or England were at all behind animosities beginning between the two countries." U.S. papers reprinted these articles in hearty agreement.[135]

Looking for a way to defuse the situation, the United States government found a solution in the arctic. In the winter of 1854, British explorer Edward Belcher abandoned four of his five vessels and fled for home, fearing that his massive crew could not survive another arctic winter. The next spring a U.S. whaler discovered one of these ships, the *Resolute*, drifting in Baffin Bay. They towed it back to New York and claimed it for themselves under international salvage laws. England, embarrassed by the whole incident, readily gave up claim to the ship. In early 1856, the U.S. government began to debate whether it should buy this ship, restore it to pristine condition, and return it to England as a goodwill gesture. At the same time, England, also wanting to ease tensions, sent medals to Dr. Kane and his crew for their efforts on the behalf of Sir John Franklin.[136]

Lady Jane saw this as a perfect opportunity for another expedition. With Henry Grinnell's help, she began pushing the U.S. government to go ahead with their plans for the *Resolute* and to appoint Dr. Kane as its captain. He could then sail it back to England with the express purpose of commanding a joint U.S.-British effort to definitively learn the story of her husband's failed expedition. To his dismay, Elisha found himself in the middle of this touchy diplomatic effort. He did not want to be involved, but felt duty-bound to do his part—his heroic persona was again dictating his life.[137] He went to Washington for several days in August 1856 to push Lady Jane's plan, but once the government agreed to send the *Resolute* and make him its captain, he wrote his father: "Looking ahead and feeling as I now do, this dream must be over. My health has gone." He also confessed, "of this transatlantic scheme—personally I don't care the toss of a copper about it—but clearly do I think that duty requires my presence, if I owe a duty to the interests of this Arctic search, which has for six years been my one topic."[138]

Ultimately, Elisha compromised. He agreed to go to England to help promote a final expedition, but he would not go via the *Resolute*. He would cross as a common passenger and spend most of his time in European spas trying to regain his health. With this decision made, he went back to New York. He had stayed with the Grinnells for most of the summer of 1856 so he could relax and take part in the nearby therapeutic Long Island bathing. This, at least, is what he told his family. The true reason he remained in New York had much more to do with the quiet third-floor apartment of 50 Twenty-Second Street and its attractive young resident. As Elisha wrote to Maggie that summer, "I regard [your third floor room] as a sort of sanctuary: a retreat to which we are driven by mischief-making eyes and tongues. There, like wounded deer, we escape from the hunters."[139]

The late summer and early fall of 1856 were golden moments for Elisha and Maggie. The Fox family finally accepted him as a legitimate suitor, and Elisha and Maggie's correspondence from this time shows them very much in love. When the Fox family went to Canada for a few weeks, Elisha watched over their house. He wrote, "I miss you; the third story room seems desolate without you.... Tommy [Maggie's dog] is a spoiled child.... Even now I hear him barking—I suppose at my picture.... If he could speak, he would say,— 'You think yourself a great man, but she loves me more than she loves you, and she never beats me or pulls my nose.'"[140] During these months he lavished time and money on Fox, taking her to the opera, buying her a diamond bracelet from Tiffany's and furniture for her room. Nothing, he said, was too good "for my betrothed."[141]

Elisha knew his family still disapproved of the relationship, so he kept it from all of them except his brother, Patterson. In the spring Elisha asked him to explain his extended stay in New York by telling their family that he was nursing a sick friend—not a total lie as Maggie was ill at the time. To ease Pat's apprehension he said, "be in no fear as to publicity. I am very careful and they are even moreso. My visits are in secret and I can only sit by the bedside at night when the outsiders are away."[142] These excuses worked for Elisha's parents, but Tom saw through them. He wrote Patterson in May, "to some [Elisha is] <u>stated</u> to be returned home—to others confined by illness; to others nursing a sick friend. But how many do you suppose are really deceived by such nonsense?"[143]

In August Elisha again wrote Patterson and this time justified his continued stay by noting that Maggie was "healing" him. The intimate therapy Elisha described must have shocked his brother:

> I was stretched out on a lounge covered with a very light silk (an old dress) and shampooed unmercifully for at least two hours, the two taking turns [Kate helped Maggie with this]. Then followed a bath, then stretched out again [and] a set of queer passes whenever I had pain, soothing me and finally, ridiculous as it may seem to you, putting me sound asleep. The whole thing lasts daily from 11 A.M. to 5 1/2 P.M. I wake up fresh and without pain or fever.[144]

Recognizing how all this must sound, he wrote Patterson, saying: "Do not think the worse of my kind little nurse. In all this there is no want of refinement in the matter and my respect for her and her position, her fidelity and sad future increases with my own humiliation at my own conduct. I will try to aid and sustain her in her efforts to do what is right."[145] Patterson did not like this relationship, but he tolerated it. He went to New York and visited Elisha and Maggie on several occasions, enough that Maggie would jokingly tease Elisha about his "handsome brother Patterson."[146]

Elisha was to leave for England on October 11, and in the days before his departure he devoted almost all his time to Maggie. They went to an opera at Niblo's, and he wrote her little love poems. These, Maggie commented later, showed that he was "a far better navigator than poet."[147] They were clearly very intimate by this time. On one occasion Maggie surprised Elisha by jumping out of a closet, "blooming and laughing, very coquettishly dressed." Elisha was duly impressed. He immediately arranged for an ambrotype to be taken of her in the costume; to the photographer he wrote, "Large plate—Figure erect—complete Profile—Eyelids drooping—Countenance pensive and looking down." On the morning the image was to be taken, he wrote to Maggie: "Don't be afraid of your neck and shoulders. I want you to look like a Circe, for you have already changed me into a wild Boar."[148]

The events that transpired in the days that followed are impossible to document with certainty, but they were to cause years of turmoil between the Kane family and Maggie Fox. According to Fox, one evening in early October, Elisha came to her house depressed and forlorn. He was worried about his health and her future if anything were to happen to him while he was in England. Suddenly, he turned to her and asked if she was willing to publicly declare their marriage that very night, adding, "Such a declaration, in the presence of witnesses, is sufficient to constitute a legal and binding marriage." When she agreed, Elisha called Kate, Mrs. Fox, and two other young women then in the house, up to the third story apartment. He then stood embracing Maggie and said, "Maggie is my wife, and I am her husband. Wherever we are, she is mine, and I am hers. Do you understand this, Maggie?" She said yes. This done, Elisha declared that they were legally man and wife and promised that their marriage would "be made public in May."[149]

This ceremony, if it occurred, is documented only in Fox's account, a book published a decade later for the express purpose of claiming part of the royalties from *Arctic Explorations*. This, far more than the letters reprinted in Fox's book, is subject to suspicion and impossible to validate; however, several surviving pieces of evidence do suggest that Elisha did officially commit himself to Maggie in significant ways before he left for England. The Grinnell family knew of Elisha and Maggie's relationship, and despite initial opposition, had come to like and respect the vivacious young woman who called occasionally at their house. The day Elisha left, he signed a will in the presence of Henry and Sylvia Grinnell, naming his brothers, Thomas and Patterson, as his executors and leaving his entire estate, namely the hefty royalties from his book, to such members of the family as his father might designate. He specified "the family" as his mother and siblings; however, he made one other provision—a $5,000 immediate payment to his brothers, Patterson and John, "in trust to be applied, used, employed and disposed of... in accordance with the trusts expressed by me in a paper writing to be found among my private papers."[150] Later, the Fox family and the Grinnells both publicly claimed that this $5,000 was intended for Maggie.[151] Even though the Kane family refused to acknowledge this publicly, privately they knew it was true—in a confidential letter Tom's wife wrote him, "We both surmise that the $5,000 of the will was for her."[152]

With little fanfare, Elisha and his faithful steward, William Morton, boarded the *Baltic* and left for England on October 11, 1856. Although the shipping line gave them a stateroom free of charge—making this by far the most elegant of Elisha's many sea voyages—the crossing was difficult for him. When they reached Liverpool on the October 22 he told Lady Jane, "I have arrived quite an invalid."[153] Despite his ill health, he traveled to London and began promoting another expedition. He hoped that if he put his weight behind a government-sponsored expedition, he might be able to get both it and a privately executed expedition funded. Showing the spark of his earlier promotional efforts, he wrote his parents and asked them to drum up support in the States by bringing the cause "before our public properly and at once."[154] On October 28 he met with the Royal Admiralty and they presented him with an award for his last expedition. The next day he physically collapsed. Hardly able to support his own weight, he retired to English merchant William Cross's country villa in Camberwell, an affluent suburb of London. Sir Henry Holland, the favorite physician of London society, found Elisha thin and weak and reported that he was suffering from rheumatic swelling, chills and fever, rapid pulse, and a dry cough.[155] Too ill to attend the Royal Geographical Society's ceremony in his honor, Elisha made plans to leave London for the West Indies in hopes that the tropical weather would help him recover. Cornelius Grinnell arrived from Paris on November 11 and accompanied him to Southampton, where less than a week later, Morton and Elisha boarded the steamer *Orinoco* bound for St. Thomas en route to Havana. Lady Jane wanted Elisha to go to the Portuguese island of Madeira off the coast of West Africa to recover, but Elisha was suspicious of her motives. In the last full letter he ever wrote to his father, Elisha finally bucked his duty as Dr. Kane. "Dear Father, this woman would use me if she could even now.... She wants me to go to Madeira simply because it ensures my return to England where she has a scheme for me to urge her case before Prince Albert." He explained that he would not be sorry when the proper moment arose to tell Lady Jane that he was through with arctic exploration, and if she were to persist in her requests, he assured his father, "I'll refuse point blank."[156]

Elisha and Morton's passage to St. Thomas went smoothly and they arrived on December 2 with Elisha feeling somewhat better. After an eighteen-day layover, they left for Havana, where Tom was already waiting for them—he had left New York for Cuba upon learning of Elisha's departure from England. During the short trip to Havana, however, Elisha suffered an apoplectic stroke. By the time Tom met them, Elisha's right side was paralyzed and he was unable to speak. In the days that followed several physicians attended to Elisha and he recovered a bit, regaining his ability to talk and sit up. By mid-January his mother and brother John were with him as well. He continued to improve and Tom booked passage to New York. He hoped to get Elisha back to Philadelphia by mid-February, but bad weather prevented them from sailing. Then, on February 10, Elisha suffered another stroke, this time rendering him completely speechless and unable to move. Though he had survived many illnesses, hardships, and injuries in the past decade, no one held out any hope for the weary adventurer now. Six days later, with his mother quietly reading the Bible at his bedside, Elisha Kent Kane died.[157]

When news of Elisha's death reached the United States, newspaper columns filled with eulogies and poetry celebrating Dr. Kane's life. In the months that followed, these grew and expanded, becoming increasingly celebratory as the nation lifted their fallen hero to higher and higher levels of fame and perfection. Elisha Kent Kane had died. Dr. Kane lived on.

1. Columbus, *Ohio Statesman* (March 9, 1857).

2. For this discussion of fame I am borrowing and expanding on the ideas of Daniel J. Boorstin, *The Image* (New York: Macmillan Publishing Co, 1987, 1961); and Leo Braudy, *The Frenzy of Renown* (New York: Vintage, 1997, 1986).

3. Thomas Leiper Kane to Elisha Kent Kane (May 31, 1855), APS Elisha Kent Kane papers; *New York Tribune* (Oct. 12, 1855), 4. Emphasis added.

4. *New York Tribune* (Oct. 13, 1855), 5; *Ohio Statesman* (March 9, 1857). This era, like today, was skeptical of people who openly pursued fame. A contemporary article entitled "Pursuit of Fame" declared, "What an empty, hollow thing it is," and compared fame to "a shaved pig with a greased tail... it is only when it has slipped through the hands of thousands, that some fellow, by mere chance, holds on to it!" See *Gleason's Pictorial Drawing Room Companion* (June 7, 1851), 93.

5. See for example Mark C. Carnes, *Secret Ritual and Manhood in Victorian America* (New Haven, CT: Yale University Press, 1989); Karen Halttunen, *Confidence Men and Painted Women* (New Haven, CT: Yale University Press, 1982); and Ann Douglas, *The Feminization of American Culture* (New York: Alfred A. Knopf Inc., 1977).

6. These statistics are cited in Carl Bode, *The Anatomy of Popular Culture*, 1840-61 (Berkeley: University of California Press, 1960), 116. For an examination of how

this literacy explosion affected the book publishing industry, see the contemporary article in *American Publishers' Circular & Literary Gazette* (June 15, 1863), 166-67.

7. See William Huntzicker, *The Popular Press, 1833-1865* (Westport, CT: Greenwood Press, 1999), 53-56.

8. The one portrait of him appeared in New York's *Illustrated News* 1 (March 5, 1853), 148. It was an engraving of Elisha in military uniform taken from a daguerreotype from 1847, before Elisha left for Mexico. Verbal descriptions of his sickly but energetic constitution appeared much more widely. See the Philadelphia *Pennsylvanian* (June 5, 1850), 2; *New York Tribune* (June 8, 1850), 7; *Spirit of the Times* (July 13, 1850), 245; and W. Parker Snow's more detailed description of Elisha in *Harper's New Monthly Magazine* 2 (April, 1851), 596-97.

9. *New York Tribune* (Oct. 12, 1855), 4.

10. Thomas Leiper Kane to John K. Kane, Jr (Oct. 15, 1855), Kane family papers, Clements Library, University of Michigan.

11. *New York Tribune* (Oct. 13, 1855), 7.

12. Thomas Leiper Kane to John K. Kane, Jr (Oct. 15, 1855), Kane family papers, Clements Library, University of Michigan.

13. Brady took an ambrotype of this scene and, as Tom instructed, it was photographically reproduced and given to select editors for reproduction as an engraving. An original photographic copy of this portrait appears in Oscar M. Villarejo, *Dr. Kane's Voyage to the Polar Lands* (Philadelphia: University of Pennsylvania Press, 1965), illustration gallery after page 128. Villarejo notes that this image is in the Isaac Israel Hayes papers of the Chester County Historical Society, West Chester, Pennsylvania, but they have no record of it as part of their Hayes collection.

14. John Kane Jr., "The Kane Relief Expedition," *Putnam's Monthly Magazine* 7 (July, 1856), 451-63.

15. *Frank Leslie's Illustrated Newspaper* 1 (Dec. 15, 1855), 1, 8-10. The portrait of Kane and his men is a mirror-image engraving of Brady's ambrotype.

16. *New York Times* (Oct. 12, 1855), 8. Though the *Times* reported this play was scheduled for immediate production, no advertisements for it appear in New York newspapers in the following months.

17. J. B. Peterson, "Dr. Kane's Arctic Polka" (Philadelphia: Lee & Walker, c. 1856); Albert W. Berg, "The Polar Bear Polka" (New York: Firth, Pond & Co., 1856).

18. Russell Potter & Douglas Wamsley "The Sublime yet Awful Grandeur: the Arctic Panoramas of Elisha Kent Kane," *Polar Record* 35 (Jan. 1999), 193-206. In later years several different manifestations of this panorama traveled through Europe and across the United States where it continued to attract audiences well into the 1860s.

19. Nicholas B. Wainwright, "Education of an Artist: The Diary of Joseph Boggs Beale, 1856-1862" *The Pennsylvania Magazine of History and Biography* 9 (Oct. 1973), 485-510. Joseph Beale later studied with James Hamilton, who did the watercolor

illustrations for both of Elisha's books.

20. *New York Times* (Oct. 16, 1855), 2. One hundred and forty-five years later, the *New York Times* would again announce that a ship had reached the north pole and found an Open Polar Sea. Scientists would again speculate about its cause, putting forth different theories, but this time with thoughts of dread about global warming. See *New York Times* (Aug. 18, 2000), A1.

21. See *London Times* (Oct. 28, 1855); Elisha Kent Kane to John K. Kane (Feb. 3, 1856), APS Elisha Kent Kane papers; and Corner, 261-62. Another Englishman, Augustus Petermann, also disputed Elisha's claim at that time, but not so adamantly. He felt that the sea, while open, was probably not "iceless." See *Littell's Living Age* 48 (Jan. 26, 1856), 205-07 (copied from the *Athenaeum* of Nov. 24, 1855). The first serious challenge to Kane's claim came after his death. At the April 12, 1858, meeting of the Royal Geographical Society the Danish Inspector in Greenland, Dr. Henry Rink, presented a paper that questioned the accuracy of Kane's far northern measurements and his conclusion that what Morton had seen was truly an Open Polar Sea. See Henry Rink, "On the Supposed Discovery of the North Coast of Greenland and an Open Polar Sea," *Proceedings of the Royal Geographical Society* 2 (1858), 195-201.

22. *New York Times* (Oct. 24, 1855), 2; and (Oct. 30, 1855), 2.

23. *American Phrenological Journal* 42 (Sept., 1856), 82-83.

24. Matthew F. Maury, *The Physical Geography of the Sea* 6th ed. (New York: Harper & Bros., 1857), 177.

25. *New York Tribune* (Oct. 19, 1855), 1. For the map see, "Chart Exhibiting the discoveries of the American Arctic expedition in search of Sir John Franklin" (New York: Ackerman Lithography, 1855).

26. "The Mythic Sea," *The Cincinnatus* 1 (Jan., 1856), 49-50.

27. *Portland* (Maine) *Transcript & Eclectic* (Oct. 20, 1855), 222. Emphasis in the original. This article attributes the statement to an unspecified New York newspaper.

28. *Troy Daily Whig* (Oct. 19, 1855), 2.

29. Accounts of this story were reprinted, expanded, and debated in the New York *Times, Herald, Evening Post,* and *Express* between Oct. 26 and Nov. 5, 1855. They also appeared in the *Portsmouth Journal of Literature & Politics* (Nov. 11, 1855), 2; Madison's *Weekly Wisconsin Patriot* (Nov. 10, 1855), 2; *New Hampshire Sentinel* (Nov. 2, 1855), 2; *Trenton State Gazette* (Oct. 30 & Nov. 2, 1855), 2; and *Weekly St. Louis Pilot* (Nov. 3, 1855), 1.

30. Maggie spent several weeks during May of 1850 in Troy and gained many followers. A reprinted article from the Buffalo, NY, *Courier* reported that since the "first visit of the Misses Fox" in 1850, spirit circles had been growing, meeting in large groups each week in upstate New York. See *Trenton State Gazette* (Jan. 5, 1854), 1.

31. *New York Times* (Nov. 3, 1854), 4; and (Nov. 5, 1854), 4.

32. Maggie Fox to Elisha Kent Kane (undated, c. Nov., 1855), *Love-Life*, 221-22. The

powerful friends Maggie alludes to could include many people: New York Supreme Court Justice John Edmonds, Wisconsin Governor N.P. Tallmadge, or, most likely, *New York Tribune* editor Horace Greeley with whom she and Kate had spent much time in the early 1850s.

33. *New York Tribune* (Nov. 6, 1855), 5.

34. See Philadelphia's *Daily Pennsylvanian* (Nov. 10, 1855); and *North American & United States Gazette* (Nov. 17, 1855), 2.

35. The *Daily Pennsylvanian* was the mouthpiece of Philadelphia Democrats and in 1855 Judge Kane was one of the party leaders and had direct editorial access to its pages. As Tom told Elisha a few years earlier, "I have the Press here, and Father can lead the party." Thomas Leiper Kane to Elisha Kent Kane (undated c. March, 1850), APS Elisha Kent Kane papers. That this article both denied the engagement and then promoted the family generally (something they needed as Judge Kane was still being attacked for his ruling in the Passmore Williamson case) strongly suggests that they had a hand in the article. That the article is attributed to "a Philadelphia correspondent of the *Boston Traveller*" is also telling; Tom often wrote for other papers and would then use such by-lines to help hide his identity while still being technically true. *Love-Life*, 217 footnote.

36. Maggie Fox to Elisha Kent Kane (undated, c. Dec., 1855), APS Elisha Kent Kane papers.

37. Maggie Fox to Elisha Kent Kane (undated, c. Nov., 1855), *Love-Life*, 210-11. The letters in *Love-Life* that address this period are largely undated but most can be placed fairly accurately by their context and by their relationship to dated letters appearing elsewhere.

38. Mrs. Fox to Elisha Kent Kane (Dec. 6, 1855), APS Elisha Kent Kane papers.

39. *Love-Life*, 203, 226. Emphasis in the original.

40. *Love-Life*, 242, 247.

41. Thomas Leiper Kane to Elisha Kent Kane (Feb. 20, 1848), APS Elisha Kent Kane papers. Tom expresses similar sentiments in several letters, see also Thomas Leiper Kane to Elisha Kent Kane (undated, c. Feb., 1847) and (Jan. 26, 1851), APS Elisha Kent Kane papers.

42. Thomas Leiper Kane to Elisha Kent Kane (May 31, 1855), APS Elisha Kent Kane papers.

43. Note his letter that instructed Patterson to keep rumors of the relationship from their mother, and that he forced Maggie to sign a statement denying their engagement "to satisfy his mother." Elisha Kent Kane to Robert Patterson Kane (June, 1853), APS Elisha Kent Kane papers; and *Love-Life*, 195.

44. Elisha Kent Kane to John K. Kane (June, 3, 1841), in folder "E.K. Kane to Jane D.L. Kane," APS Elisha Kent Kane papers.

45. Private Journal of Elisha Kent Kane (June, 1854), Special Collections, Stanford

University Libraries.

46. In several letters Kane noted his deep debt to Grinnell. This is clearly seen when he refused to have the expedition called the Kane Expedition and insisted that he was but one member of the "Second Grinnell Expedition." Elisha Kent Kane to Henry Grinnell (May 4, 1856), American Prose collection, folder, "Elisha Kent Kane," Historical Society of Pennsylvania.

47. Elisha Kent Kane to Maggie Fox (undated c. Feb. 20, 1853), *Love-Life*, 75-79. Emphasis in the original.

48. Maggie Fox to Elisha Kent Kane (undated c. March, 1853), APS Elisha Kent Kane papers.

49. Elisha Kent Kane to Maggie Fox (undated c. Nov., 1855), *Love-Life*, 204-05.

50. Braudy, *The Frenzy of Renown*, 5.

51. *Love-Life*, 204-05.

52. *Love-Life*, 207.

53. Though this agreement is not clearly articulated in any specific letter, it can be deduced from the many letters between Elisha and Maggie during the early months of 1856. See *Love-Life*, 215, 223-37.

54. Elisha Kent Kane to John K. Kane (Oct. 16, 1855), APS Elisha Kent Kane papers.

55. Elisha Kent Kane to John K. Kane (Nov. 21, 1855), APS Elisha Kent Kane papers.

56. See Harpers' ads in the *New York Evening Post* (Oct. 13 & 15, 1855), 2.

57. John K. Kane to Elisha Kent Kane (May 29, 1855), John Kane papers, Historical Society of Pennsylvania. See also letters between Cornelius Grinnell and Harpers in *The Archives of Harper and Brothers, 1817-1914* (Teaneck, NJ: Chadwyck-Healey Microfilm Edition, 1980), reels 1 and 51.

58. Elisha Kent Kane to John K. Kane (Oct. 30, 1855), letter in the private collection of Kane descendent Eliza Cope Harrison, Lebanon, Pennsylvania. Elisha's dispute with the Harpers was difficult because their contract had been destroyed in the fire.

59. Elisha Kent Kane to John K. Kane (Oct. 30, 1855), letter in the private collection of Kane descendent Eliza Cope Harrison, Lebanon, Pennsylvania. First public announcement of Elisha's publishing agreement with Childs appeared in the *New York Evening Post* (Nov. 15, 1855).

60. Piecing together Childs' history is difficult because his autobiography, *Recollections* (Philadelphia: J.B. Lippincott Co., 1890), largely ignores his pre-*Public Ledger* life and the many newspaper and magazine articles about him are hagiographic, celebrating him as a great promoter of the arts, as a philanthropist, and as a rags-to-riches hero of mid-nineteenth century America. See for example, *New York Tribune* (Feb. 2, 1894), 1; *American Literary Gazette* (April 15, 1870), 335; *Frank Leslie's Illustrated Newspaper* (April 4, 1874), 59; (Sept. 29, 1883), 91; & (June 5, 1886), 247; and *Publishers' Weekly* (Nov. 21, 1872), 544. Though some of Childs' papers do survive at Philadelphia's Drexel University, they shed little light on his life before he and his wealthy backer,

Anthony J. Drexel, purchased the *Public Ledger* in December of 1864. By far the most comprehensive history of Childs is Madeleine B. Stern's chapter, "George W. Childs: Poor Richard the Second," in her book, *Imprints on History: Book Publishers and American Frontiers* (Bloomington: Indiana University Press, 1956), 157-77. I rely heavily upon it for Childs' early history.

61. Stern, 160-61.

62. See his ads in the Philadelphia *Public Ledger* (Nov. 18, 1848), 3; (Dec. 18, 1848), 3; and (July 25, 1849), 2; and in the Baltimore *Sun* (Dec. 14, 1848) 2; (Dec. 20, 1848), 4; and (Jan. 13, 1849).

63. See *Dictionary of American Biography s.v.* "Charles Jacobs Peterson" and "Henry Petersen."

64. Stern, 161-62. Judging by surviving books and advertisements, R.E. Peterson's catalog included fifteen works—six religious texts, four school texts, three popular biographies (including *Memoranda of the life of Jenny Lind* by N.P. Willis and a biography of George Mifflin Dallas ghostwritten by Childs), Bouvier's *Institutes of American Law*, and Bouvier Peterson's *National Cook Book*.

65. Officially Childs got top billing in the company's new name so they would not be confused with T.B. Peterson publishing house, but the name change was also meant to help their religious works, which were still suffering from the accusations that Peterson was an "infidel." Apparently they tried to move entirely away from religious publications because, by the end of the 1850s, their stationary stated, "Childs and Peterson, Publishers of Law, School and Miscellaneous Books." See G.W. Childs to F.J. Dreer (Feb. 12, 1859), Clements Library, University of Michigan.

66. See *Norton's Literary Gazette* (March 15, 1852), 54; and (April 15, 1852), 72; as well as Stern, 162. Childs & Peterson sold off their book stock to C.G. Henderson and Company, juvenile booksellers.

67. Nathaniel Hawthorne to G.W. Childs (Sept. 16, 1851), reprinted in *The Library of George W. Childs* (Philadelphia: Collins Printer, 1888), 6-7.

68. G.W. Childs to F.J. Dreer (Dec. 27, 1853), Clements Library, University of Michigan. More on Childs' literary ambition is seen in the scrapbooks he kept on American books and authors. See Drexel University Archives, George W. Childs papers, clippings books 070 fC43 1-4.

69. *American Publishers' Circular & Literary Gazette* 1 (Nov. 17, 1855), 168-69. None of the images in the books actually came from daguerreotypes, for though the expedition took and used daguerreotype equipment, the extreme weather prevented the images from turning out.

70. *American Publishers' Circular & Literary Gazette* 1 (Dec. 22, 1855), 248. Childs' promotional efforts often began as articles appearing in a Philadelphia based newspaper or magazine (to which he and Peterson had many ties) and were then distributed widely. Childs was also well connected with the *American Circular &*

Literary Gazette and his projects received greater than usual attention in its pages. Childs bought and began to edit this publication in 1864.

71. Elisha Kent Kane to George W. Childs (undated, c. May, 1856), item 15, Kane-Childs album, Dreer Collection, Historical Society of Pennsylvania.

72. William Elder, *Biography of Elisha Kent Kane* (Philadelphia: Childs & Peterson, 1858), 219. Elisha was generally pleased with Hamilton's work but felt he took too many liberties with some of the sketches. He complained to Childs that Hamilton's paintings "are so commanded by waves and ships where neither wave nor ship could exist that I am seriously embarrassed in distributing the cuts." See Elisha Kent Kane to George W. Childs (Feb. 25, 1856) item 8, Kane-Childs album, Dreer Collection, Historical Society of Pennsylvania.

73. Elisha Kent Kane to George W. Childs (undated, c. Feb. 10, 1856), item 6, Kane-Childs album, Dreer Collection, Historical Society of Pennsylvania.

74. Elisha Kent Kane to George W. Childs (undated, c. Feb. 10, 1856), item 6, Kane-Childs album, Dreer Collection, Historical Society of Pennsylvania.

75. See *Magnetical Observations in the Arctic Seas; Meteorological Observations in the Arctic Seas; Physical Observations in the Arctic Seas;* and *Tidal Observations in the Arctic Seas* (Washington D.C.: Smithsonian Institution, 1858 & 1859). Charles A. Schott oversaw these publications and some of them were reprinted by mainstream presses.

76. Elisha Kent Kane to George W. Childs (May 25, 1856), item 17, Kane-Childs album, Dreer Collection, Historical Society of Pennsylvania.

77. Elizabeth Kane to Elizabeth Wood Kane (June 8, 1856), Kane family papers, Clements Library, University of Michigan.

78. Elizabeth Wood Kane journal (May 15, 1853), and (March 12, 1856), BYU Thomas Leiper Kane papers. I am indebted to Matt Grow for calling my attention to these journal entries.

79. Elisha Kent Kane to George W. Childs (June 14,1856), Kane-Childs album, Dreer Collection, Historical Society of Pennsylvania.

80. Jane Duval Leiper Kane and Bessie Kane to Thomas Leiper Kane and Elizabeth Wood Kane (June 27, 1856), BYU Thomas Leiper Kane papers.

81. Elisha Kent Kane to George W. Childs (July 4, 1856), Kane-Childs album, Dreer Collection, Historical Society of Pennsylvania.

82. There had been a push in both the newspapers and by Grinnell to name the expedition the "Kane Expedition" but Elisha refused. He sent the title page of his book to Grinnell with a note saying, "Neither the suggestions of newspapers or your own wishes will move me in doing my duty as historian of the 'Second Grinnell Expedition.'" Elisha Kent Kane to Henry Grinnell (May 4, 1856), American Prose Collection, folder, "Elisha Kent Kane," Historical Society of Pennsylvania.

83. *Archive of Harper Brothers*, Memorandum Book vol. 1, 1856-59 (Teaneck, NJ: Chadwyck-Healey Microfilm editions, 1980), reel 22.

84. *United States Magazine* 3 (Aug., 1856), 173-75 and (Dec., 1856), 560-61. These articles are part of a series on the book trade that ran during 1856.

85. See "Publishers and the Newspaper Press," *American Publishers' Circular & Literary Gazette* (Dec. 1, 1855), 197-8. This issue blew up in a dispute between publisher Ticknor & Fields and the Boston *Traveller* when the *Traveller* published a scathing review of Longfellow's *Song of Hiawatha* even after Ticknor & Fields had purchased expensive advertising space in their paper. Ticknor & Fields pulled their ads and for the next several months, newspapers and publishers argued with each other about who was extorting whom.

86. William Charvat, *Literary Publishing in America, 1790-1850* (Amherst: University of Massachusetts Press, 1993), 23.

87. Neil Harris, *Humbug: The Art of P.T. Barnum* (Boston: Little, Brown &Co., 1973), 118-24. For an in-depth look at the growth of advertising in the 19th century, see Duke University's John W. Hartman Center for Sales, Advertising & Marketing's online resource page, *Emergence of Advertising in America: 1850-1920.* (http://scriptorium.lib.duke.edu/eaa/timeline.html).

88. "The Philosophy of Advertising," *The American Whig Review* (Aug., 1852), 121-25.

89. *Frank Leslie's Illustrated Newspaper* 1 (Dec. 15, 1855), 10. Interestingly, this first issue also carried a large exposé on Spiritulism as well.

90. *Southern Literary Messenger* (Oct. 1856), 319; *Knickerbocker* (Oct. 1856), 417.

91. Scott E. Casper, *Constructing American Lives: Biography and Culture in Nineteenth-Century America* (Chapel Hill: University of North Carolina Press, 1999), 7. A copy of Judge Kane's anonymously published pro-Jackson pamphlet "A Candid View of the Presidential Question," (Philadelphia, 1828) is available at the American Philosophical Society, Philadelphia.

92. See Nathaniel Parker Willis, *Memoranda of the Life of Jenny Lind* (Philadelphia: R.E. Peterson, 1851). Childs started working for R.E. Peterson in 1849 and handled the "literary" aspects of the business while Robert Peterson handled the business end. See Madeline Stern, "George W. Childs: Poor Richard the Second," *Imprints on History: Book Publishers and American Frontiers* (Bloomington: Indiana University Press, 1956), 161-64.

93. William Elder, "Dr. Kane, a Sketch" *Graham's Illustrated Magazine* 48 (Feb., 1856), 105-08. For examples of its extensive reprinting see: *Littell's Living Age* 48 (Feb. 16, 1856), 427-30; *The Crayon* 3 (Feb., 1856), 60-61; *Waverly Magazine* 12 (Feb. 9, 1856), 85; *Portland Transcript & Eclectic* (Feb. 2, 1856), 338-39. A proof-page of this article, formatted into standard columns to be sent to multiple publishers, still exists among Childs' papers, showing he was behind the sketch's creation and wide circulation. See Drexel University Archives, George W. Childs papers, clippings books 070 fC43 1, 11.

94. See for example *Graham's Illustrated Magazine* 49 (Nov., 1856), 385-400; *American Phrenological Journal* 25 (Jan., 1857), 3-7.

95. Elisha Kent Kane to George W. Childs (Jan. 26, 1856) item 3, Kane-Childs album, Dreer Collection, Historical Society of Pennsylvania. A clipping from the *Daily Legislative Record* regarding Mr. Morris's efforts is pasted next to the above letter in the Kane-Childs album. Note that Elder's sketch of Kane in the February edition of *Graham's* reached the public in January. Like today, at that time magazines issues often came out well before the date on their cover.

96. Elisha Kent Kane to George W. Childs (Jan. 26, 1856), item 3, Kane-Childs album, Dreer Collection, Historical Society of Pennsylvania.

97. Elisha Kent Kane to Thomas H. Benton (Jan. 6, 1856), item 2, Kane-Childs album, Dreer Collection, Historical Society of Pennsylvania.

98. See John C. Frémont, *Explorations during the Years 1845, '46, '47, '48, '49, '53, '54...* (Philadelphia: Childs & Peterson, 1859). Childs & Peterson often placed ads for Kane's and Frémont's books together, using the one to promote the other.

99. Alexander Dallas Bache to Job R. Tyson (Feb. 19, 1856), Society Collection, folder "Alexander D. Bache," Historical Society of Pennsylvania.

100. Philadelphia *Public Ledger* (March 4, 1856).

101. Elisha Kent Kane to George W. Childs (March 4, 1856), item 10, Kane-Childs album, Dreer Collection, Historical Society of Pennsylvania.

102. Washington D.C. *Congressional Globe* (March 14, 1856), 1.

103. Elisha Kent Kane to John K. Kane (undated, c. March 15, 1856), APS Elisha Kent Kane papers.

104. Elisha Kent Kane to George W. Childs (April 30, 1856), item 11, Kane-Childs album, Dreer Collection, Historical Society of Pennsylvania.

105. Elisha Kent Kane to George W. Childs (July 30, 1856), item 33, Kane-Childs album, Dreer Collection, Historical Society of Pennsylvania.

106. Senate, 34th Congress, 1st Session. Rep. Com. No. 281. The Congressional debate over this funding as well as over paying officers to write after an expedition were covered in the Washington, D.C. *Daily Globe* (Aug. 19, 1856), 1-2.

107. See "Bookselling," *American Publishers' Circular & Literary Gazette* (Aug. 14, 1858), 390-92; and Michael Winship "Getting the Books Out: Trade Sales, Parcel Sales, and Book Fairs in the Nineteenth-Century United States" in *Getting the Books Out*, Michael Hackenberg ed. (Washington D.C.: The Library of Congress Center for the Book, 1987), 4-25.

108. George W. Childs, *Recollections*, 12.

109. Richmond, Virginia's *Southern Literary Review* 23 (Oct., 1856), 319, noted subscription sales going on in that city. Two surviving subscription books from Boston show that an agent went door-to-door through Boston's affluent neighborhoods. The agent also went to businesses, which often purchased multiple copies, suggesting that they bought them for gifts for employees or clients. These efforts were targeted to high-sales areas, suggesting Childs method. These subscription books are in the Shillaber

family papers, Massachusetts Historical Society. A surviving subscription card that was given to potential buyers is in the Kane-Childs album, Dreer Collection, Historical Society of Pennsylvania.

110. Childs was fond of claiming to have sold "30,000 advanced copies"; he also claimed this for Elder's *Biography of Elisha Kent Kane* and *Allibone's Dictionary of Literature*. Privately, just before the book came out, he told Elisha that his agents had sold 17,000 copies but Elisha noted, "He cannot count bonafide 10,000." See Elisha Kent Kane to John K. Kane (Sept. 9, 1856), APS Elisha Kent Kane papers. Total subscription sales for *Arctic Explorations* are hard to estimate, but it did sell well. The two surviving subscription books noted above show that one Boston agent sold over 400 copies for more than $2,400.

111. "Polar Sea Discovered by Dr. Kane," *Waverly Magazine* 12 (Feb. 2, 1856), 69; Baltimore *Commercial Advertiser* (March 12, 1856).

112. See Elisha Kent Kane to George W. Childs (Aug. 30, 1856), items 44 & 45, Kane-Childs album, Dreer Collection, Historical Society of Pennsylvania.

113. Mathew F. Maury to Elisha Kent Kane (Oct. 7, 1856) and N.P. Willis to Elisha Kent Kane (Oct. 5, 1856), APS Elisha Kent Kane papers.

114. George W. Childs to Rufus W. Griswold (Oct. 23, 1856), Rufus Griswold papers, Boston Public Library.

115. Elisha Kent Kane to George W. Childs (Sept. 18, 1856), item 46, Kane-Childs album, Dreer Collection, Historical Society of Pennsylvania.

116. Childs, *Recollections*, 12.

117. *Crayon* (Nov., 1856), 351-52; *Ladies Repository* (Dec., 1856), 756-57; *DeBow's Review* (Aug., 1857), 172-92; *Ohio Cultivator* (Jan. 15, 1857), 24; *American Phrenological Journal* (Feb., 1857), 36-38.

118. *Genesee Farmer* 18 (April, 1857), 109.

119. *Knickerbocker* (Oct., 1856), 417.

120. *Knickerbocker* (Nov., 1856), 518-21.

121. *Graham's Illustrated Magazine* (Nov., 1856), 385-400.

122. *North American Review* (Jan., 1857), 95-122.

123. *Knickerbocker* (Nov., 1856), 518-21.

124. *Crayon* (Nov., 1856), 351-52.

125. *United States Magazine* (Dec., 1856), 538-43.

126. *The Ladies' Repository* (Dec., 1856), 756-57.

127. The "terrible winter of 1856" is vividly described in J. Thomas Scharf & Thompson Westcott, *History of Philadelphia, 1609-1884* 3 vols. (Philadelphia: L.H. Everts & Co. 1884), I, 720.

128. *Knickerbocker* (Nov., 1856), 518-21.

129. John Aldrich Christie, *Thoreau as World Traveler* (New York: Columbia University Press, 1965), 198. Eddy was Ralph Waldo Emerson's son.

130. *Portland Transcript & Eclectic* (Jan. 31, 1857), 342.

131. Folder, "Kane, E.K. Poetry," (undated, c. 1856), APS Elisha Kent Kane papers.

132. Henry Grinnell to Lady Jane Franklin (July 19, 1856), reprinted in *The Life, Diaries & Correspondence of Jane Lady Franklin*, Willingham Franklin Rawnsley ed. (London: Erskine MacDonald, Ltd., 1923), 218-19.

133. Elisha Kent Kane to John K. Kane (Sept. 3, 1856), APS Elisha Kent Kane papers.

134. Wilson's narrative still remains unpublished, see John Wall Wilson, *Narrative of the Second Grinnell Expedition* (unpublished manuscript, National Archives).

135. "No Quarrel with America," *London Atlas* (Nov. 3, 1855), reprinted in *New York Evening Post* (Nov. 15, 1855), 2.

136. "Compliments to Dr. Kane and Associates," *Daily Pennsylvanian* (March 18, 1856).

137. See Henry Grinnell to Lady Jane Franklin (July 19, 1856) and Elisha Kent Kane to Lady Jane Franklin (July 24, 1856), in *The Life, Diaries & Correspondence of Jane Lady Franklin*, 218-20; and, Elisha Kent Kane to George W. Childs (Aug. 9, 1856), Kane-Childs album, Dreer Collection, Historical Society of Pennsylvania. Childs was happy about this plan because it would also serve as a promotional effort for book sales in England.

138. Elisha Kent Kane to John K. Kane (Aug. 31, 1856), APS Elisha Kent Kane papers. The conclusion of this letter matches the letter Maggie wrote Elisha about wanting to quit spiritualism: "I have given my whole time to this subject for six years. I think I have done my part." Maggie Fox to Elisha Kent Kane (undated, c. March, 1853), APS Elisha Kent Kane papers.

139. Elisha Kent Kane to Maggie Fox (undated, c. summer, 1856), *Love-Life*, 236-37.

140. Elisha Kent Kane to Maggie Fox (undated, c. Aug., 1856), *Love-Life*, 256.

141. *Love-Life*, 253, 263.

142. Elisha Kent Kane to Robert Patterson Kane (April 15, 1856), APS Robert Patterson Kane papers.

143. Thomas Leiper Kane to Robert Patterson Kane (May 5, 1856), APS Robert Patterson Kane papers.

144. Elisha Kent Kane to Robert Patterson Kane (Aug. 8, 1856), APS Elisha Kent Kane papers.

145. Elisha Kent Kane to Robert Patterson Kane (Aug. 8, 1856), APS Elisha Kent Kane papers.

146. Maggie Fox to Elisha Kent Kane (undated, c. Sept., 1856), *Love-Life*, 260-61.

147. *Love-Life*, 266. According to multiple reviews in the New York *Herald*, The German Opera Company was at Niblo's through the fall of 1856, performing multiple productions, each to great acclaim.

148. *Love-Life*, 267-68.

149. *Love-Life*, 269-72.

150. "Kane, E.K. Will," APS Elisha Kent Kane papers. This document is signed by Elisha

and both Henry and Sylvia Grinnell.

151. Mrs. Fox to Robert Patterson Kane (undated, c. March, 1857), APS Robert Patterson Kane papers. This letter notes that after the news of Elisha's death reached New York, Mrs. Grinnell came to Maggie to console her and told her not to worry as she had been "remembered to the last."

152. Elizabeth Wood Kane to Thomas Leiper Kane (April, 24, 1862), BYU Thomas Leiper Kane papers.

153. Elisha Kent Kane to Lady Jane Franklin (Oct. 22, 1856), *The Life, Diaries & Correspondence of Jane Lady Franklin,* 224.

154. Elisha Kent Kane to Jane Duval Leiper Kane (Oct. 25, 1856), APS Elisha Kent Kane papers.

155. Corner, 247. Corner, a physician who spent much time studying Elisha's illnesses, believes that he was suffering from "bacterial endocarditis with subacute bronchitis."

156. Elisha Kent Kane to John K. Kane (Nov. 15, 1856), APS Elisha Kent Kane papers.

157. Corner, 248-49.

7

The Death and Life of Dr. Kane

❧

The moment news of Elisha's illness reached the United States, people across the nation offered their hearts and homes to their arctic hero. Though he had never met Elisha, Lewis M. Hatch wrote that, like the rest of the nation, he "felt a deep interest in your welfare" and thus offered Dr. Kane his country estate outside of Charleston for his recovery. He noted proudly, "Many a stranger can bear grateful testimony to the goodness of our ladies as nurses."[1] Similarly, a young lady named Marian—who reminded Dr. Kane that they had met when she was six years old—wrote from San Francisco: "You are sick—will you not come to California this next Winter? I feel sure our climate would restore you." Not wanting him to get the wrong impression she added, "Do you think that I am a moon-struck damsel who writes to you because you are a fit hero for romance?— Far from it. I am a calm quiet woman."[2] Other people offered poetry instead of hospitality. Elizabeth H. Whittier, sister of poet John Greenleaf Whittier, pleaded to Cuba in verse, asking it to restore Dr. Kane's health,

> A noble life is in thy care,
> A sacred trust to thee is given:
> Bright Island! let thy healing air
> Be to him as the breath of Heaven.[3]

When news of Dr. Kane's death reached America, this outpouring of feeling became a deluge. A paper from Elisha's hometown proclaimed: "Wherever the news of his death has penetrated, there are the same spontaneous manifestations, which prove how deeply the public mind has been impressed by the event."[4] The day after Elisha's death, the American consul in Havana called together all the U.S. citizens on the island and announced that the captain-general of Cuba, Don José de la Concha, had offered official condolences from Spain. During the four weeks that passed between this ceremony and the body's final interment in Philadelphia, thousands of Americans in thirteen Northern and Southern states attended dozens of ceremonies organized by the small towns and cities through which Dr. Kane's funeral procession passed.[5] No one person planned this long procession, but the Kane family, with the enthusiastic support of George W. Childs, facilitated it. Instead of sending the body on steamer directly from Havana to New York and on to Philadelphia, they chose a long and winding route through the heart of the nation to provide Americans from the deep South to the Quaker state the chance to celebrate their fallen hero.[6]

On February 20, a company made up of eight hundred people and two military bands carried Elisha's body to Havana's *Plaza de Armas*. After a brief speech by the governor of Havana, Tom, John, Mrs. Kane, and Morton joined the body aboard the steamer *Cahawba*, which carried them to New Orleans, arriving on February 22.[7] City officials were awaiting their arrival and an assembled corps of "Continental Guards" carried Elisha's body to City Hall, where it lay in state for the night. The next morning a large procession of Masons, army and navy men, and civic societies and clubs marched the coffin to the Mississippi steamboat, *Woodford*. The New Orleans *Evening Delta* wrote: "Strange that even the corpse of the Arctic wanderer is traveling still. Poor Kane was a true martyr to science, and there is a genuine sanctity in his coffin, worth the prestige of a thousand conquerors."[8]

During the week-long passage up the Mississippi and Ohio rivers, people lined smalltown wharves to see Dr. Kane. Soon after the procession passed from the Mississippi to the Ohio River, the Kane family met the *Woodford* in Paducah, Kentucky, and traveled with it to greet the massive ceremony that awaited them in Louisville. A long parade of civic, professional, and social organizations carried Elisha's body from the steamer to Mozart Hall, where it lay in state, surrounded by an honor guard. The Louisville Bar members wrote Judge Kane, "We need not assure you that a nation claims a participation in your grief. You must know that the reputation of your son belongs to the American people, and will be cherished as part of the Nation's wealth."[9] Exhausted and anticipating similar ceremonies at the rest of the stops along the way, Judge and Mrs. Kane took quick passage from Louisville back to Philadelphia to prepare quietly for their son's burial. Elisha's three brothers remained with the steamer as it crossed from Louisville to New Albany, Indiana, and then chugged its way up the Ohio to Cincinnati.[10]

Cincinnati, which had a bit more time to prepare for the event, put together a massive procession that included thirty-one pall-bearers and all branches of Ohio society, ranging from the governor to the Butchers' Benevolent Association. They sent their own boats down the Ohio to accompany the body up from New Albany and, once they reached Cincinnati, they transferred the coffin from boat to rail by parading it up from the Fifth Street wharf to the depot of the Little Miami Railroad. Before being loaded onto the train, the casket—bearing the Masonic insignia and wrapped in an enormous U.S. flag—was placed on display for several hours while a series of local dignitaries made their heartfelt remarks.[11] From Cincinnati the train slowly passed through Ohio, stopping briefly at many of the small towns along the way. At several locations, the townspeople had draped the depots in black cloth. The crowds in Xenia, Ohio, were so great that they flooded the tracks and delayed the train's progress on to Columbus.

The train arrived in the state capital at midnight, where there was another procession, accompanied by the solemn sound of muffled drums, that carried Elisha's body to the senate chamber of the State House, where it again lay in state. In the days that followed, town after town in Ohio, Virginia (now West Virginia), and Maryland staged public displays of their pride and grief.[12] Ceremonies and eulogies were not limited to the towns through which the hero's body passed, however. Newspapers in Chicago celebrated Dr. Kane's illustrious career and preachers in Roxbury, Massachusetts, publicly declared his "inestimable value" to the nation. In Harrisburg, the speaker of the Pennsylvania House stopped the chamber's daily proceedings to note that Dr. Kane's name was being "spoken in every tongue," as "boys shouted it in the streets, and sages muttered it over the midnight lamp. It was canvassed by the peasant at his toil, and the monarch heard it upon his throne." To this cacophony of mourning he noted, "I cannot refrain on this occasion from adding my tribute of respect to the memory of the dead."[13]

On Tuesday, March 10, Elisha's casket, having been transferred first to the cars of the Central Ohio Railroad and then to a specially prepared car of the B&O line, arrived in Baltimore, where it was greeted by an enormous crowd. There, for the first time in the weeks of ceremonies and speeches, Elisha was eulogized by someone who actually knew him, not as the heroic image of Dr. Kane, but as himself. Former Secretary of the Navy John Pendleton Kennedy had known Elisha for years and was keenly aware of both his talents and faults. Before a packed crowd he said: "A Gentler spirit and a braver were never united in one bosom. He possessed the modest reserve of the student with the ardent love of adventure and daring, which distinguished the most romantic sons of chivalry." Kennedy wrote privately to the Kane family: "Now that these rites have been performed and time has been allowed for reflection, I trust that remembrance of them will bring solace to your sufferings.... It was the happy fortune of your son to achieve in youth a fame which the oldest and the best would be proud to win... even at the price at which it has been secured."[14] Kennedy here recognized what few others did—Dr Kane's heroic fame had cost Elisha his life.

Elisha Kent Kane lying in state in Independence Hall, Philadelphia. From William Elder, *Biography of Elisha Kent Kane* (Philadelphia: Childs & Peterson, 1858).

The next day, after two more brief stops in Wilmington, Delaware, and Chester, Pennsylvania, Elisha's body finally reached Philadelphia, the city of his birth. With great and solemn pomp, a massive procession followed eight of Elisha's former crewmembers (Bonsall, Brooks, Godfrey, Goodfellow, Hayes, Hickey, Morton, and Stephenson), who carried his casket to Independence Hall, where it lay in state for the final time. During that night and the next morning, hundreds of citizens filed through the hall to pay their last respects. At 10:00 A.M. a procession made up of six divisions and dozens of groups paraded the casket through town, placing it finally at the front of the Kane family's home church—Second Presbyterian. After a final ceremony, Elisha's body made its last journey to its resting place, the Kane family vault in the Laurel Hill Cemetery.[15]

During the solemn celebration surrounding Elisha's death, only one oblique sign of Margaret Fox's connection with Elisha attracted any public notice—a large wreath bearing the benign message "To the Memory of Dr. E. K. Kane, from Two Ladies" that Maggie and Kate sent anonymously.[16] In April 1857 Maggie's mother contacted Patterson because, after Elisha's death, Sylvia Grinnell had told her that Elisha had left provisions for Maggie in his will.[17] A few months later, Maggie also began writing. Her initial letters were friendly, even flirtatious, but when it became clear that Patterson did not intend to honor the will, they became increasingly threatening. She sought help from the Grinnells, but they distanced themselves from the ordeal, not wanting to take sides. By December she wrote Patterson disgustedly, "The fact is you are all a set of cross kings."[18]

At this time, despite the Kane family's best efforts, the American public was still aware and curious about Maggie and Elisha's relationship. Two months after Dr. Kane was laid to rest, editor and politician E. Pershine Smith wrote a friend, "I am sorry to be informed that being thoroughly in love with Miss Fox, [Dr. Kane] had not the courage to marry her against the opposition of his family. The passion and the cowardice are both strange & the latter painful as diminishing one's respect for what I had thought a heroic character."[19] Maggie used the public's curiosity to her advantage, pesenting Elisha's love letters to the Kane family as a bargaining chip. After proving their existence by sending copies of a few of them to Patterson, she wrote in May 1858, "The letters are mine to guard and cherish so long as I live and when I am no longer able to guard them, I will place them with you. But do not think me so lost as to ever allow them to be published."[20] This passive but pointed mention of publishing the letters roused Patterson's attention, and in her next letter, Maggie kept him attentive by casually mentioning her friend "Mrs. Ellet of magazine celebrity." Elizabeth F. Ellet was a New York writer and publisher who specialized in gossipy biographies and histories, exactly the sort of person to whom the Kane family did not want Maggie talking.[21] Not long after Maggie first mentioned Mrs. Ellet, Patterson began sending her funds when she requested them, usually through Father William Quinn, a New York priest whom Maggie had gone to for solace after Elisha's death.

On August 15, 1858, for the first time since Elisha's death, Maggie again made headlines when she, one of the founders of spiritualism, was baptized into the Catholic faith at New York's St. Peter's Cathedral.[22] Years earlier Elisha had encouraged her to embrace Catholicism in an attempt to keep her away from spiritualism. Her decision to honor this request in 1858 seems to have been largely designed to demonstrate her wifely compliance to these

The Kane family vault at Laurel Hill Cemetery, Philadelphia. From William Elder, *Biography of Elisha Kent Kane* (Philadelphia: Childs & Peterson, 1858).

wishes because just five days afterward she had her attorney, Rush Hawkins, write Patterson an informal but pointed letter asking for a copy of Elisha's will. Mr. Hawkins explained, "I am of the opinion that Margaretta Fox was... lawfully married to your Brother, and that she is now justly entitled to bear his name."[23] From this time forward Maggie always signed her name "Margaret Fox Kane." A few days later the Kane family received another letter, this one from an anonymous concerned friend who wondered if they were aware that Maggie had turned over her correspondence with Elisha to Mrs. Ellet. "Of course," the friend noted, "publishers would offer high for such a work as it would have an immense sale."[24] Though the anonymous author suggested that he was writing without Maggie's knowledge and completely for the benefit of the Kane family, it is likely that the opposite was true. The letter suggested that the Kane family should try to pay Maggie to be quiet (exactly what Maggie wanted) and ended almost threateningly, "I feel sorry that such a blight should come upon such a name—and should really grieve for his mother under the circumstances."[25] Adding further force to this situation was the fact that Maggie had many influential friends. Soon after Maggie's baptism, she, Kate, and their mother gave up their large house at 50 East Twenty-Second Street and moved into a home at 35 East Nineteenth Street, a residence supplied to them by Horace Greeley, editor of the *New York Tribune*.[26] Greeley had helped and housed the Fox sisters several times before, and his continuing support—he not only housed Kate and Maggie but hosted Leah's wedding in November of 1858—forced the Kane family to recognize that ignoring Maggie's demands could have serious social repercussions.

All of this caused Patterson to act quickly. Though the terms of their agreement were not clearly spelled out, after consulting with his family, Patterson agreed to cover Maggie's expenses if she promised to stop the publication of the book—a process that had been moving along quickly; a complete draft was edited and ready for press, thanks to the efforts of Ellet.[27] Maggie's next letter to Patterson was cold and blunt. In the past five years she had moved from being one of the most well-known and self-sufficient women in America to being a woman with a damaged reputation who had to resort to blackmail to get the funds she needed to live. She had trusted Elisha and abandoned spiritualism to become the "proper" woman he wanted her to be, but everything had gone wrong. She acknowledged her shame to Patterson, admitting that "to me a private marriage is quite as disgraceful as to stand in another light," but insisting that "our honorable engagement you can never deny." Her letter ended stoically: "The Margaret that Dr. Kane loved is dead. I am simply a Margaret without a heart, void of love or affection. So when you visit me, you can be as cross and bitter as you please.... No Mr. Kane, nothing now that you could say will ever cause even a frown."[28]

This arrangement between Patterson and Maggie continued smoothly for the next three-and-a-half years. Patterson sent funds to Father William Quinn, who managed Maggie's financial affairs, and Maggie turned her letters and the manuscript over to Father Quinn, who agreed to hold them in strict confidence.[29] As the years passed, however, the explosive nature of the letters lessened because the public eye turned from Dr. Kane to the horrors of the Civil War. Patterson began to ignore his family's agreement with Maggie, so in the summer of 1861 she applied to the Widow and Orphan's Court to force Tom, as Elisha's executor, to officially file his account of the arrangement between her and Elisha's estate. Tom could not respond, however, because at the start of the Civil War he had organized the Thirteenth Pennsylvania Reserves for the Union Army and by June 1861 he and his "Bucktail Regiment" were stationed at Camp Mason Dixon near Cumberland, Maryland, awaiting orders that would soon send them south into some of the bloodiest battles of the war.[30] In his absence, Patterson again stepped forward to manage Maggie for his family. At the advice of Tom's hired counsel, Constant Guillo, they refrained from addressing Fox at all and instead cited a state law that precluded soldiers from legal suits, arguing that her request of Tom was thus invalidated. The judge rejected this interpretation of the law, but ruled that the Kanes could wait until the fall of 1862 to comply with the suit.[31]

Delayed from legal action for a year, Maggie kept pressure on the Kane family by informing them that she had given her manuscript and love letters to the New York publishing company Rudd & Carleton to be stereotyped. Now it was the Kanes' turn to seek court action. Under Tom's name as executor, they filed an injunction to have the letters blocked, claiming they were legally part of Elisha's estate and thus under Tom's control, but their past legal maneuvering worked against them. Citing the same law they used to delay Fox's initial suit, the court ruled that Tom's presence was necessary to make the request and so refused to grant the injunction. This frightened the family greatly. They had only a few months left before the court would force them to explain Fox's relationship to Elisha's estate, and now Fox was publishing a manuscript that persuasively argued that she was Elisha's rightful wife. If she won her suit and the court legally ruled her his widow, she could win not just the $5,000 mentioned in the will, but potentially half his entire estate—money that the Kane family was using to support their elderly mother because Judge Kane had passed away suddenly in 1858, leaving behind much property, but also substantial debt. As Tom's wife Bessie noted in her journal, if Fox was successful in her suit, it would bring "ruin to Mother's estate, and shame and scandal upon our honored name."[32]

During this entire controversy, Bessie acted as Tom's eyes and ears, taking careful note of all that went on. Of Fox's book she wrote, "Mr. Guillo says the letters will undoubtedly be altered and <u>strengthened</u>. We do not know their contents, but Patterson and he implied their belief that they would be fulsome passion letters— I cannot say love in connection with this creature." Having been tipped off to the full content of the book, they knew Fox was claiming that, in the days before El-

Portrait of Maggie Fox. From *The Love-Life of Dr. Kane* (New York: Carleton Publisher, 1866).

isha had left for England, he had instigated a private ceremony, announcing to a group of witnesses that they were man and wife. Patterson was unable to find out who these witnesses were (he was hoping to be able to discredit them), and this alarmed him greatly because, as Bessie noted, "he tells me that saying before witnesses 'I have chosen you for my wife' or 'We have been one these two weeks' or such phrases, constitutes a lawful marriage." Bessie guessed that Patterson's panic was greatly increased because both he and Mr. Guillo thought that it was "extremely probable that Elisha was bewitched into some such weak folly." If the case went to court, she was sure Maggie would win because the decision would be made by "a jury who of course will be well filled with accounts of the proud Kanes who won't acknowledge the pretty widow in her deep needs, etc, etc."[33]

Bessie's account of this incident provides an essential glimpse into the Kane family's assumptions and actions regarding Fox. Although prominent, the Kanes were not especially wealthy during the 1860s. Elisha's book had earned well, but by 1862, according to Patterson, his estate was completely spent. He did not spell out the exact details of what had happened to the money, but it is fairly easy to guess how the estate lost its value. In 1857, the same year as Elisha's death, the nation suffered a massive economic crash. Then, with the start of the Civil War, like many other families North and South alike, the Kanes likely lost a great deal of money because of investments that were in some way rooted in Southern interests. Judge Kane and his sons were aggressive investors and speculators, which brought them great gains at times, but it also opened them to massive losses during market downturns. For example, in the months before Elisha's death, the family was heavily involved with the fledgling S & E Railroad, which they feared was going to flop, taking their money with it.[34] Once the war started, business was again disrupted to a large degree. In her journal, Bessie noted that Patterson had invested large sums, including $3,000 of Tom's money, with "B. Phillips" who then "swindled him out of all his savings."[35]

In March 1862, to prevent Maggie's suit from going before a jury, Patterson tentatively offered her the $5,000 named in the will as well as routine interest payments on another $5,000 that would be paid to her for the rest of her life. In exchange, Maggie was to deposit all the love letters and the book manuscript with Dr. Edward Bayard, who would act as their trustee.[36] This offer appealed to Maggie. As a woman well aware of the sensibilities of her era, she knew that her lawsuit could easily prove to be more damaging than beneficial. She could lose her suit and wind up with no money. Furthermore, she was not especially excited about the idea of publishing her manuscript. It was a public airing of private matters, something strictly taboo in Victorian America. The public could easily turn against such a document and view her not as a wronged and slandered victim, but as a blackmailing scoundrel deserving of the misfortune she was suffering. Just such a fate had recently befallen another prominent woman, Sara Payson Willis, the highly successful author who wrote under the pseudonym, "Fanny Fern." In 1855 she published a thinly veiled biography, *Ruth Hall*, that condemned her famous literary brother, Nathanial Parker Willis, for his mistreatment of her. The public was titillated by these details, and gobbled up her book, but at the same time they condemned her for her pride, vengefulness, vulgarity, and blatant lack of feminine virtue.[37] It is not surprising, then, that Fox accepted Patterson's offer, but she did so only on the condition that the money was "secured by mortgage." Patterson refused this request, but gave his personal security. Patterson did not have $5,000 to give, but arranged to borrow it from his father-in-law, the wealthy businessman, Joshua Francis Fisher.[38]

Observing all of this, Bessie was uncertain which course she wanted the family to follow. She was certain Elisha would have wanted them to protect his reputation and that Tom would try to "save Elisha at any cost," but Elisha was dead and they were sorely lacking in funds. Why agree to give away $5,000 that they did not have? In her journal she exclaimed, "Is it right to hazard all, nay to give away all we have, to avert this shame?" But, "On the other hand," she continued, "if she proves her claim, she can shame us by this book, and at the same time render us quite as poor."[39] Then there was another problem. After noting all the financial implications of the situation, Bessie acknowledged a fact that bothered her far more. "I only learned yesterday, she had a child. It has much altered the case to me. Whether he legally acknowledged her as his wife or not, he sold his birth right for this mess of pottage. His union with her was a sin, or a folly. If he chose to buy her body, and this child is proof that he did, he knew the price would be heavy. He is dead, thank God, and pardoned, I hope, but we know he would <u>now</u> pay any price to be rid of her. Now she demands her price... ought we not to do what he would have prayed us to do?"[40] Conflicted, she wrote to Tom for advice on how to proceed. She summed up the family's dealings with "that wretched woman," and carefully spelled out that it wasn't clear whether Fox could prove a legal marriage or not. She told Tom that if Fox could prove the marriage, she could "squeeze us well, as well as mortify us." In her mind, this was actually the better of the two scenarios because if Fox didn't prove marriage, Bessie was quite sure she could prove "what you and I call adultery," and this would cause the family to "suffer more than in the first case." In her closing comments to Tom, Bessie's understanding of Maggie's situation is remarkably perceptive and guardedly compassionate. She despised Fox and was appalled that she would threaten to make such private affairs public, but she was sure that, one way or another, Elisha had wronged Maggie and the family needed to make some sort of restitution. She wrote: "If Elisha seduced her, she sold herself and he bought her.... If he purchased all she had to sell, we can't turn round, and asserting the worthlessness of the commodity refuse to pay the price. If on the other hand she had some virtue, really loved him, and was really educating [to be] his honorable wife, and either was or was not married to him—but has suffered enough to impair her value as a wife for any one else, ought we not to maintain her?"[41]

It is important to note that even though she wrote of Maggie's child as blunt fact in her journal, Bessie made no such definite statement in her letters to Tom. This journal entry is even more intriguing because it is the only surviving document that overtly states that Maggie had Elisha's child. In later years Maggie oversaw two "tell all" books about her life, but neither mentions a child, and in the many letters between the Kane family and Fox, though she often enumerates the many wrongs done her, she never mentions a pregnancy.[42] Despite this, there is circumstantial evidence that suggests that she may have had Elisha's child. It is clear that, whether secretly married or not, Elisha and Maggie were deeply intimate in the months before his departure for England in October 1856. As discussed earlier, in the fall of 1856 they spent much time alone in Maggie's third-story private room, and in his letters to her he was explicit about his passion, calling her his Circe and exclaiming that "you have already changed me into a wild Boar."[43] Then there is also the strange silence from Maggie after Elisha's death. In her own account, she stated that she was afflicted by "an illness of many months" and that during this time she was "shut up in a dark room, utterly inconsolable, and unable to bear the light of day."[44]

It is odd that Fox did not contact the Kane family until months after Elisha's death. Her first correspondence was through her mother, who wrote to Patterson in the spring of 1857, explaining that the Grinnells had informed her that Elisha had "remembered [Maggie] to the last" by providing for her in his will. She also cryptically noted, "Her trials have been (as you must already know) greater than she could bear, and we fear that unless changes soon take place she cannot survive them much longer. I wish you would come at once."[45] Then, in the early summer of 1857, Maggie began writing Patterson. In a letter that was polite but familiar she noted that "the Dr. must have left some message for me," and asked Patterson to bring it to her.[46] In another, like her mother's letter before, she alludes to some secret. "My Dear Mr. Kane, I wish that you would call on me at your earliest convenience. Now that you know all, I can no longer wear a mask, at least in your presence."[47] Maggie left New York and headed for Cleveland shortly thereafter. Mid-June, 1857, is nine months after mid-September, 1856, when Maggie returned from Canada and spent several weeks of intimate time with Elisha. A strange bit of material culture survives from Maggie's time in Cleveland—a cross-stitched poem dated "Cleveland, June 16, 1857" and entitled "To My Sister Kate." It reads:

> I present thee a rose Kate,
> A rose I present unto thee,
> I know it is sweet and 'tis pretty
> Then wilt thou accept it of me.
> Tis fresh from the stem where it was blooming
> And filled all with nectar and dew,
> Its fragrance how sweet and presuming,
> Its blushes remind me of you.
> From your sister, Maggie[48]

While tantalizing, none of this proves that Maggie bore Elisha's child. Bessie's comment is provocative, but it cannot be substantiated. As the events surrounding Elisha's efforts to hide his lovechild with Julia Reed in 1846 show, in the mid-nineteenth century it was quite possible to conceal a pregnancy via geographical movement and the use of pseudonyms. If Maggie was pregnant, she would have wanted to conceal this fact because she had not been publically married. Given this, moving to Cleveland would have been a sensible idea. She had friends there thanks to her 1851 tour, and they could have quietly passed her off as a pregnant grieving widow. It is impossible to know if this is why she went to Cleveland, but it is clear that though documents show that Maggie was there in 1857, the press never reported her presence, which is odd.[49]

What transpired in the months immediately before and after Elisha's death remains a mystery, but although the facts are not clear, the Kane family's perceptions are. Though they publicly denied any connection between Elisha and Maggie, Bessie and Tom's correspondence shows that privately they believed just the opposite. They were certain of his engagement and sure that he had intended to leave her money in his will. Far more profoundly, they also believed that he had conducted a marriage ceremony (perhaps legal, perhaps not) to convince Maggie to consummate their relationship, and that this consummation resulted in a child. With this unpleasant predicament before them, and after much family debate, Patterson worked out a financial agreement between Maggie and his family. Backing off from his initial offer of $5,000, Patterson informed Maggie that they would pay her $2,000 up front and a yearly stipend of $450 for the rest of her life.[50] Although it was not what she wanted, Maggie agreed. As specified by the agreement, she dropped her suit against Elisha's estate and gave her letters and book manuscript to Dr. Edward Bayard of New York, a mutual friend of Maggie and the Kanes, to be held in trust until the time of her death when all the material would transfer to the Kanes. After borrowing the initial $2,000, Patterson began making payments to Maggie, but not regularly. Over the next three years Patterson become more and more delinquent in his payments, and though Dr. Bayard constantly pleaded with him to keep up his end of the bargain, by May 1865, under the pressure of an impending law suit by Mrs. Ellet at Maggie's behest, Bayard returned the letters and manuscript to Maggie in recognition of the Kanes' refusal to honor their agreement.[51] By September 1865, the book was again ready to go to press. Patterson threatened legal action against Mrs. Ellet but backed down after she reminded him of his "dishonest and disreputable" dealings with Maggie and promised that she would not be "slandered with impunity—especially by a person whom it would be so easy to unmask before the community."[52]

Under such headlines as "Curious Romance of Dr. Kane," newspapers across the country cited a correspondent for the *Rochester Union*, noting that he was "fully conversant with all that is stated," and thus able to provide a brief summary of the forthcoming book about the "Love-Life of Dr. Kane." Each paper slightly reworded the story, but most expressed sympathy toward Fox, condemnation for the Kane family, and a belief that the narrative would "show the world a singular example of faithful love, enduring through unkindness and calumny." Some contained a note that "a Philadelphia dispatch denies the whole story," but this was usually tacked on after the main article supporting Fox's narrative."[53] Then in October a correspondent from New York, claiming to be "acquainted with the persons cognizant of the entire affair," provocatively noted that Dr. Kane had been "infatuated with the girl" and that "this peculiar intimacy raised Kane in more senses than one." The writer further claimed that, "family pride was the sole reason Kane had for not wedding Margaretta openly," and insisted that he knew that the doctor had written "to some of his most confidential friends that he could not conquer his passion; that he had struggled with it in vain; that it would destroy his usefulness in life, and finally he overcame temptation by yielding to it, making her his wife." He lambasted the Kane family for denying the relationship, insisting that "they knew better," and concluded by saying, "Strange, that a strong, brave man, who dared all the terrors of an Arctic winter and a Polar sea, was not courageous enough to brave public opinion in following the promptings of his heart."[54]

The Love-Life of Dr. Kane came out at the end of 1865 and the public hardly noticed. People accepted the letters as true, but found nothing shocking about them except that Maggie had been insensitive enough to publish them. Bessie Wood Kane wrote to her sister-in-law: "The dreaded Book seems to be a molehill compared to what we feared.... If that is all, the Book will in no way detract from poor Elisha's credit." It is telling that in this letter to her family, Bessie did not question the book's account of the relationship; instead she noted that it was both endearing and accurate, "I confess," she concluded, "the description touched me."[55] In its review of the book, the *New York Times* regarded it "as an intrusion of private matters before that many-headed monster, the Public—the last body in the world that should be selected to exercise the functions of a court of appeal for the redress of individual grievances." They thus condemned Maggie for its publication while noting that the book, despite its racy title, contained "nothing in it that either party concerned need be ashamed of." In fact, they found Dr. Kane's letters to be "full of the open hearted, generous enthusiasm that might be expected from the heroic mold of his character."[56]

Though *Love-Life* did vindicate her claims and cause the public to address her as "Mrs. Kane" for the rest of her life, it was ultimately disasterous for Maggie. It earned her little money and much criticism, further estranged her from the spiritualist community, and cost her the one bargaining chip that had provided her funding during the years since Elisha's death.[57] With no other resources available to her (both her parents passed away in 1865 and she was estranged from Leah), Maggie was forced to return to the séance table. Within the year, both she and Kate were severe alcoholics. Horace Greeley and Dr. Edward Bayard offered to pay for them to enter the Swedish Movement Cure clinic to help rid them of the bottle; Kate accepted but Maggie refused.[58] Maggie's next twenty years were a constant struggle with alcoholism, depression, and financial want. She spent several years in England working as a medium, and briefly served as the medium in residence for Henry Seybert's "Spritual Mansion" in Philadelphia.[59] Seybert passed away in 1883, but he willed funds to the University of Pennsylvania for the further study of spiritual phenomena. The Seybert Commission formed in 1884 and invited Maggie to participate. The salary they offered prompted her to accept the position, but she staunchly refused to make any claim about the otherworldly nature of the "raps." She told the commission, "Leave others to judge for themselves."[60] She stayed on with the Seybert Commission for two seasons, but turned down an invitation to come back for a third because of illness.

Kate Fox faired better than her sister during this time. Dr. George Taylor, who founded the vastly successful Swedish Movement Cure clinic in New York, took Kate on as a patient in 1865. When her funds ran out, he and his wife Sarah kept her on in exchange for her serving as a medium to the spirits of their departed children, Frankie and Leila.[61] Despite this stable situation, Kate continued to struggle with alcohol, so in the fall of 1871 the Taylors and other concerned friends arranged for Kate to travel to England, hoping the trip would cure both her depression and increasingly debilitating addiction. She met respected London barrister Henry Dietrich Jencken shortly after her arrival, and they were married the next year. Jencken was a believer in spiritualism and supported his new bride fully. They soon had two children, Ferdinand and Henry, Jr., and while Jencken maintained an active professional schedule that often took him away from London Kate continued to have séances in their home, though they were always quiet, private affairs. The family split their time between Jencken's home in England and New York, where they would reside with either Leah or the Taylors. For the first time since her childhood, Kate experienced a stable, happy family life. This all came to an end in November 1881 when her husband suffered a fatal stroke, leaving her with two young children and little money. Needing to make a living, she went back to public séances, and with no good reason to remain in England, she moved back to the United States by the summer of 1885. She lived briefly with Leah, but then moved to her brother David's house in Hydesville, New York, where her rapping carreer had began nearly four decades earlier.[62]

In this same year, Leah (who in 1858 had quietly married a successful businessman, Daniel Underhill, and settled into a respectable, middle-class lifestyle) published a book entitled *The Missing Link in Modern Spiritualism*, which told her version of the Fox family's impact on the founding of modern spiritualism. The

The Fox sisters as pictured in Leah Fox Underhill's *The Missing Link In Modern Spiritualism* (New York: Thomas R. Knox & Co., 1885).

MARGARETTA FOX-KANE   KATE FOX-JENCKEN   LEAH UNDERHILL

book's fantastic stories of poltergeists and aggressive spirits that guided her and her sisters' careers troubled Kate and Maggie. Though neither initially denounced the book, their displeasure with it grew to abhorrence in the following years. Spiritualism had gained Leah fame, financial security, and, with her marriage to a prominent business man, respectability as well. When her book came out, both Maggie and Kate were nearly destitute, and this sharpened their long-held feelings that their elder sister had built her life through their exploitation; her book was just one more example of this.[63] The spiritualist movement that Leah so triumphantly celebrated in her book had not been nearly so beneficial for her younger sisters. Maggie (and Kate to a lesser extent) struggled with the implications of their involvement with spiritualism. Although they did believe, at least to some degree, in the existence of spirits, they knew that when raps echoed through their séance chambers it had far more to do with their own cunning than any spiritual communication. Maggie especially wondered what this would ultimately mean for her own immortal soul, and tried to move away from the spiritualist movement and toward a more mainstream, middle-class lifestyle. Even when she did return to the séance table for financial reasons, her cards always included the statement: "MRS. KANE DOES NOT CLAIM ANY SPIRIT POWER; BUT PEOPLE MUST JUDGE FOR THEMSELVES."[64] By 1885, Maggie and Kate were in dire financial situations and both were still struggling with alcoholism. Then in May 1888, disaster struck when Kate was arrested in Harlem for drunkenness and charged with neglecting her fourteen and twelve-year-old sons, who were sent to the Juvenile Asylum. Both Kate and Maggie suspected that Leah, who saw herself as the protector and matriarch of the family, was behind Kate's arrest and the boys' removal, and were furious that she was again meddling in their lives. When the boys were released a few weeks later, Kate immediately took them to London to join Maggie, who was there conducting séances. Once together, they launched a publicity tirade against spiritual "fanatics" in an effort to refute Leah's book and to destroy her influence over them once and for all. Writing a letter to the *New York Herald*, Maggie raged against spiritualism, calling it "a curse" and insisting that no matter what form it took (rappings, séances, spirit-writing, etc.) "it is, has been and always will be a curse and a snare to all who meddle with it."[65] Within a few months Maggie, Kate, and the boys returned to New York where Maggie immediately granted a tell-all interview to *New York Herald* reporter Reuben Davenport. Davenport described her as "a small, magnetic woman... whose face bears the traces of much sorrow and of a world-wide experience," and noted that she was much agitated, and by her own admission, in a frantic state that had very nearly led her to suicide during her passage across the Atlantic. For his report, he began with the obvious question: How could she have been so deeply involved with a movement she now so adamantly hated? Maggie immediately launched into a tirade against Leah, saying that she had "made me take up with it." "She is my damnable enemy. I hate her. My God!" she continued, "I'd poison her! No, I wouldn't but I'll lash her with my tongue." She insisted that when the rappings first began, she and Kate "were but innocent little children" and that Leah had convinced them that the raps were spirits speaking through them and had thus lured them into believing. The price this had taken on Maggie was great. She said, "I used to say to those who wanted me to give a séance, 'You are driving me into hell.' Then the next day I would drown my remorse in wine." Maggie's next accusations were more telling, for they touched on the social and financial toll that spiritualism had taken on Kate and her. "Our sister used us in her exhibitions and we made money for her. Now she turns upon us because she's the wife of a rich man, and she opposes us both whenever she can."[66]

In this interview Maggie announced that she would give one final performance of the "spirit raps" to show once and for all that they and the movement they began were based on deception. With great publicity, including the publication of a book, *The Death-Blow to Spiritualism*, Maggie staged a grand performance on October 22, 1888, in New York City's Academy of Music. Standing before a large crowd, and with Kate providing supportive approval from a box seat, she sent forth a barrage of rapping noises that sounded from all corners of the hall. Laughing bitterly, she proclaimed that this "spiritual manifestation" was nothing other than the clever manipulation of the joints in her toes.[67] Newspapers across the country ran sensational headlines proclaiming spiritualism a humbug once and for all. The spiritualist community denounced Kate and Maggie as deranged drunks.

Though this performance and its subsequent tour provided her with funds for a while, it was not long before Maggie was again forgotten and destitute. Within a year of the "death-blow to spiritualism," she pitifully recanted her denial of spiritualism and returned to the séance table.[68] Sick and bitter, she struggled on, trying to make ends meet. Five years later, at the bottom of the last page of the March 5, 1893, edition of the *New York Times* a small notice appeared:

Margaret Fox Kane Destitute.

Margaret Fox Kane, one of the Fox sisters... is sick and destitute at the rooms she has long been occupying at the tenement house 456 West Fifty-seventh street. Though she is very ill, she will be dispossessed on Tuesday.[69]

A few days later a brief obituary noted that Margaret Fox Kane, one of the "once famous Fox sisters," had died—destitute, homeless, and forgotten.[70]

❧❧❧

From the time of his return from the arctic in 1855, Dr. Kane had become the personification of the hopes of the United States. He successfully managed his grumbling and divisive crew and saftely led them out of the sublime horrors of the arctic and back to civilization and safety. This made him a hero, but his book and George Childs' promotional efforts made him a nationwide celebrity. *Arctic Explorations* was an allegory for the times. It was a story of a brave man who reunited his quarrelsome and seceding crewmembers and led them from the brink of destruction to safety. Then, when Elisha died, his heroic persona, Dr. Kane, took on a tragic hue. From the announcement of Elisha's illness in December 1856 until the time of his burial in Philadelphia's Laurel Hill Cemetery in March 1857, Dr. Kane remained constantly in the public eye, and in the months and years that followed, his fame continued to grow. No longer tied to Elisha—the sickly physician with all his faults and passions—Dr. Kane achieved what no human could, perfection. As one minister proclaimed, "He thought like a philosopher—he wrote like a poet—he acted like a hero—he felt like a child—he lived like a man—he prayed like a Christian."[71] Elisha displayed each of these attributes at times in his life, but with Dr. Kane, these qualities could exist perfectly and simultaneously, without reservation or condition. Dr. Kane was an image, not a man, and could thus perfectly embody all the qualities Americans desired in themselves and expected in their heroes. More importantly, because this image was no longer tied to any specific person, party, cause, or agenda, Dr. Kane became a fluid symbol of American heroism that transcended many of the divisions that marked this turbulent era. Dr. Kane came to represent America—all of it—and many hoped that his example of triumphing over desperate odds might prove a healing catalyst that could rescue a nation on the verge of tearing itself asunder. Dr. Kane thus became the optimistic image of the era—a symbol of hope for a divided nation.

In an article entitled "Dr. Kane, Why We Honor Him," the Philadelphia *Evening Journal* perceptively noted that what the nation commemorated during Elisha's funeral was not the death of a man, but a longing for the ideals he had come to represent. In all the ceremonies, it explained, "the people do not so much worship the individual whose inanimate and unconscious remains they follow to interment, as that abstract idea of manly virtue and magnanimity, which his life embodied." This was a clear articulation of the difference between Elisha Kent Kane and Dr. Kane. Elisha was dead; no one was following him, but Dr. Kane marched on, and the nation followed because he had come to represent something they craved. Dr. Kane, like all heroes, was a reflection of his admirers—as the *Evening Journal* noted of heroes like Kane, "We see ourselves reflected in them... they are of the essence of that nature which we have in common with the loftiest examples of manhood." The nation's praise of Dr. Kane was an "expression to that conception of greatness, that love of exalted virtue, which is inherent in every human soul, though not revealed and realized in every human life."[72]

This article demonstrates what Leo Braudy has said of heroic fame—that a hero is created when a society holds up one of its members as a representative of the qualities they admire in, and desire for, themselves.[73] In the late-1850s, Dr. Kane filled this role for the United States. Once Elisha died, the public easily forgot all aspects of his less-than-perfect life in their eager adoration of the bravery, heroism, and success personified by Dr. Kane. As Civil War soldiers noted to Tom a few bloody years later, his brother Dr. Kane had been "the last hero of the United States of America."[74] Dr. Kane became a perfect hero for an imperfect time. As one magazine noted, his persona filled the nation's "desire for repose on some strong arm, while passing through the trial of time, this winter of eternity."[75] Dr. Kane was a malleable symbol, thus allowing vastly different groups embraced him for their own ends, each convinced that they, like their hero, represented the true America. This is nowhere more evident than in how Dr. Kane was used in the sectional conflict then brewing between the North and the South.

In the same month that *Arctic Explorations* appeared before the public, the nation was deciding its future in the presidential election between the slavery-sympathetic Democratic candidate, James Buchanan, and the newly formed free-land, free-labor Republican party's candidate, John C. Frémont. Then, just six days before Elisha's burial, the Supreme Court ruled on the *Dred Scott* case, handing down a decision that allowed slavery in the territories and called into question the legality of denying slavery anywhere in the union. This explosive decision destroyed the uneasy balance between the North and South. Elisha had remained neutral on the slavery question during his life, a necessity given his need to court support from both Northern and Southern individuals and institutions.[76] Furthermore, his family was split on the issue, making it impossible to look to them to determine what Dr. Kane believed. Judge Kane was praised by the South and hated by abolitionists for his pro-slavery rulings in the *Christiana* (1850) and *Passmore Williamson* (1855) cases. Tom was a staunch supporter of free-soil issues, heavily involved in the Underground Railroad, and widely praised by reform-minded Northerners for his efforts on behalf of oppressed groups, ranging from escaped slaves to Mormons.[77]

Dr. Kane's silence on the issue of slavery allowed both North and South to embrace him as their "native son." Because he was from Pennsylvania, Northerners automatically claimed him as their own. He was raised in Philadelphia, got his medical degree from the University of Pennsylvania, and as a man of science connected with many British institutions, he was, they were sure, against slavery and its expansion. This sentiment was most pronounced in the days directly following his return from the arctic when Northern papers condemned Judge Kane, who had just ruled on the *Passmore Williamson* case, and wondered how this pro-slavery man could produce such a noble son.[78]

The South did not wonder about Dr. Kane's relationship to Judge Kane, they celebrated it. They also noted that Dr. Kane had attended the University of Virginia for most of his college career, and had sought refuge in Cuba (which many Southerners viewed as a territory that would soon be theirs) when he was ill. New Orleans's *DeBow's Review*, a fervently pro-South literary journal, found nothing about Dr. Kane to be contradictory to Southern interests; in 1856 it placed a celebratory review of *Arctic Explorations* directly before a call to the "People of the Slaveholding States," rallying them to attend a meeting of the Southern Convention to discuss the misdeeds of the North.[79] Even more telling is a poem by John Esten Cooke that appeared in the *Southern Literary Messenger*. Playing on the fact that Dr. Kane was crippled by the arctic *north* and went to the *southern* isle of Cuba to recover, Cooke turned Kane's life, death, and funeral procession into an allegory of Northern oppression of the South.

> So take him! this is all the South "gives up,"
> The lifeless body of our hero-boy;
> He went from us in glory and in joy,
> He came again to die!—
> He came far in the Sunny South to die,
> He who had braved the terrors of the North.[80]

By capitalizing "North" and "South," and depicting the North with terror and sunless winters and the South with sunlight, flowers, and warmth, Cooke used Dr. Kane to express poetically the Southern belief that the industrial North was destroying the South's genteel agrarian culture. Dr. Kane represented all that was pure and good about the South, and he was coldly consumed by his harsh work in "the North." In this long allegorical poem, Cooke used Dr. Kane to represent America at its best—its "white and perfect bride"—and then showed that this pure perfection was crushed by the "terrors of the North." Dr. Kane returned to the solace of the South to recover, but it was too late; the North had done him in. Then, adding insult to injury, the South had to "give up" the body that represented all that they held dear, and send it back to the North to be buried in the cold ground. Such regional transgressions made conflict inevitable—"A bitter drop is in the golden cup," he concluded.[81]

Dr. Kane's neutral expression of American greatness allowed his image to be used by both Northern and Southern sectionalists, but it was far more common that his name was evoked as a uniting force for the troubled nation. In the week immediately following the *Dred Scot* decision, a poem depicting Dr. Kane as a hero who could unite a divided country appeared on the cover of *Harper's Weekly*. It exclaimed that his valiant deeds were celebrated in "Maine's deep woods" and the "mild Keystone State," as well as by "Hot Southern Lips, with eloquence aflame," and the "large-lunged West" which "From its giant breast / Yelled its frank welcome." Even "Texas, wild and grim, / Proffered Its horny hand" of welcome, thus uniting the country from "main to main." Using the seceding men of the *Advance* as an analogy for calls of Southern secession, the poem further praised the unifying power of Dr. Kane. When "whispers of rebellion, faint and few... grew / Into black thoughts of murder" Kane remained noble and by "ministering aid / To all around him" he "By a mighty will" remained "defiant of the wants that kill."[82]

In those times of turmoil, both Dr. Kane and his Open Polar Sea came to represent a panacea that inspired Americans to hope for better days. John Sampson, in his cultural evaluation of arctic narratives noted that "in the context of the mid-century turmoil that threatened to destroy America," stories of incredible suffering and endurance in the arctic reassured nineteenth-century citizens of "that indomitable American spirit."[83] Unlike most arctic narratives, however, Dr. Kane's *Arctic Explorations* did not stop at just providing a tale of humanity's ability to survive great suffering. Assaulted by both arctic cold and a mutinous crew, Kane persevered, bettering both the evils of nature and society. Then, he did something more. He discovered a beautiful new ocean at the top of the world. His narrative thus represented more than America's ability to survive; it put forth the possibility of a new and better world. Kane's Open Polar Sea surrounded by the harsh arctic became an inspirational allegory of the times; it promised that a better place of peace and beauty lay beyond the harsh and brutal environment through which the nation was then struggling. As a poem entitled "Dr. Kane and the Unknown Sea" put it:

> They say that far across those waters blue,
> There is a sinless land, a strange, mysterious shore ...
> Whose bright inhabitants shall never sorrow more.[84]

This and many other poems, including the widely praised three-part epic, "The Arctic Queen," published anonymously by the popular dime-novelist Metta Victoria Fuller Victor, firmly establish Dr. Kane as a hero of mythic proportions.[85] *Harper's Weekly* explained in the first months of 1860, "Of late years we have had no man who was so popularly a hero as Dr. Kane." His adventures had turned the arctic into a magical place much like "fairy land, or the England of Arthur," and for his readers, "certain names... had a kind of clear, polar music in them, but no meaning of locality. 'Lancaster Sound,' 'Prince Regent's Inlet,' 'King William's Land,' 'Melville Bay,' were names as familiar as Camelot and Caërleon, but as exquisitely vague." Grateful for this blending of reality and fantasy, *Harper's* noted that the "great moral of the Arctic... is this, that as man was sent into the world to replenish and subdue it, so there is no obstacle that he will not overcome."[86]

Given the tide of poems, speeches, eulogies, and celebrations in his honor, Dr. Kane's ubiquitous heroism appears to have been a spontaneous outpouring of emotion, and in some cases it was, but the story is more complex than this. Elisha's death did allow people to recast the image of Dr. Kane to best fit their needs, but they had help in this endeavor. The public embraced Dr. Kane for his heroic, scientific, and humanitarian efforts, but they did this largely because that was exactly what Dr. Kane's promoters encouraged them to do. There is no doubt that antebellum Americans loved the romance of scientific exploration and that they readily held up explorers as heroes (note both Kane and Western explorer John C. Frémont, who became the Republican party's first presidential candidate in 1856), but this does not tell the whole story. If it did, then many other men should have been far greater heroes than Kane or Frémont. Matthew Maury, Louis Agassiz, Asa Gray, Charles Darwin, and Alexander Humboldt were all far greater men of science and exploration. They too went on exciting adventures to exotic lands, and yet they were not celebrated as "models of heroic manhood" for one very simple reason— they were not promoted as such.

Describing the romantic "second great age of discovery," William H. Goetzmann has noted that changes in science and public heroism created a "wonderful paradox" in the last half of the nineteenth century: "As the activities of science became even larger, more organized, and more complex... the demand for individual explorer media heroes increased tenfold."[87] During this era, when science was growing more scientific and heroes more sensational, explorers who became heroes did so not because they were men of science, but because they were men of the press. Frémont led five expeditions through the American West and made many contributions to the nation's scientific knowledge through his discoveries. This made him heroic, but it did not make him a hero. He became a hero because his young and talented wife, Jessie Benton Frémont, and her father, Senator Thomas Hart Benton, enthusiastically promoted his expeditions to the American public.[88] Another explorer from this era, Henry Morton Stanley, demonstrates the importance of publicity even more clearly. Stanley became famous thanks to his 1869 trek through Africa to find the "lost" missionary, David Livingston. As they had done with Dr. Kane, the U.S. media celebrated Stanley because he explored an unknown and exotic land in search of a long-lost Englishman. This trip made him famous, not because of his geographical discoveries, which were substantial, but because of his sensational, self-promoting journal articles that were printed and promoted by James Gordon Bennett and his *New York Herald*.[89]

The world did not weep because Elisha Kent Kane the scientist died; they wept because an incredible amount of time and effort had gone into creating and promoting the heroic image of Dr. Kane, and this heroic image became magnificently tragic with Elisha's early death. Elisha was a dedicated scientist well deserving of the nation's tears, but this does not explain a thirteen-state, month-long funeral procession attended by thousands of Americans. The nation's ecstatic mourning of Dr. Kane was the result of years of effort by Elisha, his family, and George W. Childs to create a hero worthy of such sorrow. Dr. Kane did not continue to be a hero because of Elisha's contributions to science (his Open Polar Sea theory would be dismissed by most scientific agencies within a decade), but rather because of the many people and organizations that continued to promote Dr. Kane for their own, often money-making, purposes. In Elisha's death, as in his life, George W. Childs led this effort.

In the months following Elisha's death, Childs increased his efforts to make Dr. Kane a versatile and usable hero—one that the nation could love and, more importantly, consume. From 1855 when Elisha signed on with Childs & Peterson through the mid-1860s, Childs worked tirelessly to make Dr. Kane a desirable commodity that he could sell to the whole American public. *Arctic Explorations*, Childs' first Dr. Kane product, sold very well. Even taking into account Childs' propensity to exaggerate sales figures, this book sold at least 65,000 copies in its first year and 145,000 copies by 1860.[90] Childs used several other publishers to help him distribute this book all across the country: J.B. Lippincott & Co. of Philadelphia; Phillips, Sampson & Co. of Boston; G.P. Putnam & Co. of New York; and Applegate & Co. of Cincinnati.[91] This multiprong selling technique worked well, and within a few years, *Arctic Explorations* "was said to be found along with the Bible on every parlor table in the nation."[92]

In the fall of 1856, wanting to follow up on the success of *Arctic Explorations*, Childs had worked with Elisha to buy back the publication rights for his first book, which were still held by Harpers.[93] Childs went ahead with this project after Elisha's death and had the book ready for sale by the late spring of 1857. In his ads he exclaimed, "It should be owned by all who have purchased the last Expedition, as it makes DR. KANE'S works complete."[94] But Childs did not stop with this. Once Elisha died, he recognized that a biography would be the perfect book to complete his Dr. Kane series. As he had done with the biographical sketch the year before, he again commissioned Dr. William Elder, a friend of the Kane family, to write this book. The Kane family supported this project because they trusted Elder to preserve their son's reputation. This was especially important to them at this time because Maggie Fox had started to push for public recognition of her relationship with Elisha.[95] Fortunately for them, Childs and Elder envisioned the biography in much the same way they did. They wanted it to do for Elisha what Mason L. Weems's cherry-tree-chopping biography had done for George Washington a generation earlier—turn a great man into a faultless American hero.

Elder did his job quickly, completing the book in just eight months thanks largely to Childs' constant pressure. In his introduction Elder bitterly alluded to

Childs' impatience saying, "I have worked hard, under pressure of a clamorous impatience for the publication.... I have not been unpunctual. Moreover, I have had so very, very little help that my only temptation to affect thankfulness would be a division of the responsibility, which, in the strictest justice to all parties, rests exclusively upon myself."[96] The Kane family was happy with his work because he made no mention of Maggie and assured his readers that, after going through Dr. Kane's "private letters and memoranda," he had "not been obliged to suppress a letter or a line for the sake of his fame!"[97] In August 1857, four months before he released the book, Childs ran full-page ads in magazines pushing his full line of Kane products. Besides *Arctic Explorations* and his re-release of Elisha's first book (which he

This Childs & Peterson ad appeared in the back pages of *Emerson's United States Magazine* 5 (August 1857).

re-titled *Dr. Kane's First Narrative*), Childs now added Elder's biography and noted, "In announcing the LIFE OF DR. KANE, we are but anticipating the wishes of thousands and tens of thousands of the admirers of the great man." The ad assured readers that Elder was "well qualified to do justice to the subject" because he had been a personal friend of Dr. Kane and enjoyed "a large share of his confidence." It also stressed that all fans of Dr. Kane needed this book to complete the full set of Dr. Kane's works, and that it would be a beautiful addition to their library because it would "equal in every respect the superb volumes of 'ARCTIC EXPLORATIONS.'" The other important new item Childs introduced with this ad was "A Photograph of Dr. Kane, Taken from Life." In *Arctic Explorations*, Childs included a fine steel engraving of Elisha done from a portrait by the nation's leading photographer, Matthew Brady. This image was far different from the previous images of Dr. Kane because it showed him in full profile, dressed in a suit, and clean-shaven, except for an immaculately trimmed goatee. Similarly, for the biography, Childs included another image of the hero, "a new full-face portrait, executed on steel." This engraving, also taken from a picture by Brady, returned to an arctic theme—Dr. Kane was again bearded and wearing a heavy coat, suggesting his Northern adventures. Each of these images was copied and recopied in multiple publications, showing the public's desire for images of Dr. Kane. Childs, however, also offered the ultimate in Dr. Kane likenesses, an actual photograph of America's departed hero. In 1857, this was state-of-the-art technology and sold for a premium—five dollars—the same price as the cloth-bound two volume *Arctic Explorations* (also about the same amount the average worker earned in a week).[98]

To keep Dr. Kane in the public eye, Childs used publicity tactics that rivaled P. T. Barnum's in their ingenuity and execution. A few days before Dr. Kane's Philadelphia funeral, Childs paid to have Dr. Kane's rescue boat, the *Faith*, along with several other artifacts from the expedition, brought down from New York to Childs & Peterson's offices at 124 Arch Street. Then, immediately following Elisha's burial, Childs led Henry Grinnell and the members of Kane's crew to his offices for a public ceremony. This "solemn occasion" was a highly successful media event covered by several Philadelphia newspapers. Before a crowd of eager onlookers, Childs had the eight crewmembers demonstrate how they had packed their cargo into the small ship and where each of them had slept. The crowd was moved by this display, and, as one paper noted, it required "but little of the 'vision and the faculty divine' to imagine the memories which filled [the crew's] hearts and found thronging utterance." To end the event, Henry Grinnell presented the flag of the *Advance* to Childs who, in turn, handed it to Brooks and Morton, who carefully hung it on the wall above the *Faith*.[99] This display remained in the Childs & Peterson offices for several years—a solemn memorial that attracted audiences and encouraged book sales. In October 1860, Lady Jane Franklin visited it with the

The two engravings of Elisha Kent Kane commissioned by George W. Childs for Kane's *Arctic Explorations* and Elder's *Biography of Elisha Kent Kane.* These images were reprinted ubiquitously; the two examples here come from individual prints that sold in several different portrait galleries. Collection of Author.

Kane family and, as Elisha's sister Bessie recorded in her journal that evening, after Lady Jane viewed the small boat "she took me tenderly by the hand, kissed me and said 'You must have been quite a little girl when your poor brother was first interested in these things.'"[100]

Although Childs promoted Dr. Kane heavily, and profited greatly from his efforts, he was by no means the only person who used Kane's heroic image for his own purposes. Seeing the huge potential for sales, many publishers quickly put together their own Dr. Kane books. Just months after Elisha's death, two books by members of his crew appeared, printed by small, less-reputable presses. The first was by the expedition's bad-boy, William Godfrey. In his account, Godfrey indignantly retold the events of the expedition to prove that he was its hero, not the mutinous malcontent portrayed in *Arctic Explorations.* The introduction explained that the book would lay out "circumstances to be considered in connection with this matter" and was certain that its readers would find it difficult "to overlook the deliberate wrong which [Dr. Kane] has done to William C. Godfrey by making vague charges of delinquency against this man."[101] The book was meant to vindicate his name, but Godfrey must have been less than pleased with the final product. The publisher, wanting to capitalize on Dr. Kane's fame not attack it, paired Godfrey's narrative with a glowing sketch of Kane's life and packaged the two pieces together as one book.[102] The other book that came out at this time was *Sonntag's Thrilling Narrative*. It was less sensational but more controversial than Godfrey's because its content was largely fabricated by the book's publisher and was in no way endorsed by Augustus Sonntag, who was conveniently out of the country.[103] Anticipating accusations of fraud, the book's ghostwriter and first publisher, Charles C. Rhodes, noted in his preface that he had acquired a few of Sonntag's notes from the expedition and had written the book because "it would be almost criminal for any man who possesses such information to withhold it from the world."[104] Godfrey and Sonntag's narratives included sensational etchings of battles with polar bears, swarms of attacking Eskimos, and gigantic whirlpools over the north pole. Both of these books were inexpensive, selling for a dollar or less, compared to *Arctic Explorations'* five dollar price. Thus, despite their tawdry construction and questionable veracity, both sold well.[105]

Courtesy of the American Antiquarian Society.

William H. Shuster, "Kane's Funeral
March" (Philadelphia: Wm H. Shuster,
1857). Collection of Author.

Samuel Smucker, the author of many popular histories and biographies, also
jumped on the Dr. Kane bandwagon. In 1856, Smucker wrote *Arctic Explorations
and Discoveries during the Nineteenth Century,* a book outlining the era's many arctic expeditions. After Elisha's death, he changed the book's frontispiece to an engraving of Dr. Kane and extended the title, adding, "including the Final Effort of
Dr. E. K. Kane."[106] Smucker also quickly wrote a 135-page biography of Dr. Kane.
He combined this with several previously written biographical sketches of other
explorers and released it as an impressive 406-page book entitled, *The Life of Dr.
Elisha Kent Kane, and of other Distinguished American Explorers.* Both of these books
were quite successful, and over the next decade many different publishers marketed
them, changing nothing but the title page, and, in one case, the author's name—
Smucker becoming Schmucker.[107]

Books were not the only way to capitalize on Dr. Kane's fame. Thanks to at
least four different sheet music publications, many Americans could literally sing
Dr. Kane's praises in their own homes. As noted earlier, the "Polar Bear Polka" and
"Dr. Kane's Arctic Polka" came out in 1856 in celebration of Dr. Kane's return. The

next year, after Kane's death, two requiems appeared; the first, "He Sleeps, but not 'mid the Arctic Snow," was written for single voice and piano and was to be sung "andante religioso"—slowly and religiously. The other, "Kane's Funeral March," was a proud, solemn piece, full of pomp and gallantry. It was composed for coronets, trombones, and drums and was intended for a military band, but it was published in the form of a piano score, which made it as easy to perform in a parlor as on a bandstand. These pieces appeared with large engravings of Dr. Kane on their covers; a feature that certainly helped their sales.[108] In 1859 another piece celebrating Dr. Kane appeared, "The Fair Augusta Schottisch"—a fast-moving dance piece for piano and named in honor of the masthead of the *Advance*.[109]

Like composers, poets and writers also found inspiration in Dr. Kane. Newspapers and magazines filled with dozens of anonymous and obviously amateur-written poems that celebrated the triumph and tragedy of Dr. Kane, but accomplished poets also embraced him and used his name to increase the sales of their books. Popular poet George W. Chapman entitled his 1860 book, *A Tribute to Kane, and Other Poems*, and John Greenleaf Whittier published a dual volume of poems with his sister, Elizabeth H. Whittier, that included one of her poems to Dr. Kane.[110] At the end of the century, Jules Verne began publishing his "Doctor Hatteras" stories; these were modeled on Kane's narrative. Verne's *The Field of Ice* was essentially a fictional retelling of *Arctic Explorations*, complete with an Open Polar Sea.[111]

Dr. Kane's heroic persona was marketed well beyond the confines of the printed world of books, poetry, and sheet music. Panorama and cyclorama presentations, which used gigantic canvases hundreds of feet long that were either scrolled in front of a stage or displayed in the round, were hugely popular in antebellum America. Beginning in 1855 and continuing for more than a decade, several of these shows, featuring the arctic exploits of Dr. Kane, began criss-crossing the nation, playing to large crowds in the North, South, and West. In their study of arctic panoramas, Russell Potter and Douglas Wamsley found that even though these shows attracted large audiences that were familiar with Kane's literary works, they also pulled in "a significantly different audience" because they allowed "those who lacked the rudiments of literacy or geographical education" to join in the celebration of Dr. Kane.[112] At least four Kane panoramas toured the nation during the 1850s-1860s, and they often included an additional draw, such as a life-size wax statue of Dr. Kane, a dog (there were many) purported to be "Toodles," the sled dog Kane brought home with him, or, most impressively, an actual member of his crew, dressed in arctic garb, and narrating the show. During the late 1850s William Morton, James McGary and Thomas Hickey each toured with panorama shows at different times and Morton, with financial backing from the Kane family, became part owner of one of them.[113] Even using conservative estimates, these panoramas' combined attendance from 1855 to 1864 was in the hundreds of thousands.[114]

An advertisement from one of the many panorama shows touring the nation in the late-1850s. Courtesy of the American Antiquarian Society.

Magic Lantern shows were another popular entertainment medium of the era and they too quickly catered to the Dr. Kane market. Magic Lanterns, the forerunner of modern projectors, used a magnifying lens and a candle, gaslight, or limelight to project images from painted glass slides. These shows always included a lively narrative and were often accompanied by music and audience participation. Though this technology was first developed in the mid-1600s, it flourished in America two hundred years later because it was a cheap, portable way to bring entertainment to the far-flung masses.[115] Some time before 1860, the American Stereoscopic Company produced a Dr. Kane magic lantern series that drew on the most dramatic illustrations and incidents in Kane's *Arctic Explorations*, and its presentation continued to attract audiences well into the late-1800s.[116] Another magic lantern show also toured during this time, and judging by the size and elaborate nature of its slides (it had massive 11 1/2 x 9 5/8 inch slides with hinged tin-panels to create the "special effect" of dissolving one image into another), it probably played in larger venues.[117]

After reading, singing, and watching Dr. Kane's story, the American public was then invited to "play" Dr. Kane. Gamemaker V. S. W. Parkhurst of Providence,

One of fourteen magic lantern slides from Dr. Kane's Second Grinnell Expedition series by the American Stereoscopic Company (c. 1860). Courtesy of Russell Potter.

Rhode Island, who had good success with its "Uncle Tom and Little Eva" card game in 1852, released a new card game, "Dr. Kane's Trip to the Arctic Seas," in 1858. The game was made up of dozens of illustrated cards, some of which were hand-colored, and was essentially a variation of "Go-Fish." Players traded cards to try to form sets that included matching characters and events from Kane's *Arctic Explorations*. Once a player had a complete set, they needed to get the "Jonathan Ahead" card to win. This card shows an exuberant man, tipping his top hat to the sun setting over an open polar sea while the American Flag waves prominently over the entire scene.[118] If one wanted to consume Dr. Kane further, it was not a problem because several collectable items were also available for public purchase. At least two companies minted commemorative coins in his honor, a *carte de visite* and several engravings of him were available, the Smithsonian released a stereoscopic image of Dr. Kane sitting with two Inuit, and, by the turn of the century, W. Duke, Sons & Co. and Hassan tobacco companies each produced color Dr. Kane trading cards that were available in their cigarette packs. Citizens could also participate in a more official celebration of Dr. Kane by contributing to the "Kane Monument Association." This organization of five hundred prominent men began meeting in 1857 and over the next two years held lectures and sold subscriptions to gather funds for the construction of a large bronze and stone statue honoring Dr. Kane.[119] This monument, sculpted by artist Thomas Hicks, was to be a public celebration of Dr. Kane. Because of this, newspapers recommended "the amount of individual subscriptions might be fixed so low that even those of limited means might have the pleasure of contributing."[120]

Most of these items were designed for adult audiences, but several publishers also began to produce Dr. Kane items for children by the end of the 1850s. George

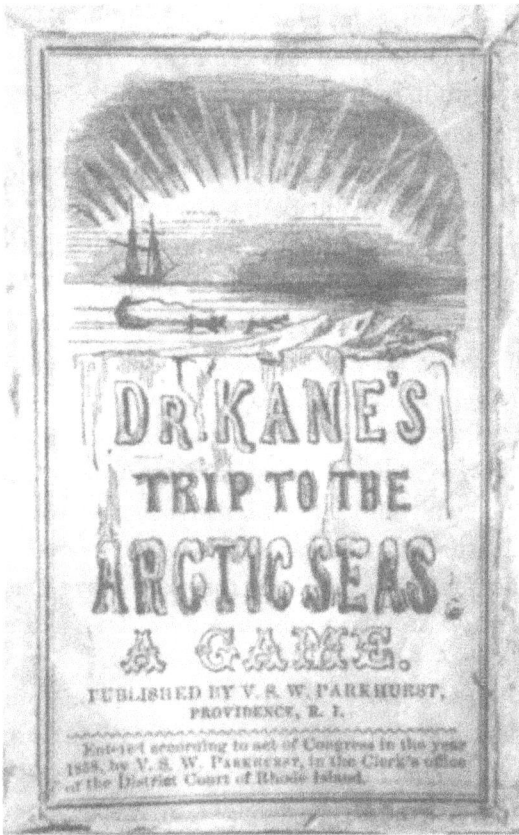

Card Game "Dr. Kane's Trip to the Arctic Seas" (Providence, Rhode Island: V.S.W. Parkhurst, 1858) courtesy of Patrice McFarland. Carte de visite "Dr. E.K. Kane" by Matthew Brady (New York: E. Anthony, 1862), and the W. Duke, Sons & Co. (1888) and Hassan (1914) tobacco companies picture cards. From collection of Author.

W. Childs began this trend—he had Elder target his biography at both the youth and adult markets. In his first chapters, Elder noted that he intended to write a work that would guide the nation's youth in their hero-worship of a man whose life could be a lesson to them. He challenged his readers to be disciplined and studious and noted of Kane's childhood, "The boy had not a vice or a fault that could spoil the man."[121] He provided a litany of stories illustrating Dr. Kane' boyhood heroism that were designed to inspire the youth of the nation. In one, when five neighborhood boys perched themselves on a roof and shot putty-wads at girls below, young Elisha ordered them to stop. When they refused, he quickly scaled the building, bested all five of them, and dragged them to the edge of the roof to apologize. In another, via a dramatic rope-swinging kick to the face, young Elisha knocked out a ruffian who was harassing a group of adult women. Later, when a harsh school master unjustly threatened to whip his younger brother, Tommy, Elisha came to his defense saying, "Don't whip him, he's such a little fellow—whip me."[122] This last tale must have been especially popular because when a new biography of George Washington written for school children came out a few years later, it included the same story with Washington substituted for Kane and a "young slave-boy" for Tommy.[123]

In these tales Elder gave his readers a view of Huckleberry Finn and Tom Sawyer twenty-five years before Twain would create them. He said of his little hero, "It was not the monkey mirthfulness... of childhood that he was chargeable with, but something more of purpose and tenacity... [that] he did not overlay with good-boy policy. He was absolutely fearless... and he had a pair of little fists that worked with the steam-power of passion in the administration of distributive justice." Elder ended these early tales with a discussion of Kane's childhood reading list— Chemistry texts, *Robinson Crusoe*, and *Pilgrim's Progress*. He celebrated Elisha's individualist spirit and claimed that he was almost entirely self-educated, a "monk of intellectual industry."[124]

From beginning to end, this biography was an instructional manual for how young men should live, and judging from reviews of the time, it was quite successful. *The Atlantic Monthly* reported that Elder's book made Kane's life "one of the moral possessions of the country, worth more to it than any new invention which increases its industrial productiveness or any new province which it adds to its territorial dominion." It concluded, "To the young men of the country we especially commend this biography, in the full belief that it will stimulate and stir to effort many a sensitive youth who feels within himself the capacity to emulate the spirit which prompted Dr. Kane's actions."[125] These sentiments did not appear in reviews alone. The instruction card for the "Dr. Kane's Trip to the Arctic Seas" card game (no doubt trying to prove its own moral worth) explicitly named Elder's book and its publisher and proclaimed that "it should be in the hands of every American youth." It assured parents that if they read the stories of Dr. Kane to their children they would be "sowing seeds which in years to come may bring forth an abundant harvest."

Throughout the remainder of the nineteenth century, Dr. Kane figured prominently in didactic adventure books such as *Dr. Kane the Arctic Hero: A Book for Boys* (1869). The 1860 book, *Famous Boys and How They Became Great Men*, included a long chapter on Dr. Kane and noted that there were many "qualities exhibited by Dr. Kane, which every boy might study and try to imitate."[126] In these books, Dr. Kane's image became more perfect than even Childs dared to make him. In one, Rev. Daniel Wise completely altered the events of the terrible winter of 1854 when half of Elisha's crew left him. In his version, the crew wanted to abandon the ship, but Dr. Kane, knowing it was a bad idea, refused to let them. This strong leadership was so impressive that "Kane's subordinates yielded gracefully, and even enthusiastically." Rev. Wise concluded that Dr. Kane was "a man who had brains to form an intelligent purpose, and nerve to execute his plans at all hazards."[127]

Dr. Kane also appeared in instructional manuals for young men. In *Getting On in the World; or, Hints on Success In Life* (1874) published in the young, boom-town of Chicago, Dr. Kane served to illustrate two important characteristics for success: to have and follow a plan systematically; and to demonstrate determination, faith and effort, even in the face of seemingly insurmountable tasks.[128] Perhaps most impressively, Dr. Kane's life even influenced how state legislatures dealt with young men. In the debates at Illinois's second constitutional convention, Dr. Kane was used as evidence to argue that young men (those under thirty) should be allowed to serve in the senate. One convention member noted (incorrectly) that Kane had done all his heroic deeds before he was thirty and then rhetorically demanded, "Was he any less a hero? Are young men, if they possess the ability to represent the people... any less fit or qualified for that position because the people choose them?"[129]

Dr. Kane's heroic image was so broad and inclusive that it crossed the strict nineteenth-century gender gap and allowed him to become an inspirational model for young women as well as young men. One "young woman from Baltimore" praised Dr. Kane not for manly virtues, but for domestic actions associated with the feminine sphere. She noted that during the expedition he was "not only commander," but also "housekeeper, and cleaner, and nurse, and everything." Acting with all the compassion of a mother, he stood "by the sick couch of his officers and crew, sharing and sympathizing in their suffering, denying himself necessary rest and food that they might have it, studying their comfort and doing their work." She concluded, "Here he shines in the purest light, presenting to my mind one of the strongest instances of *moral sublimity* that I ever read of—*for many men can do a few great actions, yet but few know the happy art of doing little things greatly.*"[130] This idea that Dr. Kane represented the best attributes of both men and women reverberated throughout the national media. When it learned of Elisha's severe illness, the *New York Tribune* explained that his death would be a huge loss because Dr. Kane represented a rare balance of the best of male and female traits: "His modest simplicity, his refined tastes, his tenderness of feeling, and his almost feminine sympathies are perpetually revealed in connection with a dauntless courage and constancy as ever nerved heroic heart to lofty prowess." This duality of male and female, they felt, made him a model of "undismayed manhood."[131] A popular magazine agreed: "A man so rarely, so delicately, and yet so manfully endowed, is not often presented to our admiration. With the fineness of perception belonging to a beautiful woman, he combined the energy and courage, the chivalry, piety and abnegation of self so renowned in the knights of the olden time."[132]

In the mid-nineteenth century, the embodiment of male and female virtues suggested the unification of two other opposite forces: science and religion. In life, Elisha was a well-recognized man of science, honored by many American and British scientific organizations.[133] After his death, however, the clergy and public alike celebrated Dr. Kane as a man of true faith, a somewhat surprising fact given Elisha's life-long ambivalence toward religion.[134] It was only in his last hours of life, with his mother reading scripture at his bedside, that, according to his sister, Elisha "came to Jesus." She confided in a letter home that this was what she had "most longed for yet scarcely dared to hope," and exclaimed, "That our prayers were answered, and that he died a Christian, is so great a cause of rejoicing that it seems almost wrong to grieve."[135] Elisha's religious ambivalence did not affect Dr. Kane's perfect piety, however. Henry Ward Beecher, the most prominent minister of the era, publicly compared Dr. Kane's attention to a small, arctic flower to God's love of a lost soul; and Rev. Bishop Clark of Providence, Rhode Island, said of Dr. Kane, "We cannot estimate the moral value of his example… it is, in short, a *victory of faith.*"[136] Summing up the totality and ubiquity of all these statements, the Dr. Kane card game minced no words and simply proclaimed that Dr. Kane was, "The greatest moral hero that ever lived."[137]

In March 1860 New York's *Cosmopolitan Journal of Art* noted that John Adam Jackson had completed his design for Dr. Kane's statue, which the five hundred-member Kane Monument Association planned to erect "upon some of the public lands of this city." The $3,000 marble slab base had already been donated by the Albert Free Stone Company of Nova Scotia, and Jackson's winning likeness of the arctic hero was to be cast as an eight-foot tall bronze statue.[138] This was the last mention of the Kane Monument Association in this publication and no statue of Dr. Kane was ever erected in New York City, or anywhere else. In the late 1850s,

From a painting by Alonso Chappel (New York: Johnson, Fry & Co., 1862). This popular image of Kane appeared in many portrait collections and seems to have also been sold as a souvenir at panorama and magic lantern shows. From collection of Author.

Americans embraced Dr. Kane as a hero capable of reuniting the nation, but the nation did not reunite. The Civil War began in April 1861, and four years and over 600,000 deaths later, the public no longer believed in or needed Dr. Kane. Though he would remain a household name for another two generations, the Civil War turned Dr. Kane into a quaint, almost fictional hero of a bygone age—a character best suited for children's morality tales—a pure, simplistic, almost naïve hero. At the time of Elisha's death, Dr. Kane had embodied the entire nation, contradictions and all. He was North and South, Young and Old, Male and Female, Science and Religion. He was the hero of the masses—he was large; he contained multitudes. The Civil War brought about a new nation that needed new heroes, however, and Dr. Kane, like the antebellum period that so celebrated him, faded into the obscurity of the past.

1. Lewis M. Hatch to Elisha Kent Kane (Jan., 18, 1857), John K. Kane papers, folder, "letters to E.K. Kane," Historical Society of Pennsylvania.
2. Miriam to Elisha Kent Kane (Feb. 9, 1857), John Kane papers, folder, "Letters of

sympathy," Historical Society of Pennsylvania.

3. "Dr. Kane in Cuba" *Littell's Living Age* 52 (Jan-March, 1857), 688. This poem was later reprinted along with other poems by Elizabeth in her brother's poetry books. See John Greenleaf Whittier, *Hazel-Blossums* (Boston: James R. Osgood & Co., 1875), 118-20.

4. *Public Ledger* (Feb. 25, 1857), Dow papers, Stefansson Arctic Collection, Dartmouth College.

5. The events of this procession are laid out in extensive detail in *Kane Obsequies* (Philadelphia: James B. Chandler, 1857), a 94-page report of the "Joint Committee appointed to receive the remains and conduct the obsequies of the late Elisha Kent Kane," which was printed and sold to the public. This report was reprinted with additional notes in a 103-page section at the end of William Elder, *Biography of Elisha Kent Kane* (Philadelphia, Childs & Peterson, 1858), 285-387.

6. Steamer passage from Havana to New York took about one week and was readily available—Elisha's mother and brother John came to Cuba via this route and Tom had booked Elisha passage home on this same route before he died. After his death, the family decided to take Elisha's body back to Philadelphia via the much longer New Orleans route. Madeleine Stern notes that this public procession came about "largely through Childs' machinations." See Madeleine Stern, *Imprints on History* (Bloomington: Indiana University Press, 1956), 167.

7. Elder, 302-06.

8. *Evening Delta* (Feb. 23, 1857), Dow papers, Stefansson Arctic Collection, Dartmouth College.

9. Louisville Bar members to John K. Kane (Feb. 28, 1857), John Kane papers, folder, "letters of sympathy,"Historical Society of Pennsylvania.

10. Elder, 307-09; George W. Corner, *Dr. Kane of the Arctic Seas* (Philadelphia: Temple University Press, 1972), 254.

11. Elder, 309-20.

12. Small ceremonies were held in Zanesville and Bellaire, Ohio; Benwood, Wheeling, Fairmount, Martinsburg, and Harper's Ferry, Virginia (now West Virginia); and Cumberland and Ellicott's Mills (now Ellicott City), Maryland. See Elder, 339-42 and Corner, 254-55.

13. See "A Long Voyage in an Unknown Sea," *Chicago Daily Journal* (Feb. 26, 1857); pamphlet "Sermon on the death of Dr. Kane. by Rev. Dr. Putnam, of Roxbury. A Beautiful Tribute" (March 8, 1857); and Harrisburg *Daily Telegraph* (Feb. 27, 1857), Dow papers, Stefansson Arctic Collection, Dartmouth College.

14. This speech and letter are reprinted in *The Life of John Pendleton Kennedy*, Henry T. Tuckerman, ed. (New York: G.P. Putnam, 1871), 231-32.

15. *Kane Obsequies*, 52-70; and Elder, 358-87.

16. This wreath, sent by Maggie and Kate Fox, was noted in *Kane Obsequies*, 61.

17. Mrs. Fox to Robert Patterson Kane (undated, c. April, 1857), APS Robert Patterson

Kane papers. In this letter Mrs. Fox said that, after Elisha's death, Mrs. Grinnell consoled Maggie and told her that Elisha had "remembered her to the last" by supplying funds for her support in his will.

18. Maggie Fox to Robert Patterson Kane (undated, c. Dec., 1857), APS Elisha Kent Kane papers. Henry Grinnell gave all of his letters regarding Elisha's affairs to the Kane family in June, 1857. See Henry Grinnell to Thomas Leiper Kane (June 19, 1857), APS Elisha Kent Kane papers.

19. E. Pershine Smith to Henry C. Carey (April 27, 1857), Henry C. Carey papers, Edward Carey Gardiner collection, Historical Society of Pennsylvania.

20. Maggie Fox to Robert Patterson Kane (May 27, 1858), APS Elisha Kent Kane papers. The letters that Maggie sent Patterson are in the APS Elisha Kent Kane papers and provide concrete evidence of the veracity of her memoir, *The Love-Life of Dr. Kane*. Aside from a bit of grammatical editing, the surviving letters in Elisha's hand exactly match the letters reprinted in the memoir.

21. The *Dictionary of American Biography* notes that Ellet was a writer of popular women's history whose prose tended to be "gossipy and superficially interesting."

22. *New York Herald* (Aug. 16, 1858), 2; and The South Carolina *Charleston Mercury* (Aug. 20, 1858), 2.

23. Rush C. Hawkins to Robert Patterson Kane (Aug. 20, 1858), APS Elisha Kent Kane papers.

24. See folder, "Letter in re: Kane-Fox correspondence," APS Elisha Kent Kane papers. This is an undated and unsigned copy of a letter sent to Robert Patterson Kane.

25. Folder, "Letter in re: Kane-Fox correspondence," APS Elisha Kent Kane papers.

26. Barbara Wiesberg, *Talking to the Dead: Kate and Maggie Fox and the Rise of Spiritualism* (New York: Harper SanFrancisco, 2004), 193-94.

27. To arrange this, Patterson wrote to Maggie's lawyer and asked for "further explanations in the matter which has formed the subject of our communication." See folder, "Kane, R.P. to Rush C. Hawkins," APS Elisha Kent Kane papers. A few weeks later Maggie tells him that Mrs. Ellet and the spiritualist community are furious with her for not publishing the book. See Maggie Fox to Robert Patterson Kane (Sept. 25, 1858), APS Elisha Kent Kane papers.

28. Maggie Fox to Robert Patterson Kane (Sept. 2, 1858), APS Elisha Kent Kane papers.

29. See the many letters between Maggie Fox, Robert Patterson, and William Quinn in the APS Elisha Kent Kane papers.

30. For Tom's Civil War career, that eventually led to his promotion to Major General, see John D. Imhof "Two Roads to Gettysburg: Thomas Leiper Kane and the 13th Pennsylvania Reserves," *The Gettysburg Magazine* 9 (July 1, 1993): 53-60; and Robert D. Hoffsommer, "The Bucktails," *Civil War Times* 4, no. 9 (Jan. 1966): 16-25.

31. Tom's wife Bessie provided a detailed account of the Kane family's response to Fox in her journal. See Elizabeth Wood Kane Journal, 1860-1863 (March 28, 1862), BYU

Thomas Leiper Kane papers. I am indebted to Matthew Grow for calling this entry to my attention.

32. Elizabeth Wood Kane Journal, 1860-1863 (March 28, 1862), BYU Thomas Leiper Kane papers.

33. Elizabeth Wood Kane Journal, 1860-1863 (March 28, 1862), BYU Thomas Leiper Kane papers.

34. Elisha noted that Tom was working for their father, manipulating the railroad's stock for their benefit. See Elisha Kent Kane to John K. Kane and Jane Duval Leiper Kane (undated, c. Sept., 1856) in folder "Elisha Kent Kane to Mother and Father," APS Elisha Kent Kane papers.

35. Elizabeth Wood Kane Journal, 1860-1863 (March 28, 1862), BYU Thomas Leiper Kane papers.

36. Elizabeth Wood Kane Journal, 1860-1863 (March 28, 1862), BYU Thomas Leiper Kane papers. Fox's book confirms this arrangement, see *Love-Life*, viii.

37. Fox tried to head off these charges in the preface to *Love-Life*. For the public response to *Ruth Hall*, see Joyce W. Warren's "Introduction" in Fanny Fern, *Ruth Hall and other Writings*, Joyce W. Warren, ed. (New Brunswick: Rutgers University Press, 1992).

38. Elizabeth Wood Kane Journal, 1860-1863 (March 28, 1862), BYU Thomas Leiper Kane papers. Patterson's in-laws were remarkably wealthy as Joshua Fisher was married to Elizabeth Izard Middleton, whose family was one of the most wealthy and powerful in the nation. See Eliza Cope Harrison, *Best Companions: Letters of Eliza Middleton Fisher and her mother, Mary Hering Middleton, from Charleston, Philadelphia, and Newport, 1839-1846* (Columbia: University of South Carolina Press, 2001).

39. Elizabeth Wood Kane Journal, 1860-1863 (March 28, 1862), BYU Thomas Leiper Kane papers.

40. Elizabeth Wood Kane Journal, 1860-1863 (March 28, 1862), BYU Thomas Leiper Kane papers.

41. Elizabeth Wood Kane to Thomas Leiper Kane (April 24, 1862), BYU Thomas Leiper Kane papers.

42. See *Love-Life* and Reuben Davenport, *The Death-Blow to Spiritualism: Being the True Story of the Fox Sisters, as Revealed by Authority of Margaret Fox Kane and Catherine Fox Jencken* (New York: G.W. Dillingham, 1888).

43. *Love-Life*, 236, 268 and passim.

44. *Love-Life*, 280.

45. Mrs. Fox to Robert Patterson Kane (undated, c. April, 1857), APS Elisha Kent Kane papers.

46. Maggie Fox to Robert Patterson Kane (June 1, 1857), APS Elisha Kent Kane papers.

47. Maggie Fox to Robert Patterson Kane (undated, c. June, 1857), APS Elisha Kent Kane papers.

48. A photograph of this artifact is reprinted in the pamphlet, R. G. Pressing, *Rappings that*

Startled the World: Facts About the Fox Sisters (Lily Dale, NY: Dale News Inc., c. 1947), 81. It notes that the item is part of the collection of "Mrs. D. H. Pond" (Miriam Buckner Pond) who married a grand-nephew of Maggie and Kate and in the late-1940s organized the Fox Memorial Society and published her version of the Fox sisters' history, *Time is Kind: The Story of the Unfortunate Fox Family* (Clinton, CT: Centennial Press, 1947).

49. A thorough search of Ohio newspapers in 1857 and 1858 shows no evidence of Maggie in the area. They do report that "the Foxes," Kate and Leah, were in Boston in July of 1857. See Columbus *Daily Ohio Stateman* (July 2, 1857), 3.

50. Elizabeth Wood Kane to Thomas Leiper Kane (May 11, 1862), BYU Thomas Leiper Kane papers.

51. See folder, "Edward Bayard," APS Robert Patterson Kane papers.

52. Mrs. E.F. Ellet to J.P. Green (Robert Patterson Kane's legal secretary) (Sept. 7, 1865), APS Robert Patterson Kane papers.

53. Versions of this story ran in the *Milwaukee Daily Sentinel* (Sept. 13, 1865), 3; *New Hampshire Sentinel* (Sept. 14, 1865), 2; *Houston Tri-Weekly Telegraph* (Sept. 25, 1865), 6; Columbus Georgia *Daily Sun* (Sept. 27, 1865), 1; San Francisco *Evening Bulletin* (Oct. 14, 1865), 6.

54. "The Fox-Kane Imbroglio" Columbus *Daily Ohio Statesman* (Oct. 18, 1865), 1.

55. Elizabeth Wood Kane to Bessie Kane Shields (undated, c. Nov., 1865), Kane family papers, Clements Library, University of Michigan.

56. *New York Times* (Dec. 15, 1865), 5.

57. One interesting outcome of this book was another book, *Sequel to the "Love-Life"; Given by the Spirit of E.K. Kane* (San Francisco: Francis, Valentine & Co., 1866). This book claimed to be literally "ghostwritten" by Elisha via the hands of a spiritual medium, Mrs. Fanny Green M'Dougal. In it, Elisha asks for forgiveness for not having publicly married Maggie, and then, uncharacteristically, preaches the wonders and truth of spiritual communication.

58. Weisberg, 209-12; and Herbert G. Jackson Jr., *The Spirit Rappers* (Garden City, NY: Doubleday & Co. Inc., 1972), 175.

59. Nancy Rubin Stuart. *The Reluctant Spiritualist: The Life of Maggie Fox* (NY: Harcourt, 2005), 268-73.

60. *Preliminary Report of the Commission by University of Pennsylvania to Investigate Modern Spiritualism* (Philadelphia: Lippincott, 1887), 42 as cited in Weisberg, 233.

61. The hundreds of hours of séances (often done through trance writing) facilitated by Kate for the Taylors are largely preserved in a book edited by the Taylors' daughter. See Sarah E.L. Taylor, ed., *Fox-Taylor Automatic Writing, 1869-1892 Unabridged Record* (Minneapolis: Tribune-Great West Printing Co., 1932).

62. Weisberg, 214-15, 222-34.

63. Leah Fox Underhill, *The Missing Link In Modern Spiritualism* (New York: Thomas R.

Knox & Co., 1885); Weisberg, 234-35.

64. Davenport, 236.

65. *New York Herald* (May 27, 1888), reprinted in Davenport, 30-31.

66. Davenport, 32-36.

67. *New York Times* (Oct. 22, 1888). For a full account of this performance as well as Maggie's reasons for doing it, see Davenport's *The Death-Blow to Spiritulaism*, which was published in conjunction with this exposé.

68. Jackson, 212.

69. *New York Times* (March 5, 1893), 20.

70. *New York Times* (March 10, 1893), 10.

71. *Evening Journal* (March 2, 1857), Dow papers, Stefansson Arctic Collection, Dartmouth College.

72. Philadelphia *Evening Journal* (March 12, 1857), 2.

73. Leo Braudy, *The Frenzy of Renown* (New York: Vintage Books, 1986, 1997), 5-7.

74. Thomas Leiper Kane to Robert Patterson Kane (May 17, 1862), APS Robert Patterson Kane papers. Tom, a Union general at this time, noted that many soldiers had said this of Dr. Kane.

75. *National Magazine* (Nov., 1858), 458.

76. Elisha's convictions on the slavery question are not clear because slavery was never one of his primary, or even secondary, concerns. He was firmly a Democrat, like his father, but as a doctor he was horrified by his investigations of the treatment of slaves in the slave trade. See folders "Examinations taken at the African Hospital" and "Whydah Slave Trade, 1842," APS Elisha Kent Kane papers. In June of 1846 he toured several of the slave factories of West Africa as well as the village of one of the "African Kings" in Dahomey. Elder claimed in his biography that, after seeing the brutality of both these places, Dr. Kane had the impression that "the slaves that are driven to the coast for shipment may very well congratulate themselves upon the commutation of their fate, even with the 'middle passage' before them." This statement, however, is more telling of Elder's beliefs than Elisha's. Elder, 104.

77. For Tom's efforts in these causes, see Matthew J. Grow's "'Liberty to the Downtrodden': Thomas L. Kane, Romantic Reformer" (PhD diss., University of Notre Dame, 2006), forthcoming by Yale University Press, 2009.

78. Portsmouth, New Hampshire *Morning Chronicle* (Oct. 15, 1855).

79. *DeBow's Review* 23 (Aug., 1857), 172-92, 193.

80. *Southern Literary Review* 23 (April, 1857), 257-60. Cooke also sent an ornately handwritten copy of this poem to the Kane family. See folder, "letters of sympathy," John Kane Papers, Historical Society of Pennsylvania.

81. *Southern Literary Review* 23 (April, 1857), 257-60.

82. *Harper's Weekly Journal of Civilization* (March 14, 1857), 1. This was reprinted in the Southern magazine, *Littell's Living Age* 17 (April 4, 1857), 122-26.

83. John Sampson, "Personal Narratives, Journals, and Diaries" in *America and the Sea: A Literary History* Haskell Springer, ed. (Athens, GA: University of Georgia Press, 1995), 90.

84. "Dr. Kane and the Unknown Sea," *Salem Register* (March 9, 1857), Dow papers, Dartmouth.

85. "The Arctic Queen," dedicated to Dr. Kane, "Discoverer of the Open Polar Sea," was an anonymous, privately-printed poem that was widely distributed as a chapbook in January 1857 and gained a good deal of public attention through multiple reviews: see, for example, the *Ohio Cultivator* (Jan. 1, 1857), 24; and *Cosmopolitan Art Journal* (Sept., 1857), 151-54. Though she never publicly acknowledged her authorship, Metta Victoria Fuller Victor had her husband write Judge Kane to let him know that she had written the poem as an "offering" to Dr. Kane and that she had sent it to "the press and literary people of the country" in hopes that it would bring greater honor to his name. See O.J. Victor to John K. Kane (Jan. 1, 1857), APS Elisha Kent Kane papers.

86. *Harper's Weekly* (March 3, 1860), 130-31.

87. William H. Goetzmann, *New Lands, New Men* (New York: Viking Penguin Inc., 1986), 421.

88. For the public nature of Frémont's expeditions, see Andrew Rolle, *John Charles Frémont: Character as Destiny* (Norman: University of Oklahoma Press, 1991); and William H. Goetzmann, *Exploration & Empire* (New York: W.W. Norton & Co., 1966), 240-41.

89. For a full telling of Stanley's explorations and self-promotion, see John Bierman, *Dark Safari: The Life Behind the Legend of Henry Morton Stanley* (New York: Knopf, 1990).

90. "Bookselling" *American Publishers' Circular and Literary Gazette* (Aug. 14, 1858), 391; and Alice Payne Hacket, *Fifty Years of Best Sellers, 1895-1945* (New York: R.R. Bowker Co., 1945), 132. The *American Publishers' Circular* article is an abstract from *Appleton's New American Cyclopaedia*. Hacket gets her numbers from articles on American book sales that were published in the *Boston Post* during 1860. *Arctic Explorations* continued to sell well during the Civil War, and perhaps very well. Elisha's estate received one dollar for each two-volume set of *Arctic Explorations* sold. In the 1866 legal proceedings between Maggie Fox and the Kane family, Maggie sued for $100,000 or one third of the book's royalties to date, suggesting a sale of 300,000 volumes. See Maggie Fox to Mr. Dougherty (Dec. 20, 1866), psychologists volume, Dreer Collection, Historical Society of Pennsylvania.

91. The title page and the text are the same in all the "first editions" of *Arctic Explorations* that I have examined—Childs & Peterson is listed as the primary publisher with all other companies listed below—but the name printed on the bottom of the spine varies. This suggests that the text was printed at one location and then each company bound the book on its own. See also the advertisement section in *American Publishers'*

Circular & Literary Gazette (Feb. 21, 1857), which suggests that the book was also promoted by Miller, Orton & Co. Each of these publishers were probably acting as "jobbers"—buying large quantities of *Arctic Explorations* from Childs & Peterson at a discount rate and then selling the books at a profit. Each of these companies ran frequent ads for *Arctic Explorations* throughout the first half of 1857. Childs & Peterson did not. They ran one or two full-page ads around the time of a book's release, but then did not run regular ads for it throughout the year. For its ad see *American Publishers' Circular* (Dec. 6, 1856), 754.

92. Carl Bode, *The Anatomy of American Popular Culture, 1840-1861* (Berkeley: University of California Press, 1960), 223. Though not as popular in England as in the United States, *Arctic Explorations* also sold well there. It was published in London by Trübner & Co., 1856.

93. After several months of negotiations, Elisha bought the copyright, plates, and remaining copies of his first book from Harpers for $1,200. See Elisha Kent Kane to John K. Kane (undated, c. May, 1856), APS Elisha Kent Kane papers; and Elisha Kent Kane to George W. Childs (undated), items 15 and 16, Kane-Childs album, Dreer Collection, Historical Society of Pennsylvania.

94. See full-page ad in the back pages of *Emerson's United States Magazine* (Aug., 1857).

95. See Mrs. Fox to Robert Patterson Kane (undated, c. April, 1857), and Maggie Fox to Robert Patterson Kane (June 1, 1857), APS Elisha Kent Kane papers.

96. Elder, 3.

97. Elder, 4. Elder was pleased that the Kane family liked the book. See William Elder to John K. Kane (Jan. 12, 1858), APS John K. Kane papers.

98. See full-page ad in the back pages of *Emerson's United States Magazine* (Aug., 1857).

99. Philadelphia *Evening Bulletin* (March 14, 1857), Dow papers, Stefansson Arctic Collection, Dartmouth College.

100. Journal of Bessie Kane (Oct. 10, 1860), reprinted in the pamphlet "Letters to B.K." A copy is in the Kane Family papers, Clements Library, University of Michigan.

101. William Godfrey, *Godfrey's Narrative of the Last Grinnell Arctic Exploring Expedition* (Philadelphia, J.T. Lloyd & Co., 1857), 6.

102. The book's complete title is: *Godfrey's Narrative of the Last Grinnell Arctic Exploring Expedition, in Search of Sir John Franklin, 1853-4-5. With a Biography of Dr. Elisha K. Kane, from the Cradle to the Grave.* This book was obviously put together quickly and without much editing as the title on the cover page contains a typo, "Arctic Exploring Txpedition."

103. Joseph Sabin in his *Dictionary of Books Relating to America* (New York: J. Sabin, 1868-1935) noted that this book was prepared by C.C. Rhodes from information in an unpublished article of Sonntag's, but that the book was repudiated by Sonntag and several other members of the expedition. The *Philadelphia Evening Journal* (May 19, 1858) reprinted a letter from Sonntag in which he said, "I did not write the book, it

is a shameful imposition."

104. [August Sonntag], *Professor Sonntag's Thrilling Narrative of the Grinnell Exploring Expedition to the Arctic Ocean* (Philadelphia: C.C. Rhodes., 1857), 7.

105. *Godfrey's Narrative* went through at least two printings; there are 1857 and 1860 editions. *Sonntag's Thrilling Narrative* appeared with many different title pages, each listing different publishers. In Philadelphia it was released by C.C. Rhodes, J.T. Lloyd & Co., J.C.H. Whiting, and D. Rulison; and both J.T. Lloyd & Co. and H.M. Rulison released it in Cincinnati. All of these publishers specialized in sensational works and C.C. Rhodes, J.T. Lloyd, and J.C.H. Whiting seem to have been connected as they published many of the same titles.

106. This book was first released in 1856 and then re-released with the longer title in 1857. See Samuel M. Smucker, *Arctic Explorations and Discoveries during the Nineteenth Century* (New York: Miller, Orton & Co, 1856, 1857). In 1859 C.M. Saxton of New York released this book and then it was revised and updated in 1886 by William L. Allison. See *Arctic Explorations and Discoveries* (New York: William L. Allison Co., and John W. Lovell Co., 1886).

107. Samuel Smucker's *The Life of Dr. Elisha Kent Kane* was released in Philadelphia in 1858 with title pages by G.G. Evans, J.W. Bradley, and John E. Potter. Bradley also had an 1859 edition and Potter an 1871 edition—Potter listed the author's last name as Schmucker instead of Smucker. A popular biography of Kane also appeared in Germany and was probably modeled loosely on Smucker's. It is exceptional for its sensational illustrations, including one of Kane in the Taal Volcano. See *Kane, der Nordpolfahrer* (Leipzig: Verlag von Otto Spamer, 1858).

108. J.C. Beckel, "Requiem: He Sleeps, But not 'mid the Arctic Snow" (New York: Firth Pond & Co. 1857); William H. Shuster, "Kane's Funeral March" (Philadelphia: Wm H. Shuster, 1857).

109. J. M. Abbot, "The Fair Augusta Schottisch" (New York: Wm. Hall & Son, 1859).

110. George W. Chapman, *A Tribute to Kane: and Other Poems* (New York: Rudd & Carleton, 1860), 17; John Greenleaf Whittier, *Hazel-Blossoms* (Boston: James R. Osgood & Co., 1875). In his introduction, Whittier noted that his sister's poem, "Dr. Kane in Cuba," arrived in Cuba "while the great explorer lay on his death-bed, and... that he listened with grateful tears while it was read to him by his mother."

111. Jules Verne, *The Field of Ice* (New York: George Rutledge & Sons, 1895).

112. Russell A. Potter & Douglas W. Wamsley, "The Sublime yet Awful Grandeur: The Arctic Panoramas of Elisha Kent Kane" *Polar Record* 35 (Jan., 1999), 193-206.

113. See folder, "William Morton papers... 1857" APS Elisha Kent Kane papers. See also the pamphlets that accompanied these shows: William Morton & James McGary, *Dr. Kane's Arctic Voyage* (New York: 1957); and Thomas Hickey, *Thomas Hickey's Narrative of the Last Arctic Expedition of the late Dr. Kane* (Baltimore: James Young, 1860).

114. Potter & Douglas, 202.

115. Howard B. Leighton, "The Days of Magic Lanterns," *Nineteenth Century* 5 (Spring 1984): 44-47.

116. Fourteen of the slides from this series are in the collection of Russell Potter of the College of Rhode Island and several of them can be seen in his book *Arctic Spectacles: The Frozen North in Visual Culture*, 1818-75 (Seattle: University of Washington Press, 2007), and on his web-site dedicated to popular images of Sir John Franklin. See Russell Potter, *Sir John Franklin in the Public Eye* (Available online at: www.ric.edu/rpotter/publiceye.html).

117. Seven of the original slides of this series are in the collection of Dr. Willem Albert Wagenaar of Leiden University, Netherlands.

118. A fine example of this now rare game is in the collection of game collector Patrice McFarland of Averill Park, New York, whom I gratefully thank for her assistance and for photographs of the game. For more on V. F. W. Parkhurst and his Uncle Tom game, see Stephen Railton, director, "Playing Uncle Tom," *Uncle Tom's Cabin and American Culture: A Multimedia Archive*, www.iath.virginia.edu/utc/tomituds/games.html.

119. "Dr. Francis' Remarks... on behalf of the Kane Monument in New York" [pamphlet] (NY: John F. Trow, 1859); and, *The Crayon* 6 (Aug., 1859), 256.

120. *New York Tribune* (Feb. 26, 1857), 4. It is unclear what became of these funds, but no monument was ever erected.

121. Elder, 29-30.

122. Elder, 19-25.

123. Morrison Heady, *The Farmer Boy, and How He Became Commander-in-Chief* (Boston: Walker, Wise & Co., 1864) as described in the introduction to Mason L. Weems, *The Life of Washington*, Marcus Cunliffe, ed. (Cambridge, MA: Harvard University Press, 1962), xxii.

124. Elder, 18-19, 35.

125. *The Atlantic Monthly* (March, 1858), 636-38.

126. M. Jones, *Dr. Kane the Arctic Hero: A Book for Boys* (New York: T. Nelson & Sons, 1869); and *Famous Boys and How They Became Great Men* (New York: R. Worthington, 1860), 74-75.

127. Rev. Daniel Wise, *Uncrowned Kings, or, Sketches of Some Men of Mark Who Rose from Obscurity to Renown* (Cincinnati: Hitchcock & Walden, 1875), 154-55. Dr. Kane was also held up as a role model in Rev. W.K. Tweedie, *The Life and Work of Earnest Men* (Cincinnati: Poe & Hitchcock, 1864).

128. William Matthews, *Getting On in the World; or, Hints on Success In Life* (Chicago: S.C. Griggs & Co., 1874), 168, 219.

129. *Debates and Proceedings of the Constitutional Convention of the State of Illinois*, vol. 1 (Springfield, IL: E. L. Merritt & Brother, 1870), 505.

130. *Baltimore Weekly Patriot* (May 9, 1857), emphasis in original.

131. *New York Tribune* (Feb. 18, 1857), 5.

132. *Emerson's United States Magazine* 5 (July, 1857), 94-95.

133. Among many others, Dr. Kane was awarded honors by the American Philosophical Society, the American Geographical Society, and the Royal Geographical Society.

134. In his letters to Tom, Elisha often made remarks suggesting his lack of faith. This is also clear in his poetry, where he addressed God, "if God there be." See folder, "Kane, E.K. Poetry," APS Elisha Kent Kane papers.

135. Bessie Kane to Mrs. George Gray Leiper (Feb. 26, 1857), cited in Corner, 250.

136. Henry Ward Beecher, *Life Thoughts* (Boston: Phillips, Sampson & Co., 1859), 127; and "Tribute to Dr. Kane," *Providence Daily Post* (March 23, 1857), Dow papers, Stefansson Arctic Collection, Dartmouth College..

137. V.S.W. Parkhurst, *Dr. Kane's Trip to the Arctic Seas, A Game* (1858) in the collection of Patricia McFarland, Averill Park, New York.

138. *Cosmopolitan Journal of Art* 4 (March, 1860), 34. Earlier information about the Kane Monument Association was reported in *The Crayon* 6 (August, 1859), 256. For a fuller account of Jackson's commission and his failure to complete it, see Lorado Taft, *History of American Sculpture* (New York, Macmillan Co., 1903), 200.

INDEX

Italicized page numbers indicate an illustration of the given term.